4

The Guthlac Poems
of the Exeter Book

Roundel 7, British Library MS Harley Roll Y.6
(approx. 3:4)

The Guthlac Poems
of the Exeter Book

EDITED WITH AN INTRODUCTION
AND COMMENTARY BY
JANE ROBERTS

CLARENDON PRESS · OXFORD
1979

Oxford University Press, Walton Street, Oxford OX2 6DP

OXFORD LONDON GLASGOW
NEW YORK TORONTO MELBOURNE WELLINGTON
KUALA LUMPUR SINGAPORE JAKARTA HONG KONG TOKYO
DELHI BOMBAY CALCUTTA MADRAS KARACHI
NAIROBI DAR ES SALAAM CAPE TOWN

Published in the United States by
Oxford University Press, New York

© *Oxford University Press 1979*

British Library Cataloguing in Publication Data

The Guthlac poems of the Exeter Book.

I. Roberts, Jane

829I'.1   PR1722   79-40418

ISBN 0-19-812462-7

Printed and bound in Great Britain by
William Clowes (Beccles) Limited
Beccles and London

Acknowledgements

I wish to express my gratitude to the many people who have advised and guided me over the years I have been preparing this edition. For much detailed information and for help involving general principles I am greatly indebted to Professor Alan Bliss, the late Professor Alistair Campbell, Professor Éamonn Carrigan, Miss Janet Cowen, Mr. John Farish, Professor M. L. Samuels, Professor E. G. Stanley, Professor Dorothy Whitelock, and Mr. Gordon Whately. I also wish to express my thanks for the generous and courteous help given me by the library staffs of King's College London and of the University of Glasgow.

Finally I cannot ever forget my deep indebtedness to the late Professor M. F. Liddell, who first taught me Old English, and to the late Professor C. L. Wrenn, who with great patience and generosity guided me to the completion of the thesis from which this edition derives.

Contents

Abbreviations

A	*Guthlac A.*
AEW	F. Holthausen, *Altenglisches etymologisches Wörterbuch* (Heidelberg, 1934).
Anglia	*Anglia. Zeitschrift für englische Philologie.*
Assmann	B. Assmann, *Bibliothek der angelsächsischen Poesie*, dritter Band (Leipzig, 1898).
B	*Guthlac B.*
BBA	*Bonner Beiträge zur Anglistik*, hrsg. von M. Trautmann.
Beiblatt	*Beiblatt zur Anglia.*
BT	J. Bosworth and T. N. Toller, *An Anglo-Saxon Dictionary* (Oxford, 1898).
BTs	T. N. Toller, *Supplement* (Oxford, 1921).
Campbell	A. Campbell, *Old English Grammar* (Oxford, 1959).
CFF	R. W. Chambers, Max Förster, and Robin Flower, *The Exeter Book of Old English Poetry* (London, 1933).
Clark Hall	J. R. Clark Hall, *A Concise Anglo-Saxon Dictionary* (4th edn. with Meritt's supplement: Cambridge, 1960).
Colgrave	B. Colgrave, *Felix's Life of Saint Guthlac* (Cambridge, 1956).
EETS (OS)	Early English Text Society (Original Series).
GK	C. W. M. Grein, *Sprachschatz*, neu hsg. von J. J. Köhler (Heidelberg, 1912).
JEGP	*The Journal of (English and) Germanic Philology.*
KD	G. P. Krapp and E. Van K. Dobbie, *The Exeter Book* (Anglo-Saxon Poetic Records, iii).
MÆ	*Medium Ævum.*
MED	H. Kurath, S. M. Kuhn, and J. Reidy, *Middle English Dictionary* (Ann Arbor, 1952–).
MLN	*Modern Language Notes.*
OED	*Oxford English Dictionary.*
PG	*Patrologia graeca* (Migne, *Patrologiae cursus completus*).
PL	*Patrologia latina* (Migne, *Patrologiae cursus completus*).
PMLA	*Publications of the Modern Language Association of America.*
RES	*The Review of English Studies.*
SB	K. Brunner's revision of E. Sievers, *Angelsächsische Grammatik* (3rd edn.: Tübingen, 1965).

Vita   Felix's *Vita sancti Guthlaci* (Colgrave's text, unless otherwise noted).

(Note: Old English poems are cited throughout from the *Anglo-Saxon
Poetic Records* texts, except for *Beowulf* where Klaeber's text is generally
used.)

The following signs and abbreviations are used in §9, the Commentary,
and the Glossary.

a, acc	accusative
adj	adjective
adv	adverb
anom vb	anomalous verb
art	article
conj	conjunction
cpv	comparative
d, dat	dative
def	definite
dem	demonstrative
dir. q.	direct question
f., fem.	feminine
g, gen	genitive
i	instrumental
imp	imperative
impers	impersonal
ind	indicative
indir. q.	indirect question
inf.	infinitive
intr	intransitive
L.	Latin
m., masc.	masculine
n	nominative
n.	neuter
N	see Commentary
neg	negative
num	numeral
obl	oblique
OHG.	Old High German
ON.	Old Norse
OS.	Old Saxon
pers	personal
pl	plural
post p.	post position
pp	passive participle
pr, pres	present
prep	preposition
pron	pronoun
pt prs vb	preterite-present verb

ptc	participle
ptc adj	participial adjective
s, sg	singular
sb	substantive
spv	superlative
stv	strong verb
subj, sj	subjunctive
tr, trs	transitive
vb	verb, verbal
wk	weak
wkv	weak verb
WS.	West Saxon
*	hypothetical form (marks doubtful headwords in Glossary)
†	marks *hapax legomena*

Introduction

§1. The legend of Saint Guthlac

The primary source for our knowledge of Guthlac is the early eighth-century life by Felix, a monk, written for the East-Anglian king Ælfwald. Although this definitive life of the saint is both highly literary and heavily indebted to earlier hagiographic writings, it has been described by F. M. Stenton as 'the one historical work which has come down from the ancient Mercian kingdom'.[1] From Felix we learn that Æthelred was already on the Mercian throne when Guthlac was born,[2] probably c. A.D. 674. The Anglo-Saxon *Chronicle* states that he died in A.D. 714.

Felix tells us how the saint, while praying one day, recognized the signs of his approaching death:

Septem enim diebus dira egritudine decoctus, octavo die ad extrema pervenit. Siquidem quarta feria ante Pascha egrotare coepit, et iterum octavo die, quarta feria, quarto etiam lumine paschalis festi, finita egritudine ad Dominum migravit.[3]

The length of Guthlac's illness and even the days of the week follow closely the events set out by Bede in his account of Cuthbert's death, but, working from the evidence of the Old English Martyrology[4] and of the later Latin calendars[5] that Guthlac's feast was celebrated on 11 April, his death can be dated to A.D. 714. In that year Easter day fell upon Sunday, 8 April.[6] Thus, the date 714 for Guthlac's death given in the Anglo-Saxon *Chronicle*[7] can be supported from Felix by consultation of the Easter tables.

[1] F. M. Stenton, *Anglo-Saxon England* (3rd edn.: Oxford, 1971), p. 178.
[2] *Vita*, §i.
[3] Colgrave, p. 152.
[4] G. Herzfeld, *An Old English Martyrology*, EETS OS cxvi (1900), 56.
[5] Most of the relevant materials have been collected together by Wormald: for a brief account of them see Jane Roberts, 'An Inventory of Early Guthlac Materials', in *Mediaeval Studies*, xxxii (1970), §8.
[6] See for example Table 18 in C. R. Cheney, *Handbook of dates for students of English history*, Royal Historical Society Guides and Handbooks, no. 4 (1945), pp. 118–19.
[7] C. Plummer, *Two of the Saxon Chronicles Parallel* (Oxford, 1952 re-issue), i. 42.

In some sources the date of Guthlac's death is given as 715,[1] which stems from the reading found only in the Douai manuscript of the *Vita sancti Guthlaci*:[2]

anno ab incarnatione Domini nostri DCCXV (*and above the numerals* septingentesimo quinto decimo).

In the Douai manuscript the chapter dealing with Guthlac's death ends with the following sentence, to which is added the above phrase:

Dixit, et extendens manus ad altare, munivit se communione corporis et sanguinis Christi, atque elevatis oculis ad caelum extensisque in altum manibus, animam ad gaudia perpetuae exultationis emisit.[3]

The influence of this Douai reading is shown not only in medieval documents, for example in the history of Ordericus Vitalis,[4] but also in modern writings, for example in the *Dictionary of Christian Biography* where Felix is given as the authority for 715 as the year of Guthlac's death.[5] C. W. Jones has noted that: 'Felix offers the unique instance in early English hagiography of a reference to the Dionysiac era: "In the seven hundred and fifteenth year from the Incarnation of our Lord."'[6] In a note for this remark, Jones observes: 'The explanation of the editors of the *Acta SS* that this is a use of the imaginary Era of the Incarnate Word because there is a mistake of one year in the notice is an early manifestation of a constant tendency to form theories to explain anachronisms.'[7] Yet a glance at Jones's own translation of Felix shows that he does not include this phrase to which he has given so much attention, perhaps because here he follows Birch's edition[8] rather than the Bollandists.[9] These quotations suggest the identification of two anachronisms

[1] E.g. by 'John of Wallingford': see R. Vaughan, 'The Chronicle attributed to John of Wallingford', *Camden Society* (third series) xxi (1958), 9.

[2] See Colgrave's collations, p. 158, fn. 19; this problem is not discussed by him beyond the statement (on p. 193) 'Guthlac died on 11 April which in 714 was the Wednesday of Easter week.'

[3] Colgrave, p. 158.

[4] A. le Prévost, 'Historiæ ecclesiasticæ libri tredecim; ex veteris codices Uticensis collatione emendavit, et suas animadversiones adjecit Augustus Le Prevost', *Société de l'Histoire de France* (Paris, 1838–55), ii. 277.

[5] W. Smith and H. Wace, *Dictionary of Christian Biography*, i (London 1877–87), 826.

[6] C. W. Jones, *Saints' Lives and Chronicles in Early England* (Ithaca, 1947), p. 86.

[7] Ibid., p. 219, n. 13.

[8] W. de G. Birch *Memorials of Saint Guthlac of Crowland* (Wisbech, 1881).

[9] *Acta Sanctorum* (Antwerp and Brussels, 1675), Aprilis ii. 38–50.

in the reading of the Douai manuscript: both the misdating of Guthlac's death and the inclusion within the text of words unlikely to have been written by Felix.

Felix emphasizes Guthlac's noble lineage, tracing his ancestry back to Icel,[1] whose name appears five generations above Penda in Mercian genealogies,[2] and alluding a second time to his kingly descent.[3] The child was christened Guthlac *ex appellatione illius tribus, quam dicunt Guthlacingas,*[4] and other evidence suggests that such a family was indeed once famous.[5] The name Guthlac lent itself usefully to an attractive symbolic interpretation which was to become one of the most popular features of the Guthlac legend,[6] even though the name is more likely to have meant 'battle-play' first and *belli munus* 'the reward of war' by religious etymologizing.

We know nothing of Guthlac's parents beyond their names and we are uncertain even about these. Both father and mother were, Felix assures his readers, noble. His father was called either Penwald (the form found in the Old English translation of Felix's *Vita* and in only two *Vita* manuscripts)[7] or Penwalh (the more generally accepted form); neither compound is elsewhere recorded as a personal name.[8] His mother's name is given as Tette. A sister, Pege, is mentioned by Felix in his account of Guthlac's death,[9] and she is supposed to have lived as a hermit at Peakirk in Northamptonshire. Other records tell of her pilgrimage to Rome where she died and was buried and of how all the church bells in Rome rang for an hour at her arrival there. Such details however come from a source

---

[1] *Vita,* §ii.

[2] See chronicle entry for A.D. 626. Stenton (*Anglo-Saxon England*, p. 39) suggests that he may have been 'the first of the race to reach Britain', and H. M. Chadwick, *The Origin of the English Nation* (Cambridge, 1907), pp. 15–16, that expressions like Felix's *ab origine Icles* indicate that 'the ancestor from whom descent is claimed is believed to have reigned in Britain.'

[3] *Vita,* §xviii.

[4] *Vita,* §x.

[5] R. M. Wilson, *The Lost Literature of Mediaeval England* (2nd edn.: London, 1970), p. 28. J. S. P. Tatlock, *The Legendary History of Britain* (Berkeley and Los Angeles, 1950), pp. 139–40, connects a Danish king Guichtlacus of Latin chronicle legends with Wihtlæg of the Mercian genealogies.

[6] See W. F. Bolton, 'The Background and Meaning of *Guthlac*', JEGP lxi (1962), 595–603 and Fred C. Robinson, 'The Significance of Names in Old English Literature', *Anglia*, lxxxvi (1968), pp. 45 ff.

[7] B. L. Harley 3097 and Douai Public Library 852 (see Colgrave, p. 176).

[8] Professor D. Whitelock has pointed out to me that -*walh*, early a common name element, went out of fashion, tending to be replaced by -*wald*.

[9] *Vita,* §l.

unreliable in many respects,[1] and have probably been elaborated from the few bits of information about Pege in Felix's life. Similar elaboration is found in a poem on Guthlac by Henry of Avranches, who introduces into his story a temptation by the devil in Pege's form,[2] and there is no evidence to support W. de G. Birch's suggestion that she may have assumed an importance as great, if not greater than, her brother's in some traditions.[3] The name Pege is uncommon in Old English, but may be cognate with P(a)ega, a man's name found infrequently.[4]

Guthlac spent nine years of his youth as a soldier before entering religious life,[5] and must have become a well-known leader in those years. This point is made by B. Colgrave, who notes that men would not otherwise have come from afar to serve under him.[6] Interestingly enough, the name Guthlac occurs among signatories to two grants supposedly made during these years by Æthelred of Mercia to Bishop Oftor of Worcester, though little reliance can be placed upon this charter evidence.[7] We are not told by Felix where Guthlac fought or even for whom and it may indeed be that he followed 'a career of warfare on his own account',[8] unless the charter references are allowed as evidence that his loyalty was to Æthelred. He is likely at this time to have fought on the western borders of Mercia, a troubled area in the seventh and early eighth centuries. He was at one time an exile among the Britons, as a hostage or to prevent his seeking the throne of Mercia or for some other reason not known, and he could as a result understand their language.[9] Despite his success in war the heroic ideal became insufficient for Guthlac, so at the age of 24 he decided to enter religion. From that time he played no further part in the political life of his age, except as counsellor and friend of those who came to him at Crowland, and Felix has therefore little to say about historical

---

[1] *Historia Ingulfi.*

[2] ll. 680 ff.

[3] See Roberts, 'Inventory', p. 211, for a note on how this view may have arisen.

[4] M. Redin, 'Studies on Uncompounded Personal Names in Old English', *Uppsala Universitets Årsskrift* (1919), pp. 106, 117.

[5] *Vita,* §xviii.

[6] Colgrave, p. 3.

[7] See Roberts, 'Inventory', p. 219.

[8] D. Whitelock, *The Audience of 'Beowulf'* (Oxford, 1951), p. 87.

[9] *Vita,* §xxxiv.

events after Guthlac's reception into Repton.[1] A few details can be gleaned about Æthelbald of Mercia because as an exile he often visited Guthlac at Crowland[2] and, after the saint's death, went to his sepulchre to mourn him.[3] Part of this exile coincided with Ceolred's reign.[4] Æthelbald was related to Guthlac for—although this fact is never stated by Felix—they shared a common ancestry.

Guthlac's connection with Repton, first as a monk and later as a hermit who apparently looked to that monastery as his mother-house, is the only evidence of any value for the existence of a double monastery there in the early Anglo-Saxon period. Although a later tradition records that St. David founded a monastery at Repton in the sixth century, this seems unlikely. Felix is therefore the sole authority for an early date for this foundation. In Guthlac's two years at Repton the abbess was a woman named Ælfthryth,[5] but later in his life Ecburgh, daughter of Aldwulf of East Anglia, had become abbess. She too appears to have regarded Crowland as a dependency of Repton. The presentation of her enquiries about the future of the hermitage at Crowland after Guthlac's death may be modelled on Ælfflæd's questioning of Cuthbert about the Nor-thumbrian succession after Ecgfrith,[6] but the chapter very likely owes its inspiration to the continuance of a close relationship between Repton and the cell at Crowland. In Felix's time Repton, no matter what its rather problematical earlier custom had been, accepted the Roman obedience, for Felix tells us twice over that Guthlac received the Petrine tonsure there.[7]

A few more people are named once or twice in Felix's life. How far they are derived from reality and how far from Felix's knowledge of the way in which a legend should be written up is impossible to say. For example, two people are named as having given Guthlac a shroud. This curious inconsistency occurs in all the extant manu-scripts of the *Vita*, and is therefore generally ascribed to Felix himself. Yet the inconsistency may have arisen through some scribal

[1] *Vita*, §xx.
[2] *Vita*, §§xl, xlii, xlv, and xlix.
[3] *Vita*, §lii.
[4] *Vita*, §xlix.
[5] *Vita*, §xx. This may be the Ælfthryth whose case for readmission to church privileges was considered at the council of Mercia in A.D. 705 (see L. Ecken-stein, *Women under Monasticism 500 A.D. to 1500 A.D.* (Cambridge, 1896), p. 109).
[6] Colgrave, p. 191.
[7] *Vita*, §xx.

omission or substitution in the early textual history of the *Vita*, for
it does not occur in either the Old English translation or in Peter of
Blois's epitome, indicating either the alertness both of translator and
of Peter, or an omission made early in the transmission of the text.[1]
At any rate, the apparent self-contradiction between Ecgburgh's
and Ecgberht's gifts need not be regarded as evidence of Felix's
carelessness in gathering together his materials.

Felix refers by name to some twelve more of the men and women
who played a part in the saint's life. Each is for the most part a
central character in a typical hagiographic episode. Among the
named companions and servants of Æthelbald are Ecga[2] and
Offa,[3] but we are told as little about them as about the unnamed
servant of God who was staying at Crowland at the time a jackdaw
stole from Guthlac the parchments he was writing on,[4] and less
about them than about the *paterfamilias* from the people of the
Wissa cured of blindness after Guthlac's death.[5] Offa may, indeed,
still have been with Æthelbald after he came to the throne of Mercia,
for a man of that name is among the witnesses of several of his
charters.[6] We assume that Wilfrid, who in one chapter accompanies
Æthelbald to Crowland,[7] is the abbot Wilfrid whom Felix twice
cites as one of his chief informants;[8] he appears also as the witness
of the obedience shown Guthlac by swallows in their choice of a
nesting-place.[9] A young East-Anglian noble, Hwætred, was freed by
Guthlac from possession,[10] but the name is common enough in
Anglo-Saxon records and similar incidents occur in other saints'
lives, so we cannot be sure if this Hwætred is anything more than a
suitable fiction.

The bishop who consecrated Guthlac and his oratory[11] had with
him a secretary Wigfrith, unknown except from the two chapters of

---

[1] See *Vita*, §§xlviii and l for Ecgburgh's gift, whereas Guthlac is wrapped in
Ecgberht's shroud in §li, *on oþre scytan* according to the Old English translation,
alia syndone according to Peter.

[2] *Vita*, §xlii.

[3] *Vita*, §xlv.

[4] *Vita*, §xxxvii.

[5] *Vita*, §liii.

[6] Stenton, *Anglo-Saxon England*, p. 303.

[7] *Vita*, §xl.

[8] *Vita*, prologue and §xxviii.

[9] *Vita*, §xxxix.

[10] *Vita*, §xli.

[11] *Vita*, §§xlvi–xlvii.

the *Vita* in which he appears. The existence of Bishop Hædda himself is attested by other documents. He was at this time Bishop of Lichfield and, as Stenton has pointed out, the fact that the Bishop of Lichfield dedicated Guthlac's oratory suggests that Crowland was within the Mercian kingdom.[1] Later, however, the monks of Crowland confused Hædda with Hæddi, a contemporary bishop of Winchester.

Four other men named in the life all have a close connection with Crowland. They are Tatwine, the old man who first ferried Guthlac to Crowland;[2] Beccel, who was tempted to kill Guthlac[3] but remained with him faithfully to his death and was entrusted with his dying confidences;[4] the anchorite Ecgberht to whom, as to Pege, the secret of the angel of consolation might be told[5] and the donor of a shroud;[6] and Cissa, Guthlac's successor (although brought up a pagan)[7] and, together with Wilfrid, the most valued of Felix's informants.[8] As in Pege's case, stories attached themselves to these men in later chronicles of Crowland history. It is perhaps as well that only Beccel acquired separate *acta* of his own, for the life printed by Wynkyn de Worde well deserves Baring Gould's description, 'a collection of curious popular legends, nothing more'.[9]

The facts Felix gives of person and incident are, when summarized in this way, few, and the over-all impression left by a reading of the *Vita* is that he has dealt in types and stock episodes. Indeed, the details of Guthlac's life are so thoroughly pieced out with borrowings still recognizable that we are in danger of wondering if Guthlac ever existed. Within the *Vita*, however, there are some indications of the material from which Felix worked. A very striking break in narrative occurs between chapters xxvii and xxviii. At the beginning of §xxviii Felix declares: 'Igitur ut de sancti Guthlaci solitaria vita,

---

[1] Colgrave, p. 190; Stenton, *Anglo-Saxon England*, p. 50, n. 1; Ann Dornier, 'The Anglo-Saxon monastery at Breedon-on-the-hill, Leicestershire', *Mercian Studies* (Leicester, 1977), p. 157, suggests that he was earlier first a priest and then abbot of Medeshamstede.

[2] *Vita*, §xxv.

[3] *Vita*, §xxxv.

[4] *Vita*, §l.

[5] Ibid.

[6] *Vita*, §li.

[7] *Vita*, §xlviii.

[8] *Vita*, prologue and §xxviii.

[9] S. Baring Gould, *The Lives of the Saints* (London, 1897), x. 139; for an examination of these *acta* see J. Crawford, 'St Bertellin of Stafford', *The Downside Review*, cclxxxii (1968), 56–67.

sicut proposui, scribere exordiar, quae a frequentatoribus eius Wilfrido et Cissan audivi, eodem ordine, quo conperi, easdem res narrare curabo.' These words imply that for many the main events of the story of Guthlac began with his arrival at Crowland, an implication noted by Colgrave.[1] Similarly, the homilist who excerpted material from the Old English translation of the *Vita* chose not to include any of the introductory materials of the life in his sermon. Indeed, his homily opens without a conventional formula of the sort customary in so many Old English sermons (although it is not alone among the Vercelli Book sermons in opening abruptly).[2] Further support may be found for this identification of the beginning of the main episodes in the Guthlac legend in Felix's double reference to St. Bartholomew's Day as the date of Guthlac's arrival at Crowland.[3] Again, the choice of ending-point made by the Vercelli homilist may be significant. He diverges from Felix's account with the appearance of Bartholomew:

þa he ða se eadiga wer his þone getrywan freond geseah ða wæs he mid gastlicre gefeannesse 7 on heofoncundre blisse swiðe gefeonde 7 þa æfter þam fleah se haliga guðlac mid þam apostole *sancte* bartholomei to heofona rices wuldre 7 hine se hælend þær onfeng 7 he þær leofað 7 rixaþ in heofona rices wuldre a butan ende on ecnesse amen fiat:7[4]

These lines should be compared with the final sentence of §xxxii in the *Vita* and the opening of the following chapter:

Sanctus vero Guthlac adventum fidelissimi auxiliatoris sui persentiens, spiritali laetitia repletus, gavisus est.
    xxxiii. Tunc deinde sanctus Bartholomaeus catervis satellitum iubet, ut illum in locum suum cum magna quietudine, sine ulla offensionis molestia, reducerent.[5]

The clauses following *swiðe gefeonde* provide a separate ending for the homilist's extract from the *Vita*, and it cannot be said that he is here anticipating Felix's description of Guthlac's death, for Bartholomew plays no part in that scene. However, it could be

---

[1] Colgrave, p. 182.
[2] M. Förster, 'Der Vercelli-Codex CXVII nebst Abdruck einiger altenglischer Homilien der Handschrift', *Festschrift für Lorenz Morsbach* (Halle, 1913), p. 86, compares homilies xv and xxii.
[3] See J. Roberts, 'St Bartholomew's day: a problem resolved?' *MÆ*, xlvi (1977), 16–19.
[4] Text from *The Vercelli Book*, fo. 135ᵛ (ed. Celia Sisam, *Early English Manuscripts in Facsimile*, vol. xix, 1976).
[5] Colgrave's text.

argued that he knew some account of Guthlac's life which ended with his being taken to heaven by Bartholomew immediately after his journey to the gates of hell.[1] These chapters of the *Vita*, dealing with Guthlac's fights against devils, are very much in the Antonian tradition, so much so that only the saint's actual journey to hell-gates to behold the sufferings of the damned differs strikingly in content from the Evagrian and Athanasian lives of St. Anthony.[2] Perhaps this section of the *Vita*, in which Guthlac's patron saint plays so large a part, reflects the most important of the materials available to Felix for the life of St. Guthlac.

All that is known of Felix himself is to be found in the *Vita*. He was a monk, but little can be deduced from the phrase in which he refers to himself as *catholicae congregationis vernaculus*[3] beyond the recognition of this vocation. The same phrase appears also in a preface written by Aldhelm, his contemporary, whose style he obviously greatly admired,[4] and the words may be no more than a phrase conventional in Latin writing of that period. There is indeed scarcely anything in the preface to the life of Guthlac, where we might hope to find some information about the author, which cannot be paralleled in some earlier text, though the terms of the opening dedication suggest that Felix lived and worked in East Anglia, at any rate at the time he put together the *Vita*.[5] His method of composition, so far as its derivative aspect is concerned, is well described by B. J. Kurtz, who visualizes

... Felix at work, with the *Vita Antonii*, the *Vita Cuthberti*, and the *Dialogi Gregorii* open before him, and perhaps the *Vita Martini* as well, while with the plan and spirit of the *Antonius* as model he pieces out the details of the Guthlac oral tradition with passages and phrases from his four manuscripts, drawing at first most largely from Evagrius, later most often from Bede.[6]

[1] See further pp. 23 ff., 41, and 49.
[2] B. J. Kurtz, 'From St. Anthony to St. Guthlac', *University of California Publications in Modern Philology*, vol. xii, no. 2, (1926), p. 113.
[3] *Vita*, prologue.
[4] Colgrave, p. 15.
[5] Not only is the *Vita* dedicated to Ælfwald, but Ecburgh of Repton is described as *Adulfi regis filia* (§xlviii) without the name of Aldwulf's kingdom being given. Aldwulf ruled in East Anglia from 664 to 713 when he was succeeded by Ælfwald, apparently the last of the local dynasty in that region (see Stenton, *Anglo-Saxon England*, p. 210). There is some uncertainty as to the relationship between these men, but the length of Ælfwald's reign would suggest father and son or uncle and nephew rather than brothers.
[6] Kurtz, 'From St. Anthony to St. Guthlac', p. 126.

A useful list of sources used by Felix is available in B. Colgrave's edition,[1] demonstrating clearly the breadth of his reading. From the scanty details of Guthlac's life known to him and with the help of this wide reading Felix put together an instructive biography which remained popular even after twelfth-century simplified revisions of it were in circulation.

Felix's life of Guthlac places the saint in the Antonian rather than the Benedictine monastic tradition. Like Cuthbert and other western followers of the desert fathers, Guthlac imposed austerities upon himself and chose the life of a separate cell rather than the membership of a brotherhood; and after his death Cissa succeeded him as anchorite at Crowland. Apart from Felix's *Vita* the only early documents of any length concerned with Guthlac are the old English materials of the Exeter Book[2] and the Vercelli Book,[3] all glorifying the same tradition. Whether or not we believe in the existence of an early monastery at Crowland, sacked by the Danes, we must recognize that Felix does not mention it.[4] Most of the other references to and stories about Guthlac come from the period of Dunstan's reforms and from later centuries.[5] Thurkytel's foundation, some time after A.D. 971,[6] was a Benedictine abbey, and all the writings which emanated from it are informed with the ideals of the Benedictine way of life.

There may, however, be indications of early traditions embedded in the later Guthlac materials. For example, a scourge must at one time have played an important part in the local stories about the saint. Two of the eighteen illustrations in the Harley Roll[7] give emphasis to scourges. The eighth roundel is particularly interesting for, as well as hell being labelled *Infernus*, two other headings appear. Usually each episode represented in the roll has one title only, but in this picture two things are described, both that Bartholomew is giving a scourge to Guthlac and that the devils are carrying him to the gates of hell. In the next picture Guthlac has a whip in his right hand

---

[1] Colgrave, pp. 16–17.

[2] *Guthlac A* and *Guthlac B*.

[3] The Old English homily. The materials of the Old English life and martyrology derive ultimately from Felix.

[4] See *Vita*, §li, and Colgrave, p. 194.

[5] See Roberts, 'Inventory', §§3(b) ff.

[6] D. Whitelock, 'The Conversion of the Eastern Danelaw', *Saga-Book of the Viking Society*, xii (1941), 174.

[7] Sir George Warner, *The Guthlac Roll*, Roxburghe Club (Oxford, 1928). For scourges in the demons' hands, see frontispiece.

and, holding a devil by the neck, is about to use it. Bartholomew also gives Guthlac a scourge in the hell-gates scene in the poem by Henry of Avranches, and that incident was important enough for the scribe of the extant manuscript to direct special attention to it, writing in his margin: *De aduentu Bartholomei cum flagro*.[1] The tradition that Bartholomew gave Guthlac a scourge is again illustrated on the Longchamp seal,[2] and Guthlac holds a whip both in the statue on the west front of Crowland abbey[3] and in the central compartment of the quatrefoil over the great west door.[4] Three whips and knives quarterly, presumably in honour of Guthlac and his patron Bartholomew, became the arms of the abbey and appear on stones erected in the Crowland area. These arms were even adopted as the assay mark for Crowland in the seventeenth century. Such details attest at least to the persistence of this legend, but do not prove that it was already known in Felix's time. Some such tradition may have been known to the *Guthlac A* poet, who seems at any rate to have known stories in which Guthlac revealed more fighting spirit than in the *Vita* by Felix.

Whatever the local traditions may have been at an early period, and it is unlikely that they can be deduced reliably from the evidences now available,[5] they have given way to Felix's highly literary defini- tive life of Guthlac. His *Vita* must always be regarded as the primary source for the saint's cult, though whether it was used by the *Guthlac A* poet remains a problem open to debate. Sections were used by the *Guthlac B* poet. Stories without the authority of Felix, for example of Guthlac's scourge and his psalter,[6] might as easily be late inven- tions as early traditions. After all, even though Felix is heavily indebted to earlier hagiographic writings, this in his own day would not have reflected badly upon him. Students of English literature may tend to view his *Vita* merely as the source of one or both Old

---

[1] See text given by W. F. Bolton, 'The Middle English and Latin Poems of Saint Guthlac' (doctoral thesis, Princeton, 1954), l. 526.

[2] Warner, *The Guthlac Roll*, p. 23.

[3] W. Stukeley, *Itinerarium Curiosum* (London, 1724), p. 31, J. J. Gresley, *Some Account of Croyland Abbey, Lincolnshire* (Ashby-de-la-Zouche, 1886), p. 8, J. Schnebbelie, *The Antiquary's Museum* (London, 1800), p. 18.

[4] Gresley, *Croyland Abbey*, p. 4.

[5] An extreme instance is the tradition that Guthlac 'enclosed the devil in a boiling pot' (*The Acts and monuments of John Foxe*, I. ii (Townsend edn. in Cattley revision, London, 1837–41), p. 357).

[6] See Roberts, 'Inventory', p. 224.

English Guthlac poems, but should remember its value to historians who extract from among the elegancies of Felix information about Guthlac, his contemporaries, and the area in which he lived.

§2 *The manuscript*

A full description of the Exeter Book is to be found in the 1933 facsimile edition.[1] Useful supplementary material is available in N. R. Ker's review of the facsimile[2] and in his *Catalogue of Manuscripts containing Anglo-Saxon*. Kenneth Sisam's review of the facsimile is also important,[3] as are his later writings on the Exeter Book.[4] A detailed account of the manuscript and its contents is given also in the third volume of The Anglo-Saxon Poetic Records series.[5] Professor Pope's recent discussion of some Exeter Book problems is invaluable.[6]

The manuscript is generally ascribed to the latter half of the tenth century, as are the other great codices which contain the bulk of surviving Old English poetry. It now consists of 131 folios, of which the first eight are later than the 123 folios (numbered 8 to 130) which remain from the original collection of Old English verse. The eight additional folios, the first containing a title given to the book in post-medieval times and the number 3051, and the other seven containing eleventh- and twelfth-century materials in both English and Latin from Cambridge University MS. Ii, ii. 11, are reproduced in the facsimile of the manuscript, together with a discussion of them by M. Förster. Only the 123 leaves numbered 8–130 therefore constitute the Anglo-Saxon poetic manuscript.

These leaves were apparently written by a single scribe who was perhaps responsible also for two other manuscripts at one time in Exeter, MS. Lambeth 149 (which left Exeter in 1018) and MS. Bodley 319 (given to Oxford by the cathedral Chapter in 1602). The folios are c. 310–20 × 218–25 mm (written space 240 × 160 mm),

---

[1] CFF.

[2] *MÆ* ii (1933), 224–31.

[3] *RES* x (1934), 338–42.

[4] *Studies in the History of Old English Literature*, esp. chapter 6 and n. C.

[5] KD.

[6] John C. Pope, 'Palaeography and poetry: some solved and unsolved problems of the Exeter Book', *Medieval Scribes, Manuscripts & Libraries*, Essays presented to N. R. Ker, edited by M. B. Parkes and Andrew G. Watson (London, 1978), pp. 25–65.

with 21 to 23 long lines of writing per page (approximately 36 verse lines). As well as the loss from the beginning of the manuscript, leaves have disappeared after folios 15, 37, 69, 73, 97, 105, and 111, 118, 125(2), and 130(1 or 2), and the top part of folio 53 has been cut away. The seventeen gatherings of the manuscript now vary in size from 5 to 8 folios and are not provided with signatures (unlike the Vercelli Book gatherings).

The Guthlac poems, filling folios 32^v to 52^v, appear in the gatherings numbered IV, V, and VI by Förster. Gatherings IV and VI are among those gatherings of the manuscript still made up of 8 folios; VI, containing 3 full sheets and 2 half-sheets folded in, is the only complete gathering of the manuscript not made up of the usual 4 folded sheets. Gathering V has lost its first folio, i.e. some 70 lines of *Guthlac A* (between lines 368 and 369) which is otherwise complete. *Guthlac B*, which begins part of the way down folio 44^v, ends in mid-sentence with the last folio (52^v) of gathering VI. The top part of folio 53 has been cut away, so that now the first line of script on folio 53^r corresponds to the fifth line normally, and four script lines (i.e. about six verse lines) have gone with the top portion of 53^r. It has often been suggested that a whole gathering has fallen out between folios 52 and 53, that is between gatherings VI and VII, for in this part of the manuscript the beginning of a new poem is signalled by one or two free lines followed by a line filled with large capitals.[1] The first line of script remaining on folio 53^r is, however, marked out as the beginning of a fitt, a conclusion supported by the appearance of the lower tips of two letters from what must have been the fourth line of script immediately above. Recently an ingenious attempt has been made to treat the two fitts called *Azarias* which begin on folio 53^r as 'really a pair of songs of supplication and praise . . . to be related to *Guðlac*',[2] in an avowed attempt to 'put to rest the disquieting idea of a lost gathering in the Exeter book',[3] but in the end it may prove less disquieting to assume the now traditional lost gathering.[4]

The longer poems of the Exeter Book, if it is accepted that some

[1] Ker, *MÆ* review, p. 227.

[2] R. T. Farrell, 'Some remarks on the Exeter Book *Azarias*', *MÆ*, xli (1972), 5.

[3] Ibid., p. 7.

[4] J. Roberts, '*Guðlac* A, B, and C?', *MÆ*, xlii (1973), 43–6; see also Pope, 'Palaeography and poetry', pp. 35–41.

considerable material has been lost from the beginning of *Azarias*, are all in the first part of the manuscript on folios 8ʳ–76ʳ. The opening of each is distinguished by a line almost entirely filled with bold capitals and their endings by heavy punctuation followed by one or two lines blank. It is probable that the collection of Advent hymns which make up *Christ I* had such introductory capitals, and *Azarias* too if a lost gathering is assumed. In the latter part of the manuscript such lines of capitals are used erratically, appearing only at the beginning of *The Gifts of Men*, *Widsith*, and *Soul and Body II*, and spacing between shorter poems is frequently lacking. Sections within the longer poems, like the shorter poems, the riddles, and fragments, open with one or two large introductory capitals and end with heavy punctuation; a free part-line, line, or lines may follow. These fitts are not numbered, unlike the sections of *Beowulf* which show that at some time the divisions within that poem were fully numbered. The only punctuation within fitts or short poems is a low dot (sometimes with an accompanying small capital) used sparingly and normally coincident with a verse ending. N. R. Ker has pointed out[1] that it is difficult to be sure of the scribe's dots on certain folios where post-medieval stops have been added (fos. 14ᵛ–15ᵛ, 16ᵛ–20ʳ, 21ʳ, 32ᵛ, and 35ʳ). 'Accent' marks occur throughout the manuscript, five-sixths over vowels etymologically long in words frequently so marked. Often where the accent is placed over a short vowel, it falls on a syllable obviously stressed. Sometimes a preposition, either free or a verbal prefix, may carry an accent and be unstressed: in such cases the accent may have served to indicate syllabic division, facilitating reading in the same way as the presence of small capitals, low dots, and variations in letter forms. Abbreviations are sparingly used and are those generally found in Old English manuscripts. Used in these poems are the stroke (usually to indicate the omission of a nasal consonant and sometimes of *e*, as *ḡþonc* 368), 7 for *ond*, and *þ̄* for *þæt*. Nowell's hand has been identified in the post-medieval interlinear English gloss to seven lines on folio 9ʳ,[2] but whether or not he is responsible for the finer script which appears on folios 10ʳ, 20ᵛ, 32ᵛ, and 44ᵛ is uncertain.

---

[1] *MÆ* review, p. 228.
[2] Robin Flower, 'Laurence Nowell and the Discovery of England in Tudor Times', *Proceedings of the British Academy*, xii (1935), 70.

§3. *Editorial history of the Guthlac poems*

The Exeter Book, which Leofric gave among other donations to the cathedral at Exeter at some time in the middle of the eleventh century, is the only one of all his books still in Exeter. It is described in the catalogue of his donations as: '.i. mycel Englisc boc be ge-hwilcum þingum on leoðwisan ge-worht'.[1] For years it lay neglected, occasionally used as a store for gold-leaf or as a stand for a drinker's mug. It must have seemed of little value to an age which, unable even to translate its description in this Old English list, labelled it *a mochel englys boke of meny thyngys*.[2] Apparently the book was not recognized as a collection of verse in Middle English times. In the sixteenth century too it attracted little attention. Although Laurence Nowell is thought responsible for some interlinear glossing and other marginalia[3] he did not apparently draw on poetic texts to any significant extent for his lexicographical work.[4] It is likely also that John Joscelyn, Archbishop Parker's secretary, consulted the manuscript in Exeter, for he uses some of the preliminary matter in his preface to Parker's *A testimonie of antiquitie* (1566).[5] However, Joscelyn and his contemporaries were interested in finding and examining books and charters concerned with law, customs, the church, and English history, and the book remained virtually unknown outside catalogues of the cathedral's possessions until 1705. From Wanley's *Catalogus*[6] of that year we learn that the Exeter Book was already bound and foliated as it was to remain until its rebinding in 1930 when the facsimile edition was put in hand.

Early in the nineteenth century J. J. Conybeare, who was Professor of Poetry and Anglo-Saxon at Oxford, read three papers on the Exeter Book before the Society of Antiquaries. With their publication in *Archaeologia*[7] a sizeable amount of the verse of the Exeter Book was for the first time available in print,[8] for Conybeare

---

[1] CFF, p. 28, ll. 38–9.

[2] CFF, p. 31, l. 35.

[3] See CFF, p. 34.

[4] A. H. Marckwardt, *Laurence Nowell's 'Vocabularium Saxonicum'* (Ann Arbor, 1952), p. 8.

[5] CFF, p. 91; Ker, *Catalogue*, no. 116.

[6] See pp. 279–81.

[7] Conybeare, 'Account of a Saxon Manuscript preserved in the Cathedral Library at Exeter', *Archaeologia* xvii (1812), 180–97.

[8] *c*. 100 lines in all, from *Christ*, *The Phoenix*, and *Soul and Body II*.

was interested not only in runic curiosities but also in 'our early Poetry'. Conybeare died in 1824 and the only other memorial to his interest in Old English is an edition of some of the more important minor poems of the manuscript, made from his papers and lecture notes by his brother.[1]

N. F. S. Grundtvig, sent to England by the Danish government to study Old English manuscripts, visited Exeter in 1830. A year earlier he had made enquiries in London about the Exeter Book, with the result that by the time he reached Exeter the manuscript had been requested by the British Museum for a copy to be made of it. However, it had not yet been sent to London and Grundtvig, to his great amazement, was locked into a room daily with the manuscript for as long as he wished. His many interests prevented him from ever completing his proposed edition and only a little of his transcript was eventually published.[2]

With Benjamin Thorpe's arrival in Exeter in 1832 the textual history of the Guthlac materials in the Exeter Book begins. He found the codex had at last been sent to the British Museum for transcription by Robert Chambers, and it was hurriedly returned to Exeter for Thorpe to prepare his edition. In his *Codex Exoniensis* of 1842 the 1,379 lines of verse now generally accepted as relating to Guthlac are divided into three separate poems. Thorpe marks out the first twenty-nine lines as the second part of a poem 'Of Souls after Death etc.'. Lines 30 to 92 are identified as a separate and complete 'Poem Moral and Religious', of which he writes: 'This poem is highly unintelligible. It is probably, like many others, a translation from a Latin original by one ill-qualified for the task; and this I suspect to be a chief cause of the numerous obscurities attending similar productions in Anglo-Saxon.'[3] 'The Legend of Saint Guthlac' begins with *Guthlac A*, l. 93, i.e. with the second fitt of that poem. Loss (a leaf is suggested) is recognized between folios 38 and 39 (*A*, ll. 368–9), but no further division of the Guthlac material is made. The heavy capitals of the opening of *Guthlac B* which had caused Wanley to label this material a new book[4] do

---

[1] W. D. Conybeare, *J. J. Conybeare's Illustrations of Anglo-Saxon Poetry* (London, 1826).

[2] Two riddles (5, 26) and ll. 1–29 of *Christ* were published by Müller in 1835, and Grundtvig himself published an edition of *The Phoenix* in 1840.

[3] Thorpe, *Cod. Ex.*, p. 503.

[4] Wanley, *Catalogus*, p. 281.

not stop Thorpe from treating it as the continuation of a single poem. His explanation of the first sixty lines of *Guthlac B* runs: 'This digression, though in appearance a clumsy interpolation is, nevertheless, a portion of the poem, as is evident from lines 29 and 30, page 154 [line 878], where it is connected with the rest by the alliterating words *sigorlean sohtun* and *secgað*.'[1] At the end of the Guthlac material he notes the excision of the upper part of folio 53[2] and in his commentary remarks: 'The rest of the legend, which is void of interest, may be seen in Felix.'[3]

It may perhaps seem that too much attention is here given to an early editor, but it must be remembered that Thorpe's *Codex Exoniensis* was Grein's chief source for the material of the Exeter Book when in 1857 and 1858 he included it in his *Bibliothek der angelsächsischen Poesie*, providing the first definitive edition of the Exeter Book poems. The opening twenty-nine lines of *Guthlac A*, which Thorpe had taken as the second part of his 'Of Souls after Death etc.', were now taken as the end of *Christ*. Grein treats Thorpe's 'Poem Moral and Religious' (*Guthlac A* ll. 30–92) as the beginning of one Guthlac poem. This new division of the Guthlac material has had a long-lasting effect upon the critical history of *Guthlac A* and *Guthlac B*. Grein's decisions,[4] although already disputed by Gollancz as early as 1892,[5] are responsible both for the consecutive numbering of the poems and for the instigation of an unnecessarily protracted consideration of the unity of *Guthlac A*. His lineation of the texts is followed in the two most important Anglo-Saxon dictionaries.[6]

Some of the emendations Grein suggested for Thorpe's readings were later to prove to be the actual manuscript readings, but where he attempted to fill in lacunae he was less successful. For some time German scholars followed his lead, trying to fill up inductively the gaps in damaged parts of the Exeter Book. With the publication in 1874 of Schipper's notes from his collation of the manu-

---

[1] Thorpe, *Cod. Ex.*, p. 505.

[2] Ibid., p. 184.

[3] Ibid., p. 507.

[4] Note especially that his *Christ* and the disputed 29 lines of *Guthlac A* appear in *Dichtungen der Angelsachsen*, i, thus firmly detached from the single Guthlac poem of volume ii.

[5] I. Gollancz, *Cynewulf's Christ* (London, 1892), p. xix.

[6] References to both Thorpe and Grein are given in BT. Köhler's dictionary of 1912, a revision of Grein's own *Sprachschatz* (1861–4), retains the references to Grein's *Bibliothek*.

script against the editions of Thorpe and Grein, a fairly detailed account of the manuscript, together with corrections of many things misreported by Thorpe, became available. So far as other parts of the Exeter Book are concerned, it is unfortunate that Schipper did not use Chambers's transcript which could have provided a few readings that had since his day been obscured by binding strips; for the 1,379 lines of Guthlac material, however, Schipper notes only a few incorrect readings, some misplaced accents, and occasional emendations made within the manuscript itself. To note these things he did not need the help of the British Museum transcript.

The first part of a new edition of the Exeter Book, edited by Israel Gollancz for the Early English Text Society, appeared in 1895. In this volume Gollancz, following his own earlier suggestion, prints the twenty-nine lines taken by both Thorpe and Grein with preceding materials of the manuscript as the opening of the first of two Guthlac poems. He justifies this departure from earlier editorial practice by a consideration of the scribe's presentation of the poems in the earlier part of the manuscript, noting the importance of the row of capitals which opens these lines on folio 32^v. His identification of the beginning of the first Guthlac poem did not gain immediate acceptance and was not followed three years later in the third volume of the revision of Grein's *Bibliothek*. In this last volume of the new series, largely devoted to the Exeter Book collection, new readings drawn from Assmann's examination of the relevant manuscripts are to be found, but no change is made in Grein's distribution of the Guthlac material. So, as in Grein's edition, the first twenty-nine lines of *Guthlac A* are the end of *Christ*. Two Guthlac poems are identified.[1]

Gollancz, in his edition of poems from the Exeter Book, gives both his own new consecutive numbering for the Guthlac poems and references to the *Bibliothek* numbering, a practice followed also in the 1933 facsimile. Both systems are widely used to-day, despite the appearance in 1936 of *The Exeter Book* as the third volume of The Anglo-Saxon Poetic Records series, in which only the newer line references are given. The results of this confusion are apparent, not only in the identification of extracts and citations in

---

[1] Assmann, p. 78, recognizes the break between the two poems in the manuscript.

the critical writings on these poems but also in translations.[1] The question of the unity of *Guthlac A* will be surveyed in a later section of this Introduction, but it should be noted here that the often discussed opening twenty-nine lines are not included in the edition of 'The Old English Poem of St Guthlac' presented by Bertha Thompson for a Leeds University doctorate in 1931 and that that editor did not recognize the existence of two separate and very different poems about Guthlac.

§4. *The sources of* Guthlac A

The relationship of *Guthlac A* to Felix's life of St. Guthlac has been much discussed and, though this is a question on which there is little agreement, it is generally held that the poet must have known the *Vita*.[2] Certainly a great part of the poem (ll. 93–748) loosely resembles Felix's account of the saint's struggles against demons.[3] However, Rieger, the earliest critic to give this question more than a cursory glance, argues for the poem's independence of the *Vita*, noting especially that the passage in which Guthlac is shown and taunted with the lax behaviour of monks (ll. 412–512) is a tale of which Felix knows nothing, and suggesting that the poet must have owed much to oral tradition.[4] Following Fritzsche's observation that the poet's ignorance of the *Vita* cannot be argued much beyond line 529,[5] both D'Ham and Lefèvre examine and contrast two parts of *Guthlac A*. D'Ham[6] is unable to identify any of the parallels between the latter part of the poem and the *Vita* inferred by Fritzsche. Lefèvre[7] notes that the description of the arrival of Bartholomew (ll. 685–9) and of the terror of the demons

[1] E.g. G. K. Anderson, *The Literature of the Anglo-Saxons* (Princeton, 1949), pp. 126 and 151, manages to follow the older lineation within his text and the newer in his notes.
[2] There is a useful summary of attitudes in T. Wolpers, *Die englische Heiligenlegende des Mittelalters* (Tübingen, 1964), p. 112.
[3] *Vita*, §§xxviii–xxxiii.
[4] M. Rieger, 'Über Cynevulf', *Zeitschrift für deutsche Philologie*, i (1869), 325, n. 1.
[5] A. Fritzsche, 'Das angelsächsische Gedicht Andreas und Cynewulf', *Anglia*, ii (1879), 461.
[6] O. D'Ham, *Der gegenwärtige Stand der Cynewulf-Frage* (Limburg, 1883), pp. 25, 45.
[7] P. Lefèvre, 'Das altenglische Gedicht vom hl. Guthlac', *Anglia*, vi (1883), 227 ff.

(ll. 692–5) may owe something to the *Vita*, without pointing to passages in the life from which these may stem.

Three close verbal similarities between *Guthlac A* and Felix, advanced by Liebermann,[1] are still widely quoted in summaries of this problem, though generally without sufficient examination. The first is the poet's account of the place where Guthlac built his home:

> nales þy he giemde þurh *gitsunga*
> *lænes lifwelan*
>
> (ll. 150–1b)

Guthlac has chosen to become an anchorite and will strive to keep his chosen dwelling-place *on beorhge*[2] for God's glory because he does not look for worldly riches. Liebermann compares with this passage Felix's reference to the mound where Guthlac lived as a

> ... tumulus agrestibus glaebis coacervatus, quem olim *avari* solitudinis frequentatores *lucri* ergo illic adquirendi defodientes scindebant, in cuius latere velut cisterna inesse videbatur.[3]

The poet makes no allusion to others having sought treasure in that place. Indeed, any resemblance here between the poem and *Vita* is slight and probably due to coincidence. The poet is recounting how Guthlac followed the advice of his two guardian angels, despising the wordly possessions which one suggested he should seek and working towards *þa longan gód*[4] as the other prompted, so there is no need to look beyond the immediate context to find a reason for the inclusion of the phrase *lænes lifwelan*. The other two similarities noted by Liebermann are closer. With the words of caution addressed by Bartholomew to the demons:

> Ne sy him banes bryce ne blodig wund,
> lices læla *ne laþes wiht*
>
> (ll. 698–9)

he compares a phrase in the instructions given by Bartholomew to the demons in the *Vita*:

> ... ut illum in locum suum cum magna quietudine, *sine ulla* offensionis molestia, reducerent.[5]

---

[1] F. Liebermann, 'Über ostenglische Geschichtsquellen', *Neues Archiv*, xviii (1892), 247; the phrases actually cited as close parallels are italicized in the quotations in this paragraph.

[2] l. 140.

[3] *Vita*, §xxviii.

[4] l. 120.

[5] *Vita*, §xxxiii.

The third of Liebermann's parallels occurs in the poet's account of how Guthlac was returned to his dwelling-place. The demons carry him carefully, guarding him from falling:

> wæron hyra gongas under Godes egsan
> smeþe 7 gesefte.

(ll. 731–2b)

The wording is at once simpler and more dramatic than in the Latin compared:

Nam illum revehentes cum nimia *suavitate*, velut *quietissimo* alarum remigio, ita ut nec in curru nec in navi modestius duci potuisset, subvolabant.[1]

It is evident that the poet echoes neither the structure nor the imagery of the *Vita* in this place.

The next examination of the relationship between *Guthlac A* and the *Vita* to contain any detail is found in Forstmann's dissertation upon this problem.[2] Forstmann begins by summarizing both the poem (for him a poem of 790 lines) and the *Vita*, detailing in a running commentary what Felix material is not used by the poet and listing five features of the poem not present in the Latin life.[3] Of these the most important is the observation that Guthlac's home is *auf einem einsamen Berge* in the poem. The poet's first description of Guthlac's hermitage as a *beorgseþel* 'a dwelling-place in the hills',[4] following as it does upon his discussion of *ánbuendra . . . on westennum*,[5] recalls rather the lives of the desert fathers than of Felix's Guthlac. A well-argued attempt to equate the use of *beorg* in *Guthlac A* with Felix's *tumulus* fails to convince because textual reinforcement is lacking.[6] The pervasive imagery is of hills and waste places and, as Paul F. Reichardt has recently pointed out, the *beorg* is 'as much a symbol of interior spiritual achievement as a geographical location

---

[1] *Vita*, §xxxiii.

[2] Printed in 1901 and reprinted as the first section of Forstmann, 'Untersuchungen zur Guthlac-Legende', *BBA*, xii (1902).

[3] Ibid., pp. 15–16.

[4] l. 102; cf. with this nonceword the phrase *beorges setl* 383.

[5] ll. 81–92.

[6] L. K. Shook, 'The Burial Mound in *Guthlac A*', *Modern Philology*, lviii (1960), 4 ff., and see Commentary for ll. 140, 274, and 384. Father Shook's interpretation is elaborated by Karl P. Wentersdorf '*Guthlac A*: The Battle for the *Beorg*' *Neophilologus*, lxii (1978), 135–42, who describes Crowland as 'a latter day Calvary', arguing that the word *bearu* 'not only designates an ordinary grove but is also a technical term for a sacroneme, the combination of *beorg* and *bearu*'.

in the fens of Crowland'.[1] Guthlac's tormentors mourn for the *grene beorgas*[2] that his constancy made them forgo, a phrase perhaps indicating that the site of his hermitage was in the poet's eyes a green rising set among hills. Fred C. Robinson indeed suggests that Crowland (*cruglond* 'the land of the hump (or mound)') where by tradition Guthlac lived as a hermit could have 'fostered the poet's imagination to make the mound a focal image'.[3]

The four other features noted by Forstmann as absent from the *Vita* are the saint's erection of a cross, the different temptations in the poem, the statement of Guthlac's unworthiness made by the demons,[4] and their intent to drive him away from their territory. He also draws attention to the different handling of bird and fish motifs in the two works, concluding from his negative evidence that *Guthlac A* is independent of the *Vita*. G. H. Gerould at first decides for the independence of *Guthlac A* from Felix,[5] but later changes his mind[6] and at some length relates the poem to the *Vita*, seizing on casual similarities, minimizing differences. He can therefore equate the end of the poem[7] with the conventional eulogistic part of Felix's account of Guthlac's body being found incorrupt after twelve months[8] and point out that, although Felix is concerned only with Guthlac, the spirit is in both poem and *Vita* similar.[9] B. J. Kurtz judges the passages cited by Gerould as 'not sufficiently similar to prove derivation'[10] and cannot find any indication that the poet was trying to recast the material presented by Felix.[11] Instead he recognizes the poet's originality in dealing with two important themes, Guthlac's

---

[1] '*Guthlac A* and the Landscape of Spiritual Perfection', *Neophilologus*, lviii (1974), 335.

[2] l. 232; cf. *beorgas* 209.

[3] F. C. Robinson, 'The Significance of Names in Old English Literature', *Anglia*, lxxxvi (1968), 48–9 and n. 92.

[4] ll. 579–89; and perhaps the preceding lines of reported speech are to be noted here.

[5] Review of Forstmann's 'Untersuchungen' in *Englische Studien*, xxxiv (1904), 96.

[6] Gerould, *Saints' Legends* (Boston and New York, 1916), p. 80, and 'The Old English Poems on St. Guthlac and their Latin Source', *MLN*, xxxii (1917), 77–89.

[7] ll. 790–818.

[8] *Vita*, §li.

[9] Gerould, 'The Old English Poems', p. 84.

[10] 'From St. Anthony to St. Guthlac', *University of California Publications in Modern Philology*, vol. xii, no. 2 (1926), p. 143, n. 63.

[11] Ibid., p. 145.

setting up of his hermitage and the demonic attacks, and finds the differences between *Vita* and poem 'so great as indeed to cast serious doubt upon the assumption of literary indebtedness'.[1] C. Schaar, apparently independently of Kurtz, comes to much the same conclusions,[2] finding a resemblance between *Vita* and *Guthlac A* only in the arrival of St. Bartholomew. Colgrave may well be right in concluding that 'the poet had a vague knowledge of Felix's work',[3] but it is surprising that the proof of such a relationship is so difficult to find.

Developing a suggestion put forward by Grau,[4] Father Shook looks at *Guthlac A* against the patristic traditions of psychopomps[5] and finds some general correspondences between the poem and the *Visio sancti Pauli*.[6] He singles out in particular the fourteenth chapter of the *Visio*, a chapter that has long been recognized as a manifestation of the 'soul journey' motif (itself part of the larger eschatological conception, the otherworld journey) in Christian writings. The theme is treated elsewhere in Old English, both in verse[7] and prose.[8] It was well known to Anglo-Saxon and Irish Latinists in such forms as the otherworld visions related by Gregory in his *Dialogues*,[9] and became widely used by hagiographers for death scenes.[10] The theme was familiar also to the artist of the Harley Roll.[11] In his picture of Guthlac's death he draws one angel who receives the saint's soul as it leaves his mouth and another who hovers nearby with an outstretched cloth. The distinction between

---

[1] Ibid.

[2] C. Schaar, *Critical Studies in the Cynewulf Group*, Lund Studies in English, xvii, (1949), 39–42.

[3] Colgrave, p. 20 and n. 2; his suggestion that the saint has 'his dwelling on a barrow' in *Guthlac A* may have influenced Shook's reading of the poem.

[4] G. Grau, 'Quellen und Verwandtschaften der Älteren Germanischen Darstellungen des Jüngsten Gerichtes', *Studien zur englischen Philologie*, xxxi (1908), 87.

[5] L. K. Shook, 'The Prologue of the Old English *Guthlac A*', *Mediaeval Studies*, xxiii (1961), 294–304.

[6] Ibid., p. 302, and see Commentary for ll. 4 ff.

[7] The *Soul and Body* poems are, as pointed out by M. W. Bloomfield, *The Seven Deadly Sins* (Michigan, 1952), p. 20, within this tradition.

[8] See the homilies discussed by R. Willard, 'Two Apocrypha in Old English Homilies', *Beiträge zur englischen Philologie*, xxx (1935).

[9] Bloomfield, *The Seven Deadly Sins*, p. 14.

[10] L. Dudley, *The Egyptian Elements in the Legend of the Body and Soul* (Baltimore, 1911), p. 44.

[11] Ibid., p. 171, and see Harley Roll, plate xiv.

anima and *spiritus*, important in the *Visio sancti Pauli* texts cited
by Shook, can be fitted into *Guthlac A* only with an unusual manipulation of both syntax and vocabulary,[1] and it is not a constant feature
in stories of the soul journey convention.[2] It is not found in the Old
English *Soul and Body* poems, nor in the sermons based on the
exemplum of the three utterances.[3]

There are few resemblances in imagery and phrasing between
Guthlac A and the two *Soul and Body* poems beyond those to be
expected among any Old English poems. The soul journey traditions
have given the *Guthlac A* poet his opening scene in which an angel
greets the soul of a just man, whereas in the *Soul and Body* poems a
debate is waged between a soul and its body. In the sermons based
on the exemplum of the three utterances, an angel (or, in some
versions, angels) arrives to receive the soul which, if a good man's
soul, exclaims that it sees light, joy, and a pleasant way before it,
but if a bad man's soul, that it sees shadows, sorrow, and a hard
way. The soul is then escorted, either by an archangel or with the
support of choirs of angels before and behind it, to God for judgement; the wicked depart into eternal fire and the good are taken to
Paradise where they will remain until Judgement Day. It is possible
to glimpse in this summary some of the themes which appear in the
opening twenty-nine lines of *Guthlac A* and again at the end. These
homilies may therefore give us a clearer idea than does the *Visio
sancti Pauli* of the themes which the poet may have drawn from the
soul journey tradition.

Willard brings together five such homilies, in Latin, Irish, and
late Old English, and he suggests that these share features which
presuppose a brief and well-known narrative of the events which
occur between the soul's separation from the body and its judgement
by God. All the texts assembled by him contain utterances which
obviously stem ultimately from one source, although they differ
from version to version in order and form:

Certainly there has been much freedom, not only in the order of the
utterances, but in the wording, as well, and in the association of response
to utterance. In each of our texts the story of the Three Utterances is
inserted as an exemplum; it is there to make a point. It is not used

[1] See Commentary, ll. 4ff.
[2] Bloomfield, *The Seven Deadly Sins*, p. 17.
[3] Willard, 'Two Apocrypha in Old English Homilies', pp. 31 ff.

twice in the same way or under the same circumstances. It is a short, easily apprehended piece, which is not hard to remember in its main outline.[1]

At the beginning of *Guthlac A* a good man is dying. His soul leaves his body, and so it comes about that angel and soul first meet. The angel announces God's message to the blessed soul, affirming that the soul will travel on pleasant ways, that it will see glory's bright light and that it will arrive at a home where there is no sorrow. It seems likely that the poet knew some source[2] in which the utterances of the good soul appeared and that this may have furnished him with the material for his angel's speech. At any rate, he returns to these same themes towards the end of the poem, assuring all who love truth that God will make life's ways pleasant for them[3] and that they will have no sorrow after death.[4]

Father Shook[5] suggests that elsewhere in the poem than the opening section there are indications of the poet's knowledge of apocryphal materials,[6] citing lines 557–68 as 'strong evidence' that there were available to him sources which 'Felix either did not know or preferred not to employ'. Although he singles out as particularly noteworthy lines 560–3, the following passage is perhaps as striking:

> Hy hine bregdon, budon orlege,
> egsan 7 ondan arleaslice,
> frecne fore: swa bið feonda þeaw
> þon*ne* hy soðfæstra sawle willað
> synnum beswican 7 searocræftu*m*.
> (ll. 564–8)

Guthlac's journey to hell-door is surely to be contrasted with the poet's opening account of the greeting given to the blessed soul, an impression reinforced by the content of the speech of accusation made by the demons to Guthlac.[7] This account of the further journey offered him by the demons may owe something to the

---

[1] Willard, 'Two Apocrypha in Old English Homilies', p. 125.
[2] An example is given in Appendix I.
[3] ll. 760 ff. and 790 ff.
[4] ll. 811 ff.
[5] Shook, 'The Prologue of the Old English *Guthlac A*', p. 302.
[6] F. R. Lipp, '*Guthlac A*: an Interpretation', *Mediaeval Studies*, xxxiii (1971), 46, points out that *Guthlac A* lacks the descriptive qualities of apocryphal apocalyptic literature.
[7] ll. 579–89.

utterances of the wicked soul in the three utterances exemplum. It can at least be said that Grau and Shook are right in placing this poem within the soul journey tradition.

   More agreement is found among the critics on the source for *Guthlac A* 30 ff. than for the rest of the poem, though even here two sources are in competition. Gerould suggests that the content of this passage may derive from either the tenth chapter of the *Vitae Patrum* of Gregory of Tours[1] or from the second book of Lactantius's *De ira dei*:[2]

Multi variique sunt gradus per quos ad cœlorum regna conscenditur. . .
(*Gregory*)

Nam cum sint gradus multi per quos ad domicilium ueritatis ascenditur
. . .   (*Lactantius*)

Either of these passages, or similar phraseology in another writer, could have prompted:

> Monge sindon geond middangeard
> hadas under heofonum þa þe in haligra
> rim arisað.
>
> (ll. 30–2a)

The following elegiac passage does not, however, come from either of these sources.[3] With line 59[4]

> he fela findeð, fea beoð gecorene,

obviously based on Matthew 22: 16, the poet chooses to describe two ways in which men may serve God on earth (at the same time answering his own question of ll. 26–9). The distinction between monastic and anchoritic life is often drawn in early medieval religious writings, but there are now some striking similarities between lines 60–92 and the tenth chapter of the *Vitae Patrum*:

Nam si ad martyrium mens accensa est, hujus adjutorii opem poposcit martyr ut vinceret; si jejunii observantiam adhibere studiit, ut ab eo confortaretur afflictus est; si castitati artus reservare voluit impollutos, ut ab illo muniretur oravit; si post ignorantiam pœnitendo converti desideravit, ut ab eo nihilominus sublevaretur cum lacrymis flagitavit; et si quid operis boni exercere eorum quispiam meditatus est, ut ab hoc adjutorio juvaretur expetiit.

[1] *PL* lxxi, 1054–5.
[2] S. Brandt and G. Laubmann, 'L. Caeli Firmiani Lactanti opera omnia', *Corpus Scriptorum Ecclesiasticorum Latinorum*, xxvii (1893–7), ii. 69.
[3] l. 50 may possibly suggest the poet's return to some such source.
[4] See also the Commentary.

Lines 60–80 describe the behaviour suited to those who *non modo martyres* serve God among their fellow men, and lines 81–92 tell over briefly the perils that beset those with mind *ad martyrium . . . accensa.* The division between *fela* and *fea* of line 59 is carefully developed, so that the poet can now turn to the struggles of one of God's chosen champions. Moreover, Gregory's words may have remained in his mind as he worked through his account of Guthlac's struggles with devils, for the passage cited above is in tune with his view of Guthlac as a man who *martyrhád mode gelufade*[1] and as a *martyre* who was *from moncynnes synnum asundrad.*[2] This Guthlac does not endure passively the persecutions which come upon him, but fights to continue in his chosen dwelling-place as a champion of God.

Although the *Guthlac A* poet's familiarity with the writings of the church fathers and with much hagiographical literature is apparent, specific sources for other passages within his poem cannot easily be found. Occasionally well-known phrases spring to mind on a reading of the poem, for example from the Evagrian life of St. Anthony.[3] The demons of *Guthlac A*, like the demons whom Anthony strove against, think the lonely hermitage chosen by the saint their own and advise him:

> Geswic þisses setles
> (l. 278a)

just as Anthony is advised:

abscede a finibus alienis, non potes nostras insidias sustinere.   (§13)

Or again, when Guthlac has undergone many temptations from demons and withstood them all, the poet tells us:

> wæs seo æreste earmra gæsta
> costung ofercumen;
> (ll. 437–8a)

The words are reminiscent of Evagrius's account of Anthony's first victory:

Hæc autem Antonii contra diabolum fuit prima victoria . . .   (§7)

Even the poet's description of Guthlac's hermitage recalls Evagrius's

---

[1] l. 472.
[2] ll. 514–15a.
[3] *PG* xxvi 837–976.

picture of Anthony's dwelling-place—at the foot of a mountain by a clear running spring, in a plain which held a few uncared-for trees [1]— rather than the marshy Crowland countryside of Felix's *Vita*.

Wolpers [2] finds resemblances between *Guthlac A* and other hagiographic writings, but they are of much the same sort as these, coincidental parallels due to similarity of subject matter. Towards the end of the poem he finds the tone reminiscent of the psalms of praise and of the *Vita Pauli* of Jerome but, though he suggests that lines 748b–51 recall the final chapter of the *Vita Pauli*, he is unwilling to press this similarity much further. He notes also that the poet might have looked to chapter xxii of the Sulpicius Severus *Vita sancti Martini* for inspiration for his passage on monastic corruption, [3] but he could as easily have found hints for this from St. Anthony's sermon to his monks. According to Evagrius, Anthony warned his followers that demons attack all Christians and especially monks, [4] sometimes indeed taking on the appearance and speech of holy men so that they may deceive their victims as they will. [5] However, although no satisfactory source for these lines of the poem has been found, they need not be regarded as necessarily inspired by some particular piece of writing, for they look back to lines 60 ff. in the introductory section of the poem itself.

No single source has been found for *Guthlac A* as a whole, and it is unlikely that there ever was a single source. Resemblances of the sort summarized in the last few paragraphs could be multiplied considerably, but observation of themes and materials common to many medieval writers does little to illumine either the poet or the composition of his poem. Nor indeed is the truism that the *Guthlac A* poet refers specifically to oral sources helpful. [6] The saint is described four times as a hero *ussum tidum* [7] or a man whose history was widely known or often told, but the allusions, perhaps no more than conventional formulae, can hardly be allowed as evidence that the *Guthlac A* poet was 'a Mercian, who knew Crow-

---

[1] §49.

[2] Wolpers, *Die englische Heiligenlegende*, pp. 114–15.

[3] ll. 412 ff.

[4] §23.

[5] §25.

[6] See discussions in Rieger, 'Über Cynevulf', p. 325, n. 1, Kurtz 'From St. Antony to St. Guthlac', p. 144, and C. A. Hotchner, *Wessex and Old English Poetry* (New York, 1939), p. 97.

[7] l. 401, and cp. ll. 108, 153 ff., and 752–4.

land well'.[1] By contrast, as is first noted by Rieger, the poet refers to *bec*[2] which reveal God's wisdom to us all, and he was probably as dependent upon books, whether consciously or unconsciously, as was Felix in his composition of the *Vita*. It is curious, however, that the *Vita* material which B. J. Kurtz identifies as without parallel in the Evagrian life of St. Anthony and as comparable rather with accounts of Fursey's otherworld visions[3] is the sort of Guthlac material on which the poet has chosen to concentrate his attention. The attack of the demons on Guthlac's constancy and the following journey to hell-gates provide a suitable narrative for a poem on the merits of the souls of the just, so much so that it might even be argued that the poet was influenced in lines 699 and 732[4] by memories of the three utterances exemplum:

Suscitate eam leniter de suo corpore, et ut nichil timoris, nichil doloris uideat.[5]

As for the relationship of *Guthlac A* to the *Vita sancti Guthlaci*, the problem with which this discussion of sources opened, all that can be said is that there is insufficient proof either for or against placing the *Vita* among the sources used by the poet. There are, in this poem, no indications that the poet followed any part of the *Vita* closely.

§5. *The structure of* Guthlac A

The poet's main concern is the souls of just men and he chooses Guthlac in illustration of one of the many ways in which a man may aspire to the kingdom of heaven. The purpose is didactic, with Guthlac as *bysen*. Although the greater part of the poem is a slowly moving narrative of encounters between Guthlac and his demon attackers, the poet does not lose sight of his wider subject. Various temptations are described, but there is little suspense, for the outcome of the struggles is never in doubt. Once the saint has chosen his lonely hermitage, the presiding demons must leave. Their taunts and assaults cannot win them back this resting-place. The poet does

---

[1] F. Tupper, 'The Philological Legend of Cynewulf', *PMLA*, xxvi (1911), 262.
[2] l. 528.
[3] 'From St. Anthony to St. Guthlac', p. 113 and n. 19.
[4] Liebermann's most convincing verbal parallels between poem and *Vita*.
[5] See Appendix I, ll. 22–3.

not present a simply ordered and straightforward series of encounters, but mixes narrative with lengthy discursive reflection. The many arguments between the devils and Guthlac cannot fairly be termed debate. The attacks are cogent enough, but Guthlac's speeches might be shortened with advantage, were they intended only as replies. Reply and more generalized praise of God intermingle so gently that the narrator is able to interpose his own affirmation of Guthlac's words without being noticed.[1] The reflective quality of the poem is not generally acknowledged, but then neither is its unity,[2] and recognition of the former can only follow the acceptance of *Guthlac A* as something more than a collection of disparate entities.

The opening twenty-nine lines have only grudgingly been recognized as part of the poem.[3] The editorial history of this part of the Exeter Book is to a large extent responsible[4] for the tendency to isolate these lines from the rest of the poem to which they are attached. They are not 'an unnecessary prelude to a prelude',[5] nor do they bear 'a closer verbal resemblance to *Christ III* than to *Guthlac A*',[6] for they introduce themes which pervade the poem. The parallels to be found between these lines and other parts of *Guthlac A*[7] are many of them the stock phrases of a religious poet, but some important correspondences in matter are often overlooked. These occur not only between the opening twenty-nine lines and the closing lines,[8] but within the rest of the poem too.[9] Yet, whether or not these lines form part of *Guthlac A* has so dominated discussion of them that a smaller and curious point of interpretation within them has gone unnoticed. The editors and translators mostly agree

---

[1] E.g. ll. 620b–2, and see Commentary.

[2] As recently as 1966, Rosemary Woolf (in her essay in E. G. Stanley, *Continuations and Beginnings*, p. 56) suggests that ll. 1–107 'seem to be an accretion'; and F. R. Lipp, '*Guthlac A*: an Interpretation', 1971, pp. 57–9, agrees with this judgement.

[3] T. A. Shippey, *Old English Verse* (London, 1972), 130–1, recognizes the '*purposeful*' nature of the poem's 'long and sinuous prologue'. A positive attitude is taken by D. G. Calder, '*Guthlac A* and *Guthlac B*: Some Discriminations', *Anglo-Saxon Poetry: Essays in Appreciation*, ed. L. E. Nicholson and Dolores Warwick Frese (Notre Dame, 1975), pp. 65–80.

[4] See §3.

[5] E. J. Howard, 'Cynewulf's Crist 1665–1693', *PMLA*, xlv (1930), 354.

[6] Ibid., p. 362.

[7] See the good survey by A. Adams, 'Christ (?) 1665–1693', *MLN*, xxi (1906), 240.

[8] Cp. ll. 7/781, 8/768, 10/811, 12/816, 22/790, etc.

[9] Cp. ll. 18/485, 24/120 ff., 22/567, 6 ff./579 ff., etc.

that the angel's speech begins at line 6,[1] but there is considerable tacit disagreement as to where this speech ends. The favourite ending-places are in the middle of either line 10[2] or line 11,[3] though neither of these is entirely satisfactory. Perhaps as a result of dissatisfaction with these solutions we find one translator closing his inverted commas twice, both in the middle of line 11 and at the end of line 17.[4] The inference to be drawn from this editorial confusion is that as the poet expands on the great happiness the soul will have, he loses sight of the angel. However, both the excursus and the speech[5] end neatly with line 25, if lines 26–9 are read as a rhetorical question, though line 17 must also be regarded as a good breaking-point.

In effect there is no new beginning at line 30. Attention shifts from the heavenly home which righteous souls will attain to ways of serving God in the world so as to be numbered among the holy. The reverie of lines 35–58 contains many of the conventional ideas of Old English 'elegiac' verse, for example the passing and failing of *eorþan blæd*,[6] the unrest of the world and a falling off in God's worship,[7] and the impossibility of improvement before the end of creation.[8] The similarity of these lines to better-known passages of verse has often been noted,[9] but they are not inapposite.[10] They lead naturally into the statement:

> he fela findeð, fea beoð gecorene   (l. 59)

with which the poet returns to his consideration of the ways in which the chosen few serve God. After this long passage on that familiar Anglo-Saxon theme, the transience of all things upon earth, men who place *eorðwela* above *þæt ece lif*[11] are unfavourably contrasted with those who yearn for *þa mæran gód*,[12] whether in daily life or as anchorites. Such men, the poet declares in the last lines of his first

---

[1] Only Shook, 'The Prologue', disagrees, giving the angel l. 4b also.
[2] As in Grein's edition and Assmann and KD.
[3] Gollancz, *The Exeter Book*.
[4] Gollancz, *The Exeter Book*.
[5] See Commentary for l. 26.
[6] l. 43.
[7] l. 38.
[8] l. 50.
[9] Cp. for example, *The Wanderer*, esp. ll. 62b–5a, 73–7, and 106–7.
[10] They may be balanced by ll. 742 ff. in the final fitt.
[11] l. 62.
[12] l. 71.

fitt, are God's chosen warriors,[1] and in his closing lines he will
remind us again of their behaviour on earth and their heavenly
reward.[2]

Guthlac is introduced at the beginning of the next fitt as a man
who despised *eorðlic æþelu*,[3] whose thoughts turned heavenwards
once he had gained enlightenment. As a young man he had loved
danger, but the time came when the arguments of his good angel
prevailed over his bad angel's incitement to wordly daring.[4] The
rest of this fitt is eulogistic in tone. The poet reflects on the nature
of Guthlac's *beorgseþel* and its loneliness. Here there is no guide,
no Tatwine, to ferry the saint to a remote corner of the water-logged
fens. This hermitage is God-revealed to Guthlac alone, and he
dwells there *feara sum*;[5] human companions play no part in *Guthlac
A*, unless possibly as disciples who *þrowera þeawas lufedon*.[6] The
emphasis here, as throughout the poem, is very much on Guthlac's
solitariness, except for his *frofre gæst*,[7] despite these concluding
lines of the second fitt which return to an elaboration of its opening
remarks on the saint. He was a man who abjured comforts, feast-
days, worldly clothing—the demons will tempt him by showing him
men under monastic discipline who behave otherwise.

What might be called the action of the poem begins in the third
fitt, but only after further introductory material, part explanatory
(adding to earlier information), part eulogistic. Guthlac has taken
up his position to do battle as Christ's champion in a secret place,
eþelriehte feor.[8] He puts to flight the devils for whom these deserted
hills had been a retreat, unmoved by their threats, and resolutely
declares the disputed land his and theirs no longer. At the beginning
of the next section the outcast devils cluster about the hills nearby.
They threaten attack, accusing Guthlac of arrogance and asking

[1] ll. 91–2.
[2] ll. 790 ff.
[3] l. 97.
[4] ll. 110 and 128, and see Commentary.
[5] l. 173; see Commentary.
[6] l. 161; the desert fathers are portrayed as having bands of disciples, but
the emphasis here resembles rather Jerome's account of Paul.
[7] l. 136. Contrast in *Vita*, §l, Guthlac's brief explanation of the *angelum
consolationis meae* to Beccel.
[8] l. 216. The suggestion of Wentersdorf 'Guthlac A: The Battle for the *Beorg*',
Neophilogus, lxii, p. 136, that Guthlac is playing his part in 'the unremitting
campaign by the Church to suppress the lingering remnants of heathendom in
England', seems without textual support.

how he plans to deal with hunger and thirst. Now they offer not to wound or kill him, not to level his home or tear him to bits, if he will have a care for his life and go to some place where he can hope for friends.[1] In reply Guthlac observes that, no matter how bitterly they attack, they cannot gain victory, for, having no desire for *eorðwelan*[2] or anything more than his daily needs,[3] he will not use weapons against them. He announces that his trust is in his *sawelcund hyrde*[4] and his hope with God. The poet now reflects on Guthlac's victory which has gained him a brief respite, and describes his steadfast devotion to God in his solitary home. The devils, visiting by night, find him resolute. Guthlac follows the teaching of his guardian angel with whom he often talked. The text breaks off, where a folio is missing from the manuscript, with Guthlac speaking to the angel:

> Hu sceal min cuman
> gæst to geoce nemne ic Gode sylle
> hyrsumne hige þæt him heortan geþonc . . .
> (ll. 366b–8)

These few verses are perhaps sufficient to show that the poet recalls the themes of the opening section of the poem.[5]

About seventy verse lines have been lost. After this gap (the numbering carries on without interruption in the editions) we find Guthlac speaking, but his words are now addressed to demons. A new attack must have been mounted by the devils,[6] and this may be a reply to bodily torture by fire and weapons. There is little new in this incomplete speech, but it is again an effective declaration of faith. Guthlac is unmoved by the thought of death, for then his soul

> in gefean fareð þær he fægran
> botles bruceð.[7]
> (ll. 382–3b)

In the final lines of this fitt the poet reflects on Guthlac's victory,

---

[1] ll. 266–91.
[2] l. 319.
[3] l. 322.
[4] ll. 317–18.
[5] ll. 26–9 and 81 ff.
[6] The fitt length in *Guthlac A* ranges between 77 lines and 126, so it is likely that the fourth fitt drew quickly to an end and that a new fitt began in the lost folio.
[7] Cp. the soul journey theme of the first fitt.

reminding us that this was a man who set his mind on glory and, in a closing rhetorical question, extolling his merits.

The sixth fitt[1] makes explicit a contrast between the monastic and eremitical life suggested in the first section of the poem.[2] The demons lift Guthlac up into the air, revealing to him the unworthy life led by many in monasteries,[3] but this temptation fails. The attackers, though beaten, try subtler arguments, telling Guthlac that he has gained their enmity by ignoring their friendly advice and by putting his faith in *þam myrcelse*.[4] Many men with that same sign upon them, *se werga gæst*[5] reminds Guthlac, betray it in their lives (and, for a few lines, the poet himself suddenly directs similar accusations at his audience[6]), and they, wishing that Guthlac should recognize the truth of their accusations, have therefore raised him into the air. However, God gives Guthlac the strength and wisdom to answer, and in his reply the criticism of lax monastic discipline is again tempered.[7] With years wisdom will come and the young men of God's houses will change:

> þæt se gæst lufað
> onsyn 7 ætwist yldran hades.
> (ll. 499b–500)

For such men, Guthlac points out, there is hope, but none for his tormentors. The section ends with praise for Guthlac's words and deeds, and for the deeds of righteous men.[8]

The seventh and eighth fitts relate Guthlac's temptation at the gates of hell and the arrival of one of the apostles to command his safe return to his chosen dwelling-place. This messenger of God is named in the opening lines of the final fitt of *Guthlac A*, and the saint's triumphant home-coming follows. Little attempt is made to visualize the horrors of hell,[9] for the appeal of the devils is to Guthlac's mind. The poet reminds us that hell's door is where, after death, the journey of doomed souls begins.[10] The devils try to betray

---

[1] The fitts are newly numbered.
[2] Cp. ll. 60–80 with ll. 81–92.
[3] ll. 412–26.
[4] l. 458 and see Commentary.
[5] l. 451.
[6] ll. 460–6.
[7] l. 420.
[8] l. 525. Cp. l. 506.
[9] Contrast the account of Felix, *Vita*, §xxxi.
[10] ll. 559 ff.

Guthlac into *accidie*,[1] accusing him of being an unworthy servant of God:

> nu þu in helle scealt
> deope gedufan, nales dryhtnes leoht
> habban in heofonum, heahgetimbru,
> seld on swegle.
>
> (ll. 582b–5a)

The echoes of the message brought by an angel to the departing soul at the beginning of the poem are effectively ironical. Guthlac is not moved by these threats, but reveals his true submission to God in a long speech that straddles two sections of the poem.[2] In this profession of faith Guthlac denounces the devil and all his works. His love of God and his determination to observe His will and walk in His ways does not pass without some words of commendation from the poet:

> IC þone deman in dagum minum
> wille weorþian wordum 7 dædum,
> lufian in life.' (Swa is lar 7 ar
> to spowendre spræce gelæded
> þam þe in his weorcum willan ræfnað.)
>
> (ll. 618–22)

The poet's comment reinforces the attention drawn to this particular sentence by its position at the beginning of the eighth fitt. Guthlac now taunts the demons with the horrors of hell which they must endure, whereas he will possess *dreama wyn*[3] in the kingdom of Heaven. Bartholomew arrives promptly at the end of this speech, to command Guthlac's safe return to the place from which he had been taken. He has command of that field,[4] and his steadfast soul will journey into God's keeping.[5]

Guthlac's victorious return to his *beorge*[6] opens the final fitt. That battlefield is now a field of victory, and Guthlac's triumph is emphasized in what is at first glance pathetic fallacy:

> Smolt wæs se sigewong 7 sele niwe,
> fæger fugla reord, folde geblowen;
> geacas gear budon; Guþlac moste,
> eadig ond onmod, eardes brucan.
>
> (ll. 742–5)

[1] l. 575.
[2] ll. 592–684a.
[3] l. 680.
[4] l. 702.
[5] ll. 689a–91a.
[6] l. 733.

Guthlac's return from the gates of hell can, however, be regarded
as a resurrection. Up to this point of the poem there has been no
mention of seasons, and this description of Guthlac's hermitage and
especially the phrase *sele niwe* suggests that the symbolism of the
reawakening of plant life is being used to mark Guthlac's achievement of salvation.[1] The *grena wong*[2] is now in God's protection,
and His messenger, Bartholomew, has banished from it the fiends.

The rest of the poem is explanatory. The poet asks if his audience
has heard of any nobler accomplishments

>   in wera life
>   þara þe yldran usse gemunde
>   oþþe we sylfe siþþan cuþen?
>   (ll. 749b–51)

These things, he reminds them, happened in their own time and
cannot be doubted. They reveal God's love for *ealle gesceafte*.[3]
Guthlac lived faithfully in God's service until a better life was
granted him, and he was led *on engla fæðmum*[4] into His presence
and a seat in heaven was given him for ever. And in the same way
just souls will earn their places in heaven because they follow God's
teachings here on earth.[5] In this final passage the poet carefully
and explicitly picks up his first subject, using again the themes of
the opening fitt. At the end the inner eye lingers meditatively, as it
does in *The Dream of the Rood*, on Jerusalem, the home of the
righteous.[6]

§6. *The sources of* Guthlac B

In contrast with the great amount of dispute over the relationship
of *Guthlac A* to the *Vita sancti Guthlaci* there is general agreement
that the main source for *Guthlac B* is Felix's fiftieth chapter. The
poet restricts himself to this part of the *Vita*, except in ll. 894–
932a where he draws upon some episodes related in earlier chapters
of the life.[7] The opening section of the poem is based on a theme

[1] See the Commentary on l. 744.

[2] l. 746.

[3] l. 760.

[4] l. 782.

[5] ll. 790–818.

[6] The excellent article by Thomas D. Hill, 'The Middle Way: *idel-wuldor*
and *egesa* in the Old English *Guthlac A*', *RES*, n.s. xxx (1979), 182–7, appeared
too late for consideration in this section.

[7] An interesting account of this passage is to be found in J. L. Rosier,
'Death and Transfiguration: *Guthlac B*', *Philological Essays* (1971), p. 83.

which arises early in Felix's account of Guthlac's death: 'Nam sicut mors in Adam data est, ita et in omnes dominabitur. Quisquis enim huius vitae saporem gustaverit, amaritudinem mortis evitare nequit.'[1] These phrases, worked over with great freedom, account for about a sixth of the extant poem. The intention may have been other than biographical, for it is possible that this theme played a greater part in the presentation of Guthlac's death than is evidenced by the poem's present truncated form. Already in the opening lines of the poem the simple platitudes of Felix have been transmuted to become an effective account of the reason for death in this world, but the emphasis is not solely on death. This illness occurred during Easter, and the poet later expatiates on Christ's resurrection[2] where Felix merely mentions that Easter Day was the fourth day of Guthlac's illness.

Only in the opening sections does the *Guthlac B* poet diverge from the *Vita* at great length and with considerable originality, so it has often been suggested that here his choice and order of imagery may be shaped by his remembrance of some earlier treatment of the fall of mankind. Grau[3] suggests that he may have been inspired by parts of the *Carmen de Resurrectione Mortuorum*,[4] but the parallels drawn between *Guthlac B* and verses from this *Carmen* and other similar *carmina* point only to their common indebtedness to such traditions of the fall and resurrection. The most striking feature of the *Guthlac B* account, the poet's use of the *poculum mortis* figure, is absent from all versions of the source adduced by Grau. Certain of Felix's words in the sentences quoted above could have prompted the poet's use of this figure, the collocation of the verb *gustaverit* with the phrase *amaritudinem mortis* perhaps calling to mind

> þone bitran drync
> þone Eue fyrn Adame geaf,
> (ll. 868b–9)

and the clause *ita et in omnes dominabitur* may underlie the personification of death.

---

[1] Cp. 1 Corinthians 15: 22. The importance of the phrase *sicut mors in Adam data est* was first noted by Rieger, 'Über Cynevulf', pp. 314–15.
[2] ll. 1098b–1104.
[3] Grau, 'Quellen und Verwandtschaften', pp. 94–8.
[4] The versions in *PL* iv. 1053–60, ii. 1147–56, and lix. 1004–6 have been consulted, as have clxxi. 1715–16 and lxxxix. 297–300.

A popular hymn, often appended to early English psalters, the *Rex aeterne domine*, brings together in a few verses many of the thoughts developed by the poet in the opening sections of *Guthlac B*. It has been shown[1] that versions of this hymn, incorporating the *poculum mortis* figure, must have been well known in early Anglo-Saxon England, although the relevant verses are preserved in an English compilation only in an early eleventh-century collection of hymns and canticles.[2] If Felix's words called into the poet's mind the figure of the *poculum mortis* and with it the words of the *Rex aeterne domine*, he would then have had available to him many of the features of the creation and fall theme used in the opening sections of the poem. It is at any rate possible to set against phrases from this hymn passages from *Guthlac B* and to find between them more verbal resemblances than can be found in a comparison of the poem with the *Carmen de resurrectione mortuorum*. The opening verses of this hymn will be found in Appendix III; here an attempt is made to list some of the more striking similarities:

Rex aeterne Domine (1)	cyning ælmihtig (822)
Rerum Creator omnium (2)	frymþa God (820)
Qui mundi in primordio (5)	þone ærestan ælda cynnes
Adam plasmasti hominem (6)	of þære clænestan . . . foldan geworhte. (821–3a) ða was fruma niwe, ęlda tudres, etc . . . Fæder wæs acenned Adam ærest (823b–6a)
Quem diabolus deceperat (9)	wyrmes larum (846)
Hostis humani generis (10)	þurh deofles searo (850)
Per pomum ligni vetiti (11)	feond (864) blede forbodene 7 of beame ahneop wæstm biweredne (847–8a)
Mortis propinans poculum	deaðberende gyfl / þæt ða sinhiwan to swylte geteah. (850b–1) þone bitran drync (868)

---

[1] C. Brown, '*Poculum Mortis* in Old English', *Speculum*, xv (1940), 389–99.
[2] Durham, Cathedral MS. B. III. 32; see Ker, *Catalogue*, no. 107. A fuller account of the MS. appears in Helmut Gneuss, *Hymnar und Hymnen im englischen Mittelalter* (Tübingen, 1968), pp. 85–90.

Quique clausis in tenebris
Gemebat in suppliciis
(13–14)

Siþþan se eþel uðgenge wearð
Adame 7 Euan, eardwica cyst,
beorht, oðbroden (852–4a)
þa hy ón úncyððu,
scomum scudende, scofene wurdon
on gewinworuld; weorces onguldon
deopra firena þurh deaðes cwealm . . .
(855b ff.)

In a following stanza God is addressed as having assumed human form to redeem mankind, thematically relevant to both the Felix passage and *Guthlac B*, but there are no verbal similarities of the sort indicated. Later the Anglo-Saxon poet again takes up the theme of the bitter taste of death, once more relating the effect on humanity of the *poculum mortis*:

> bryþen wæs ongunnen
> þætte Adame Eue gebyrmde
> æt fruman worulde.
>
> (ll. 980b–2)

The bitter cup which is poured out for Adam and Eve by the devil is a *bitter bædeweg*,[1] and Guthlac could not defend himself from *þone bleatan drync deopan deaðweges*.[2] Here, as in the earlier use of the image, Eve's part in bringing death into the world is described. In the first passage the actual plucking of the apple at the devil's instigation is narrated,[3] but in the second figurative terms only are used. The theme has been sufficiently developed for it to be used in this more telling manner.

The personification of death, owing much to 1 Corinthians 15, is probably the most striking feature of *Guthlac B*.[4] Death is emphasized as a warrior coming to claim Guthlac, to achieve dominion over him as over all men.[5] Death is an enemy[6] who rules mankind,

---

[1] l. 985.
[2] ll. 990–1.
[3] ll. 846 ff.
[4] This is well treated by Rosier, 'Death and Transfiguration', pp. 86–7, who, however, thinks that the personification is not made 'a figure of major narrative interest'.
[5] Felix's use of the phrase *mors in Adam data est*, from 1 Corinthians 15: 22, could have helped along the personification.
[6] l. 864, ambiguous between 'death' and 'devil'.

pressing in upon men[1] and prevailing over them:[2]

> ne mæg ænig þam
> flæsce bifongen feore wiðstondan
> ricra ne heanra ac hine ræseð on
> gifrum grapum:[3]
> (ll. 993b–6a)

Death is described in a chilling manner. He is an *enge anhoga*,[4] a *wiga wælgifre*,[5] and Guthlac himself refers to him in these terms[6]—a poetic licence without any authority in Felix. When four days of the saint's illness have passed we are reminded how all the time death is drawing nearer to him:

> stop stalgongum, strong 7 hreðe
> sohte sawelhus.
> (ll. 1140–1a)

With the seventh day of the illness death attacks:

> him in gesonc
> hat, heortan neah, hildescurun,
> flacor flanþracu, feorhhord onleac
> searocægum gesoht.
> (ll. 1142b–5a)

Except for the *intimorum stimulatio* which signalled the onset of the saint's death, there is nothing in §1 of the *Vita* from which the poet might have derived inspiration for his use of the figure of the darts of death. Yet the image occurs three times in *Guthlac B*,[7] continuing the battle theme introduced by the poet. The personification of death appears twice elsewhere in Old English poetry, in *The Phoenix* and in the *Meters of Boethius*, but only in *Guthlac B* is it sufficiently developed to include the darts of death.[8]

Despite his great elaboration of introductory sentences from §1 of the *Vita*, the poet does not lose sight of the subject of that chapter in the first fitt of his poem. The universal rule of death affects all men, but there are *fela . . . gæsthaligra*[9] to seek a *sigorlean*:[10] a

---

[1] l. 863.   [2] l. 871.
[3] Cp. also the opening sentence of *Vita*, §1.   [4] l. 997.
[5] l. 999.   [6] ll. 1033–4b.
[7] ll. 1142–4, 1154, and 1286.
[8] See also Commentary on ll. 999 and 1154.   [9] ll. 872–3.
[10] l. 878. Thorpe, *Cod. Ex.*, p. 505, first notes the linkage of materials in this line.

simple bridge has been built and rather generalized eulogy of Guthlac follows as a suitable climax for this fitt. The second fitt begins with a passage of some thirty lines more closely dependent upon earlier material from Felix. In lines 894–915 the poet uses material from *Vita* §xxxvi, at some points following the Latin very closely.[1] He does not, however, describe the particular shapes taken by the demons, but recalls how at times they assumed human shape, at times serpent form, emphasizing Guthlac's patience through all such attacks, even when threatened with death. Lines 916–19a recall the episodes of the *Vita* which centre upon birds, but more specifically the swallows of §xxxix who obeyed Guthlac's commands as to where to build their nest.[2] Lines 919b–32a contain more praise for the help and comfort given by the saint to all who visited him and, through their similarity to lines 878b–93 of the preceding fitt, clearly round off a summary of Guthlac's achievement in life.

It has sometimes been argued that the *Guthlac B* poet knew *Guthlac A* and was providing a companion-piece for it from Felix's life of the saint. Certainly the description of Guthlac's death in *Guthlac A* is brief[3] and might have seemed woefully inadequate to anyone familiar with the *Vita*, in which the striking death scene occupies eleven per cent of the entire text.[4] Those parts of the first two sections of *Guthlac B* dealing with events of the saint's life show similarities in content and phrasing with *Guthlac A*, and the possibility that the *B* poet had heard or read *Guthlac A* cannot be ruled out. Attention has been focused upon the appearance of *sigewong* in both poems, although the word occurs in other late Old English poetry.[5] At most, a knowledge of *Guthlac A* might have suggested to the author of *Guthlac B* some themes by which to illustrate the saint's life, but if so, these were supplemented from and shaped by the accounts in Felix. The hosts of devils who crowd in upon Guthlac may remind us of the struggles in *Guthlac A*, but their taking on of different shapes is a detail worked up from the *Vita*.

---

[1] E.g. the correlative clauses of ll. 903–4 may owe something to the Latin.

[2] Rosier, 'Death and Transfiguration', p. 83, suggests §xxxviii here and §§xli–xlii for the following lines.

[3] These lines, 781 ff., are rather an account of Guthlac's reception into heaven; see further p. 49.

[4] This figure is given by Kurtz, 'From St. Antony', p. 122, n. 42, who notes also the continuing appeal of this chapter in the Middle English period.

[5] See Commentary on *Guthlac A* 742–3.

The reference to birds in *Guthlac B* is hardly similar to the symbolic appearance of *geacas*[1] in *Guthlac A*. And the miracles performed by Guthlac after his victory over the hosts of devils, entirely neglected in *Guthlac A*, lie behind the two rather general passages of eulogy in the *B* poet's summary of Guthlac's life. It does not seem likely that *Guthlac A* provided much in the way of actual source-material for the *Guthlac B* poet.

From line 932b the poet follows Felix's account of the saint's death closely, interweaving and reintroducing the themes developed from Felix's use of the Corinthians text *sicut mors in Adam data est*. Sometimes his dependence is so close that the structures of the Latin original are reproduced,[2] but generally he elaborates the *Vita* narrative. The dramatization of speeches, comparable with the treatment of the *Elene* source by Cynewulf, accounts for a great deal of the expansions. For example, if Guthlac's words in lines 1064–93 are compared with the *Vita*, only lines 1067b–76a are not implicit within Felix: Guthlac firmly announces that he has no fear of death,[3] perhaps a further incursion of the warrior death into the saint's speech. Next he points out that he fears neither the devil nor his ministers who must themselves lament and suffer hellfire, a passage which recalls his earlier struggles against demons.[4] Here the additions are thematically apt and well handled, and the saint's courage as he grows weaker physically is reiterated.[5] This Guthlac is far less impassive than Felix's in dying. Otherwise the greatest elaboration is in the description of Beccel's journey to Pege with news of her brother's death. Sources other than Felix have not been found for this episode, and there is nothing in it which might not have been suggested by some phrase or clause in the *Vita*. The passages so often labelled original are those in which the poet draws most freely on formulaic phrases and ornamental kennings. The journey scene and the following speech have in particular led critics to assert that *Guthlac B* is clearly in 'the vernacular tradition' of Anglo-Saxon verse.[6] Descriptions of natural phenomena have been singled out for admiration and are indeed 'in the Anglo-Saxon

---

[1] *Guthlac A* 744.
[2] See, for example, ll. 1114–15, 1118–19, 1122.
[3] ll. 1064 ff.
[4] Both in the *Vita* and in this poem, ll. 894–915.
[5] Note the passages in which his *ellen* is emphasized, e.g. ll. 1226, 1271 and 1294.
[6] Schaar, *Critical Studies in the Cynewulf Group*, p. 42.

poetic tradition',[1] but they are also literary and very much in the spirit of Felix.

The poem breaks off with little more of *Vita* §l to run: the sister's grief, the return to Crowland, three days of prayer, and Guthlac's burial. How much of *Guthlac B* has disappeared is impossible to say. From the poet's use of his main source we can, however, guess that he would not have spared us an account of Pege's swoon, of Beccel's return journey with her, of the ambrosial odours found in all the Crowland buildings, of the prayers and praise and Guthlac's burial on the third day after his death.[2] Indeed, the poet's use of the *sicut mors in Adam data est* theme and his development of the figure of death might have made attractive to him the following chapter, which tells of the discovery a year later of Guthlac's incorrupt body.[3] And if the poet were versifying the octave of the saint,[4] the poem could have carried on to the end of chapter lii.

§7. *The organization of* Guthlac B

Guthlac B is incomplete. It has often been assumed that only a few lines of script, the amount which might have filled the excised top portion of folio 53[r], are missing, although a gathering (or more) has dropped out of the manuscript between folios 52 and 53. For the earlier critics these lines contained the end of Beccel's message to Pege, or the poem was considered unfinished or fragmentary, but from 1885 Wülcker's suggestion that the 'lost lines' held a Cynewulf signature is an important factor in all discussions of the Cynewulf question, with the result that *Guthlac B* is still today the poem most

---

[1] Ibid.

[2] R. T. Farrell, 'Some Remarks on the Exeter Book *Azarias*', *MÆ*, xli (1972), 5, suggests that the Azarias songs which follow in the MS. are 'to be taken as the praises uttered by Guthlac's sister, or (as seems more likely) the songs sung by Guthlac's sister and retainer when they return to discover the odour of sanctity in Guthlac's place of death', adding that perhaps this appropriate addition is better ascribed to the Exeter Book compiler. See further Roberts, 'Guðlac A, B, and C?', pp. 43–6, and Pope, 'Palaeography and poetry', pp. 37–41.

[3] In favour of this suggestion it is worth noting that no break between the materials of §§l and li occurs in the Old English translation of the *Vita*.

[4] Rosier, 'Death and Transfiguration', p. 82, notes that lection divisions in two *Vita* manuscripts place the saint's death in prominence, but there is no equivalence between the materials so marked and those parts of Felix used by the poet.

likely to be placed in the greatly attenuated Cynewulf canon with *Elene, Juliana, Christ II*, and the *Fates of the Apostles*. The once general acceptance of such views has meant that *Guthlac B* is frequently discussed as if it were virtually complete. This attitude is stronger than the ascription of Cynewulfian authorship, which lost ground with the realization that four lines of script (i.e. some six lines of verse) are not enough for a Cynewulf signature and that in any case these lines probably belonged to some earlier part of *Azarias*.

Because the unity of what remains of *Guthlac B* is generally accepted, a lengthy discussion of its contents is unnecessary. The poet's use and elaboration of themes selected principally from Felix's account of Guthlac's death have been examined in the account of the sources of the poem, but certain important changes in his use of this material have not yet been noted. His method is narrative, and he does not think to mention Beccel as the authority from whom his account of Guthlac's death is ultimately derived.[1] In some ways he simplifies the account given in the *Vita*. Felix's references to Ecgburgh and Ecgberht are, for example, omitted and, though it could be argued that these omissions are made because of a self-contradiction within his source,[2] this argument may misinterpret the poet's intention. For him there is only one person in the story he tells, Guthlac, and only he is named. Beccel is reduced to a faithful servant and messenger, and the absence of his name is indicative of this change. His words and feelings are retained and developed, because they are relevant to the fact of Guthlac's death, but his identity is not made clear. Even Pege remains anonymous, alluded to as Guthlac's sister or in such poetic periphrases as *wuldres wynmæg*[3] and *leofast mægða*,[4] and the saint's instructions to Beccel, to keep secret from all *nisi Pegae aut Ecgberhto anachoritae* that God sent him every morning and evening an *angelum consolationis*, are omitted.

There are many signs that the poet gave careful thought to the organization of his materials.[5] He works in sections of approximately

---

[1] If we accept Felix's note on his source for Guthlac's death, §l.

[2] See pp. 5–6.

[3] l. 1345.

[4] l. 1376.

[5] Recently T. D. Hill, 'The Typology of the Week and the Numerical Structure of the Old English *Guthlac B*', *Mediaeval Studies*, xxxvii (1975), 531–6, has argued for the poet's awareness of 'the traditional typology of the week' from the fitt arrangement.

the same length, apparently distributing the contents with some idea of how they are to add together. At first it seems almost that he is as much concerned with death as with Guthlac,[1] and the achievement of deliverance as an overt theme is held over to the fourth day of the saint's illness. The first fitt is an account of the coming of death into the world, and the universality of death's rule is emphasized. The bitter potion of death is unavoidable:

> Deað ricsade
> ofer foldbuend þeah þe fela wære
> gæsthaligra.
>
> (ll. 871b–3a)

Guthlac is introduced towards the end of this section in illustration of such blessed men, and the second fitt is devoted to establishing his death as the narrative centre of the poem. A brief and allusive summary of the saint's life in his cell and of his miracles indicates the holiness of Guthlac's spirit in his life in the world[2] and leads quickly to his final illness. The greater part of the fitt is then given over to the description of trust and hope, despite the coming separation of *se bliþa gæst*[3] from the pain-racked body, and closes with a reminder of the inevitability of death purchased by our first ancestors.[4]

Guthlac's courage and resoluteness in the face of great pain is stressed in the opening lines of the next section. Excitement is lent to the narrative by a heightened account of *þone bleatan drync deopan deaðweges*[5] poured out for Eve by the devil:

> swa wæs Guðlace
> enge anhoga ætryhte þa
> æfter nihtscuan, neah geþyded,
> wiga wælgifre.
>
> (ll. 996b–9a)

From this point Felix's narrative order is followed, but the poet does not lose sight of the changes and subtleties he has introduced. Guthlac is slow in answering his companion's question about his

---

[1] See Rosier, 'Death and Transfiguration', p. 84: '*Guthlac B* might as readily be termed a poem on the subject of death, or the coming of Death, as a poetic account of the last days of a particular saint.'
[2] ll. 894 ff.
[3] l. 944.
[4] ll. 970b ff.
[5] ll. 990b–1a.

illness, so heavily is he afflicted, but he speaks bravely, *eadig on elne,*[1] telling of the approach of death, that *wiga . . . unlæt laces,*[2] and the longed-for separation of body and soul. The closing lines of the fitt, by contrast with Guthlac's *mægen*[3] in its opening lines, is filled with his follower's great sorrow, grief depicted traditionally in terms of loss of one's *hlaford,*[4] and the poet ends with a suitable generalization on the inexorability of fate. The fourth section begins with Guthlac's reply to his sorrowing servant and moves to Easter Day. In the poet's handling of this piece of information from Felix, Christ's resurrection is explicitly introduced, in terms of arising from death, of mounting to the heavens, of ascending from hell, so that when Guthlac gets up despite his great sickness his achievement is in Christ's model which has bought for him his own resurrection. And on that day he preaches most memorably to his servant-companion. It is tempting to think of this fourth fitt as the turning point of the poem, the half-way mark, with its teaching to be entrusted to the saint's sister in a final lost fitt, but we have no way of knowing how the poet chose to draw his themes together.

The fifth fitt at its outset states that Easter Day was the fourth day of Guthlac's suffering, emphasizing the importance of the events of that day by the delaying of this detail. Death now comes closer with stealthy paces. By the seventh day death is at hand and his servant finds Guthlac *awrecen wælpilum.*[5] In conversation Guthlac reveals that he will soon die, giving instructions about his burial and messages for his sister. At the end of this section his servant asks about a mysterious visitor he has often heard talking with Guthlac at night. In a long speech which opens the next section Guthlac tells him about his angel of consolation, though he has always concealed that *þeodnes þrymcyme*[6] until now. At the end of this speech he sinks against the wall, owning his great weariness, yet holding *ellen on innan.*[7] The poet has not forgotten that for him a warrior saint is bravely confronting the warrior death. The following passages show that he can work in Felix's decorative manner, recasting his source-material in an even higher literary style. His descriptions of Guthlac's

[1] l. 1026.
[2] ll. 1033a–4b.
[3] l. 977.
[4] l. 1053.
[5] l. 1154.
[6] l. 1256.
[7] l. 1271a.

sweet dying breath, of the onset of night, and of the fiery light which envelops his cell are among the most admired parts of the poem, and are revisualized with a good command of simile and ornate diction. Felix's careful explanation that these marvels were seen by Beccel is replaced by straightforward narrative in which the Latin account is lengthened and elaborated. A few phrases remind the audience that the struggle between Death and Guthlac is nearly over, and again the characterization is much more active than in Felix's account. Guthlac gets up, *eadig, elnes gemyndig*,[1] for his final words to his servant, by contrast with the *Vita* presentation in which he manages to raise himself for a few moments, *velut exsurgens*. There is no need to argue that the poet has misunderstood the Latin, for his changes are consistent with the way in which he has reorganized his source from the beginning.

At the end of this sixth fitt Guthlac's death follows on from his final words to his companion and, as in Felix, he is depicted as sending his spirit into perpetual bliss. In the introduction to the next section a few lines are provided by the poet in explanation of the fate of the body and soul at death. His statement that angels carried Guthlac's soul to heaven and that his body grew cold makes clear the final dissolution of body and soul which Death has been trying to bring about. In the event the chilling figure of Death is absent, very likely because his advent held no terrors for a man ready and eager for eternal bliss. A marvellous light, sweet smells, and angelic song surround Guthlac's cell. While these miraculous things terrify Felix's Beccel, a new detail is found in the Old English poem:

> Beofode þæt ealond,
> foldwong onsprong.
> (ll. 1325b–6a)

in explanation of his fear.[2] The grief of Guthlac's companion is then greatly elaborated by the poet, as is the journey to the saint's sister. The poet's use of his source becomes more and more free in this section, so that the merest hints, a couple of clauses to make known a boat journey or a reference to a speech, are worked up into blocks of some twenty or thirty verse lines. It is therefore impossible to estimate how many more sections the poet might have needed to

---

[1] l. 1294a.

[2] Cp. the movement of the earth and the cross's fear in the *Dream of the Rood*, ll. 35 ff., and see Hill, 'The Typology', p. 535, n. 10.

finish dealing with even the few sentences remaining in Felix's
account of Guthlac's death, and the final scope of *Guthlac B* cannot
be gauged.

Though *Guthlac B* is by no means a close or compact translation,
in the techniques of description the poet owes much to Felix. The
extent of the indebtedness is somehow the clearer because of the very
different handling of themes and materials in its companion poem
Guthlac A, and the *B* poem has generally had greater acclaim. Thorpe
first pointed admiringly to its 'great beauty of diction',[1] establishing
what has become a widely held critical attitude. In particular, the
presentation of the friendship between the saint and his companion
is singled out for praise (too often accompanied by a comparison
of the final speech with the sorrow expressed by Wiglaf at the death
of Beowulf[2]). Most literary historians, perhaps because the shadow
of Cynewulf lies over the poem, rate *Guthlac B* highly, veering more
to adulation[3] than to criticism,[4] but, despite the appearance of
selections in many well-known anthologies, the poem has had
curiously little attention in recent years.[5]

§8. *Diction, metre, and affiliations of the poets*

The separate authorship of the Guthlac poems has so far been
assumed throughout this introduction, and it is hoped that the
rigorous attempts to avoid comparison have resulted in the recognition
of their great dissimilarity both in source-material and form.
Although their extent and interdependence have been much debated
there can be little doubt that the scribe of the Exeter Book (or his
director) marked out two poems, just as he made three major
divisions of the *Christ* material which precedes them. However, in
placing the poems side by side in his anthology he has made it
necessary to discuss whether or not he meant them to be read as a

[1] Thorpe, *Cod. Ex.*, p. vi.
[2] See M. B. Price, *Teutonic Antiquities in the Generally Acknowledged Cynewulfian Poetry* (Leipzig, 1896), p. 51, for details of the excessive praise given this passage by the earliest critics.
[3] See, for example, Gerould, *Saints' Legends*, p. 83.
[4] See D. C. Collins, 'Kenning in Anglo-Saxon Poetry', *Essays and Studies*, n.s. xii (1959), 15.
[5] Apart from writings already mentioned, see D. G. Calder, 'Theme and Strategy in *Guthlac B*', *Papers on Language and Literature*, viii (1972), 227–42.

sequence. Once this question is framed, there arise problems of interpretation which can only be answered subjectively. For example, it has been suggested that the Guthlac poems, read as a sequence, are structurally comparable with *Beowulf*,[1] but, though few would quarrel with the statement that *Beowulf* and the Guthlac poems share the 'same thought-world', the dependence of a poem *Guthlac* 'upon *Beowulf* as a model' is less easy to accept. After all, Guthlac dies in *Guthlac A*, so to argue that his death 'is not treated *as such* in this part of the sequence, though he is taken up to heaven' is a bit of special pleading that overlooks the coherence of that poem. Guthlac's struggles against the taunts and temptations of devils serve the poet as a parable of the good soul whose journey to heaven is fully deserved, so the emphasis is very properly more on his being taken up to heaven than on his death. He is, all the same, dead. And he dies again in *Guthlac B*, with all the detail ascribed by Felix to the eye-witness account of a named companion. The poems can well be read in sequence, but not as a single narrative with linear progression, and the sequence should be extended backwards. Sisam has pointed out that 'arrangement by subject is apparent in the first five' poems of the Exeter Book, 'but it is external'.[2] It is as important for us to know that *Guthlac A* follows *Christ III* as it is for us to know that it is followed by *Guthlac B*. Some critics have, indeed, found more links in subject matter between *Christ III* and *Guthlac A* than between the Guthlac poems.[3] That Judgment Day poem, dealing more with the deserts of the wicked than with good souls, ends with a passage in which the seven joys of heaven are described,[4] and *Guthlac A* may have been chosen to follow it not just for its interest rather in the souls of the righteous but because the account of heaven in its opening lines resembles the closing description of *Christ III*.

The essentially homiletic and reflective *Guthlac A* is succeeded by a contrasting poem on Guthlac, an account of the saint's death after the definitive Latin life. Unfortunately the loss of at least a gathering after *Guthlac B* means that *Azarias* may not always have

[1] M. E. Goldsmith, *The Mode and Meaning of 'Beowulf'* (London, 1970), pp. 257–9, following a point made by Professor E. V. Gordon in his edition of *The Battle of Maldon*.

[2] Sisam, *Studies*, p. 291.

[3] Grau, 'Quellen und Verwandtschaften', pp. 83–7.

[4] See Thomas D. Hill, 'The Seven Joys of Heaven in *Christ III* and Old English Homiletic Texts', *Notes and Queries*, ccxiv (1969), 165–6.

followed that poem, and though its thematic relevance to the
Guthlac poems has been advanced[1] the essential evidence that
Azarias always followed *Guthlac B* is lacking. In its turn *Azarias*,
perhaps 'basically a complete poem'[2] centres on a furnace from
which three young men emerge unscathed, to be followed rather
aptly by *The Phoenix* and *Juliana*, three poems in a row on deliverance
from flames. Any attempt to abstract two from this series, whether
interrupted or not by some lost poem(s) before *Azarias*, and treat
them as a larger unit, is forced. Stylistic differences from one poem to
another are great and must not be discounted. It is easier, for example,
to assume common authorship for *Guthlac B* and *The Phoenix*[3] than
for the two Guthlac poems, surely a strong argument against a
two-part Guthlac poem on the model of *Beowulf*.

Close examination of *Guthlac A* and *Guthlac B* throws up marked
differences between them, especially as regards those verse types
whose occurrence depends for the most part on the presence of
compound words. For example, the *Guthlac B* poet chooses to fill
his half-line with one word considerably more often than the *Guthlac
A* poet, so that it is hardly surprising to find the total number of
poetic compounds much greater in his poem than in *Guthlac A*. This
disproportion in the distribution of poetic compounds reflects also
over-all differences in the vocabulary of the poems. It seems therefore
that stylistic questions cannot usefully be treated in separate sections
on metre and diction, and an attempt will be made here to include
both these topics in one chapter.[4]

Two groups of specialized vocabulary not general in Old English
verse may be distinguished in *Guthlac A*:

(i) legal: *bisæce* 217, *eþelriehte* 216, *edergong* 11, *fealóg* 246,
gestalum 510, *on his sylfes dóm* 706, *sibbe ryht* 197, *socne* 716,
wergengan 594, 713, and *woruldryhte* 57; words containing the
first element *wræc-* should perhaps be included.

These words are only tentatively grouped together and, though
a few more examples might be given, these instances are the

[1] Farrell, 'Some Remarks', pp. 5 ff.

[2] J. W. Kirkland and C. E. Modlin, 'The Art of Azarias', *MÆ*, xli (1972), 9.

[3] Sisam, *Studies*, p. 291, notes that they are 'closely related in style'.

[4] For a scansion of the poems and the figures on which many of the assump-
tions made in this section are based see Jane Roberts, 'A Metrical Examination
of the Poems *Guthlac A* and *Guthlac B*', *Proceedings of the Royal Irish Academy*,
lxxi, Section C, no. 4 (1971), 91–137.

most striking.[1] Two of the forms (*edergong* and *fealóg*) are not elsewhere recorded in Old English, but cognate forms occur in legal texts in other Germanic languages; their use may point to the conservative nature of the poet. The interpretation of *socn* 'visitation, persecution', paralleled in *Beowulf* 1777 *þære socne*, as a use of the simplex peculiar to these two poems, is drawn from the compound *hamsocn*. The phrase *on his sylfes dóm* 706, cognate with Old Norse *sjálfdæmi*, resembles the *Chronicle* entry for 755 *hiera agenne dom*, and *Battle of Maldon* 38 *on hyra sylfra dom*; and phrases containing *dom* in *Guthlac A* 111, 135, and 601 may also have legal associations. Previous editorial emendations of *bisæce* 217 are shown to be unnecessary once similar words in laws are taken into account. The compound *wergengan* has cognates in the laws of other Germanic peoples, though its only other Old English occurrence is also poetic (*Daniel* 662). Legal use of *riht* is likely in the phrase *sibbe ryht* 197, as in the compounds *woruldryhte* 57 (found also in Edgar's laws and in a latish homily) and *eþelriehte* 216 (otherwise recorded only in poetry, *Exodus* 211 and *Beowulf* 2198).

(ii) religious: *ælmessan* 77, *ánbuendra* 88, *ealdres* 420, *hades* 60, *hyrda* 415, *husulbearn* 559, *husulweras* 796, *ombiehthera* 599, *regulas* 489, *spelbodan* 40, *þegn* (in phrases) 693, 708, *þeow* (in phrases) 157, 314, 386, 579, 600, *þrowera* 161, 182, *æfter þrowinga* 471, *in þrowingum* 385, 778, *in Godes templum* 490.

Among the words listed above are a few poetic coinages not found outside this poem: *ánbuendra* 88, *husulbearn* 559, *husulweras* 796, *ombiehthera* 599. Poetic also is *spelbodan* 40, a word quite widely recorded. The learned word *martyre* 514 does not have much currency in verse texts (otherwise *Andreas* 876, *Menologium* 69 and *Christ and Satan* 653), and *martyrhád* 472 penetrates poetry only here, but the scarcity of these forms in the poetry may be as much the result of subject matter as convention, for the native word *þrowere* does not appear in any other poem. Native words and phrases reflecting extensions of meaning under Christian influence are numerous in *Guthlac A* (for example *had*, *þegn*, *þeow*, *þrowing*), but such words can for the most part be interpreted without knowledge of the possible specialized applications. Sometimes the extension is more opaque, as in *husul-* 559, 796, *-hera* 599, *hyrda* 415, *þrowera* 161, 182.

---

[1] A few further possible examples are noted in the Commentary.

Keiser[1] is unwilling to recognize any monastic terms in *Guthlac A* other than *mynsterum* 416 in its original sense 'dwelling-places of monks' (two further examples of this word in the poetry, *Menologium* 106 and *Durham* 17, he takes as 'church'). He suggests that, apart from *mynsterum* 416 and the 'general statements' of lines 60–1 and 790–810, there are no monastic terms in the poem.[2] Monastic terms are indeed rare in Old English poetry, but there may well be more than Keiser allows. The *rume regulas* 489 of young men in God's houses must refer to monastic discipline,[3] and contextually it seems very likely that *þæs ealdres* 420 should be interpreted 'superior, prior', even though *ealdor* is not otherwise known in poetry for men of ecclesiastical authority. As the content of the poem indicates that its author was interested in the monastic way of life and that he may even have expected the poem to have a monastic audience, it is not surprising to find in it these monastic terms.

Though there may be little significance in his use of legal terminology, except by contrast with the *Guthlac B* poet, the great amount of religious terminology of a sort not often found in Old English poetry is noteworthy, especially for its unobtrusive nature. The poem is, perhaps, nearer than many others to the group freely admitting 'prosaic words' in which E. G. Stanley places the *Meters of Boethius* and *Judgment Day*.[4] In addition to *ege* 686, *hyrsumne* 368, *hearsume* 705, 725, *gelimpe* 268, and *meodumre* 384[5] identified by Professor Stanley as 'prosaic' words in this poem, there are examples of two more at least of the forms cited for other poems: *bidinge* 209[6] and *mynsterum* 416;[7] and the putative 'monastic' terms might be allowed as further evidence that this, like *Judith*,[8] is a poem which admits prosaic words. Other similarities to *Judith*, both in diction and metre, suggest that this too could be a southern poem, an interesting

---

[1] A. Keiser, *The Influence of Christianity on the Vocabulary of Old English Poetry*, Univ. of Illinois Studies in Lang. and Lit., v (1919), p. 41.

[2] Ibid., p. 36.

[3] Keiser excludes 'the clergy proper' from this allusion, as from *Menologium* l. 44, *rincas regolfæste*, but does not make it clear how he thinks these passages are to be interpreted.

[4] E. G. Stanley, 'Studies in the Prosaic Vocabulary of Old English Verse', *Neuphilologische Mitteilungen*, lxxii (1971), 387.

[5] Ibid., p. 389; on p. 415 he takes *gestalum* 510 out of his significant forms.

[6] Ibid., p. 392.

[7] Ibid., p. 387, n. 4.

[8] Ibid., p. 390.

possibility when its apparent lack of knowledge of fenland country is considered.

The kennings in *Guthlac A* are generally descriptive and rarely metaphorical. Of the *hapax legomena* few merit the description 'poetic'. Perhaps the most noteworthy of the compounds are *edergong* 11, *flygereowe* 349, *husulbearn* 559, *husulweras* 796, *ryneþragum* 213, *teonsmiðas* 205, and *tidfara* 9. There is in the poem nothing by way of a set-piece, no obvious purple passage. The account of Guthlac's return to his hermitage is a fitting climax. Structurally it is suitable, providing a satisfactory balance with the rather more pessimistic 'elegiac' material of the opening fitt of the poem; and in its use of the topos of the reawakening of plant-life together with other conventional motifs of the lyrical mode, the passage has many of the qualities of *The Seafarer*. It cannot be dismissed as 'pretty' or 'slight and obvious', the epithets chosen by Sisam[1] to describe Cynewulf's facility in elaborating, for example, a voyage for Elene or descriptions of battle. Rather this is a poet who is content with something nearer to 'the plain staple'[2] of Cynewulf's verse, recognizing clarity and simplicity as sufficient for his poem of meditation and instruction. The diction is indeed over all so plain that readers of *Guthlac A* have often been unwilling to allow the poet his one striking image, *lege biscencte* 624,[3] even though the ironic use of metaphors of serving drink is well attested in Old English poetry. Humour is denied the poet in lines 308 ff., where proffered emendations again remove a brief but by no means unsuitable heightening of the style. And a familiar enough use of litotes,[4] to emphasize the solitariness of Guthlac's hermitage, by and large goes unrecognized.

Parallels between this poem and *Andreas* are much remarked, despite the even greater differences between the two. Verbal similarities examined by Schaar[5] are advanced as evidence that *Guthlac A*, like *Beowulf*, was among the dominant literary influences on the *Andreas* poet. Schaar argues that in at least five places the *Andreas* poet has borrowed from *Guthlac A* without giving sufficient attention

[1] Sisam, *Studies*, p. 15.
[2] Ibid., p. 16.
[3] The phrase is termed 'a rather violent metaphor' for the poet by KD; see Commentary.
[4] *feara sum* 173; see Commentary.
[5] Schaar, *Critical Studies in the Cynewulf Group*, pp. 291–5 and 'On a New Theory of Old English Poetic Diction', p. 304.

to the suitability of the plagiarized phrases in his own narrative.[1]
He compares *Guthlac A* 404–7a with *Andreas* 1330b–5a:

> Lætað gares ord,
> earh ættre gemæl, in gedufan
> in fæges ferð. Gað fromlice,
> ðæt ge guðfrecan gylp forbegan."
> Hie wæron reowe, ræsdon on sona
> gifrum grapum.

but it is difficult to see why the last three verses in this *Andreas*
passage are thought out of place. Here Schaar compares also a
couple of verses from *Guthlac B*:

> ac hine ræseð on
> gifrum grapum:
> (ll. 995b–6a)

suggesting that both Guthlac poets were inspired in their use of
grap by *Beowulf*. Again he argues that the *Andreas* poet has 'badly
rendered' *Guthlac A* 514–17a in the following sentence:

> Hæfde him on innan
> ellen untweonde, wæs þæt æðele mod
> asundrad fram synnum, þeah he sares swa feala
> deopum dolgslegum dreogan sceolde.
> (*Andreas* 1241b–4)

drawing attention to a likeness in alliterative pattern between the
two passages. With *Guthlac A* 574–6 he compares a couple of lines:

> woldon aninga ellenrofes
> mod gemyltan. Hit ne mihte swa!
> (*Andreas* 1392–3)

which he regards as 'inappropriate to *Andreas*', although the
similarity consists mainly in the exclamatory line-filler. The opening
of Bartholomew's instructions to the demons:

> 'Ne sy him banes bryce ne blodig wund,
> lices læla ne laþes wiht
> þæs þe ge him to dare gedon motan . . .'
> (*Guthlac A* 698–700)

is thought to lie behind two passages in *Andreas*:

> No þe laðes ma
> þurh daroða gedrep gedon motan,
> þa þe heardra mæst hearma gefremedan.
> (*Andreas* 1443b–5)

---

[1] Schaar, 'On a New Theory', p. 304.

and

>ne ban gebrocen, ne blodig wund
>lice gelenge, ne laðes dæl.
>
>   (*Andreas* 1473-4)

The spear-motif is especially noted as appearing suddenly in *Andreas* 'for no good reason'. Here the resemblance is greater than Schaar actually indicates, for *Andreas* 1443a *lices lælan* (the usual emendation from the manuscript *liclælan*) may give a second instance of the word *læl* in poetry. The phrase *laþes wiht* occurs also in *Guthlac A* 313 and *Panther* 32, and in prose texts collocates with words like *noht*; many examples of the genitive singular dependent upon other nouns are found in both verse and prose texts. Even the *Guthlac A* poet's description of the triumphant plain (*Guthlac A* 742-3) is deemed to have had a shaping influence on *Andreas* 1581-2:

>Smeolt wæs se sigewang, symble wæs dryge
>folde fram flode, swa his fot gestop.

Schaar points out that the alliterative patterns are similar in both poems and that the *Andreas* lines are unsuitable contextually because the ground has just been flooded. The lines are, however, by no means unsuitable, for the poet is describing the miraculous path which opens through the waters for Andreas; and Schaar himself notes the likeness of *Phoenix* 33a *Smylte is se sigewong* to *Andreas* 1581a and *Guthlac A* 742a. In all these cases it seems possible that the correspondences occur because the poets, dealing with similar themes from time to time, draw upon the same stock phrases in expressing their ideas. Yet, a passage where the correspondences with *Guthlac A* 637-41 are particularly close has been singled out as 'an instance of the complex series, which is otherwise rare in the poem':[1]

>Ic gelyfe to ðe, min liffruma
>þæt ðu mildheort me for þinum mægenspedum,
>nerigend fira, næfre wille,
>ece ælmihtig, anforlætan.

>   (*Andreas* 1284-7)

Professor Stanley suggests that the introduction here of the 'prosaic' word *mildheort* 'may be regarded as supporting evidence for the view that the poet of *An* has borrowed from *Gu*, and that the borrowing is not in the opposite direction'.[2]

---

[1] Schaar, *Critical Studies*, p. 293.
[2] Stanley, 'Studies in the Prosaic Vocabulary', p. 410.

By contrast with the *Guthlac A* poet the poet of *Guthlac B* has an easy command of the poetic vocabulary typical of Cynewulfian poems. Of the longer Old English poems it stands closest to *The Phoenix* and *Andreas* in diction, rather nearer to the former than the latter. Moreover, the similarities in diction between *Guthlac B* and *Andreas* are so striking that there seem stronger grounds for comparison between these two poems than between *Andreas* and *Guthlac A*. In particular they share the only examples of certain compounds (see Commentary on *wrohtsmiðas* 905, *dægredwoma* 1292, and compare *bryþen* 980 with *Andreas* 1532 *sorgbyrþen*) and indeed the only references to lame devils in Anglo-Saxon poetry (see Commentary on *adloman* 912). These resemblances cannot, however, be distinguished in any convincing manner from resemblances held in common particularly within the 'Cynewulfian' school of poetry (see for example the notes for *halge heafdes gimmas* 1302, *wæghengest* 1329, *wopes hring* 1339). *Guthlac B*, *The Phoenix*, and *Andreas* must come from the same literary background as the 'signed poems' of Cynewulf, from poets who seem determined to please an audience which loved ornament, both in imagery and sound. And for many readers today this style of Old English verse-making has great attractions, though for others the expressions used by Cynewulf and his followers have 'for the most part in the translation from one poetic tradition to another lost almost all their intrinsic effectiveness'.[1] The relative simplicity so pleasing in other Old English poems, most obviously in *Beowulf*, perhaps in *Judith* and *Guthlac A*, is absent here, for these writers have evolved their own 'fixed apparatus of stylistic devices'.[2] Of the poems in this group *Guthlac B* has come in for much praise. The shadow of a putative lost Cynewulf signature has sometimes led to its being treated as more Cynewulfian than any other poem outside the recognized canon, though this position is hard to defend.

There is, however, a lot of justice in the criticism that lines 1330–9, from a much-anthologized part of the poem,[3] are 'representative of any pedestrian passage of Old English poetry',[4] except for a

---

[1] Collins, 'Kenning in Anglo-Saxon Poetry', p. 17.
[2] The phrase is Professor Smithers's, in 'Five Notes on Old English Texts', *English and Germanic Studies*, iv (1951–2), 73.
[3] See the anthologies listed in the Select Bibliography, below, section 2(b), edited by Bolton, Campbell and Rosier, Craigie (1926), Williams, and Wyatt.
[4] Collins, 'Kenning in Anglo-Saxon Poetry', p. 15.

lingering feeling that the numerous decorative compounds descriptive
of ships are strung together more effectively than in, for example,
Elene. And the adjective 'pedestrian' seems strangely chosen, for
the poet is attempting a high style, with ornateness its most distinctive feature.[1] In these lines alone the compounds *lagumearg* 1332
and *hærnflota* 1333 are peculiar to *Guthlac B*, and the phrase *æfter
sundplegan* 1334 is found otherwise only in *Phoenix* 111 (there
differently used, of the bird bathing). The compound *sondlond* 1334
may have been invented both for its meaning and to rhyme with
grond at the head of the following verse; and in addition there is
the assonance with *sund-* 1334. Cosijn too attacks the passage[2] for
the incongruousness of the phrase *ofer burgsalo* 1331 in the description of a journey through the fens, and points out another assumed
oddity, the inconsistency between the adjectives *leoht* 1332 and
gehlæsted 1333 applied to the boat, but may misread the account.
The boat moves quickly, and is light although heavy-laden with
sorrows; and all the time the journey takes place the sky is clear
above the dwelling-places of men. (After all, that is the meaning of
the phrase in its earlier occurrence, *Guthlac B* 1284, and a similar
sense is to be assumed for the compound in *Panther* 49–50 *of
ceastrum and of cynestolum/and of burgsalun.*) The subject of grief
allows the poet to use what must have become a highly conventional
piece of poetic stock, the *wopes hring* image, and in developing it he
happens upon the unparalleled poetic archaism *teagor* 1340. A few
lines further on the phrase *fusleoð agol* 1346 is again familiar, and
carries reverberations from stronger poems than Cynewulf's. Then
follows the well-known, incomplete 'elegy'.

So cursory a glance at the diction of this passage does more to
indicate its conventionality than its originality, for its effectiveness
is to some extent the result of the quick recognition of known or
simple imagery reinforced by assonance, rhyme, and the repetitions
of decorative variation. The *Guthlac B* poet used poetic compounds
lavishly throughout, especially, as Schaar has pointed out, to
describe natural phenomena. Yet I cannot agree with him that such
descriptions are 'Anglosaxonisms' and 'in the Anglo-Saxon poetical

[1] Even the sentences are more complex by far than in *Guthlac A* (see §9, p. 70).
[2] P. J. Cosijn, 'Anglosaxonica. IV', *Beiträge zur Geschichte der deutscher Sprache und Literatur*, xxi (1898), 120.

tradition',[1] and for me their independence of the source is in question.
For example, Schaar suggests lines 1271ff. are typical of the Anglo-
Saxon tradition, but on comparison of them with the parallel
section of the *Vita sancti Guthlaci*

cum parumper anhelaret, velut melliflui floris odoratus de ore ipsius
processisse sentiebatur, ita ut totam domum, qua sederet, nectareus
odor inflaret[2]

it becomes apparent that the germ for the poet's elaboration of the
passage is in Felix. Whereas in the Latin the scent of sweet-smelling
flowers seems to proceed from Guthlac's mouth, the poet states that
the sweetest of smells came from his mouth, then adds a new simile
(probably triggered off by the *velut* in his source) which is his working
of the clauses from *ita ut*. The stylistic influence is, as J. L. Rosier has
pointed out,[3] on the whole 'indirect'. In his sympathetic study of the
poem he notes that its 'patterns of repetition, recomposition and
balance' are typical of Old English poetry in general, 'but they are
not often to be found in other individual poems with such consistency, in such density and profusion'.

   It has been argued that the account of the fall of man in *The
Phoenix* (ll. 393–423) is drawn from 'the more detailed and expanded
statement in the *Guthlac*',[4] but literary dependence of the shorter
Phoenix passage upon material from *Guthlac B* (ll. 819–71a) cannot
be proved or disproved. The treatment of the fall and redemption is
differently slanted in *The Phoenix*. The tree and its fruit are described
and, as a tree is important in the poem's structure, its poet may
conflate the tree of knowledge and the phoenix's home. Certainly the
fruits of the phoenix's tree symbolize the good deeds by which man
can achieve salvation.[5] The forbidden fruit is emphasized, but the
figurative extension common to the *Guthlac B* poem and the *Rex
aeterne domine*[6] does not follow. The *Phoenix* poet is concerned
more with redemption than death at this point, and he moves on to

   [1] Schaar, *Critical Studies*, p. 41.
   [2] Colgrave, pp. 156–8. This passage is one of six looked at by Edward M.
Palumbo, *The Literary Use of Formulas in 'Guthlac II' and their Relation to
Felix's 'Vita Sancti Guthlaci'* (The Hague, 1977), in his attempt to show how
the poet 'used formulas not only to translate his prose source . . . but also to
expand it'.
   [3] Rosier, 'Death and Transfiguration', pp. 88–9.
   [4] H. G. Shearin, 'The *Phoenix* and the *Guthlac*', *MLN*, xxii (1907), 263.
   [5] N. F. Blake, *The Phoenix* (Manchester, 1964), p. 80.
   [6] See §6.

consider the significance of Christ's coming. The *Guthlac B* poet,
however, develops metaphorically the forbidden fruit theme, and
then emphasizes death, the warrior who is coming to claim Guthlac.
Both poets, it seems, are using and adapting to contextual needs
themes widely available to medieval religious writers, so it is hardly
surprising, given the similarity of wordstock which lies behind these
two poems, that some fairly close parallels in phrasing occur.[1] W. P.
Ker[2] singles out 'the use of rhyme for the "Paradise" motive'[3] as
'something found out by an artist, before it was repeated by the
school'. His confidence that we can recognize 'Cynewulf's modes'
has its roots in nineteenth-century biography of a largely mythical
bishop, but the comparison of the use of rhyme in these three poems
holds good to-day. The three are still regarded as 'school of Cynewulf', but not Cynewulf's, and in all rhyme is used to a greater
extent perhaps than in the signed poems (the end of *Elene* being
exceptional). Comparable with them in the use of occasional
rhyming verses of this sort are some shorter poems of the Exeter
Book, e.g. *The Panther* and *The Ruin*, but these are not long enough
to play a significant part in modern discussions of the 'Cynewulf
group'.

As an account of the metre of both Guthlac poems is available,[4]
some of the more interesting features only will be noted in this
chapter. For example, a marked difference between the poems is
obvious as regards forms generally contracted in 'later' Old English
verse. In *Guthlac A* uncontracted forms are necessary metrically in
ealdfeonda 475, *hean* 412, *hyhst* 63, and in the present tense of the
contracted strong verbs *tweoþ* 252, *áteoð* 301, and *aflihð* 504. Three
forms should be read aloud without syncopation: *hyhsta* 16, *fægran*
382, and *æfstum* 712 (see Commentary). It has long been accepted
that 'decontraction' cannot be used as a hard and fast dating test
for Old English poetry, for original hiatus can be restored sporadically
in Old as in Modern English.[5] Again, it can be argued that the
persistence of metrical formulae may give rise to metrically deficient

[1] E.g. *Guthlac B* 827–8a: *Phoenix* 397–8a; *Guthlac B* 852 ff.: *Phoenix* 404b–8a.
[2] W. P. Ker, *The Dark Ages* (1904; Mentor text, 1958), p. 171.
[3] See *Guthlac B* 829–30a; *Phoenix* 15–16; *Andreas* 867 (the closeness between the *Guthlac B* and *Phoenix* examples is particularly striking).
[4] Roberts, 'A Metrical Examination'.
[5] See especially R. Quirk, 'On the Problem of Morphological Suture in Old English', *Modern Language Review*, xlv (1950), 5.

phrases.[1] Yet these forms seem to indicate affinities between *Guthlac A* and a few other of the longer Old English poems, *Genesis A*, *Beowulf*, *Exodus*, and *Daniel*. Its author apparently worked within the older narrative traditions, whereas the *Guthlac B* poet is in this respect more in line with the 'Cynewulfian school'. There are no obvious 'contracted' forms in *Guthlac B*: in line 876 the metre demands *ussera*, the form of the possessive adjective usual in verse (compare *Guthlac A* 753), instead of the scribe's *urra*; and though an uncontracted form might perhaps be advanced for *frea* 1222, the reconstructed form is unnecessary.[2]

As the presence of these 'contracted forms' may point only to a manner of composition and not to a firm dating, it must be admitted that *Guthlac A* could be contemporaneous with the Cynewulfian poems or even later than them. Certainly the themes and sources of the poem are more in line with latish homilies than with *Beowulf* and *Genesis A*; and there are parallels in content and wording between *Guthlac A* and the first part of *Christ and Satan*, though these may indicate little more than the dependence of both poets on the alliterative tradition and on similar stories of the devil.[3] A possible pointer towards a late dating for the poem is the alliteration on *w* of *hwearfum* 263, for which there is a parallel in *Judith* 249b *hwearfum bringan*.[4] Another line which presents difficulties of scansion is *for þam oferhygdum þe eow in mod astag* 661: stress is unusual on a dative pronoun in normal syntactic position and, if recognized, involves accepting a syllable of anacrusis, unparalleled in a verse of this type. Although a simple emendation (the addition of *-e*) removes a further troublesome verse, *no hy hine to deað* 549a, the presence of *þæs þe ge him to dare* 700a supports retention of the manuscript reading, and both verses may be held late. It then becomes possible to group with them two more verses in which decontraction is otherwise argued necessary: *ge her áteoð* 301a and *Woldun hy geteon* 574a.[5] The unusual *gæstlicne goddream* 630a, a pattern which

[1] F. P. Magoun, 'Oral Formulaic Character of Anglo-Saxon Narrative Poetry', *Speculum*, xxviii (1953), 461 ff.

[2] Cp. 1035b, 1186a, 1227a, and see Roberts, 'A Metrical Examination', p. 116.

[3] See M. D. Clubb, *Christ and Satan*, Yale Studies in English, lxx (New Haven and London, 1925), xxviii–xxix.

[4] Cp. *reþe* 489 (see Commentary).

[5] See Roberts, 'A Metrical Examination', p. 109.

recurs in the hypermetric *genom him to wildeorum wynne* 741a (where Cosijn's substitution of *wildrum* for *wildeorum* would remove one of these anomalous verses), is paralleled by a verse from the tenth-century *Battle of Brunanburh* 64a *grædigne guðhafoc*.[1]

Certain features distinctive of *Guthlac A* as opposed to *Guthlac B* have little bearing on the question of dating. For example, completely absent from *Guthlac B* is the use of alliterating finite verbs in the first half-line, often with co-ordinate verbs in following verses, as in lines 24, 76, 82, 138, 160, 249, 288, 395, 663, and 767, but such verses are found in all periods of Old English poetry.[2] So too the *A* poet's greater dependence on 'light' verses in the first half-line is striking,[3] but within the corpus of Anglo-Saxon poetry may do little more than help to distinguish his poem from the Cynewulfian group with which *Guthlac B* has so many affinities. Again, there are considerably fewer verses containing only one word in *Guthlac A* than in *Guthlac B*,[4] in part the natural consequence of the less decorative style of this poem. The two stand apart also in the distribution of hypermetric verses, the *A* instances exceeding the *B* in the approximate ratio 2:1,[5] and, more interestingly, in the patterns used in the first half of the line. A. J. Bliss has well summarized the general distribution of hypermetric verse patterns—'normal and heavy verses in the *a*-verse, light verses in the *b*-verse'.[6] This distribution is carried through strictly in only a very few poems: Bliss lists *Beowulf*, *Guthlac B*, and *The Seafarer*, to which I would add *The Phoenix*;[7] whereas the practice of the *Guthlac A* poet resembles the *Christ* poems, *The Dream of the Rood*, and *The Meters of Boethius* in having a high proportion of light verses in the first half-line.

Some of the noteworthy verses in *Guthlac B*, strange though they seem by comparison with the practice of the *Beowulf* poet, are paralleled within at least the Vercelli and Exeter books. For example, the light verses *asanian* 1175a, *asundrien* 1177a, *bideaglian* 1252a, and *acennedne* 1361a (a pattern absent from *Guthlac A*) are among

---

[1] Ibid., p. 112.
[2] Ibid., pp. 107–8.
[3] See Roberts, 'A Metrical Examination', p. 118, n. 137. (Bliss's term 'light' includes such patterns as Sievers A3.)
[4] A rough ratio is 2:5.
[5] See Roberts, 'A Metrical Examination', p. 118.
[6] *The Metre of 'Beowulf'* (Oxford, 1968), p. 96.
[7] Roberts, 'A Metrical Examination', p. 118, n. 133.

some thirty-five instances in these codices;[1] and such verses may point to a later period of composition for much of the poetry contained in these collections.[2] A pattern $(\times \times) \times \times //$ was apparently available at this time and is seen in *þonne seofon niht* 1035b, *þæt wit unc eft* 1186a, *ær þu me, frea min* 1222a and *Hwæt! þu me, wine min* 1227a, but is less well represented than the *asanian* type in the Exeter and Vercelli books.[3] A couple of long-recognized infringements of Kuhn's law,[4] paralleled in *Andreas*, *Elene*, and *Juliana*, have sometimes been considered indicative of the Cynewulfian nature of *Guthlac B*,[5] and a further example occurs in line 951a. There are four times as many 'heavy' verses in *Guthlac B* as in *Guthlac A*,[6] but a full examination of these verses within the corpus is lacking and they may only reflect the *B* poet's liking for weight, as evidenced by eight examples of the *wiceard geceas* 935b pattern. *Swa se burgstede wæs* 1317b is anomalous, for, though resolution of the two short syllables in *stede* might be argued, the actual presence of secondary stress in a B verse is unusual, and, alternatively, classification as an E-type is with anacrusis unlikely.[7] One line is without alliteration: *bi me lifgendum. Huru ic nolde sylf* 1234 (see Commentary); but may be held together by assonance.[8] And the use of the weak genitive plural *dagena* to fill out the verse *on his dagena tid* 949a is thought distinctive of later Old English poetry.[9]

Just as this poet loads his poem with ornate diction, so somehow he achieves a far greater degree of decorativeness in the sound of his lines. Instinctively the part played by assonance in *Guthlac B* must be acknowledged great, as in *The Phoenix* too, and in this both accord with the Cynewulfian group against the longer poems of MS. Junius 11 and *Beowulf*, but assonance, though it may be demonstrated

---

[1] In *Andreas*, *Dream of the Rood*, *Elene*, *Christ*, *Juliana*, *Gifts of Men*, *Riddles*, and *Descent into Hell* (see Roberts, 'A Metrical Examination', p. 108, n. 92).

[2] Cp. *Battle of Maldon* 109a.

[3] Roberts, 'A Metrical Examination', p. 116, n. 117, lists five further examples from *Andreas*, *Soul and Body I*, *Elene*, and *Soul and Body II*.

[4] ll. 1163b and 1224b.

[5] See D. Slay, 'Some Aspects of the Technique of Composition of Old English Verse', *Transactions of the Philological Society* (1952), 13–14.

[6] Roberts, 'A Metrical Examination', pp. 113–14.

[7] Cp. ll. 947b, 1026b, 1029a, 1144b, 1326a, 1334b, 1343b. By contrast *Guthlac A* has only one such verse, l. 174a.

[8] See Roberts, 'A Metrical Examination', pp. 115–16.

[9] See further the Commentary on this line.

at length, remains immeasurable. Allied, however, is the poet's love of extra alliteration and of rhyme, both features which can be described,[1] and in his use of these devices he is again strikingly at variance with the *Guthlac A* poet and the 'early' longer Old English poems. Successive alliteration,[2] for example, occurs about three times more often in *Guthlac B* than in *Guthlac A*, and instances of rhyme and word-repetition have often been singled out for admiration in *Guthlac B*. Rhyme in *Guthlac A* has the appearance of accident about it, whether in the formulaic phrases *ealra cyninga cyning* 17a and *swa is lar 7 ar* 620b, or between half-lines, as *se næfre þa lean alegeð þam þe his lufan adreogeð* 92 and *se þæt hluttre mód | in þæs gæstes gód* 106b–7a; and must indeed be accidental in *7 þær ær fela* 143b. Though statistically negligible, the instances of rhyme in *Guthlac B* appear intended, whether a jingling verse like *leof mon leofum* 1164a[3] or a grouping of three verses like *breahtem æfter breahtme. Beofode þæt ealond, | foldwong onsprong* 1325–6a.[4] In *sume ær, sume sið, sume in urra* 876 the positioning of the repeated forms within the unstressed portions of the line is a trick found also in *Phoenix* 296 *sum brun, sum basu, sum blacum splottum* but not elsewhere extended across a whole verse-line. Perhaps the best word for summarizing the appeal of this poem is 'aureate'. Beside its showiness the solemnity and depth of *Guthlac A* has too often gone unappreciated.

§9. Language

The relative linguistic conformity of the Exeter Book by comparison with the other major codices of Old English poetry is widely acknowledged, and valuable accounts of its language are available.[5] Both Guthlac poems are in the late WS. dialect, but with a sprinkling of Anglian and Kentish forms which may result from successive stages of copying or from the normal presence of such forms in WS. poetic manuscripts.

Some of the WS. features are uncharacteristic of late WS. The

---

[1] A summary appears in Roberts, 'A Metrical Examination', pp. 104–8.
[2] Examples in *Guthlac B* are ll. 845–6, 848–9, 852–3, etc.
[3] Cp. ll. 882b, 897b, 1103a.
[4] Cp. ll. 829–30a and 1334–5a.
[5] See especially K. Sisam, *Studies*, pp. 97–108 and N. F. Blake, 'The Scribe of the Exeter Book', *Neophilologus*, xlvi (1962), 316–19.

digraph *ie* is found frequently in these poems as throughout the manuscript, most often in the group *gie-* where it indicates the
palatal nature of the consonant (e.g. *agiefen* 660, *feorhgiefa* 1239),
but occasionally it is not the result of initial palatalization (e.g.
eþelriehte 216 and *siex* 51 reflect the WS. or Kentish palatal mutation
of *eo* and *ombiehthera* 599 the WS. *i*-mutation of *ea*); and the spelling
i appears for *ie* after palatal consonants (e.g. *cirm* 264, 393, *gifran*
375). Most, however, of the WS. features give little indication of
date, for example: the characteristic retraction of primitive Germanic
æ before *u* (as in *gesawe* 468), its breaking (as in the *neah-* forms),
and its mutation (as in *nyhstan* 445, etc); the WS. *i*-mutation of *ēa*
(*lig* 193, *-e* 1072) and of primitive Germanic *iu* (e.g. *hiw* 710, 909,
-es 900, *niwe* 742, 823); the dative *gehwam* 321, 1242, peculiar to this
dialect; loss of *g* between front vowel and dental consonant (as in
anhydig 897, 978, *gebredan* 1165, and, analogically, *gefrunen* 1360
and *oðbroden* 854). Other changes frequently evidenced in WS. texts
are shown by *dalum* 54, *gestalum* 510 (Campbell, §162), *geara* 40,
-o 630 (Campbell, §172), the *sel-* group where *syl-* is usual and a
manuscript correction to *y* indicated for *sylfe* 751 (Campbell, §§325,
326), and the preterite *geræhte* 171 with *æ* levelled from the present
system (Campbell, §753 (9) b.2).

Typical rather of late WS. is the rounding of *i* in the neighbourhood
of labials and before *r* (e.g. *byscyrede* 145, 895, *fyra* 988). Apparent
rounding occurs sporadically in a few other positions, for example
gynnwised 867, *hyne* 127, 552, and *synd* 91, but here the closeness of
n would seem to suggest that *y* may be a late spelling variant used
for clarity among a succession of minims (compare *nyðgista* 540,
where an original *i* has been altered to *y*, and *þrynesse* 646, where
alternatively *y* may reflect the early WS. contraction of *ī* + e). Late
WS. unrounding of *ȳ* is seen in *inðriceð* 285, *ligesearwum* 228, and
wiscað 223, and smoothing of *ea* (< *æ*) in *gerehte* 96. The general
restoration of *a* in WS. is seen in *hraðe* 422, 687, and *late* 1164, 1225.
Late OE. monophthongization of *ĕa* is indicated by *scæd* 675 (an
interpretation supported by the general development of initial
palatalization of *æ* in these texts), *ætstælle* 179, *onstæl* 824, and by the
back spelling *eahteð* 88. The effects of late OE. monophthongization
are perhaps to be seen also in *wolde* 517(N).

Certain features, given the over-all character of the manuscript,
are more likely than not WS. The *meahte* forms (10 instances) and
meahton 187, for example, have been termed either WS. or Kentish,

as has the palatal mutation of *eo* reflected in *sihste* 1150, *ætryhte* 997, 1152, *ryht-* (6 instances), and *woruldryht* 57. The digraph *io* appears in *hio* 2, 3, *biorg* 175, and *spiowdon* 912(N), all forms unusual in late WS. but not restricted to non-WS. texts (Campbell, §296). Such forms as *waldend* 594, 666, 763, 800, *-es* 845, and *onwald* 482, 1102 (both with *e* subpuncted before *al*) are not uncommon in WS.,[1] *galdrum* 1207 is one of those words which appear more often than not in Anglian form in poetry,[2] and *halsige* 1203 may reflect an unshortened root vowel rather than an Anglian change.[3] The irregular front mutation of *mæcges* 1219, *-as* 861, and *wræcmæcgas* 129, 231, 263, 558, though frequent in the Lindisfarne and Rushworth glosses, is found also in WS. The forms *sceþþan* 226 and *sceðþenra* 404, reflecting a mutation of *æ* which has not undergone initial palatalization, invade WS. prose and are thus not significant of dialect (Campbell, §188 and n.3). It is possible to see reflected in *Geofu* 530 and *geofona* 1303 WS. back mutation of *ie* to *io* (Campbell, §220) rather than Anglian back mutation of *e*, and *geafena* 1042 displays the *ea* for *eo* frequent in ninth-century Kentish but sporadic also in WS. and Mercian (Campbell, §§280, 281). Such forms as *nelle* 1259, reflecting a vowel developed under low sentence stress, though found in early WS. and Kentish, are frequent in late WS. The hooked *ę* of *ęlda* 824, *ręste* 363, *węgan* 370 and *genęged* 1013 is a mere orthographic variant of *æ*.

A small number of forms may point to a non-WS. element within these poems. Non-WS. *e* for *æ* occurs, e.g. *bædeweg* 985, *blede* 847 (here *i*-mutation of *ō* can be argued), *ceargesta* 393(N), *deaðweges* 991, *efna* 1242, *forsegon* 630, and the *æ* of *forsæcen* 377(N) may be a back spelling. Second fronting of *æ* to *e* is found in *meþelcwide* 1219, *-a* 1007, *meðelcwidum* 1015, and back mutation of *æ* arising from second fronting of *a* in *eaferum* 855, *heafelan* 1270, and perhaps *sceaðena* 127 (which may however, like *-sceaþan* 650 and 909, have a glide vowel between palatal *sc* and following back vowel) and *þeara* 398 (Campbell, §708, n. 5). The *i*-mutation of *a* restored in Anglian dialects before the velar group *l* + consonant appears in *ældu* 109, *ælda* 755, 821, 835, 926, 975, *ældum* 1142, and *sorgwælmum* 1262,

---

[1] E. G. Stanley 'Spellings of the *Waldend* Group', *Studies in Language, Literature, and Culture of the Middle Ages and Later*, ed. E. Bagby Atwood and A. A. Hill (Austin, 1969), p. 47.

[2] Ibid., p. 65.

[3] Ibid., p. 48.

but *wærc* 1028, the apparent solitary example of similar Northumbrian mutation, is a noun which penetrates WS. in this form (Campbell, §193 (a), n. 4). Non-WS. *i*-mutation of *ea* (< *æ* before *r* + consonant) is found in *ermþu* 447, *tergað* 288, and *werga* 451, and of *ea* (< *æ* before [χ]) in *behlehhan* 1357, *onbehtþegn* 1146, *-e* 1294, *ombehtþegn* 1000, and *-e* 1199, but such forms appear in Ælfric; *sinnehte* 678 may also reflect this mutation or its levelling (Campbell, §628(3)). Further examples of non-WS. *i*-mutation are *heorde* 747 (of *io < i*); *steor* 510, *þeostorcofan* 1195, and *þeostra* 696 (of *io < iu*); and *geeþe* 1206 (of *ēa < au*). Non-WS. back mutation of *e* appears in *heolstrum* 83, *meodumre* 384, *meotud-* forms, etc., analogically in *breodwiað* 287, and even before *c* in *wiþerbreocum* 294; and of *i* in *freoþað* 243, *freoðade* 396, *heonan* 1036, etc. Examples of Anglian smoothing are *degle* 952, *gehþa* 1208, *leg* 595, *-e* 375, 624, *geræhte* 768, *þegan* 169(N), *þigað* 461 and *wærnysse* 671(N).

Many consonantal and inflectional features often emended in editions of Anglo-Saxon poetry have been retained in this edition[1] and are generally noted in the Commentary or in the Glossary. A few such features, thought significant for dating or provenance, should be included in this section. Final unvoicing, a fairly common trait of both Anglian and late WS., appears in *gestah* 175, and inverted spellings in *feorg* 243, 1058 and *feorggedal* 1178 (Campbell, §446); the compromise symbol of *beorhge* 140 is of little significance as it is found in late WS., Northumbrian, and Rushworth[1] (Campbell, §58). Medial *-ig-* in *bewitigian* 199 and *hyrcnigan* 1006, though not restricted to WS. texts, may reflect the early WS. interchange of *-ig-* and *-i-* in class II weak verbs (Campbell, §§267, 757); the appearance of *g* for *i* in class I weak verbs of the *herian* type, e.g. *herge* 611, *nergan* 553, *-ende* 598, is of no dialect significance. Unusual for WS. are the poetical present participles of class II weak verbs *gnornende* 232, 679, 1209, *drusendne* 1061, 1379 and perhaps *neosendes* 1217 (but see Sievers[2]), with loss of *i* between main and secondary stress after a long syllable (Campbell, §757). Loss of *w* from the preterite *Com* 1141 is apparently exceptional in

---

[1] See G. L. Brook, 'The relation between the textual and linguistic study of Old English', *The Anglo-Saxons, Studies presented to Bruce Dickins*, (ed. P. Clemoes (1959), pp. 280–91) on some of the disadvantages of less conservative editions.

[2] E. Sievers, 'Zur Rhythmik des germanischen Alliterationsverses', *Beiträge zur Geschichte der deutschen Sprache und Literatur*, x (1885), 233.

this MS.;[1] in *neole* 563 the consonant has dropped out between back vowels which have contracted; and the consonant is absent from the reduced forms of proclitic *swa* (*se* 409, 961). The absence of glide vowel between *sc* and back vowel, a feature of Mercian and Kentish texts (Campbell, §183 and n. 4), is well evidenced, e.g. *scadu* 1288, *scome* 204, 633, the glide appearing only in the preterite forms of *sculan*.

The doubling of *t* before *r* usual in early WS. appears in *attre* 668, 912, *uttor* 126 (Campbell §453), and the doubling of *d*, a late WS. change (Campbell, §453), in *tuddor* 735; a curious doubling of post tonic *ð* appears in *ferðþes* 923. The prosthetic *g*- of *geadwelan* 1091, subpuncted in the manuscript, and perhaps merely scribal dittography, though sometimes considered indicative of Kentish colouring, reflects at most the late southern levelling of initial *ea*- and *gea*- (Campbell, §303). The forms *foldærne* 1031 and *hærnflota* 1333 reflect the movement of *r* from before to behind the vowel after the period of breaking (Campbell, §459(1)), a metathesis occurring also in low stress, e.g. *tintergum* 211, -*u* 649. The metathesis of *þl* through [*ðl*] with voiced spirant to *ld*, predominantly Anglian though common in poetic texts (Campbell, §425), appears in *ánseld* 1240, *bold* 140, -*es* 84, *melda* 1230, and *seld* 585, and the Anglian retention of *þl* with voicing of the spirant after a short vowel (Campbell, §402) in *beorgseþel* 102, *mæðlan* 1202, *meþelcwide* 1219, etc.; examples of WS. *tl* after a short vowel are *botles* 329, 383, *bytla* 148. Assimilation in groups consisting of a consonant followed or preceded by a liquid or nasal is found sporadically, e.g. *lareow* 1004, -*es* 359, *usse* 750, 973, g/dsf. *þisse* (6 times), gpl *þissa* 752, and the comparative *sellan* 278, 492, and 1268, typical of late WS. but found also in late Northumbrian texts (Campbell, §484). Other common assimilations are *þs* > *ss* (*bliss*- and *liss*- forms) and *dt* > *tt* (*latteowes* 364). Simplification with the loss of the second of three successive consonants occurs in *flæshoman* 374, *sceðþenra* 404, *wærnysse* 671, and in both simplex and compound forms of *ferð*.

The Guthlac poems, like the other verse of the Exeter Book and indeed of the other codices of Old English poetry,[2] contain many

---

[1] Sisam, *Studies*, p. 101, points out that *cw*- is found throughout the Exeter Book in the past tense of *cuman*.

[2] K. Malone 'When did Middle English begin?', *Curme Volume of Linguistic Studies* (Philadelphia, 1930), pp. 110–17.

examples of inflectional levelling. Most striking is the weakening that affects even the *-um* ending in *hildescurun* 1143 and *wyrdstafun* 1351; and the *-u-* is a manuscript correction of *-o-* in *onfengum* 405. In one place similar weakening is shown by a weak noun form (ds *þeowon* 922), and *-an* may appear for *-um* in dsm. *gifran* 375. In *forþon* forms *-on* appears 8 times and *-an* only in *Forðan* 378, whereas *siþþam* 136(N) contrasts with the *-an* usual for this adverb. Verb forms ending in a nasal consonant also indicate levelling: *-on* occurs in five infinitives (*bregdon* 676, *leton* 520, 948, *ongyldon* 861, and *semon* 511); *-an* for *-on* (e.g. *binoman* 342, *brucan* 417, or even class II weak verbs *leofedan* 139, *wundredan* 1232); *-un* for *-on* (e.g. *agun* 79, *ahofun* 229, and *feredun* 1306 where *u* is a manuscript correction from *o*); and *-um* for *-on* (*mostum* 210, *motum* 13, *widhog-dum* 631, *woldum* 663, and *wurdum* 181). The plural subjunctive *-en* is often retained (e.g. *gebiden* 509, *cuþen* 751, *demen* 527) beside *-e* (e.g. *cwome* 237, *gelumpe* 194, and the emendation *gedælde* 969(N)), but in some five places an inflexion with back vowel appears (*sorgedon* 238, *onstældun* 468, *gutan* 1233, *sceoldan* 664, and *wundredan* 1232). Weakening is evident also in those endings which characteris-tically have a back vowel, and *-a* appears occasionally for *-e* (e.g. *þrowinga* 471, *ealra* 68, *mara* 384, 521, *ænlicra* 1320, *wynsumra* 1321, and *soþra* 1123).

The metre demands that 23 of the 35 instances of the second and third person present indicative forms of strong verbs be uncontracted, but points neither to short nor long forms for the remaining 12; only *cwið* 4 is short, and it is a form often found in Anglian texts (Campbell, §733(a)). The forms are for the most part unaffected by *i*-mutation, a mutated vowel appearing in *cymeð* 1350. It is hardly significant that only 2 of the 23 forms shown by the metre to be uncontracted are in *Guthlac B*, for the present tense is seldom used in that poem. In any case, this use of long forms cannot be con-sidered evidence of the Anglian origin of the Guthlac poems, but shows only that they are unlikely to have been written by the 'late composers of prosaic verse'.[1]

A few further verb forms are worth mention in this summary. Medial *-ad-* and participial *-ad* are prevalent in the preterite of weak verbs class II but, though a feature particularly of Anglian and Kentish texts, are found often in late WS.; by contrast, medial *-o-*

[1] Sisam's phrase, *Studies*, p. 125.

occurs 12 times (e.g. *Beofode* 1325, *campode* 643, *colode* 1307). Late weakening is reflected in *leofedan* 139, *wundredan* 1232, and perhaps *gynnwised* 867(N); the participle *belifd* 1308(N) shows a more radical weakening. Certain distinctive forms of *habban* occur: *hafu* 1067 and *hafað* 4, 87, and 647; but these are common in Anglian and poetic texts and *hafað* is found also in WS. prose (Campbell, §762). Twice *-es* appears for the more general *-est*, in *meahtes* 469 and *gefremedes* 586.

Both poems contain forms which have been regarded as safe evidence for Anglian origin in prose texts:[1] *gen* 515, 521, 538, *-a* 155, 233, 446, 1270, *nemne* 367, *oferleordun* 726, *wærc* 1028, *wepe* 8, *wælan* 425, *wiþerbreocum* 294, and *wló* 1154; but they have little significance in the 'general Old English poetic diction'.[2] Indeed, many other 'Anglian' features are found indifferently in both poems, e.g. the prepositions *in* and *on* in roughly equal proportions, *mid* with the accusative, the *-c* forms of oblique personal pronouns, words such as *heht* 703, *meorde* 1086, *-a* 1041, but are similarly uninformative. The *hapax legomena* are indicated in the Glossary, and there are proportionately many more of these in *Guthlac B* than in the *A* poem. The vocabulary of *Guthlac A* is remarkable for two groups of specialized vocabulary, legal and religious, which are examined in §8.

Syntactically there is little that is unusual in these two poems. Noteworthy in *Guthlac A* is the relative *se mec* 703: paralleled only in *Exodus* 380, *Maxims I* 37 and 38 in Old English verse, it has been considered a relic of 'an older construction'[3] with *se* as a demonstrative rather than a relative pronoun. Again in *Guthlac A* the relative is twice completed by a dative pronoun (*se þe him* 72 and *þa þe him* 361), and a discontinuous relative, rare in verse, appears in *þe . . . his* 716–17. The two examples of the phrase *ecan lifes* 172 and 795 may indicate that the *Guthlac A* poet was familiar with the use of weak adjectives unpreceded by a demonstrative, but otherwise the construction occurs in stereotyped phrases which contain the form *widan* 636 and 817, so little weight can be given this

---

[1] R. Jordan, *Eigentümlichkeiten des anglischen Wortschatzes*, Anglistische Forschungen, xvii (1906), 63.

[2] Sisam, *Studies*, p. 138, from the important discussion of this problem in pp. 119–39.

[3] B. Mitchell, 'Pronouns in Old English Poetry', *RES*, n.s. xv (1964), 134.

point in any consideration of dating. In any case the test is now thought to have less value than formerly. Only two examples of a weak adjective without preceding article occur in the *B* poem: the conventional formula *to widan feore* 840 found in poems of all periods; and *þone bleatan drync | deoþan deaðweges* 990b–1a (where the adjective in question modifies a dependent genitive within a phrase headed by an article). One instance of an uninflected participial adjective in variation has been found in *Guthlac B* (*gesoht* 1019(N)) and sporadic examples can be found in verse from all periods;[1] and there is a possible second instance (*soden* 1150(N)). Though parallels need not be similar syntactically, the variation of the phrase *frean feorhgedal* 1200(N) by a clause is unusual in this poem. It is worth noting that the collocation *from . . . oþ* 1291(N), paralleled only three times in the Anglo-Saxon poetic corpus, may reflect *a . . . usque* in the *Vita*, but that *Guthlac B* does not have any other syntactic peculiarities which may be explained by reference to its source.

The features gathered together in this section tell us little about the place of origin of these poems. They do indicate an earlier rather than later time of composition within the Anglo-Saxon period, particularly for *Guthlac A* which also contains features judged 'old' on metrical grounds.[2] Yet the metrical evidence points only to the common origin of both poems within the earlier Old English period. A few things suggest that *Guthlac B* may be later than Guthlac *A*,[3] but they need reflect nothing more than the use of different conventions by men working in the same period. For the same reason, the comparative plainness of *Guthlac A* is hardly proof that it was not written in the same age as *Guthlac B*. It has indeed been pointed out that in sentence structure *Guthlac A* comes closer to 'Cædmonian' poetry and *Beowulf* and *Andreas*, whereas *Guthlac B* stands with the Cynewulfian poems,[4] but even here the grouping deals rather with likenesses among poems than with their chronological relationships to one another. Though it might be comforting to argue that *Guthlac A*, because of its apparent independence from the

---

[1] See A. Campbell, 'The Old English Epic Style', *English and Medieval Studies*, ed. N. Davis and C. L. Wrenn (London, 1962), p. 20.

[2] See particularly the uncontracted forms discussed in §8.

[3] E.g. the use of *dagena* 949 (N).

[4] A. Rynell, 'Parataxis and Hypotaxis as a Criterion of Syntax and Style especially in Old English Poetry', *Lunds Universitets Årsskrift*, xlviii (1952), 36.

Vita sancti Guthlaci, must have been written before *c.* 730 and the *B* poem after that date, the suggestion lacks any firm support.

The manuscript forms indicate a shared transmission for the Guthlac poems. Some forms can be described as Anglian, a few as Kentish, but, although it was once customary to regard such forms as proof of Anglian origins, the recognition of a poetic *koinē* entails that taken by themselves they are inconclusive. The Anglian characteristics reflected in the spellings of accented syllables seem to be reinforced by the appearance of class II weak verb present participles with loss of *-i-*, but such details tend only to strengthen the metrical evidence for a *terminus ad quem* not much later than the Alfredian period.[1] Given the linguistic conformity of the Exeter Book, this assumption is probably true of much of the verse it contains. A few 'early' WS. spellings, for example the pervasive *ie* digraph, just as much as the Anglian characteristics, have been regarded as evidence that the miscellany was first put together by Alfred's time, but it should be emphasized that late WS. forms predominate.

Because both poems deal with the life of a Crowland saint it has been thought likely that they were composed in East Mercia.[2] The use in *Guthlac A* of sources and story-material strikingly different from that to be found in Felix's *Vita sancti Guthlaci* can be seen as indication of a Crowland origin for this poem. Yet, if a non-Crowland, indeed non-Mercian provenance were to be suggested, some western centre such as Glastonbury, Hereford, or Worcester[3] might seem as strong a contender as Crowland. With *Guthlac B*, because the principal source is Felix's *Vita*, the assumed probability of East Mercian authorship is diminished. Neither place nor date of composition can be established.

---

[1] Cp. Nicolas Jacobs, 'Anglo-Danish Relations, Poetic Archaism and the Date of *Beowulf*', *Poetica*, VIII (1977), 23–43, for a reconsideration of the evidence for dating *Beowulf.*

[2] As argued by Sisam, *Studies*, p. 134.

[3] These centres are suggested by Dr. Gradon, *Elene*, p. 4.

Select Bibliography

1. THE MANUSCRIPT

CHAMBERS, R. W., FÖRSTER, MAX, and FLOWER, ROBIN. *The Exeter Book of Old English Poetry* (London, 1933).

CHAMBERS, R. W. 'The British Museum Transcript of the Exeter Book', *Anglia*, xxxv (1912), 393–400.

CONYBEARE, J. J. 'Account of a Saxon Manuscript preserved in the Cathedral Library at Exeter', *Archaeologia*, xvii (1812), 180–97.

HOLTHAUSEN, F. 'Vergleichung des Gūðlāc-Textes mit der Hs.', *Anglia*, xl (1916).

KER, N. R. Review of CFF in *MÆ* ii (1933), 224–31.

——. *Catalogue of Manuscripts containing Anglo-Saxon* (Oxford, 1957).

PHILIP, A. 'The Exeter Scribe and the Unity of *Christ*', *PMLA*, lv (1940), 903–9.

POPE, JOHN C. 'Palaeography and poetry: some solved and unsolved problems of the Exeter Book', *Medieval Scribes, Manuscripts & Libraries*, Essays presented to N. R. Ker, edited by M. B. Parkes and Andrew G. Watson (London, 1978), pp. 25–65.

SCHIPPER, J. 'Zum Codex Exoniensis', *Germania*, xix (1874), 327–38.

SISAM, K. Review of CFF in *RES* x (1934), 338–42.

——. 'The Exeter Book' (incorporating much of the above review), *Studies in the History of Old English Literature* (Oxford, 1953), 97–118.

——. 'The Arrangement of the Exeter Book', *Studies*, pp. 291–2.

Times Literary Supplement, 1629 (20 April 1933), p. 272 (anon. review of CFF).

Tupper, Frederick. 'The British Museum Transcript of the Exeter Book', *Anglia*, xxxvi (1912), 285–8.

Wanley, H. *Catalogus Historico-Criticus* (1705), 279–81.

2. EDITIONS

(a) *Complete Texts*

GOLLANCZ, ISRAEL. *The Exeter Book*, an Anthology of Anglo-Saxon Poetry. Part I: Poems I–VIII (includes both Guthlac poems), EETS (OS) civ (London, 1895).

GREIN, CHRISTIAN W. M. *Bibliothek der angelsächsischen Poesie*, vols. i and ii (with *Guthlac A* 1–29 attached to *Christ* and otherwise one Guthlac poem) (Göttingen, 1857–8).

KRAPP, G. P. and DOBBIE, E. VAN K. *The Exeter Book*, Anglo-Saxon Poetic Records, iii (New York, 1936).

THORPE, BENJAMIN. *Codex Exoniensis*. A collection of Anglo-Saxon Poetry . . . (Guthlac material printed consecutively under various headings) (London, 1842).

WÜLKER, RICHARD P. *Bibliothek der angelsächsischen Poesie* 1 Band (Kassel, 1881); 2 Band (Leipzig, 1894); 3 Band. Edited by Assmann (Leipzig, 1898).

(b) *Selections and Partial Editions*

BOLTON W. F. *An Old English Anthology* (*Guthlac B* 1141b–325a) (London, 1963).

CAMPBELL, JACKSON J. and ROSIER, JAMES C. *Poems in Old English* (*Guthlac B* 1335–79) (New York and Evanston, 1962).

COOK, ALBERT S. *The Christ of Cynewulf* (*Guthlac A* 1–29 as the end of *Christ*) (Boston, 1900).

CRAIGIE, W. A. *Specimens of Anglo-Saxon Poetry*, vol. i: Biblical and Classical Themes (*Guthlac B* 819–59) (Edinburgh, 1923).

——. *Specimens of Anglo-Saxon Poetry*, vol. ii: Early Christian Lore and Legend (*Guthlac A* 93–183, 215–61, 393b–445, 530–91, 623–36, 663–702, 722–59; *Guthlac B* 999b–1059 and 1269b–1378a (Edinburgh, 1926).

GOLLANCZ, ISRAEL. *Cynewulf's Christ*. An Eighth Century English Epic (*Guthlac A* 1–29 in an appendix) (London, 1892).

KLAEBER, F. *The Later Genesis and Other Old English and Old Saxon Texts Relating to the Fall of Man* (*Guthlac B* 819–71a and 976–96a) (Heidelberg, 1913).

KLIPSTEIN, LOUIS F. *Analecta Anglo-Saxonica*, vol. ii (*Guthlac A* 30–92) (New York, 1849).

THOMPSON, BERTHA. 'The Old English Poem of St. Guthlac' (*Guthlac A* 30–818 and *Guthlac B* as one poem (an unpublished Ph.D. thesis, Leeds University, 1931).

WARREN, KATE M. *A Treasury of English Literature*, Origins to Eleventh Century. *Guthlac B* 1257–1304 (London, 1908).

WILLIAMS, O. T. *Short Extracts from Old English Poetry* (*Guthlac A* 201b–61; *Guthlac B* 819–71a, 999b–1047a, 1139b–96, and 1278b–1343 (Bangor, 1909).

WYATT, ALFRED J. *An Anglo-Saxon Reader* (*Guthlac B* 1305–78a) (Cambridge, 1919).

3. TRANSLATIONS

GOLLANCZ, ISRAEL. *The Exeter Book* (under 2(a) above).

GORDON, ROBERT K. *Anglo-Saxon Poetry* (*Guthlac A* 1–29 as the end of *Christ*, *Guthlac A* 30–818; *Guthlac B* 819–25a and 878b–1379 (London and Toronto, 1926, rev. edn., 1954).

GREIN, C. W. M. *Dichtungen der Angelsachsen stabreimend übersetzt* (*Guthlac A* 1–29 as end of *Christ* in vol. i, *Guthlac A* 30–818 and *Guthlac B* as one poem in vol. ii) (Göttingen, 1857–9).

KENNEDY, CHARLES W. *The Poems of Cynewulf Translated into English Prose* (Christ, Guthlac, Phoenix, and Juliana) (London and New York, 1910).

OLIVERO, FREDERICO. 'Sul Poemetto Anglosassone *Guthlac*', *Memorie*

della Realle Accademia delle Scienze di Turino, lxx, Serie II (1942), 223–65.

SPAETH, J. DUNCAN. *Old English Poetry*. Translations into Alliterative Verse (*Guthlac B* 894–923a, 932b–40a, 954b–75, 999b–1038a, 1047b–57a, 1060–1117, 1141b–1250, and 1269b–1379) (Princeton, 1921).

THORPE, BENJAMIN. *Codex Exoniensis* (under 2(a) above).

WARREN, KATE M. *A Treasury of English Literature* (under 2(b) above).

4. SOURCES AND BACKGROUND MATERIAL

(a) *Legend and Cult of St. Guthlac*

BIRCH, W. DE G. *Memorials of Saint Guthlac of Crowland* (Wisbech, 1881).

COLGRAVE, BERTRAM. *Felix's Life of Saint Guthlac* (Cambridge, 1956).

GONSER, P. *Das angelsächsischen Prosa-Leben des hl. Guthlac*, Anglistische Forschungen, xxvii (Heidelberg, 1909).

GOODWIN, C. W. *The Anglo-Saxon Version of the Life of St. Guthlac* (London, 1848).

GOUGH, R. *The History and Antiquities of Croyland Abbey in the County of Lincoln*, Bibliotheca Topographica Britannica, no. 11, vol. iii (London, 1783).

ROBERTS, JANE. 'An Inventory of Early Guthlac Materials', *Mediaeval Studies*, xxxii (1970), 193–233.

(b) *Other Principal Materials Consulted*

ASSMANN, BRUNO. *Angelsächsiche Homilien und Heiligenleben*, Bibliothek der angelsächsischen Prosa, iii (1889).

ATKINSON, ROBERT. 'The Passions and the Homilies from *Leabhar Breac*', *Publications of the Royal Irish Academy*, Todd Lecture Series, vol. ii, part ii (Dublin, 1887).

BROOKS, KENNETH R. '*Andreas*' and '*The Fates of the Apostles*' (Oxford, 1961).

CLUBB, MERREL DARE. *Christ and Satan*, Yale Studies in English, lxx (1925).

COLGRAVE, BERTRAM. 'The Earliest English Saints' Lives written in England', *Proceedings of the British Academy*, xliv (1958), 35–60.

DUDLEY, LOUISE. *The Egyptian Elements in the Legend of the Body and Soul* (Baltimore, 1911).

GRADON, P. O. E. *Cynewulf's 'Elene'* (London, 1958; repr. 1966).

GRAU, GUSTAV. 'Quellen und Verwandtschaften der älteren germanischen Darstellungen des jüngsten Gerichtes', *Studien zur englischen Philologie hrsg. von L. Morsbach*, xxxi (1908).

KRAPP, G. P. and DOBBIE, E. VAN K. *The Anglo-Saxon Poetic Records*, vols. i–vi (New York, 1931–53).

KURTZ, B. J. 'From St. Anthony to St. Guthlac', *University of California Publications in Modern Philology*, xii, no. 2 (1926), 103–46.

LIEBERMANN, F. 'Über ostenglische Geschichtsquellen des 12., 13., 14. Jahrhunderts, besonders den falschen Ingulf', *Neues Archiv der Gesellschaft für ältere deutsche Geschichtskunde*, xviii (1892), 225–67.

MARSTRANDER, CARL. 'The Two Deaths', *Eriu*, v (1911), 120–5.

PLUMMER, C. *Bedae Opera Historica* (Oxford, 1952 Re-issue).

SEYMOUR, ST. J. D. 'The Bringing Forth of the Soul in Irish Literature', *Journal of Theological Studies*, xxii (1921), 16–20.

WHITELOCK, DOROTHY. 'Anglo-Saxon Poetry and the Historian', *Transactions of the Royal Historical Society*, 4th Series, xxxi (1949), 75–94.

WILLARD, R. 'Two Apocrypha in Old English Homilies', *Beiträge zur englischen Philologie*, xxx (1935).

WOLPERS, THEODOR. *Die englische Heiligenlegende des Mittelalters* (Tübingen, 1964).

5. TEXTUAL CRITICISM AND INTERPRETATION

ABBETMEYER, C. 'The *Phoenix* and the *Guthlac*', a letter in *MLN*, xxiii (1908), 32.

ADAMS, ARTHUR. 'Christ(?) 1665–1693', *MLN*, xxi (1906), 240.

BINZ, G. Review of Buttenwieser, *Studien* (see 6 below), in *Englische Studien*, xxix (1901), 108–14.

BLACKBURN, F. A. 'Is the *Christ* of Cynewulf a Single Poem?', *Anglia*, xix (1897), 89–98.

BRADLEY, HENRY. 'Some Emendations in Old English Texts', *Modern Language Review*, xi (1916), 212–15.

BROOKS, K. R. 'Old English *wopes hring*', *English and Germanic Studies*, ii (1948–9), 68–74.

BROWN, CARLETON. '*Poculum Mortis* in Old English', *Speculum*, xv (1940), 389–99.

CHARITIUS, P. J. 'Über die angelsächsischen Gedichte vom hl. Guðlac', *Anglia*, ii (1879), 265–308.

COSIJN, P. J. 'Anglosaxonica', *Tijdschrift voor Nederlandsche Taal- en Letterkunde*, i (1881), 143–58.

'Anglosaxonica. III', *Beiträge zur Geschichte der deutschen Sprache und Literatur*, xxi (1896), 8–26.

'Anglosaxonica. IV', *Beiträge zur Geschichte der deutschen Sprache und Literatur*, xxiii (1898), 109–30.

GREIN, C. W. M. 'Zur Textkritik der angelsächsischen Dichter', *Germania*, x (1865), 416–29.

HOLTHAUSEN, F. 'Beiträge zur Erklärung und Textkritik altenglischer Dichtungen', *Indogermanische Forschungen*, iv (1894), 379–88.

——. Review of Assmann in *Beiblatt*, ix (1899), 353–8.

——. 'Zur altenglischen Literatur IV', *Beiblatt*, xviii (1907), 201–8.

——. 'Zu englischen Wortkunde III', *Beiblatt*, xxxii (1921), 17–23.

——. 'Wortdeutungen', *Indogermanische Forschungen*, xlviii (1930), 254–67.

——. 'Zu den AE. Gedichten der HS. von Vercelli', *Anglia*, lxxiii (1955), 276–8.

HOWARD, E. J. 'Cynewulf's Christ 1665–1693', *PMLA*, xlv (1930), 354–67.

KLAEBER, F. 'The Christ of Cynewulf', review of Cook (see 2(b) above) in *JEGP*, iv (1902), 101–12.

KLAEBER, F. 'Emendations in Old English Poems', *Modern Philology*, ii (1904), 141–6.

——. 'Guðlac 1252 ff.', *Beiblatt*, xv (1904), 345–7.

KOCK, ERNST A. 'Jubilee Jaunts and Jottings', *Lunds Universitets Årsskrift*, N.F., Avd. 1, Bd. xiv, Nr. 26 (1918).

——. 'Interpretations and Emendations of Early English Texts', pt. IV, *Anglia*, xlii (1918), 98–124; Pt. VI, *Anglia* xliv (1920), 97–114; Pt. VII, *Anglia*, 245–60; Pt. XI, *Anglia*, xlvii (1923), 264–73.

SHEARIN, H. G. 'The *Phœnix* and the *Guthlac*', a letter in *MLN*, xxii (1907), 263.

SMITHERS, G. V. 'Five Notes on Old English Texts', *English and Germanic Studies*, iv (1951–2), 65–85.

6. LITERARY AND GENERAL CRITICISM

BOLTON, W. F. 'The Background and Meaning of *Guthlac*', *JEGP*, lxi (1962), 595–603.

BUTTENWIESER, ELLEN C. *Studien über die Verfasserschaft des Andreas* (Heidelberg, 1898).

CALDER, DANIEL G. 'Theme and Strategy in *Guthlac B*', *Papers on Language and Literature*, viii (1972), 227–42.

——. '*Guthlac A* and *Guthlac B*: Some Discriminations', *Anglo-Saxon Poetry: Essays in Appreciation*, ed. L. E. Nicholson and Dolores Warwick Frese (Notre Dame, 1975), pp. 65–80.

CAMPBELL, A. 'The Old English Epic Style', *English and Medieval Studies presented to J. R. R. Tolkien*, ed. Norman Davis and C. L. Wrenn (London, 1962), pp. 13–26.

COLLINS, D. C. 'Kenning in Anglo-Saxon Poetry', *Essays and Studies*, n.s. xii (1959), 1–17.

CREMER, MATTHIAS. *Metrische und sprachliche Untersuchung der altenglischen Gedichte Andreas, Gûðlâc, Phoenix (Elene, Juliana, Crist)* (Bonn, 1888).

DAS, S. K. *Cynewulf and the Cynewulf Canon* (Calcutta, 1942).

DIAMOND, R. E. 'The Diction of the Signed Poems of Cynewulf', *Philological Quarterly*, xxxviii (1959), 228–41.

FARRELL, R. T. 'Some Remarks on the Exeter Book *Azarias*', *MÆ*, xli (1972), 1–8.

FORSTMANN, HANS. *Das altenglische Gedicht 'Guthlac der Einsiedler' und die Guthlac-Vita des Felix* (Halle, 1901).

——. 'Untersuchungen zur Guthlac-Legende', *Bonner Beiträge zur Anglistik*, xii (1902).

FRITZSCHE, A. 'Das angelsächsische Gedicht Andreas und Cynewulf', *Anglia*, ii (1879), 441–500.

GARDNER, THOMAS. 'The Old English Kenning: a Characteristic Feature of Germanic Poetical Diction?', *Modern Philology*, lxvii (1969), 109–17.

GEROULD, G. H. *Saints' Legends* (Boston and New York, 1916).

——. 'The Old English Poems on St. Guthlac and their Latin Source', *MLN*, xxxii (1917), 77–89.

HILL, THOMAS D. 'The Typology of the Week and the Numerical Structure of the Old English *Guthlac B*', *Mediaeval Studies*, xxxvii (1975), 531–6.

——. 'The Middle Way: *Idel-wuldor* and *egesa* in the Old English *Guthlac A*', RES, n.s. xxx (1979).

JANSEN, KARL, 'Die Cynewulf-Forschung von ihren Anfängen bis zur Gegenwart', *Bonner Beiträge zur Anglistik*, xxiv (1908).

LEE, ALVIN A. *The Guest-Hall of Eden* (New Haven and London, 1972).

LEFÈVRE, P. 'Das altenglische Gedicht vom hl. Guthlac', *Anglia*, vi (1883), 181–240.

LEO, H. *Quæ de se ipso Cynevulfus Poeta Anglo-Saxonicus tradiderit* (Marburg, 1857).

LIPP, FRANCIS RANDALL. '*Guthlac A*: an Interpretation', *Mediaeval Studies*, xxxiii (1971), 46–62.

MAGOUN, F. P. 'Oral Formulaic Character of Anglo-Saxon Narrative Poetry', *Speculum*, xxviii (1953), 446–67.

MATHER, F. J. 'The Cynewulf Question from a Metrical Point of View', *MLN*, vii (1892), 97–107.

REICHARDT, PAUL F. '*Guthlac A* and the Landscape of Spiritual Perfection', *Neophilologus*, lviii (1974), 331–8.

RIEGER, MAX. 'Über Cynevulf', *Zeitschrift für deutsche Philologie*, i (1869), 215–26 and 313–34.

ROBERTS, JANE. 'A Metrical Examination of the Poems *Guthlac A* and *Guthlac B*', *Proceedings of the Royal Irish Academy*, vol. lxxi, Section C, no. 4 (1971), 91–137.

ROBINSON, FRED C. 'The Significance of Names in Old English Literature', *Anglia*, lxxxvi (1968), 14–68.

ROSIER, JAMES L. 'Death and Transfiguration: *Guthlac B*', *Philological Essays*, Studies in Old and Middle English Language and Literature in Honour of Herbert Dean Meritt (The Hague, 1971), pp. 82–92.

RYNELL, ALARIK. 'Parataxis and Hypotaxis as a Criterion of Syntax and Style especially in Old English Poetry', *Lunds Universitets Årsskrift*, N.F., Avd. 1, Bd. xlviii, Nr. 3 (1952).

SCHAAR, C. *Critical Studies in the Cynewulf Group*, Lund Studies in English, xvii (1949).

——. 'On a New Theory of Old English Poetic Diction', *Neophilologus*, xl (1956), 301–5.

SHIPPEY, T. A. *Old English Verse* (London, 1972).

SHOOK, L. K. 'The Burial Mound in *Guthlac A*', *Modern Philology*, lviii (1960), 1–10.

——. 'The Prologue of the Old English *Guthlac A*', *Mediaeval Studies*, xxiii (1961), 294–304.

SISAM, KENNETH. *Studies in the History of Old English Literature* (Oxford, 1953).

SMITHERS, G. V. 'The Meaning of *The Seafarer* and *The Wanderer*', *MÆ*, xxvi (1957), 137–53 and xxviii (1959), 1–22, 99–106.

STANLEY, E. G. 'Old English Poetic Diction and the Interpretation of

The Wanderer, The Seafarer, and *The Penitent's Prayer',* Anglia, lxxiii (1956), 413–66.

STANLEY, E. G. (editor). *Continuations and Beginnings* (London, 1966).

THUNDYIL, Z. 'A Study of the Anglo-Saxon Concept of Covenant and its Sources with special reference to Anglo-Saxon Laws and the Old English Poems: *The Battle of Maldon* and *Guthlac'* (unpublished thesis, Notre Dame, 1969).

TUPPER, F. 'The Philological Legend of Cynewulf', *PMLA,* xxvi (1911), 235–79.

WENTERSDORF, KARL P. '*Guthlac A*: The Battle for the *Beorg',* Neophilologus, lxii (1978), 135–42.

WHITELOCK, DOROTHY. *The Audience of 'Beowulf'* (Oxford, 1951).

WILLARD, RUDOLPH. 'Vercelli Homily VIII and the Christ', *PMLA,* xlii (1927), 314–30.

——. 'The Address of the Soul to the Body', *PMLA,* l (1935), 957–83.

WRENN, C. L. *A Study of Old English Literature* (London, 1967).

7. LANGUAGE

BAUER, HERMANN. *Ueber die sprache und mundart der ae. dichtungen Andreas, Guðlac, Phoenix, hl. Kreuz und Höllenfahrt Christi* (Marburg, 1890).

BLAKE, N. F. 'The Scribe of the Exeter Book', *Neophilologus,* xlvi (1962), 316–19.

BLISS, A. J. *The Metre of 'Beowulf'* (Oxford, 2nd edn., 1968).

BOSWORTH, J. and TOLLER, T. N. *An Anglo-Saxon Dictionary* (Oxford, 1898); *Supplement* by T. N. Toller (Oxford, 1921); *Enlarged Addenda and Corrigenda* by Alistair Campbell (Oxford, 1972).

BRUNNER, K. *Altenglische Grammatik nach der angelsächsischen Grammatik von Eduard Sievers neubearbeitet* (Tübingen, 3rd edn., 1965).

CAMPBELL, A. *Old English Grammar* (Oxford, 1959).

FURKERT, MAX. *Der syntaktische Gebrauch des Verbums in dem angelsächsischen Gedichte vom heiligen Guthlac* (Leipzig, 1889).

GREIN, C. W. M. *Sprachschatz der angelsächsischen Dichter.* Unter mitwirkung von F. Holthausen neu hsg. von J. J. Köhler (Heidelberg, 1912).

HALL, J. R. CLARK and MERITT, H. D. *A Concise Anglo-Saxon Dictionary* (Cambridge, 4th edn., 1960).

HOLTBUER, FRITZ. *Der syntaktische Gebrauch des Genitivs in dem Andreas, Gûðlâc, Phönix, dem heiligen Kreuz und der Höllenfahrt* (Halle, 1884); also in *Anglia,* viii (1885), 1–40.

HOLTHAUSEN, F. *Altenglisches etymologisches Wörterbuch* (Heidelberg, 1934).

JORDAN, R. *Eigentümlichkeiten des anglischen Wortschatzes,* Anglistische Forschungen, xvii (Heidelberg, 1906).

KEISER, A. *The Influence of Christianity on the Vocabulary of Old English Poetry,* University of Illinois Studies in Language and Literature, v (1919), 1–150.

LEHMANN, W. P. and DAILEY, VIRGINIA F. *The Alliterations of the 'Christ' 'Guthlac' 'Elene' 'Juliana' 'Fates of the Apostles' 'Dream of the Rood'* (Texas, 1960).

MACGILLIVRAY, H. S. *The Influence of Christianity on the Vocabulary of Old English*, Studien zur englischen Philologie hrsg. von L. Morsbach, viii (1902).

MALONE, KEMP. 'When did Middle English Begin?', *Curme Volume of Linguistic Studies*, Language Monographs, no. 7 (Philadelphia, 1930), pp. 110–17.

MARQUARDT, H. *Die altenglischen Kenningar, ein Beitrag zur Stilkunde altgermanischer Dichtung* (Halle, 1938).

MITCHELL, BRUCE. 'Pronouns in Old English Poetry', *RES*, n.s. xv (1964), 129–41.

——. 'Adjective Clauses in Old English Poetry', *Anglia*, lxxxi (1963), 298–322.

QUIRK, R. 'On the Problem of Morphological Suture in Old English', *Modern Language Review*, xlv (1950), 1–5.

RANKIN, J. W. 'A Study of the Kennings in Anglo-Saxon Poetry', *JEGP*, viii (1909), 357–422 and ix (1910), 49–84.

SCHOLTZ, H. VAN DER M. *The Kenning in Anglo-Saxon and Old Norse Poetry* (Utrecht, 1928).

SIEVERS, E. 'Zur Rhythmik des germanischen Alliterationsverses', I and II, *Beiträge zur Geschichte der deutschen Sprache und Literatur*, x (1885), 209–314 and 451–545.

——. 'Zu Cynewulf', *Anglia*, xiii (1891), 1–25.

——. *Altgermanische Metrik* (Halle, 1893).

——. 'Zu Cynewulf', *Neusprachliche Studien. Festgabe Karl Luick* (*Die Neueren Sprachen*, 6 Beiheft) (Marburg, 1925), 60–81.

SLAY, D. 'Some Aspects of the Technique of Composition of Old English Verse', *Transactions of the Philological Society* (1952), 1–14.

STANLEY, E. G. 'Studies in the Prosaic Vocabulary of Old English Verse', *Neuphilologische Mitteilungen*, lxxii (1971), 385–418.

TEXTS

Note on the Texts

THE texts are presented in a conservative edition. Emendations, and words whose manuscript form is doubtful, are marked with a dagger. Expansions are italicized. The footnotes present the more important readings and emendations of those who have printed full versions of the two poems, but the spellings normalized by these earlier editors are not generally treated as variants. The opinions of other collators and annotators are to be found either in the introduction or in relevant parts of the Commentary.

The scribe's punctuation lacks consistency and is thin. In addition, it has been occasionally supplemented by a sixteenth-century hand. I have therefore given the texts a modern punctuation. The sectional divisions of the Exeter Book are retained, the capital letters at the beginning of each fitt standing for the large capitals of the manuscript. Otherwise capitals are used to mark the opening of sentences and, in accordance with modern standards, for proper names. No attempt is made to reflect the small capitals of the manuscript, for it is often impossible to decide if these are really no more than overlarge minuscules. The sporadic accents are printed, as it is easier to judge their value when reading aloud from the texts. Foliation is marked by an asterisk.

GUTHLAC A

I

*SE BIÐ GEFEANA FæGrast þonne hy æt
  frymðe gemetað,
engel 7 seo eadge sawl; ofgiefeþ hio þas eorþan
  wynne,
forlæteð þas lænan dreamas 7 hio wiþ þam lice
  gedæleð;
ðonne cwið se engel —hafað yldran hád—
greteð gæst operne, abeodeð him Godes ærende: 5
'Nu þu most feran þider þu fundadest
longe 7 gelome: ic þec lædan sceal.
Wegas þe sindon weþe 7 wuldres leoht
torht ontyned. Eart nu tidfara
to þam halgan hám þær næfre hreow cymeð,   10
edergong fore yrmþum, ac þær biþ engla dream,
sib 7 gesælignes 7 sawla ræst,
7 þær á to feore gefeon motum,
dryman mid dryhten, þa þe his domas her
æfnað on eorþan. He him ece lean   15
healdeð on heofonum þær se hyhsta,
ealra cyninga cyning, ceastrum wealdeð.
ðæt sind þa getimbru þe nót tydriað,
ne þam fore yrmþum þe þær in wuniað
lif aspringeð ac him bið lenge hu sel;   20
geoguþe brucað 7 Godes miltsa;
þider soðfæstra sawla motun
cuman æfter cwealme þa þe her Cristes æ
lærað 7 læstað 7 his lof rærað,
oferwinnað þa awyrgdan gæstas, bigytað him
  wuldres ræste.'
                                 25
Hwider sceal þæs monnes mod astigan

---

17 ealra: *Thorpe, Grein, Gollancz, and Assmann place at the end of 1.16*
18 nó, *MS*, nú: *Thorpe emends* ne, *Grein, Gollancz, Assmann, and KD emend*
no *or* nó   20 lenge hu sel: *Thorpe emends* lengþu. sin-geoguþe brucað, *Grein*
and Assmann lenge husel   25 gæstas, *MS.* gæsᵗᵃˢ

ær oþþe æfter þon*ne* he his ænne her
gæst bigonge þ*æt* se Gode mote
womma clæne *in geweald cuman?
Monge sindon geond middangeard   30
hadas under heofonum þa þe in haligra
rim arisað; we þæs ryht magun
æt æghwylcum anra gehyran
gif we halig bebodu healdan willað.
Mæg nu snottor guma sæle brucan   35
godra tida 7 his gæste forð
weges willian; woruld is ónhrered,
colaþ Cristes lufu; sindan costinga
geond middangeard monge árisene
swa þ*æt* geara iú Godes spelbodan   40
wordum sægdon 7 þurh witedóm
eal ánemdon swa hit nu gongeð.
Ealdað eorþan blæd æþela gehwylcre
7 of wlite wendað wæstma gecyndu;
bið seo siþre tíd sæda gehwylces   45
mætrę in mægne. Forþon se mon ne þearf
to þisse worulde wyrpe gehycgan
þ*æt* he us fægran gefean bringe
ofer þa niþas þe we nú dreogað
ær þon endien ealle gesceafte   50
ða he gesette on siex dagum,
ða nu under heofonum hadas cennað
micle 7 mæte. Is þes middangeard
dalum gedæled; dryhten sceawað
hwær þa eardien þe his ǽ healden;   55
gesihð he þa domas dogra gehwylce
wonian 7 wendan of woruldryhte
ða he gesette þurh his sylfes wórd:
he fela findeð, fea beoð gecorene.
Sume him þæs hades hlisan willað   60
wegan on wordum 7 þa weorc ne doð:
bið him eorðwela ofer þ*æt* ece lif
hyhta hyhst se gehwylcum *sceal

33ʳ (left of line 30 area)

33ᵛ (left of last line)

31 in haligra: *Thorpe* unhaligra *which Grein emends* on haligra   57 woruldryhte: *Grein fn.* woruld-dryhte   63 se gehwylcum sceal: *Thorpe fn.* hi
gehwylcum sceolon?

foldbuendra fremde geweorþan.

Forþon hy nú hyrwað haligra mod 65
ða þe him to heofonum hyge staþeliað;
witon þæt se eðel† ece bideð
ealra þære mengu þe geond middangeard
dryhtne þeowiað 7 þæs deoran ham
wilniað bi gewyrhtum: swa þas woruldgestreon 70
on þa mæran gód bimutad† weorþað
ðonne þæt gegyrnað þa þe him Godes egsa
hleonaþ ofer heafdum. Hy þy hyhstan beoð
þrymme geþreade, þisses lifes
þurh bibodu brucað 7 þæs betran forð 75
wyscað 7 wenaþ, wuldres bycgað,
sellað ælmessan, earme frefrað,
beoð rúmmode ryhtra gestreona,
lufiað mid lacum þa þe læs agun,
dæghwam dryhtne þeowiaþ: he hyra dæde
    sceawað. 80
Sume þa wuniað on westennum
secað 7 gesittað sylfra willum
hamas on heolstrum, hy ðæs heofoncundan
boldes bidað. Oft him brogan tó
laðne gelædeð se þe him lifes ofónn, 85
eaweð him egsan, hwilum idel wuldor,
brægdwis bona, —hafað bega cræft—
eahteð ánbuendra; fore him englas stondað
gearwe mid gæsta wæpnum, beoþ hyra geoca
    gemyndge,
healdað haligra feorh, witon hyra hyht mid
    dryhten: 90
þæt synd þa gecostan cempan þa þam cyninge
    þeowað
se næfre þa lean alegeð þam þe his lufan
    adreogeð.

---

67 eðel, MS. eleð: *Thorpe fn.* eleð *for* hæleð, *for the sake of the alliteration;*
Grein, Gollancz, Assmann, and KD emend eðel   71 bimutad, MS. bimutað:
Thorpe fn. bemiðen; *Grein, Gollancz, Assmann, and KD emend* bimutad
76 bycgað: *Thorpe emends* hycgað   77 frefrað: *Thorpe fn.* r. frefriað
89 geoca: *Thorpe fn.* geoce?   91 þeowað: *Thorpe fn.* r. þeowiað   92 alegeð: *Thorpe* aleogeð?; adreogeð *Thorpe fn.* r. adreogað

II

MAgun we nu nemnan þæt us neah gewearð
þurh haligne *hád gecyþed,
hu Guðlac his in Godes willan   95
mod gerehte, mán eall forseah,
eorðlic æþelu, úpp gemunde
ham in heofonum; him wæs hyht to þam
siþþan hine inlyhte se þe lifes weg
gæstum gearwað 7 him giefe sealde   100
engelcunde þæt he ana ongan
beorgseþel bugan 7 his blæd Gode
þurh eaðmedu ealne gesealde
ðone þe he ón geoguðe bigan sceolde
worulde wynnum; hine weard† biheold,   105
halig of heofonum, se þæt hluttre mód
in þæs gæstes gód georne trymede.
Hwæt we hyrdon oft þæt se halga wer
in þa ærestan ældu gelufade
frecnessa fela; fyrst wæs swa þeana   110
in Godes dome hwonne Guðlace
on his ondgietan engel sealde
þæt him sweðraden synna lustas.
Tid wæs toweard; hine twegen ymb
weardas wacedon þa gewin drugon—   115
engel dryhtnes 7 se átela gæst;
nalæs hy him gelice lare bæron
in his modes gemynd mongum tidum;
oþer him þas eorþan ealle sægde
læne under lyfte 7 þa longan gód   120
herede on heofonum þær haligra
salwa gesittað in sigorwuldre
dryhtnes dreamas— he him dæda lean
georne gieldeð þam þe his giefe willað
þicgan to þonce 7 him þas woruld   125
uttor lætan þonne þæt ece líf;
oþer hyne scyhte þæt he sceaðena gemot

---

105 weard, *MS*, wearð: *Thorpe, Grein, Gollancz, Assmann, and KD emend*
weard   123 dreamas: *Thorpe fn.* dreames?

nihtes sohte 7 þurh neþinge
wunne æfter worulde swa doð wræcmæcgas
þa þe ne bimurnað *monnes feore   130
þæs þe him to honda huþe gelædeð
butan hy þy reafe rædan motan.
Swa hy hine trymedon on twa healfa
oþþæt þæs gewinnes weoroda dryhten
on þæs engles dóm ende gereahte.   135
Feond wæs geflymed; siþþam frofre gæst
in Guðlaces geoce gewunade,
lufade hine 7 lærde, lenge hu geornor,
þæt him leofedan londes wynne,
bold on beorhge. Oft þær broga cwom,   140
egeslic 7 uncuð ealdfeonda nið,
searocræftum swiþ; hy him sylf hyra
onsyn ywdon 7 þær ær fela
setla gesæton þonan sið tugon,
wide waðe, wuldre byscyrede,   145
lyftlacende. Wæs seo londes stow
bimiþen fore monnum oþþæt meotud onwrah
beorg ón bearwe. þa se bytla cwom
se þær haligne hám áraerde;
nales þy he giemde þurh gitsunga   150
lænes lifwelan ac þæt lond Gode
fægre gefreoþode siþþan feond oferwon
Cristes cempa. He gecostad† wearð
in gemyndigra monna tidum
ðara þe nu gena þurh gæstlicu   155
wundor weorðiað 7 his wisdomes
hlisan healdað þæt se halga þeow
elne geeode þa he ana gesæt
dygle stowe ðær he dryhtnes lof
reahte 7 rærde. Oft þurh reorde abead   160
þam þe þrowera þeawas lufedon

128 neþinge: *Thorpe fn.* r. niþinge   136 siþþam: *Grein emends* siððan
138 lenge hu: *Grein fn.* leng þy   140 beorhge: *Grein emends* beorge
153 gecostad, *MS.* gecostað: *Thorpe, Grein, Gollancz, Assmann, and KD
emend* gecostad   155 ðara þe nu: *Thorpe fn.* hine *seems wanting after* þe
156 wundor weorðiað: *Grein, Gollancz, Assmann, and KD emend* wundor
hine weorðiað

Godes ærendu† þa him gæst onwrah
lifes snyttru, þæt he his lichoman
wynna forwyrnde 7 woruldblissa,
seftra setla 7 symbeldaga,   165
swylce eac idelra eagena wynna,
gierelan gielp*lices: him wæs Godes egsa
mara in gemyndum þonne he menniscum
þrymme æfter þonce þegan wolde.

35ʳ

III

God wæs Guðlac! He in gæste bær   170
heofoncundne hyht, hælu geræhte
ecan lifes; him wæs engel neah,
fæle freoðuweard, þam þe feara sum
mearclond gesæt þær he mongum wearð
bysen on Brytene siþþan biorg gestah.   175
Eadig oretta, *ond*wiges heard,
gyrede hine georne mid gæstlicum
wæpnum [7 wædum], wong bletsade,
him to ætstælle ærest arærde
Cristes rode; þær se cempa oferwon   180
frecnessa fela. Frome wurdum monge
Godes þrowera: we þæs Guðlacest†
deorwyrðne dæl dryhtne cennað.
He him sige sealde 7 snyttrucræft,
mundbyrd meahta, þonne mengu cwom   185
feonda færscytum fæhðe ræran;
ne meahton hy æfeste anforlætan
ac to Guðlaces gæste gelæddun
frasunga fela: him wæs fultum neah,
engel hine elne trymede. Þonne hy him yrre
    hweopan   190
frecne fyres wylme, stodan him on feðehwearfu*m*,
cwædon þæt he on þam beorge, byrnan sceolde

---

162 ærendu, *MS. with* o *changed to* u: *Thorpe and Grein* ærendo   169 æfter
þonce: *Thorpe fn.* æfþonce?   177–8 *No MS. break; older editors place*
wæpnum *at end of l.* 177 *and surmise half-line loss or more; KD* wæpnum
* * * wong bletsade *178*   181 Frome wurdum *Thorpe fn.* from-wordum?
182 Guðlaces, *MS.* guðlace: *KD emend* Guðlaces   190 hweopan, *MS.*
hwoopan *with first* o *changed to* e

7 his lichoman, lig forswelgan
þæt his earfeþu eal gelumpe,
módcearu, mægum, gif he monna dream   195
of þam orlege eft ne wolde
sylfa gesecan 7 his sibbe ryht

35ᵛ mid moncynne *maran cræfte
willum bewitigan, lætan wræce stille.
Swa him yrsade se for ealle spræc   200
feonda mengu; no þy forhtra wæs
Guðlaces gæst ac him God sealde
ellen wiþ þam egsan þæt þæs ealdfeondes
scyldigra scolu scome þrowedon;
wæron teonsmiðas tornes fulle,   205
cwædon þæt him Guðlac eac Gode sylfum
earfeþa mæst ana gefremede
siþþan he for wlence on westenne
beorgas bræce; þær hyt bidinge
earme ondsacan æror mostum   210
æfter tintergum tidum brucan
ðonne hy of waþum werge cwoman
restan ryneþragum; rowe gefegon:
wæs him seo gelyfed þurh lytel fæc.
Stod seo dygle stow dryhtne in gemyndum   215
idel 7 æmen, eþelriehte feor,
bád bisæce betran hyrdes.
To þon ealdfeondas ondan noman
swa hi singales sorge dreogað;
ne motun hi on eorþan eardes brucan   220
ne hy lyft swefeð in leoma ræstum
ac hy hleolease hama þoliað,
in cearum cwiþað, cwealmes wiscað,
willen þæt him dryhten þurh deaðes cwealm
to hyra earfeða ende geryme;   225
ne mostun hy Guðlaces gæste sceþþan
ne þurh sarslege sawle gedælan
wið lichoman ac hy ligesearwum
ahofun hearmstafas, hleahtor alegdon,

---

209 beorgas bræce: *Thorpe fn.* beorges breace?; hy, *MS.* he: *Thorpe's* hy
followed by Grein; Gollancz, Assmann, and KD emend hy   224 willen: *Thorpe*
fn. willað?   225 earfeða: *Grein fn.* earfeðum?

sorge seofedon þa hi swiðra oferstag   230
weard on wonge; sceoldon wræcmæcgas
ofgiefan gnornende grene beorgas.

36ʳ   Hwæþre hy þa *gena Godes *ond*sacan
sægdon sarstafum, swiþe geheton
þæt he deaþa gedal dreogan sceolde   235
gif he leng bide laþran gemotes
hwonne hy mid mengu maran cwome
þa þe for his life lyt sorgedon.
Guðlac him ongean þingode, cwæð þæt hy
      gielpan ne þorftan
dædum wið dryhtnes meahtum: 'Þeah þe ge
      me deað gehaten,   240
mec wile wið þam niþum genergan se þe
      eowrum nydum wealdeð.
An is ælmihtig God se mec mæg eaðe gescyldan,
he min feorg freoþað. Ic eow fela wille
soþa gesecgan: mæg ic þis setl on eow
butan earfeðum ana geðringan†;   245
ne eam ic swa fealóg, swa ic eow fore stonde,
monna weorudes ac me mara dæl
in godcundum gæstgerynum
wunað ⁊ weaxeð se me wraþe healdeð.
Ic me anum her eaðe getimbre   250
hus ⁊ hleonað; me on heofonum sind
lare gelonge: mec þæs lyt tweoþ
þæt me engel tó ealle gelædeð
spowende sped spreca ⁊ dæda.
Gewitað nu awyrgde, werigmode,   255
from þissum earde þe ge her on stondað,
fleoð on feorweg. Ic me frið wille
æt Gode gegyrnan; ne sceal min gæst mid eow
gedwolan dreogan ac me dryhtnes hond
mundað mid mægne. Her sceal min wesan   260
eorðlic eþel, nales eower leng.'

---

233 hy: *Grein emends* hym   241 se þe eowrum: *Grein* se eowrum
245 geðringan, *MS.* gedrin / gan *with second* g *altered from* c; *Thorpe* gedringan
fn. geþringan?, *Grein* geþringan; *Gollancz, Assmann, and KD emend* geðringan
252 tweoþ, *MS.* þ *changed from* w

IV

ðA wearð breahtm hæfen; beorg ymbstodan
hwearfum wræcmæcgas; woð up astag,
cearfulra cirm; cleopedon *monige
feonda foresprecan, firenum gulpon:
'Oft we ofersegon bi sæm tweonum   265
þeoda þeawas, þræce modigra,
þara þe in gelimpe life weoldon,
no weƚ oferhygdu anes monnes
geond middangeard maran fundon.   270
ðu þæt gehatest þæt ðu ham on usƚ
gegan wille: eart ðe Godes yrming.
Bi hwon scealt þu lifgan þeah þu lond age?
Ne þec mon hider mose fedeð;
beoð þe hungor 7 þurst hearde gewinnan   275
gif þu gewitest swa wilde deor
ana from eþele: nis þæt onginn wiht.
Geswic þisses setles. Ne mæg þec sellan ræd
mon gelæran þonne þeos mengu eall.
We þe beoð holde gif ðu us hyran wilt   280
oþþe þec ungearo eft gesecað
maran mægne þæt þe mon ne þearf
hondum hrinan ne þin hra feallan
wæpna wundum; we þas wic magun
fotum afyllan: folc inðriceð   285
meara þreatum 7 monfarum.
Beoð þa gebolgne þa þec breodwiað,
tredað þec 7 tergað 7 hyra torn wrecað,
toberað þec blodgum lastum; gif þu ure
    bidan þencest
we þec niþa genægað. Ongin þe generes
    wilnian,
far þær ðu freonda wene gif ðu þines feores 290
    recce.'

---

264 cleopedon, *with* pedon. *below ruled lines in MS.*   269 we, *MS* þe:
Thorpe ðe, *fn.* we *for* ðe?, *Grein, Gollancz, Assmann, and KD emend* we
271 us, *MS.* hus: *Thorpe, Grein, Gollancz, Assmann, and KD emend* us
272 ðe: *Thorpe fn.* ðu?; *Grein* eart þe; *KD emend* ðe eart   281 ungearo:
Grein fn. ungeara   285 inðriceð, *with MS. change of first* ð *from* d *and
erasure after second* i   288 tergað: *Thorpe fn.* teрað?   291 recce: *Grein
and Assmann emend* rece

Gearo wæs Guðlac —hine God fremede-
on ondsware 7 on elne strong;
ne wond he for worde ac his wiþerbreocum
sorge gesægde, cuðe him soð genog: 295
'Widt is þes westen, wræcsetla fela,
eardas onhæle earmra gæsta;

37ʳ   sindon wærlogan þe þa *wic bugað:
þeah ge þa ealle ut abonnet
7 eow eac gewyrce widor sæce   300
ge her áteoð in þa tornwræce
sigeleasne sið. No ic eow sweord ongean
mid gebolgne hond oðberan þence,
worulde wæpen, ne sceal þes wong Gode
þurh blodgyte gebuen weorðan   305
ac ic minum Criste cweman þence
leofran lace nu ic þis lond gestag.
Fela ge me earda þurh idel word
aboden habbað; nis min breostsefa
forht ne fæge ac me friðe healdeð   310
ofer monna cyn se þe mægna gehwæs
weorcum wealdeð; nis me wiht æt eow
leofes gelong ne ge me laþes wiht
gedon motun: ic eom dryhtnes þeow,
he mec þurh engel oft afrefreð.   315
Forðon mec longeþas lýt gegretað,
sorge sealdun, nu mec sawelcund
hyrde bihealdeð. Is min hyht mid God
ne ic me eorðwelan owiht sinne
ne me mid mode micles gyrne   320
ac me dogra gehwam dryhten sendeð
þurh monnes hond mine þearfe.'
Swa modgade se wið mongum stod
awreðed weorðlice, wuldres cempa,

292 fremede: *Thorpe fn.* trymede (*Kemble*)   294 wond he: *Thorpe fn.* won-
dode ('*fear'd*')   296 Wid, *MS.* wið *Thorpe, Grein, Gollancz, Assmann, and
KD emend* wid   299 abonne, *MS.* abunne; *Grein, Gollancz, and KD emend*
abanne, *Assmann emends* abonne   300 eow eac: *Grein fn.* ic eow? *oder and
Præp.* (gegen)?; widor sæce: *Thorpe fn.* wiðersace?, *Grein emends* wiðorsæce;
Gollancz widorsæce   317 sealdun: *Grein fn.* seldan (*raro*)?

engla mægne. Gewat eal þonan 325
feonda mengu: ne wæs se fyrst micel
þe hi Guðlace forgiefan þohtan.
He wæs on elne 7 on·eaðmedum,
bad on beorge —wæs him botles neod—
forlet longeþas lænra dreama; 330
no he hine wið monna miltse gedælde
ac gesynta bæd sawla gehwylcre
þon*ne* he to eorðan on þam anade

37ᵛ hleor *onhylde: him of heofonum wearð
onbryrded breostsefa bliðe gæste. 335
Oft eahtade —wæs him engel neah—
hu þisse worulde wynna þorfte
mid his lichoman læsast brucan:
no him fore egsan earmȧa gæsta
treow getweode ne he tid forsæt 340
þæs þe he for his dryhtne dreogan sceolde
þæt hine æreste elne binoman
slæpa sluman oþþe sæne mod.
Swa sceal oretta á in his mode
Gode compian 7 his gæst beran 345
oft on ondan þam þe eahtan wile
sawla gehwylcre þær he gesælan mæg.
Symle hy Guðlac in Godes willan
fromne fundon þon*ne* flygereowe
þurh nihta genipu neosan cwoman 350
þa þe onhæle eardas weredon,
hwæþre him þæs wonges wyn sweðrade.
Woldun þæt him to mode fore monlufan
sorg gesohte þæt he siþ tuge
eft to eþle: ne wæs þæt ongin swylc 355
ðonne hine engel on þam anade
geornast grette 7 him giefe sealde
þæt hine ne meahte meotudes willan
longað gelettan ac he on þæs lareowes
wære gewunade. Oft worde bicwæð: 360
'Huru þæs bihofað se þe him halig gæst
wisað on willan 7 his weorc trymað,

343 slæpa: *Thorpe fn.* slæpes?   362 trymað: *Grein emends* trymeð

laþaðð hine liþum wordum, gehateð him lifes
   reste
þæt he þæs latteowes larum hyre
ne lete him ealdfeond eft oncyrran   365
mod from his meotude. Hu sceal min cuman
gæst to geoce nemne ic Gode sylle
hyrsumne hige þæt him heortan geþonc*

V

38^r

. . ær oþþe sið ende geweorðe
þæt ge mec to wundre wegan motun.   370
Ne mæg min líchoma wið þas lænan gesceaft
deað gedælan ac he gedreosan sceal
swa þeos eorðe eall þe ic her on stonde.
ðeah ge minne flæshoman fyres wylme
forgripen gromhydge, gifran lege,   375
næfre ge mec of þissum wordum onwendað þendan
   mec min gewit gelæsteð
þeah þe ge hine sarum forsæcen: ne motan
   ge mine sawle gretan
ac ge on betran gebringað. Forðan ic gebidan
   wille
þæs þe min dryhten demeð; nis me þæs deaþes
   sorg.
ðeah min bán 7 blód butu geweorþen   380
eorþan to eacan, min se eca dæl
in gefean fareð þær he fægran
botles bruceð. Nis þisses beorges setl
meodumre ne mara þonne hit men duge†
se þe in þrowingum þeodnes willan   385
dæghwam dreogeð; ne sceal se dryhtnes þeow
in his modsefan mare gelufian
eorþan æhtwelan þonne his anes gemet

---

368 *a folio is here missing from the MS.*   370 wundre: *Thorpe fn.* wuldre?
372 deað: *Thorpe fn.* deaðe?   374 flæshoman: *Thorpe, Grein, Gollancz,*
Assmann, and KD emend flæschoman   377 forsæcen: *Thorpe fn.* forsæten?
(*Kemble*)   382 fægran: *Grein fn.* fægerran?   384 meodumre: *Thorpe fn.*
r. meodumra; mara: *Grein emends* mare; duge, *MS.* buge: *Grein, Gollancz,*
Assmann, and KD emend duge, *Thorpe suggests* hine man *for* men   387 mare:
Grein fn. ma ne?

þæt he his lichoman lade hæbbe.'
ða wæs eft swa ær ealdfeonda nið   390
wroht onwylled†, woð† oþerne
lythwon leoðode þonne in lyft astag
ceargesta cirm. Symle Cristes lof
in Guðlaces godum mode
weox 7 wunade 7 hine weoruda God   395
freoðade on foldan; swa he feora gehwylc
healdeð in hælo þær se hyra gæst
þihð in þeawum. He wæs þeara sum;

38ᵛ

ne won he *æfter worulde ac he in wuldre áhof
modes wynne. Hwylc wæs mara þonne se?   400
An oretta ussum tidum,
cempa, gecyðeð þæt him Crist fore
woruldlicra má wundra gecyðde.

VI

HE hine scilde wið sceðþenra
eglum onfengum earmra gæsta;
wæron hy reowe to ræsanne   405
gifrum grapum. No God wolde
þæt seo sawl þæs sar þrowade
in lichoman; lyfde se þeana
þæt hy him mid hondum hrinan mosten
7 þæt frið wið hy gefreoþad wære.   410
Hy hine þa hofun on þa hean lyft,
sealdon him meahte ofer monna cynn
þæt he fore eagum eall sceawode
under haligra hyrda gewealdum
in mynsterum monna gebæru   415
þara þe hyra lifes þurh lust brucan
idlum æhtum 7 oferwlencum,

---

391 onwylled, *MS.* onwylleð: *Thorpe fn.* onweced, *Grein, Gollancz, Assmann, and KD emend* onwylled; woð, *MS.* soð: *Thorpe, Grein, Gollancz, Assmann, and KD emend* woð; oþerne: *Grein, Gollancz, Assmann, and KD place* ne *in l.* 392, *Gollancz inserting* þær *at end of l.* 391   400 se: *Thorpe and Gollancz place in l.* 401, *as do Grein and Assmann who insert* he *at end of l.* 400   402 gecyðeð: *Gollancz emends.* gecyðed   404 sceðþenra: *Grein emends* sceððendra, *Gollancz, Assmann, and KD emend* sceðþendra   405 onfengum, *with* u *changed from* o *in MS.*

gierelum gielplicum: swa bið geoguðe þeaw
þær þæs ealdres egsa ne styreð.   420
No þer þa feondas gefeon þorfton
ac þæs blædes hraðe gebrocen hæfdon
þe him alyfed wæs lytle hwile
þæt hy his lichoman leng ne mostan
witum wælan; ne him wiht gescod   425
þæs þe hy him to teonan þurhtogen hæfdon.
Læddun hine þa of lyfte to þam leofestan
earde on eorðan þæt he eft gestag
beorg on bearwe; bonan gnornedon,
mændon murnende þætt hy monnes bearn   430
þream oferþunge 7 swa þearfendlic
him to earfeðum *ana cwome
gif hy him ne meahte maran sarum
gyldan gyrnwræce. Guðlac sette
hyht in heofonas, hælu getreowde,   435
hæfde feonda feng feore gedyged;
wæs seo æreste earmra gæsta
costung ofercumen; cempa wunade
bliþe on beorge: wæs his blæd mid God.
ðuhte him on mode þæt se moncynnes   440
eadig wære se þe his anum her
feore gefreoðade þæt him feondes hond
æt þam ytmestan ende ne scode
þonne him se dryhtnes dom wisade
to þam nyhstan nydgedale.   445
Hwæþre him þa gena gyrna gemyndge
edwitsprecan ermþu geheton
tornum teoncwidum. Treow wæs gecyþed
þætte Guðlace God leanode
ellen mid arum þæt he ana gewon.   450
Him se werga gæst wordum sægde:
'No we þe þus swiðe swencan þorftan
þær þu fromlice freonda larum
hyran wolde; þa þu heant 7 earm

39ʳ

421 þer: *Grein, Assmann, and KD emend* þær   430 þæt, *MS.* þæ: *Thorpe,*
Grein, Gollancz, Assmann, and KD emend þæt   454 hean, *MS.* heam: *Thorpe,*
Grein, Gollancz, Assmann, and KD emend hean

on þis orlege ærest cwome
ða þu gehete þæt þec halig gæst   455
wið earfeþum eaðe gescilde
for þam myrcelse þe þec monnes hond
from þinre onsyne æþelum áhwyrfde.'
(In þam mægwlite monge lifgað   460
gyltum forgiefene, nales Gode þigað,
ac hy lichoman fore lufan cwemað
wista wynnum: swa ge weorðmyndu
in dolum dreame dryhtne gieldað.
Fela ge fore monnum miþað þæs þe ge in
    mode gehycgað,
                                                      465
39ᵛ   ne beoð eowre *dæde dyrne þeah þe ge hy in
        dygle gefremme.)
'We þec in lyft gelæddun, oftugon þe londes
    wynna,
woldun þu þe sylfa gesawe þæt we þec soð
    onstældun;
ealles þu þæs wite awunne forþon þu hit
    onwendan ne meahtes.'
ða wæs agongen þæt him God wolde   470
æfter þrowinga þonc gegyldan
þæt he martyrhád mode gelufade;
sealde him snyttru on sefan gehygdum,
mægenfæste gemynd. He wið mongum stod
ealdfeonda elne gebylded,   475
sægde him to sorge þæt hy sigelease
þone grene wong ofgiefan sceoldan:
'Ge sind forscadene! On eow scyld siteð!
Ne cunnon ge dryhten duguþe biddan
ne mid eaðmedum are secan   480
þeah þe eow alyfde lytle hwile
þæt ge min onwald agan mosten;
ne ge þæt geþyldum þicgan woldan
ac me yrringa up gelæddon
þæt ic of lyfte londa getimbru   485
geseon meahte. Wæs me swegles leoht

458 þec: *Gollancz omits in emendation; Thorpe thinks a 'couplet' missing*
481 þeah þe: *Grein fn.* þeah he?   482 onwald, *MS.* onweald *with e subpuncted*

torht ontyned þeah ic torn druge.
Setton me in edwit þæt ic eaðe forbær
rume regulas 7 reþe mod
geongra monna in Godes templum,   490
woldan þy gehyrwan haligra lof,
sohtun þa sæmran 7 þa sellan nó
demdan æfter dædum. Ne beoð þa dyrne swa
   þeah.
Ic eow soð wiþ þon secgan wille:
God scop geoguðe 7 gumena dream;   495
ne magun þa æfteryld in þam ærestan
blæde geberan ac hy blissiað
worulde wynnum oððæt wintra rim
gegæð *in þa geoguðe þæt se gæst lufað
onsyn 7 ætwist yldran hades   500
ðe gemete monige geond middangeard
þeowiað in þeawum; þeodum ywaþ
wisdom weras, wlencu forleosað,
siððan geoguðe geað gæst aflihð.
þæt ge ne scirað ac ge scyldigra   505
synne secgað, soþfæstra nó
mod 7 monþeaw mæran willað,
gefeoð in firenum, frofre ne wenað
þæt ge wræcsiða wyrpe gebiden.
Oft ge in gestalum stondað; þæs cymeð   510
   steor of heofonum;
me þonne sendeð se usic semon mæg,
se þe lifa gehwæs lengu wealdeð.'
Swa hleoþrade halig cempa:
wæs se martyre from moncynnes
synnum asundrad; sceolde he sares þa gen   515
dæl adreogan ðeah þe dryhten his
witum wolde. Hwæt þæt wundra sum
monnum þuhte þæt he ma wolde

491 þy: *Thorpe suggests* ge   494 wiþ þon: *Thorpe, Gollancz* siþþon, *Grein* siððon, *Assmann and KD emend* siþþon   511 me þonne sendeð: *Grein adds* mund *after* þonne; se usic semon mæg: *Thorpe reads* wæg, *suggesting in fn.* usic *or* us is? mon-wæg = lif-weg, *Grein* se us is se monweg, *Gollancz and Assmann* se usic se mon wæg, *KD as above*   517 wolde: *Thorpe fn.* r. weolde? *Grein, Assmann, and KD emend* weolde

afrum onfengum earme gæstas
hrinan leton 7 þæt hwæþre gelomp.   520
Wæs þæt gen mara þæt he middangeard
sylfa gesohte 7 his swat ageat
on bonena hond; ahte bega geweald,
lifes 7 deaðes, þa he lustum dreag
eaðmod on eorðan ehtendra nið.   525
Forþon is nu arlic þæt we æfæstra
dæde demen, secgen dryhtne lof
ealra þara bisena þe us bec fore
þurh his wundra geweorc wisdóm cyþað.

VII

Geofu wæs mid Guðlac in godcundum   530

40ᵛ mægne gemeted. *Micel is to secgan,
eall æfter orde, þæt he on elne adreag;
ðone foregengan fæder ælmihtig
wið onhælum ealdorgewinnum
sylfa gesette þær his sawl wearð   535
clæne 7 gecostad. Cuð is wide
geond middangeard þæt his mod geþah
in Godes willan; is þæs gen fela
to secgenne þæs þe he sylfa adreag
under nyðgista† nearwum clommum.   540
He þa sár forseah, a þære sawle wel
[gemunde] þæs mundboran þe þæt mod† geheold,
þæt him ne getweode treow in breostum
ne him gnornunga gæste scodun,
ac se hearda hyge halig wunade   545
oþþæt he þa bysgu oferbiden hæfde.
Þrea wæron þearle, þegnas grimme,
ealle hy þam feore fyl gehehton;
no hy hine to deað deman moston,
synna hyrdas, ac seo sawul bád   550
in lichoman leofran tide.

520 leton: *Grein and Assmann emend* lætan   521 mara: *Grein emends* mare
540 nyðgista, MS. *y altered from* i   541–2 mod. MS. mond: *Thorpe emends*
wel *to* hwile, þe þæt *to* þe þa; *Grein inserts a line and emends* mond *to* mod;
Gollancz notes a line omitted; Assmann and KD emend mond *to* mod *and leave*
a line free. gemunde *not in MS.*   549 deað: *Thorpe, Grein, Assmann, and*
KD emend deaðe

Georne hy ongeaton þæt hyne God wolde
nergan wið niþum 7 hyra nýdwræce
deope deman. Swa dryhten mæg,
ana ælmihtig, eadigra gehwone   555
wið earfeþum eaðe gescildan.
Hwæðre hine gebrohton bolgenmode
wraðe wræcmæcgas, wuldres cempan,
halig husulbearn, æt heldore
þær firenfulra fæge gæstas   560
æfter swyltcwale secan onginnað
ingong ærest in þæt atule hús,
niþer under næssas neole grundas.
Hy hine bregdon, budon orlege,
egsan 7 ondan arleaslice,   565
frecne fore: swa bið feonda þeaw
þon*ne* hy *soðfæstra sawle willað
synnum beswican 7 searocræftu*m*.
Ongunnon gromheorte Godes orettan
in sefan swencan, swiþe geheton   570
þæt he in þone grimman gryre gongan sceolde,
hweorfan gehyned to helwarum
7 þær in bendum bryne þrowian.
Woldun hy geteon mid torncwidum,
earme aglæcan, in orwennysse   575
meotudes cempan —hit ne meahte swa;
cwædon cearfulle Criste laðe
to Guðlace mid grimnysse:
'Ne eart ðu gedefe ne dryhtnes þeow
clæne gecostad ne cempa gód   580
wordum 7 weorcum wel gecyþed,
halig in heortan: nu þu in helle scealt
deope gedufan, nales dryhtnes leoht
habban in heofonum, heahgetimbru,
seld on swegle, forþon þu synna to fela   585
facna gefremedes in flæschoman.
We þe nu willað womma gehwylces
lean forgieldan þær þe laþast bið,
in ðam grimmestan gæstgewinne.'

588 þær: *Thorpe emends* þæt

Him se eadga wer *ond*swarode,   590
Guðlac, in gæste mid Godes mægne:
'Doð efne swa gif eow dryhten Crist,
lifes leohtfruma, lyfan wylle,
weoruda waldend, þæt ge his wergengan
in þone laðan leg lædan motan.   595
Þæt is in gewealdum wuldorcyninges
se eow gehynde 7 in hæft bidraf
under nearone clom, nergende Crist.
Eom ic eaðmod, his ombiehthera,
þeow geþyldig. Ic geþafian sceal   600
æghwær ealles his anne dom
7 him geornlice gæstgemyndum
wille *wideferh wesan underþyded,
hyran holdlice minum hælende
þeawum 7 geþyncðum 7 him þoncian   605
ealra þara giefena þe God gescop
englum ærest 7 eorðwaru*m*,
7 ic bletsige bliðe mode
lifes leohtfruman 7 him lof singe
þurh gedefne dom dæges 7 nihtes,   610
herge in heortan heofonrices weard.
Þæt eow æfre ne bið ufan alyfed
leohtes lissum þæt ge lof moten
dryhtne secgan ac ge deaðe sceolon
weallendne wean wope besingan,   615
heaf in helle, nales herenisse
halge habban heofoncyninges.

VIII

IC þone deman in dagum minum
wille weorþian wordum 7 dædum,
lufian in life.' (Swa is lar 7 ar   620
to spowendre spræce gelæded
þa*m* þe in his weorcum willan ræfnað.)
'Sindon ge wærlogan: swa ge in wræcsiðe
longe lifdon, lege biscencte,

592 efne: *Thorpe and Grein* efen   605 geþyncðum: *Thorpe emends* geþ-
eahtum, *Grein* geþyncdum   614 deaðe: *Grein fn.* deade?   622 in his:
Grein emends his in   624 biscencte: *Grein and KD emend* bisencte

swearte beswicene, swegle benumene,   625
dreame bidrorene, deaðe bifolene,
firenum bifongne, feores orwenan,
þæt ge blindnesse bote fundon.
Ge þa fægran gesceaft in fyrndagum,
gæstlicne goddream, gearo forsegon,   630
þa ge wiðhogdum halgum dryhtne.
Ne mostun ge a wunian in wyndagum
ac mid scome scyldum scofene wurdon
fore oferhygdum in ece fýr
ðær ge sceolon dreogan deað 7 þystro,   635
wóp to widan ealdre *—næfre ge þæs wyrpe
    gebidað—
7 ic þæt gelyfe in liffruman,
ecne onwealdan ealra gesceafta,
þæt he mec for miltsum 7 mægenspedum
niðða nergend næfre wille   640
þurh ellenweorc anforlætan
þam ic longe in lichoman
7 in minum gæste Gode campode
þurh monigfealdra mægna gerynu.
Forðon ic getrywe in þone torhtestan   645
þrynesse þrym se geþeahtingum
hafað in hondum heofon 7 eorðan
þæt ge mec mid niþum næfre motan
tornmode teon in tintergu
mine myrðran 7 mánsceaþan,   650
swearte, sigelease. Eom ic soðlice
leohte geleafan 7 mid lufan dryhtnes
fægre gefylled in minum feorhlocan,
breostum inbryrded to þam betran hám,
leomum inlyhted to þam leofestan   655
ecan earde þær is eþellond
fæger 7 gefealic in fæder wuldre,
ðær eow næfre fore nergende
leohtes leoma ne lifes hyht
in Godes rice agiefen weorþeð   660

<hr>

631 wiðhogdum: *Thorpe, Grein, Gollancz, Assmann, and KD emend* wiðhogdun
633 scome scyldum: *Thorpe fn.* scomu-?

42^r

for þam oferhygdu*m* þe eow in mod astag
þurh idel gylp ealles to swiðe.
Wendun ge 7 woldum wiþerhycgende
þæt ge scyppende sceoldan gelice
wesan in wuldre. Eow þær wyrs gelomp   665
ða eow se waldend wraðe bisencte
in þæt swearte susl þær eow siððan wæs
ád inæled attre geblonden
þurh deopne dom, dream afyrred
engla gemana. Swa nu awa sceal   670
wesan wideferh þæt ge wærnysse
brynewylm hæbben, nales bletsunga;
*ne þurfun ge wenan wuldre biscyrede
þæt ge mec synfulle mid searocræftum
under scæd sconde scufan motan   675
ne in bælblæsan bregdon on hinder,
in helle hus, þær eow is hám sceapen,
sweart sinnehte, sacu butan ende,
grim gæstcwalu, þær ge gnornende
deað sceolon dreogan 7 ic dreama wyn   680
agan mid englum in þam uplican
rodera rice þær is ryht cyning,
help 7 hælu hæleþa cynne,
duguð 7 drohtað.' ða cwom dryhtnes ár,
halig of heofonum, se þurh hleoþor abead   685
ufancundne ege earmum gæstum,
het eft hraðe unscyldigne
of þam wræcsiðe wuldres cempan
lædan limhalne þæt se leofesta
gæst gegearwad in Godes wære   690
on gefean ferde. ða wearð feonda þreat
acol for ðam egsan. Ofermæcga spræc,
dyre dryhtnes þegn dæghluttre scán,
hæfde Guðlaces gæst in gewealdu*m*,
modig mundbora meahtum spedig,   695

***

671 wærnysse: *Thorpe fn.* r. werinesse *or* werigness   676 bregdon: *Grein
emends* bregdan   692 Ofermæcga: *Thorpe* ofer mæcga, *fn.* ofermettum?,
Grein fn. ?ofermægne

42ᵛ

þeostra þegnas þreamedlum bond,
nyd onsette 7 geneahhe bibead:
'Ne sy him banes bryce ne blodig wund,
lices læla ne laþes wiht
þæs þe ge him to dare gedon motan   700
ac ge hine gesundne ásettaþ þær ge hine sylfne
    genoman:
he sceal þy wonge wealdan, ne magon ge him þa
    wic forstondan.
Ic eom se dema se mec dryhten heht
snude gesecgan þæt ge him sara gehwylc
hondum gehælde 7 him hearsume   705
on his sylfes dóm *siþþan wæron;
ne sceal ic mine onsyn fore eowere
mengu miþan: ic eom meotudes þegn.
Eom ic þara twelfa sum þe he getreoweste
under monnes hiw mode gelufade.   710
He mec of heofonum hider onsende,
geseah þæt ge on eorðan fore æfstum†
on his wergengan wite legdon.
Is þæt min broþor, mec his bysgu gehreaw.
Ic þæt gefremme, þær se freond wunað   715
on þære socne þe ic þa sibbe wið hine
healdan wille nu ic his helpan mot,
þæt ge min onsynn oft sceawiað;
nu ic his geneahhe neosan wille,
sceal ic his word 7 his weorc in gewitnesse   720
dryhtne lædon: he his dæde conn.'

IX

ÐA wæs Guðlaces gæst geblissad
siþþan Bartholomeus aboden hæfde
Godes ærendu. Gearwe stodun
hæftas hearsume þa þæs halgan word   725
lyt oferleordun. Ongon þa leofne sið
dragan domeadig dryhtnes cempa

---

696 þreamedlum: *Thorpe and Grein* þreaniedlum, *Gollancz, Assmann, and KD emend* þreaniedlum   712 æfstum, *MS.* æftum *Thorpe, Grein, Gollancz, Assmann, and KD emend to* æfstum

43ʳ

to þam onwillan eorðan dæle.
Hy hine bæron 7 him bryce heoldon,
hofon hine hondum 7 him hryre burgun;   730
wæron hyra gongas under Godes egsan
smeþe 7 gesefte. Sigehreðig cwom
bytla to þam beorge; hine bletsadon
monge mægwlitas meaglum reordum,
treofugla tuddor tacnum cyðdon   735
eadges eftcyme; oft he him æte heold
þonne hy him hungrige ymb hond flugon,
gradum gifre geoce *gefegon.
Swa þæt milde mod wið monncynnes
dreamum gedælde, dryhtne þeowde,   740
genom him to wildeorum wynne siþþan he þas
    woruld forhogde.
Smolt wæs se sigewong 7 sele niwe,
fæger fugla reord, folde geblowen;
geacas gear budon; Guþlac moste,
eadig and onmod, eardes brucan.   745
Stód se grena wong in Godes wære,
hæfde se heorde se þe of heofonum cwom
feondas afyrde. Hwylc wæs fægerra
willa geworden in wera life
þara þe yldran usse gemunde   750
oþþe we sylfe† siþþan cuþen?
Hwæt we þissa wundra gewitan sindon;
eall þas geeodon in ussera
tida timan. Forþon þæs tweogan ne þearf
ænig ofer eorðan ælda cynnes   755
ac swylc God hwyrceð gæsta lifes
to trumnaþe þy læs þa tydran mod
þa gewitnesse wendan þurfe
þonne hy in gesihþe soþes brucað.
Swa se ælmihtiga ealle gesceafte   760
lufað under lyfte in lichoman
monna mægðe geond middangeard.

43ᵛ

---

738 grædum: *Thorpe fn.* grædgum (grædigum)?   750 gemunde: *Thorpe fn.*
r. gemunden (gemundon)   751 sylfe, *with* y *placed below* e *in MS.*
756 swylc, *with* y *below* i *in MS.*

Wile† se waldend þæt we wisdom a
snyttrum swelgen þæt his soð fore ús
on his giefena gyld genge weorðe   765
ða he us to are 7 to ondgiete
syleð 7 sendeð, sawlum rymeð
liþe lifwegas leohte geræhte.
Nis þæt huru læsast þæt seo lufu cyþeð
þonne heo in monnes mode getimbreð   770

44^r gæstcunde *gife: swa he Guðlaces
dagas 7 dæde þurh his dóm ahóf.
Wæs se fruma fæstlic feondum ón óndan
geseted wið synnum; þær he siþþan lyt
wære gewonade; oft his word Gode   775
þurh eaðmedu up onsende,
let his ben cuman in þa beorhtan gesceaft,
þoncade þeodne þæs þe he in þrowingum
bidan moste hwonne him betre lif
þurh Godes willan agyfen worde.   780
Swa wæs Guðlaces gæst gelæded
engla fæðmum in uprodor
fore onsyne eces deman:
læddon leoflice. Him wæs lean geseald,
setl on swegle, þær he symle mot   785
awo to ealdre eardfæst wesan,
bliðe bidan: is him bearn Godes
milde mundbora, meahtig dryhten,
halig hyrde, heofonrices weard.
Swa soðfæstra sawla motun   790
in ecne geard, up gestigan,
rodera rice, þa þe ræfnað her
wordum 7 weorcum wuldorcyninges
lare longsume on hyra lifes tid,
earniað on eorðan ecan lifes,   795
hames in heahþu: þæt beoð husulweras,
cempan gecorene Criste leofe;
berað in breostum beorhtne geleafan,
haligne hyht, heortan clæne;

---

763 Wile, *with an* l *erased before* l *in MS.*   780 agyfen, y *changed from* i
in MS.: worde: Grein, Assmann, *and* KD *emend* wurde

weorðiað waldend; habbað wisne geþoht 800
fusne on forðweg to fæder eðle;
gearwaþ gæstes hús 7 mid gleawnesse
feond oferfeohtað 7 firenlustas
44ᵛ   forberað *in breostum; broþorsibbe
georne bigongað in Godes willan; 805
swencað hi sylfe; sawle frætwað
halgum gehydgum; heofoncyninges bibod
fremmað on foldan; fæsten lufiað;
beorgað him bealoniþ 7 gebedu secað;
swincað wið synnum; healdað soð 7 ryht. 810
Him þæt ne hreoweð æfter hingonge
ðonne hy hweorfað in þa halgan burg,
gongað gegnunga to Hierusalem
þær hi to worulde wynnum motum
Godes onsyne georne bihealdan, 815
sibbe 7 gesihðe, þær heo soð wunað
wlitig, wuldorfæst, ealnet widan ferh
on lifgendra londes wynne.

817 ealne, *MS.* ealdne: *Thorpe, Grein, Gollancz, Assmann, and KD emend*
ealne

GUTHLAC B

I

ĐÆT IS WIDE CVĐ WEra cneorissum,
folcum gefræge, þætte frymþa God 820
þone ærestan ælda cynnes
of þære clænestan, cyning ælmihtig,
foldan geworhte. ða wæs fruma niwe
ęlda tudres, onstæl wynlic,
fæger 7 gefealic. Fæder wæs acenned 825
Adam ærest þurh est Godes
on neorxnawong þær him nænges wæs
willan onsyn ne welan brosnung
ne lifes lyre ne lices hryre
ne dreames dryre ne deaðes cyme 830
ác he on þam lande lifgan moste
ealra leahtra leas, longe neotan
niwra gefeana; þær he *nó þorfte
lifes ne lissa in þam leohtan ham
þurh ælda tid ende gebidan 835
ac æfter fyrste to þam færestan
heofonrices gefean hweorfan mostan
leomu lic somud 7 lifes gæst
7 þær siþþan á in sindreamum
to widan feore wunian mostun 840
dryhtne on gesihðe butan deaðe forð
gif hy halges word healdan woldun,
beorht in breostum, 7 his bebodu læstan,
æfnan on eðle; hy to ær aþreat
þæt hy waldendes willan læsten; 845
ac his wif genom wyrmes larum
blede forbodene 7 of beame ahneop
wæstm† biweredne ofer word Godes,
wuldorcyninges, 7 hyre were sealde
þurh deofles searo deaðberende gyfl 850

45ʳ

---

835 ælda tid: *Thorpe fn.* r. ælde tide   836 færestan: *Thorpe, Grein, Gollancz,*
Assmann emend fægrestan   848 wæstm, *MS.* wæsten *with* m *written above* en

þæt ða sinhiwan to swylte geteah.
Siþþan se eþel uðgenge wearð
Adame 7 Euan, eardwica cyst,
beorht, oðbroden, 7 hyra bearnum swa,
eaferum æfter, þa hy ón úncyððu,   855
scomum scudende, scofene wurdon
on gewinworuld; weorces onguldon
deopra firena þurh deaðes cwealm
þe hy unsnyttrum ær gefremedon;
þære synwræce siþþan sceoldon   860
mægð 7 mæcgas morþres ongyldon,
godscyldge gyrn, þurh gæstgedal,
deopra firena. Deað in geþrong
fira cynne, feond rixade
geond middangeard. Nænig monna wæs   865
of þam sigetudre siþþan æfre
Godes willan þæs georn ne gynnwised†
þæt he bibugan mæge þone bitran drync

45ᵛ *þone Eue fyrn Adame geaf,
byrelade bryd geong: *þæt* him bam gescód   870
in þam deoran hám. Deað ricsade
ofer foldbuend þeah þe fela wære
gæsthaligra; þær hi Godes willan
on mislicum monna gebihþum
æfter stedewonga stowum† fremedon,   875
sume ær, sume sið, sume in urra
æfter tælmearce tida gemyndum,
sigorlean sohtun. Us secgað bec
hu Guðlac wearð þurh Godes willan
eadig on Engle —he him ece geceas   880
meaht 7 mundbyrd, mære wurdon
his wundra geweorc wide 7 side,
breme æfter burgum geond Bryten innan,
hu he monge oft þurh meaht Godes
gehælde hygegeomre hefigra wita   885
þe hine unsofte adle gebundne

---

856 scudende: *Thorpe fn.* sceadende? scriðende? (*Kemble*)   867 gynnwised,
MS. gynnwiseð: *Thorpe emends* gen wisod, *Grein emends* gynn-wised, *as
following editors*   875 stowum, *MS.* stopum: *Thorpe* stopum, *Grein,
Gollancz, Assmann, and KD emend* stowum

sarge gesohtun of sidwegum†
freorigmode. Symle frofre þær
æt þam Godes cempan gearwe fundon,
helpe 7 hælo. Nænig hæleþa is   890
þe areccan mæge oþþe rím wite
ealra þara wundra þe he in worulde her
þurh dryhtnes giefe dugeþum gefremede.

II

OFT to þam wicum weorude cwomun
deofla deaðmægen, duguþa byscyrede,   895
hloþum þringan þær se halga þeow,
elnes anhydig, eard weardade;
þær hy mislice mongum reordum
on þam westenne woðe hofun,
hludne herecirm, hiwes binotene,   900
46ʳ dreamum *bidrorene. Dryhtnes cempa,
from folctoga, feonda þreatum
wiðstod stronglice. Næs seo stund latu
earmra gæsta ne þæt onbid long
þæt þa wrohtsmiðas wóp áhofun,   905
hreopun hreðlease, hleoþrum brugdon.
Hwilum wedende swa wilde deor
cirmdon on corðre, hwilum cyrdon eft
minne mansceaþan on mennisc hiw
breahtma mæste, hwilum brugdon eft   910
awyrgde wærlogan on wyrmes bleo,
earme adloman, attre spiowdon.
Symle hy Guðlac gearene fundon,
þonces gleawne; he geþyldum bad
þeah him feonda hloð feorhcwealm bude.   915
Hwilum him to honda, hungre geþreatad,
fleag fugla cyn þær hy feorhnere
witude fundon 7 hine weorðedon
meaglum stefnum; hwilum mennisce
aras eaðmedum eft neosedon   920

---

887 sidwegum, MS. siðwegum: emendation proposed by Thorpe but not
incorporated into any edition   903 stund latu: Grein stund-latu   913 gearene: Thorpe and Grein emend gearone

7 þær siðfrome on þam sigewonge
æt þam halgan þeowon helpe gemetton,
ferðþes frofre. Nænig forþum wæs
þæt he æwiscmód eft siðade,
hean, hyhta leas, ac se halga wer   925
ælda gehwylces þurh þa æþelan meaht
þe hine seoslige sohtun on ðearfe,
hæleð hygegeomre, hælde butu
lic 7 sawle þenden lifes weard,
ece ælmihtig, unnan wolde   930
þæt he blædes her brucan [moste]†,
worulde lifes. Wæs gewinnes þa
yrmþa for eorðan endedogor
þurh nydgedal neah ge*þrungen
siþþan he on westenne wiceard geceas   935
fiftynu gear; þa wæs frofre gæst
eadgum æbodan ufan onsended,
halig of heahþu; hreþer innan born,
afysed on forðsið. Him færinga
adl in gewod —he on elne swa þeah   940
ungeblyged bad beorhtra gehata,
bliþe in burgum— wæs þam bancofan
æfter nihtglome neah geþrungen,
breosthord ónboren: wæs se bliþa gæst
fús on forðweg. Nolde fæder engla   945
in þisse wonsælgan worulde life
leahtra leasne longfyrst ofer þæt
wunian leton þe him on weorcum her
on his dagena tid, dædum gecwemde,
elne unslawe. ða se ælmihtiga†   950
let his hond cuman þær se halga þeow,
deormod on degle, domeadig bád,
heard 7 hygerof. Hyht wæs geniwad,
blis in breostum; wæs se bancofa
adle onæled, inbendum fæst   955

46ᵛ

---

923 forþum: *Grein suggests* furðum?   931 [moste]: *supplied by all editors*
942 bancofan: *after this word Grein supplies* untrymnes adle gongum *and
Assmann allows for one missing line*   950 ælmihtiga, *MS.* hælmihtiga: *all
editors emend to* ælmihtiga

lichord onlocen; leomu hefegedon,
sarum gesohte. He þæt soð gecneow
þæt hine ælmihtig ufan neosade
meotud fore miltsum; he his modsefan
wið þam færhagan fæste trymede   960
feonda gewinna. Næs he forht se þeah
ne seo adlþracu eglet on mode
ne deaðgedal ac him dryhtnes lof
born in breostum, brondhat lufu
sigorfæst in sefan, seo him sara gehwylc   965
symle forswiðdet; næs him sorgcearu
on þas lænan tid þeah his lic 7 gæst
hyra somwiste sinhiwan tú
deore ge*dældet. Dagas forð scridun,
nihthelma genipu. Wæs neah seo tid   970
þæt he fyrngewyrht fyllan sceolde
þurh deaðes cyme, domes hleotan,
efne þæs ilcan þe usse yldran fyrn
frecne onfengon swa him biforan worhton
þa ærestan ælda cynnes.   975

III

ðA wæs Guðlace on þa geocran tid
mægen gemeðgad, mod swiþe heard,
elnes anhydig: wæs seo adl þearl,
hat 7 heorogrim, hreþer innan weol,
born banloca; bryþen wæs ongunnen   980
þætte Adame Eue gebyrmde
æt fruman worulde. Feond byrlade
ærest þære idese 7 heo Adame,
hyre swæsum were, siþþan scencte
bittor bædeweg þæs þa byre siþþan   985
grimme onguldon gafulrædenne
þurh ærgewyrht þætte ænig ne wæs

fyra cynnes from fruman siððan,
món ón moldan, þætte meahte him
gebeorgan 7 bibugan þone bleatan drync   990
deopan deaðweges ac him duru sylfa
on þa sliðnan tid sona ontyneð,
ingong geopenað; ne mæg ænig þam
flæsce bifongen feore wiðstondan
ricra ne heanra ac hine ræseð on   995
gifrum grapum: swa wæs Guðlace
enge anhoga ætryhte þa
æfter nihtscuan, neah geþyded,
wiga wælgifre. Hine wunade mid
an ombehtþegn se hine æghwylce   1000
daga neosade. Ongan ða deophydig
gleawmod gongan to Godes temple
þær he eþelbodan *inne wiste
þone leofestan lareow gecorenne
7 þa in eode eadgum to spræce—   1005
wolde hyrcnigan halges lara,
mildes meþelcwida; fonde þa his mondryhten
adlwerigne; him ðæt in gefeol
hefig æt heortan, hygesorge wæg,
micle modceare. Ongan ða his magu frignan: 1010
'Hu gewearð þe þus, winedryhten min,
fæder, freonda hleo, ferð gebysgad,
nearwe geneged. Ic næfre þe,
þeoden leofesta, þyslicne ær
gemette þus meðne. Meaht þu meðelcwidum   1015
worda gewealdan? Is me on wene geþuht
þæt þe untrymnes adle gongum
on þisse nyhstan niht bysgade,
sarbennum gesoht; þæt me sorgna is
hatost on hreþre ær þu hyge minne,   1020
ferð, afrefre. Wast þu, freodryhten,
hu þeos adle scyle ende gesettan?'
Him þa sið oncwæð, sona ne meahte
oroð up geteon: wæs him in bogen

47ᵛ

1007 fonde: *Grein emends* fond, *fn.* funde?   1019 sorgna, *with* n *changed from* a *in MS.*

bittor bancoþa. Beald reordade,   1025
eadig on elne *ond*cwis ageaf:
'Ic wille secgan þæt me sar gehran,
wærc in gewod in ðisse wonnan niht,
lichord onleac; leomu hefegiað,
sarum gesohte. Sceal þis sawelhús,   1030
fæge flæschoma foldærne biþeaht,
leomu, lames geþacan, legerbedde fæst
wunian wælræste. Wiga nealæceð,
unlæt laces: ne bið þæs lengra swice
sawelgedales þonne seofon niht   1035
fyrstgemearces þæt min feorh heonan
on þisse eahteþan ende geseceð,

48^r dæg scriþende. Þonne dogor *beoð
on moldwege min forð scriþen,
sorg gesweðrad†, 7 ic siþþan mot   1040
fore meotudes cneowum meorda hleotan,
gingra geafena, 7 Godes lomber
in sindreamum siþþan awo
forð folgian. Is nu fus ðider
gæst siþes georn, nu þu gearwe const   1045
leoma lifgedal: long is þis onbid
worulde lifes.' ða wæs wop 7 heaf,
geongum geocor sefa, geomrende hyge
siþþan he gehyrde þæt se halga wæs
forðsiþes fus; he þæs færspelles   1050
fore his mondryhtne modsorge wæg
hefige æt heortan —hreþer innan swearc,
hyge hreowcearig, þæs þe his hlaford geseah
ellorfusne; he þæs onbæru
habban ne meahte ac he hate let   1055
torn þoliende tearas geotan,
weallan wægdropan. Wyrd ne meahte
in fægum leng feorg gehealdan
deore frætwe þonne him gedemed wæs.

1032 leomu, lames: *Thorpe* leomu-lames   1040 gesweðrad, *MS.* geswedrad:
Thorpe and Grein gesweðrad, *Gollancz, Assmann, and KD emend* gesweðrad
1053 þe his; *Thorpe, Grein, Gollancz, and Assman emend* þe [he] his; geseah:
Gollancz places in following verse

IV

ONgeat gæsta halig geomormodes   1060
drusendnet hyge. Ongan þa duguþa hleo,
glædmod, Gode leof, geongran retan,
wine leofestan wordum negan:
'Ne beo þu unrot; ðeah þeos adl me
innan æle, nis me earfeðe   1065
to geþolianne þeodnes willan,
dryhtnes mines, ne ic þæs deaðes hafu
on þas seocant tid sorge on mode,
ne ic me herehloðe helleþegna
swiðe onsitte, ne mæg synne on me   1070
facnes frumbearn fyrene gestælan,
lices leahtor; *ac in lige sceolon
sorgwylmum soden sár wanian,
wræcsið wepan, wilna biscirede
in þam deaðsele, duguða gehwylcre,   1075
lufena 7 lissa. Min þæt leofe bearn,
ne beo þu on sefan to seoc. Ic eom siþes fus
upeard niman, edleanat georn
in þam ecan gefean ærgewyrhtum,
geseon sigora frean. Min þæt swæse bearn,   1080
nis me wracu ne gewin þæt ic wuldres God
sece, swegelcyning. Þær is sib 7 blis,
domfæstra dream, dryhten *ond*weard
þam ic georne gæstgerynum
in þas dreorgan tid, dædum cwemde,   1085
mode 7 mægne. Ic þa meorde wat
leahtorlease, lean unhwilen,
halig on heahþu þær min hyht myneð
to gesecenne; sawul fundað
of licfate to þam longan gefean   1090
in eadwelan. Nis þes eþel me
ne sar ne sorg. Ic me sylfum wat

1061 drusendne, *MS.* drusende: *Thorpe fn.* r. drusendne, *Grein, Gollancz, Assmann, and KD emend* drusendne   1068 seocan, *MS.* seocnan: *Thorpe fn.* seocan?   1078 edleana, *MS.* edlea/nan: *Thorpe, Grein, Gollancz* edleanan, *KD emend* edleana   1088 heahþu: *Grein* heahðum   1091 eadwelan, *MS.* geadwelan *with* g *super- and subpuncted*: þes eþel: *Grein fn.* þeos adl?

æfter lices hryre lean unhwilen.'
ða se wuldormaga worda gestilde,
rof rúnwita: wæs him ræste neod   1095
reonigmodum. Rodor swamode
ofer niðða bearn, nihtrim scridon
deorc ofer dugeðum. Þaᵗ se dæg bicwom
on þam se lifgenda in lichoman
ece ælmihtig ærist gefremede,   1100
dryhten mid dreame, ða he of deaðe aras,
onwald of eorðan in þa eastortid,
ealra þrymma þrym —ðreata mæstne
to heofonum ahóf, ða he from helle astag.
Swa se eadga wer in þa æþelan tid   1105
on þone beorhtan dæg, blissum hremig,
milde 7 gemetfæst mægen unsofte

*elne geæfnde; aras ða eorla wynn,
heard, hygesnottor, swa he hraþost meahte,
meðe for ðam miclan bysgum; ongon þa
    his mod staþelian   1110
leohte geleafan, lac ónsægde
deophycgende dryhtne to willan
gastgerynum in Godes temple,
7 his þegne ongon (swa þam þeodne geras)
þurh gæstes giefe godspel bodian,   1115
secgan sigortacnum 7 his sefan trymman
wundrum to wuldre in þa wlitigan gesceaft,
to eadwelan, swa he ær ne sið
æfre to ealdre oðre swylce
on þas lænan tid lare gehyrde   1120
ne swa deoplice dryhtnes geryne
þurh menniscne muð areccan
on sidum sefan. Him wæs soþra geþuht
þæt hit ufancundes engles wære
of swegldreamum, swiþor micle   1125
mægenþegnes word þonne æniges monnes lar
wera ofer eorðan; him þæt wundra mæst
gesewen þuhte þæt swylc snuttrucræft

1098 Þa, *with* e *changed to* a *in MS.*   1102 onwald, *MS.* onweald *with* e *subpuncted*   1128 snuttrucræft, *MS.* snuttocræft *with* o *changed to* u

ænges hæleða her hreþer weardade
dryhta bearna, wæs þæs deoplic eall   1130
word 7 wisdom 7 þæs weres stihtung,
mod 7 mægencræft, þe him meotud engla,
gæsta geocend, forgiefen hæfde.

V

WÆRon feowere ða forð gewitene
dagas on rime þæs se dryhtnes [þegn]†   1135
on elne bad, adle gebysgad,
sarum geswenced; ne he sorge wæg,
geocorne sefan gæstgedales,
dreorigne hyge. Deað nealæcte,
49ᵛ   stop stalgongum, *strong 7 hreðe   1140
sohte sawelhus. Com se seofeða dæg
ældum *ond*weard þæs þe him in gesonc
hat, heortan neah, hildescurun,
flacor flanþracu, feorhhord onleac
searocægum gesoht. Ongon ða snottor hæle,   1145
ár, onbehtþegn, æþeles neosan
to þam halgan hofe; fond þa hlingendne,
fusne on forðsiþ, frean unwenne,
gæsthaligne, in Godes temple
soden sarwylmum: wæs þa sihste tid   1150
on midne dæg, wæs his mondryhtne
endedogor ætryhte þa;
nearwum genæged nydcostingum,
awrecen wælpilum, wló ne meahte
oroð up geteon, ellenspræce,   1155
hleoþor ahebban. Ongon ða hygegeomor,
freorig 7 ferðwerig, fusne gretan,
meðne, modglædne; bæd hine þurh mihta
   scyppend
gif he his wordcwida wealdan meahte,
spræce ahebban, þæt him on spellum gecyðde,   1160
onwrige worda gongum hu he his wisna
   truwade

1135 se: *Grein* þe; þegn: *inserted by all editors*   1148 unwenne: *Thorpe and*
Gollancz emend unwemne   1154 wló ne: *Thorpe emends* wlonc ne

drohtes on ðære dimman adle, ær ðon hine
deað onsægde.
Him se eadga wer ageaf *ond*sware,
leof mon leofum, þeah he late meahte
eorl ellenheard oreþe gebredan: 1165
'Min þæt swæse bearn, nis nu swiþe feor
þam ytemestan endedogor
nydgedales þæt ðu þa nyhstan scealt
in woruldlife worda minra
næfre leana biloren lare gehyran   1170
noht longe ofer þis. Læst ealle well

50^r wære 7 winescype word *þa wit spræcon
leofast manna.' 'Næfre ic lufan sibbe
þeoden æt þearfe þine forlæte
asanian.' 'Beo þu on sið gearu   1175
siþþan lic 7 leomu 7 þes lifes gæst
asundrien somwist hyra
þurh feorggedal. Fyr æfter þon
þæt þu gesecge sweostor minre
þære leofestan on longne weg   1180
to þam fægran gefean forðsið minne
on ecne eard 7 hyre eac gecyð
wordum minum þ*æt* ic me warnade
hyre onsyne ealle þrage
in woruldlife, for ðy ic wilnode   1185
þæt wit unc eft in þam ecan gefean
on sweglwuldre geseon mostun
fore onsyne eces deman
leahtra lease: þær sceal lufu uncer
wærfæst wunian, þær wit wilna á   1190
in ðære beorhtan byrig brucan motun,
eades mid englum. ðu hyre eac saga
þ*æt* heo þis banfæt beorge bifæste,
lame biluce, lic orsawle
in þeostorcofan þær hit þrage sceal   1195
in sondhofe siþþan wunian.'

1174 þeoden æt þearfe: *Thorpe emends* þeodnes þearfe   1175 asanian:
Thorpe emends aswanian, *Grein* asanian, *fn.* a sanian?   1178 feorggedal:
Grein emends feorhgedal; Fyr: *Thorpe emends* fer, *Grein, Assmann and KD
emend* fys

ða wearð modgeþanc miclum gebisgad,
þream forþrycced þurh þæs þeodnes word
ombehtþegne þa he ædre oncneow
frean feorhgedal, *þæt* hit feor ne wæs   1200
endedogor; ongon þa ofostlice
to his winedryhtne wordum mæðlan:
'Ic þec halsige, hæleþa leofost
gumena cynnes, þurh gæsta weard
þæt þu hygesorge heortan minre   1205
geeþe, eorla wyn. Nis þe ende feor
þæs þe ic on galdrum ongieten hæbbe.
Oft mec geomor sefa gehþa gemanode

50ᵛ   hat æt heortan *hyge gnornende
nihtes nearwe 7 ic næfre þe,   1210
fæder, frofor min, frignan dorste.
Symle ic gehyrde þon*ne* heofones gim,
wyncondel wera, west onhylde,
sweglbeorht sunne, setlgonges fus
on æfentid† oþerne mid þec   1215
þegn æt geþeahte. Ic þæs þeodnes word,
áres uncuþes oft neosendes
dægwoman bitweon 7 þære deorcan niht,
meþelcwide mæcges 7 on morgne swa
ongeat geomormod gæstes spræce   1220
gleawes in geardum. Huru ic giet ne wat
ær þu me, frea min, furþor cyðe
þurh cwide þinne hwonan his cyme sindon.'

VI

ðA se éadga wer ageaf *ond*sware
leofum æfter longre hwile, swa he late
    meahte,   1225
elnes oncyðig, oreþe gewealdan:
'Hwæt, þu me, wine min, wordum nægest,
fusne frignest þæs þe ic furþum ær
æfre on ealdre ængum ne wolde
monna ofer moldan melda weorðan,   1230

1215 æfentid, *MS.* hæfentid: *emendation as all editors*   1226 oncyðig:
Thorpe and Grein uncuðig

þegne on þeode, butan þe nu ða
þy læs þæt wundredan weras 7 idesa
7 on geað gutan, gieddum mænden,
bi me lifgendum. Huru ic nolde sylf
þurh gielpcwide gæstes mines   1235
frofre gelettan ne fæder mines
æfre geæfnan æbylg Godes.
Symle me onsende sigedryhten min,
folca feorhgiefa, siþþan ic furþum ongon
on þone æfteran ánseld bugan   1240
geargemearces, gæsthaligne
engel ufancundne se mec efna gehwam,
meahtig meotudes þegn, 7 on morgne eft
51ʳ   sigor*fæst gesohte 7 me sara gehwylc
gehælde hygesorge 7 me in hreþre bileac,   1245
wuldres wilboda, wisdomes giefe—
micle monigfealdran þonne ænig mon wite
in lifeȝ her —þe me alyfed nis
to gecyþenne cwicra ængum
on foldwege fira cynnes   1250
þæt me ne meahte monna ænig
bideaglian hwæt he dearninga
on hyge hogde heortan geþoncum
siþþan he me fore eagum onsyne wearð.
Á ic on mode mað monna gehwylcne   1255
þeodnes þrymcyme oð þisne dæg,
leofast monna. Nu ic for lufan þinre
7 geferscype þæt wit fyrn mid unc
longe læstan nelle ic lætan þe
æfre unrotne æfter ealdorlege,   1260
meðne, modseocne, minre geweorðan
soden sorgwælmum. Á ic sibbe wiþ þe
healdan wille. Nu of hreþerlocan
to þam soþan gefean sawel fundað.
Nis seo tid latu: tydrað þis banfæt,   1265
greothord gnornað, gæst hine fyseð
on ecne geard utsiþes georn

1233 geað: *Thorpe emends* gehþum?   1234 *Grein makes up two b-verses,*
Assmann leaves two b-verses free   1248 life, MS. lifes: *all editors emend* life

on sellan gesetu. Nu ic swiðe eom
weorce gewergad.' ða to þam wage gesag,
heafelan onhylde. Hyrde þa gena   1270
ellen on innan; oroð stundum teah
mægne modig. Him of muðe cwom
swecca swetast swylce on sumeres tid
stincað on stowum, staþelum fæste,
wynnum æfter wongum, wyrta geblowene,   1275
hunigflowende; swá þæs halgan wæs
ondlongne dæg oþ æfen forð
oroð uphlæden. Þa se *æþela glæm
setlgong sohte; swearc norðrodor,
won under wolcnum, woruld miste oferteah,   1280
þystrum biþeahte; þrong niht ofer tiht
londes frætwa; ða cwom leohta mæst,
halig of heofonum, hædre scinan
beorhte ofer burgsalu. Bad se þe sceolde
eadig on elne endedogor,   1285
awrecen wælstrælum. Wuldres scima,
æþele ymb æþelne, *ond*longe niht
scan scirwered; scadu sweþredon
tolysed under lyfte: wæs se leohta glæm
ymb þæt halge hus heofonlic condel   1290
from æfenglome oþþæt eastan cwom
ofer deop gelad dægredwoma,
wedertacen wearm. Aras se wuldormago,
eadig, elnes gemyndig, spræc to his
   onbehtþegne,
torht to his treowum gesiþe: 'Tid is þæt þu
   fere
                         1295
7 þa ærendu eal biþence,
ofestum læde, swa ic þe ær bibead,
lac to leofre. Nu of lice is,
goddreama georn, gæst swiðe fus.'
Ahof þa his honda, husle gereorded,   1300

51ᵛ

1280 woruld: *Thorpe emends* worulde; miste: *Grein suggests* mist   1281 tiht:
Thorpe reads tiht-londes *in next verse; Grein places emendation* tihte *in next
verse, alternatively suggesting* liht   1284 beorhte: *Thorpe and Grein* beorht

eaðmod þy æþelan gyfle; swylce he his eagan
  ontynde,
halge heafdes gimmas, biseah þa to heofona
  rice,
glædmod to geofona leanum 7 þa his gæst
  onsende
weorcum wlitigne in wuldres drea*m*.

VII

ÐA wæs Guðlaces gæst gelæded   1305
eadig on upweg; englas feredun
to þam longan gefean; lic colode,
belifd under lyfte. ða þær leoht ascan,
beama beorhtast; eal þæt beacen wæs
ymb þæt halge hus, heofonlic *leoma   1310
from foldan up swylce fyren tor
ryht ar. æred oð rodera hrof,
gesewen under swegle, sunnan beorhtra,
æþeltungla wlite. Engla þreatas
sigeleoð sungon, sweg wæs on lyfte,   1315
gehyred under heofonum haligra dream.
Swa se burgstede wæs blissum gefylled,
swetum stencum 7 sweglwundrum,
eadges yrfestol engla hleoðres;
eal innanweard þær wæs ænlicra   1320
7 wynsumra þon*n*e hit in worulde mæge
stefn areccan, hu se stenc 7 se sweg,
heofonlic hleoþor, 7 se halga song
gehyred wæs, heahþrym Godes,
breahtem æfter breahtme. Beofode þæt
  ealond,   1325
foldwong onsprong†. ða afyrhted wearð
ar elnes biloren; gewat þa ofestlice
beorn unhyðig þæt he bat gestag,
wæghengest wræc; wæterþisa† fór
snel under sorgum. Swegl hate scan   1330

52ʳ

1306 feredun, *with* u *changed from* o *in MS.* 1308 belifd: *Thorpe emends* belifen 1308 leoht ascan: *Thorpe* leohta scan 1326 onsprong, *MS.* onþrong: *Grein fn.* onþrom? 1328 unhyðig: *Thorpe and Grein emend* unhydig 1329 wæterþisa, *MS.* wæterþiswa *with* w *subpuncted: Thorpe emends* wæterþissa, *Grein* wæterþiswa 1330 sorgum: *Grein emends* sargum

blac ofer burgsalo; brimwudu scynde,
leoht, lade fus; lagumearg snyrede
gehlæsted to hyðe þæt se hærnflota
æfter sundplegan sondlond gespearn,
grond wið greote. Gnornsorge wæg   1335
hate æt heortan hygegeomurne,
meðne modsefan, se þe his mondryhten
life bilidene last weardian
wiste wine leofne. Him þæs wopes hring
torne gemonade, teagor yðum weol,   1340
hate hleordropan, ⁊ on hreþre wæg
micle modceare: he þære mægeð sceolde
láce gelædan, laðspel *to soð.
Cwom þa freorigferð þær seo fæmne wæs,
wuldres wynmæg; he þa wyrd ne máð   1345
fæges forðsið fusleoð agol
wine þearfende ⁊ þæt word acwæð:
'Ellen biþ selast þam þe oftost sceal
dreogan dryhtenbealu, deope behycgan
þroht, þeodengedal, þonne seo þrag cymeð   1350
wefen wyrdstafun. Þæt wat se þe sceal
áswæman sarigferð, wat his sincgiefan
holdne biheledne; he sceal hean þonan
geomor hweorfan þam bið gomenes wana
ðe þa earfeða oftost dreogeð   1355
on sargum sefan. Huru ic swiðe ne þearf
hinsiþ behlehhan. Is hlaford min,
beorna bealdor ⁊ broþor þin,
se selesta bi sæm tweonum
þara þe we on Engle æfre gefrunen   1360
acennedne þurh cildes had
gumena cynnes to Godes dome,
werigra wraþu, worulddreamum of,
winemæga wyn, in wuldres þrym,
gewiten, winiga† hleo, wica neosan,   1365
eardes on upweg. Ne se eorðan dæl,

52ᵛ

1338 bilidene: *all editors except Gollancz emend* bilidenne   1351 wyrdstafun:
Thorpe, Grein, and Gollancz wyrdstafum, *Assmann and KD emend* wyrdstafum
1365 winiga, *MS.* wiinga(?): *Thorpe and Grein emend* wonga, *Gollancz,
Assmann, and KD emend* winiga

[*Texts*]

banhus abrocen, burgum in innan
wunað wælræste, 7 se wuldres dæl
of licfæte in leoht Godes
sigorlean sohte; 7 þe secgan het   1370
þæt git a mosten in þam ecan gefean
mid þa sibgedryht somud eard niman,
weorca wuldorlean, willum neotan
blædes 7 blissa. Eac þe abeodan het
sigedryhten mín þa he wæst† siþes fus   1375
þæt þu his lichoman, leofast mægða,
eorðan biðeahte. Nu þu ædre const
siðfæt minne. Ic sceal sarigferð
heanmod hweorfan hyge drusendne*

1375 wæs, *MS. þæs: Thorpe and Grein* wæs, *Gollancz, Assmann, and KD emend* wæs   1379* *This is the last word on fo. 52ᵛ.* 'Azarias' *follows in the MS.(see Commentary)*

Commentary

Note: within the Commentary the textual forms and notes of previous editors and the interpretations found in translations are usually cited without further reference than the editor's or translator's name (see Select Bibliography, sections 2 and 3); fuller references are given only where their views might not easily be traced.

GUTHLAC A

1 On fo. 32^r of the MS. the script ends three-quarters of the way along the nineteenth line, and the last three lines are empty. Fo. 32^v opens with a line filled chiefly with capitals: *SE BIÐ GEFEANA FæGrast*. The large capital *S* is approximately four times the height of the other capitals which stand on the second ruled line of the folio, touching the first line. At the top of the folio a (?)sixteenth-century hand has scrawled words which correspond closely to Wanley's account of the following material (*Catalogus*, p. 280). A title in the same hand occurs midway down fo. 44^v, over the beginning of *Guthlac B*, and a title and some glosses on fo. 10^r. The interlinear glossing of fo. 9^r has been attributed to Nowell (Robin Flower, 'Laurence Nowell and the Discovery of England in Tudor Times' *Proc. Brit. Acad.*, xxi (1935), 70), but whether or not he is responsible for the finer script which appears in these headings and on fo. 10^r is uncertain.

æt frymðe. Shook, 'The Prologue of the Old English *Guthlac A*', *Mediaeval Studies*, xxiii (1961), 297, translates this phrase 'at the going out from the body', but there is no evidence to support this interpretation (suggested by the source he adduces for this part of the poem) of *frymð*. The equivalent usually accepted is some such adverbial phrase as 'at first'.

4 ff. Shook, 'The Prologue', p. 297, translates his division of these lines: 'Then the angel says: "Receive ye higher rank". The spirit greets the other (i.e. the soul) and declares to it God's message: "Now mayest thou go whither . . ."', introducing into the text a distinction between *anima* and *spiritus* important in the *Visio sancti Pauli*. His reading of these lines unfortunately entails a unique use of the imperative plural for the singular and the transference of the psychopomp's function from angel to *spiritus*, difficulties he himself notes (p. 300). The resemblances he finds between these lines and the *Visio sancti Pauli* are due to their common background, and no closer relationship can be argued convincingly (see also §4, pp. 23–4).

9 *tidfara.* This nonceword shares its base element with two other poetic compounds, *Beowulf* 502 *merefara* 'seafarer' and *Exodus* 208 *nydfara* 'one forced to journey'. Either of the interpretations suggested

in BT, 'a traveller the time of whose journey is come' and 'one who journeys for a (short) time', can be supported from among the meanings found for the adjective *tidlic*, its related adverb *tidlice*, and the other compounds in *tid-*. Shook, 'The Prologue', p. 297, apparently prefers the first of these alternatives, translating the passage 'thou art now travelling under summons to that heavenly home' and, though we cannot be sure that the author did not visualize for the soul of the dying man a journey which would have taken some period of time, this is contextually the more attractive reading.

11 *edergong fore yrmþum*. Thorpe's translation of *edergong* as 'refuge' foreshadows BT 'a home-seeking' which KD favour. BTs 'a going into an enclosed place(?), a taking refuge' requires no manipulation of the syntax, whereas simple 'refuge' makes necessary the insertion of an affirmative verb, e.g. Shook, 'The Prologue', p. 297, 'there is shelter from miseries'. A second, tentative interpretation of *edergong* in BTs connects it with the Gothic words *idreigōn* 'to repent' and *idreiga* 'repentance', because it parallels *hreow* 10, but Bradley, 'Some Emendations in Old English Texts', *Mod. Lang. Rev.*, xi (1916), 212, points out that there is no trace of either **edergian* or **edergung* elsewhere in OE. In his turn Bradley puts forward the emendation **eargung* (based on the verb *eargian* 'grow timid' which is often followed by *for*), translating 'failing of heart for afflictions' and assuming a misreading of *ear-* as *edr-* with subsequent respelling of the word as a compound. Perhaps this interpretation lies behind Toller's further suggestion, in his additions and corrections to BTs, **ed-eargung* 'renewed discouragement'; the proposed emendation *edergung* is explained as having Anglian smoothing in the second syllable. GK interpret the compound *edergong* 'das Umhergehen der Bettler von Haus zu Haus', comparing with it the ON. legal term *húsgangr* 'mendicatio', an explanation attractive for two reasons. First, there are in the poem some words which may have had a technical use in law (see §8). It is not therefore improbable that an unusual word should have such a restricted technical meaning in *Guthlac A*. Secondly, poverty, hardship, the giving of alms, etc., are dominating images in the poem and thus support the interpretation 'beggary, penury'.

13 *motum*: see §9.

16 *hyhsta*. A form without syncopation is necessary here for the metre (see §8).

17 *ealra*. The word is not needed by the metre of l. 16b where it is placed by all editors before KD. A dot separates ll. 16b and 17a in the MS., showing that *ealra* is to be grouped with *cyninga cyning*. (This stop is not recorded by Gollancz who, taking *ealra* into l. 16, translates 'the most high, the King of Kings'.) Forms of *eall* often appear in the introductory dip of a verse, e.g. *Elene* 483a *eallra þrymma þrym*; see Sievers, 'Zur Rhythmik des germanischen Alliterationsverses', *Beiträge zur Geschichte der deutschen Sprache und Literatur*, x (1885), 479.

18 *nó*. MS. *nú*. *nú* can be defended only if *þær* 19 is regarded as contrasting with *þa getimbru* 18, but this mode of defence breaks down

with the succession of *þider* 22 and *Hwider* 26. Generally a negative is offered in emendation, the earlier editors preferring *ne*, the particle usual before a finite verb. Two things point to the reading *nó*: the adverb is so marked elsewhere in the Exeter Book, e.g. *Christ* 1097, *Guthlac A* 492, 506, *B* 833, *Phoenix* 72, 157, etc., but the particle *ne* is not; and there are thoughout the Exeter Book indications of scribal confusion of *o* and *u* (in some instances there are manuscript changes, in others excuses such as dittography, transposition of letters, and anticipation are advanced). The adverb *no* negates a finite verb only in poetry and then infrequently (B. Mitchell, 'Subordinate Clauses in Old English Poetry', (Oxford, D. Phil. thesis, 1958), i.868, lists *Christ* 1639, *Guthlac A* 492, 506, *B* 833, *Phoenix* 72, *Elene* 837, *Beowulf* 2585, *Wanderer* 96, and *Solomon and Saturn* 203).

18 *tydriað*. The only other occurrence of this verb in the corpus of OE. verse is *Guthlac B* 1265 *tydrað*, but it appears in prose, e.g. the *Leechdoms* and the translation of Gregory's *Dialogues*.

20 *lenge hu sel*. Thorpe places *hu sel* as one word in the following verse, but for his translation of ll. 20b–1a, 'but shall to them be length, / ... youth *they* shall enjoy', puts forward (p. 503) the emendation ... *lengþu. sin-geoguþe brucað*. The compound *husel-geoguðe* 'Abendsmahljugend', suggested by Dietrich, 'Cynevulfs Crist', *Zeitschrift für deutsches Altertum*, ix (1853), 207, is rightly criticized as metrically improbable by Grein, who equates *lenge* with the adjective *gelenge* 'ready, attainable', taking as one word *husel* 'Eucharist'. The word division now generally accepted is first found in Cosijn, 'Anglosaxonica', *Tijdschrift voor Nederlandsche Taal- en Letterkunde*, i (1881), 150. Cp. *lenge hu geornor* 138.

24 For the joining of two finite verbs by the simple connective in the a-verse, with or without a following string of short clauses containing co-ordinate verbs, as a feature of the *A*-poet by contrast with *Guthlac B*, see §8, p. 61.

26 ff. Here two problems, to some extent interdependent, arise. The first, the extent of the angel's address to the soul, is usually decided silently, whereas the second, the interpretation of *Hwider*, is widely discussed. The length of the angel's speech varies greatly both in editions and translations. Those who regard the opening twenty-nine lines of the poem either as a separate complete poem or as the end of *Christ III* for the most part end the speech with the twenty-ninth line, though of the earlier editors Grein and Assmann close the speech in the middle of l. 10, the division adopted by KD. So early an ending for the speech interrupts an account of heaven complete only at the end of l. 25, the choice of R. K. Gordon, *Anglo-Saxon Poetry* (London, 1954), p. 164, who treats ll. 26–9 (for him the end of *Christ*) as a question. This question is answered in what follows (see §5, pp. 30–1) and *Hwider* is an interrogative adverb. Other divisions of the material require an unusual interpretation of *hwider*, either as a relative 'to which' (as KD), or as a correlative with *þider* (as Schaar, *Critical Studies*, pp. 78–9), but the word does not in OE. introduce any clause which cannot be taken as a

dependent question rather than an adjectival or adverbial clause of place. Mitchell, 'Subordinate Clauses', i. 258, suggests that 'from a formal grammatical point of view *hwider* introduces a dependent question parallel to *ræste*', an opinion difficult to reconcile with his decision that in translation into Modern English the KD interpretation 'seems the best way out'. It seems therefore that ending the angel's speech with l. 25 removes from the text an unparalleled syntactical construction.

30 For an account of the early editorial practice of beginning the Guthlac poem(s) here see §3. Cosijn's comparison ('Anglosaxonica. IV', p. 115) of this line with the opening line of *The Panther* is often advanced in support of this practice, despite the many non-initial lines in which the formula *geond middangeard* answers to a verse with one of its main lifts supplied by some form of *monig*, e.g. *Christ* 644, *Guthlac* 39, 501, *Phoenix* 4. A discussion of the relationship of ll. 30 ff. to the preface to the tenth chapter of Gregory's *Vitæ Patrum* is to be found in §4; see also n. for l. 59.

31 *hadas*. A translation 'ranks, grades' is supported by the comparisons drawn between this passage and passages in Gregory and Lactantius (see §4), where the word *gradus* occurs in similar contexts. See also nn. for ll. 60 and 94.

35 ff. Parallels can be adduced for these 'elegiac' lines both from OE. homilies and from other poems, e.g. *Wanderer* 58 ff., *Seafarer* 64 ff. Such passages reflect the belief that 'the world was to come to an end in the sixth age of its history, and that this age was already in progress and indeed far gone' (Smithers, 'The Meaning of *The Seafarer* and *The Wanderer*', *MÆ*, xxvi (1957), 144); see also §5.

36 *forð*. This word must supply the second lift of l. 36b and to regard it as the first element of a compound *forðweges* would in any case disturb the alliterative pattern of l. 37. It is however curious that the poet should have chosen *forð* for the second stress of a *b*-verse when the first word of the following line is one often compounded with it. Syntactic ambiguity of *forð* is less likely in l. 75.

40 *Godes spelbodan*. H. S. MacGillivray, *The Influence of Christianity on the Vocabulary of Old English*, §46, notes that *spelboda* is used only here for 'apostle', but some more general translation such as 'prophet, witness' is better contextually (cp. A. Keiser, *The Influence of Christianity on the Vocabulary of Old English Poetry*, p. 25). The compound collocates with *Godes* (*Genesis* 2496, *Daniel* 229, 464, 532, 742, *Christ* 336, *Phoenix* 571), except for *Paris Psalter* 105.10 *an spellboda*.

46 *mætrę*. The hook is unnecessary here for, no matter whether a comparative nominative singular feminine or, by attraction of *mægne*, a comparative nominative singular neuter, the form to be expected is *mætre*. Otherwise the hooked *ę* is used by the scribe only twice in inflexional syllables, *Christ* 91 *solimę* and *Phoenix* 673 *letitię*, where it must be recognized as intended for *æ* (as in the accented syllables of many OE. words). Perhaps the scribe was misled into dittographing *æ*, the symbol represented in the vowels of both metrical stresses of the verse.

48 *he*. Cosijn, 'Anglosaxonica. IV', p. 115, suggests *he* 48 stands for *heo*, an interpretation followed in KD who relate the pronoun to *worulde* 48. Rather than argue a sporadic use of *he* for *heo* in late OE. or a dubious masculine gender for *woruld* beside the usual feminine, it seems easiest to take *he* 48, like *he* 51, as referring forward to *dryhten* 54.

51 *he*. Explained by Cosijn, 'Anglosaxonica. IV', p. 115, as anticipating *dryhten* 54; cp. n. on l. 48.

54 *dalum gedæled*. Cp. *Vainglory* 22.

57 *woruldryhte*. The context makes it clear that 'the law that should govern the world' (BT) is intended here and that Grein's suggestion **worulddryhte* is unnecessary. No distinction here is made between church and secular law, by contrast with two tenth-century instances of the compound where reference also to *Godes riht* reflects a growing recognition of the separate functions of *woruld bote* and *godcunde bote* in the later Anglo-Saxon period (see D. Bethurum, *The Homilies of Wulfstan* (Oxford, 1957), p. 73).

59 The line recalls words from Matthew 20:16 *multi enim sunt vocati, pauci vero electi*, and looks back also to l. 30. If it is accepted that ll. 30 ff. show similarities in content to the introduction to Gregory's life of Friardus (see §4), l. 59 may indicate that the poet's mind has returned to this material. At any rate, what remains of this section, ll. 60–92, describing two ways men may choose to serve God on earth, answers the question of ll. 26–9.

60 *þæs hades*. The contrast implicit between ll. 60–80 and 81–92 suggests the specialized connotation 'Holy Order' here, an interpretation borne out both by the high proportion of religious words in *Guthlac A* and by passages of censure directed at slackness in monastic life.

63 *hyhst*. The metre requires a form without contraction; see §8.

67 *eðel*, MS. *eleð*. Thorpe's metrically improbable suggestion, adopted by Klipstein, that the MS. *eleð* appears for *hæleð*, 'for the sake of the alliteration', has given way to Grein's emendation. Occasional transpositions of letters elsewhere, e.g. *Christ* 1100, *Phoenix* 64, *Vainglory* 3, can be cited in support of *eðel*. As there is no trace in OE. of a form similar to the OHG *alod*, Grein's alternative suggestion that we have here its OE. equivalent is not accepted.

69 *þæs deoran ham*. The verse is cited in GK under *wilnian* as an example of this verb used with the genitive, and under *ham* as a place where the genitive singular of the noun is to be found, an interpretation reflected in the translations (e.g. C. W. Kennedy, *The Poems of Cynewulf*, p. 265, 'these await their heavenly home' and Gordon, *Anglo-Saxon Poetry*, p. 257, 'they wait for the heavenly home'). Only one instance of *wilnian* followed by an accusative is listed in BT, BTs, and GK for the four major codices of verse (*Riddles* 49.7, where it is sometimes argued that *þa* has replaced the relative particle *þe*), but many examples occur in translations from Latin (see Wülfing, *Die Syntax in den Werken Alfreds des Grossen*, i (Bonn, 1894–1901), 33, 132, 260), indicating that, if the construction of *wilnian* and the accusative was not original to OE., at least it must have become an established alternative by the Alfredian

period. The phrase should be interpreted 'the home of that dear one', *deoran* referring back to *dryhtne* with which it is closely linked by alliteration: *ham* is nowhere recorded as an alternative genitive singular for *hames*. Although Klipstein's emendation to *hames* is metrically possible (cp. 71b, 88b, 363b, etc.), it is unnecessary.

71 *bimutad*, MS. *bimutað*. Thorpe's emendation *bemiðen* 'hidden' is taken over by Klipstein as *Bimiðne*, but later editors all make the simple graphical change from *ð* to the *d* to be expected in a passive participle. The verb **mutian* is not otherwise recorded, and the vowel quantity of the second syllable of *bimutad* must remain uncertain (for the possibility of both A and C classification see Roberts, 'A Metrical Examination', p. 95 and n. 18). Building on the passive participle of *mūtāre* would have produced a short vowel, but a long vowel might have arisen from use of the present stem. Because the common ON. noun *mūta* 'fee, bribe' < L. *mūtuum* is paralleled by the gloss *Mutuum, mutung* siue *wrixlung* (T. Wright and R. P. Wülcker, *Anglo-Saxon and Old English Vocabularies*, i (London, 2nd edn., 1884), 449.30) *ū* is selected also for this form.

72 *þa þe him*. Cp. *se þe him* 361 and see §9, p. 69.

76 *bycgað*. Thorpe's emendation to *hycgað* 'strive after' is attractive, especially as *bycgan* does not appear followed by the genitive in verse (GK note an example in *Solomon and Saturn* 203, but it is based on a mistaken reading of the MS. *hycgge* as *byccge*). The senses of *bycgan* and *sellan* are however as closely related to one another as are *wenan, wyscan*, and *hycgan*, and such arguments could almost be allowed to cancel each other out. No emendation is needed if *wuldres* is explained either as the partitive genitive or as an unconscious repetition of the case taken by the object in the preceding clause, where the order of elements is similar.

80 *þeowiaþ*. The poem contains forms from both the second and third conjugation of weak verbs. Sievers, 'Zur Rhythmik', p. 490, points out that the metre indicates a short stem vowel here. Cp. l. 502a and see Roberts, 'A Metrical Examination', pp. 112–13, for examples of similar verses.

89. *geoca*. Although cited by Malone, 'When did Middle English Begin?', pp. 110–17, as one of his two examples of inflexional levelling characteristic of Middle English in *Guthlac A*, the *-a* might here be genitive plural.

90 *witon hyra hyht mid dryhten*. The clause recalls a famous verse from *Psalms* 123:8, if not also the Gregory passage in which that verse is quoted (see also §4).

92 *alegeð* and *adreogeð*. Thorpe changes the first of these verbs to *aleogeð* (which Klipstein prints) translating l. 92a 'who never wrongs of their rewards'. Though *alecgan* 'belie' governs the accusative and takes the dative for the person to whom a pledge is given, the MS. form can be interpreted rather more simply as from *alecgan* 'deprive of, lessen'. If end-rhyme is thought desirable within the line, it can easily be obtained by substituting for *adreogeð* a form showing Anglian smoothing.

Thorpe's further suggestion that for *adreogeð* a plural present indicative form should be substituted has not gained acceptance into any conservative text, although the verbs of l. 89 and the inflexional levelling widely recognized in the Exeter Book show that his interpretation can be supported.

93 A new section begins here on the last line of fo. 33ᵛ, the preceding line being empty except for *adreogeð* which is placed at the end of it. In *MAgun* the first letter is a large capital, as high as three lines of script, with *A* slightly more than a third its size. A seventeenth-century hand has written *Guðlac* in the outer margin of fo. 34ᵛ against the first line of script, which may have influenced Thorpe in starting *The Legend of Saint Guthlac* with this fitt.

94 *þurh haligne hád.* Klaeber, in his review of Cook, *The Christ of Cynewulf*, in *JEGP*, iv (1902), 104, argues convincingly for the interpretation 'in a holy (or edifying) manner', deploring the customary equation of *hád* 94 with *clerus* as a collective (e.g. Gollancz 'by men of holy state'; MacGillivray 'The Influence of Christianity', §123, n. 1, and Kennedy, *The Poems of Cynewulf*, p. 266, 'by holy men').

108 *Hwæt we hyrdon oft.* This is the first of four formulaic phrases curiously used by commentators as evidence of the poet's dependence on oral sources. See also §4, pp. 28–9.

110 *frecnessa fela. frecnes* here and at l. 181 should be taken in the sense 'danger, peril'. Although the meaning 'gluttony' is shown for it in glosses, the interpretation of the phrase as 'many vicious courses' (Thorpe and Gollancz, and justified tenuously in KD by reference to ll. 128–32) seems both overfree and unsuitable. Guthlac is introduced in the second section of the poem as a man who had sought danger in his youth and, in the following section, the poet points out that later as a warrior under Christ's standard he again overcame many hazards.

114 ff. The doctrine that every man has two angels, one good and one bad, lies behind this passage and perhaps *Elene* 894–966 (see in particular ll. 935b–8). For a discussion of the development of this doctrine and its scriptural authority see Jean Daniélou, *Théologie du Judéo-Christianisme* (Paris, 1958), p. 144.

123 *dryhtnes dreamas.* Thorpe's interpretation 'of *the* Lord's Joy', with genitive singular *dreames*, is unnecessary. The phrase may be treated as the object of *gesittað* 122 (as Gollancz, Kennedy, and KD).

127 *scyhte.* For the infinitive **scyccan* advanced in the Glossary see SB §407, n. 12. Cognate with this preterite (found also in *Genesis* 898) are OE. *scucca*, ON. *skykkjum* (dative plural), and Middle High German *schucken*, and *Regius Psalter* 87.19 *þu ascihtest* translates *elongasti*. *Ancrene Wisse*, fo. 85a.17 *schuhteð* (ed. Tolkien EETS (OS), ccxlix (1962)), though apparently similar, is probably from an OE. **scyhtan* cognate with *scēoh*, Middle High Germany *schüchteren*, and Modern German *schüchtern*.

128 *neþinge.* This is the noun *neþing* 'daring' found also in Orosius (Sweet, *King Alfred's Orosius*, EETS (OS), lxxix (1883), 136.24) and cognate with OHG. *nendigi* and ON. *nenning*. Thorpe's emendation

niþinge 'villains', in any case difficult to interpret, would introduce into the poem a Scandinavian loanword first found in late law codes and the eleventh-century part of the Anglo-Saxon *Chronicle*.

136 *siþþam*. Is regarded as the adverb *siððan*, with levelling of *n* and *m* in unstressed syllables. Grein, 'Zur Textkritik der angelsächsischen Dichter', *Germania*, (1865), 423, suggests printing *sið þam* as an adverbial phrase and is followed by Assmann, BT, and GK; KD read *siþ þam* 'after that'.

139 *leofedan*. The meaning and etymology of this class 2 weak verb are obvious even without reference to the cognate OHG. *kiliubit* 'commendatur' cited in GK (cp. the unique example of the related weak verb class I in *Christ* 1644 *gelyfde*).

140 *on beorhge*. L. K. Shook, 'The Burial Mound', pp. 4 ff., equating the use of *beorg* in this poem with Felix's *tumulus*, attributes to it the specialized sense 'barrow, grave-mound'. This meaning for the word apparently dropped out of literary use in English before 1400, except in the northern dialects where forms of *bargh* (probably reinforced by the Old Norse *bjarg* 'rock-face') occur and in the South-West, where forms of *barrow* survive. Its continued use there to describe such topographical features as the 'barrows' of Salisbury Plain may have led to the word's being taken into archaeological and general use with the sense 'grave'. The OE. *beorg* is used both in verse and prose for 'grave, burial mound', but with contextual reinforcement for this interpretation. Its meaning, for example, is never ambiguous in *Beowulf* in the way suggested by Shook for *Guthlac A* (see K. Stjerna, 'Essays on questions connected with the Old English poem of *Beowulf*', *Viking Club Extra Series*, iii (1912), 242), and is similarly unambiguous in *Guthlac B* (e.g. ll. 1193–6). Also, it is strange that the author of *Guthlac A* should have failed to select from the large conventional vocabulary for mound- and cave-dwellings (e.g. *moldern, eorðscræf, eorðsele*) if he were closely visualizing the account of Guthlac's hermitage given by Felix.

144a Cp. ll. 209 ff. where the poet tells how the empty hills about Guthlac's dwelling-place had before his coming been the resting-places of fallen angels.

147 *bimiþen fore monnum*. The hermitage is divinely revealed in *Guthlac A*, by contrast with the help given by Tatwine in the *Vita sancti Guthlaci* and subsequent Crowland traditions.

148 *bytla*. This noun appears again at l. 733 and in another Exeter Book poem, *The Gifts of Men* 75 *bylda*. Close attention to this third instance (*Sum bið bylda til | ham to hebbanne*, MS. *habbenne*) may account for the uncertainty as to the word's meaning expressed in GK (*architectus? domus possessor?*). Occasional transposition of letters is found throughout the MS., giving support to the emendation *hebbanne*, and makes unnecessary for *bytla* the second of the equivalents put forward by Grein. Cognate are *botl, gebytlu, bytlung, bytlian*, etc.

153b ff. This is the second of the four passages thought to point to the poet's dependence on oral sources.

155–7a All who have edited this passage, except Craigie, supply an object for *weorðiað* 156 (Thorpe inserting *hine* after *þe* 155, and the others *hine* after *wundor* 156), but *his wisdomes hlisan* may serve as the object for both of the finite verbs here linked.

162 *ærendu*. In some six places the scribe (or perhaps a later reviser) indicates *u* by two short lines that slant outwards from the top of his *o* (cp. *Christ* 1280, *Guthlac* 405, 1128, 1306, and *Phoenix* 407). The MS. form of *Phoenix* 407 *wurdon* may account for Flower's statement (CFF, p. 85) that 'a hook sometimes develops at the left hand shoulder' of *o*.

167b–9 'there was too great a fear of God in his mind for him to wish to devote himself to the pursuit of pleasure in worldly grandeur'.

mara in gemyndum. The formula occurs twice again in the Exeter Book. In *Juliana* 36 it follows on a b-verse virtually identical with *Guthlac* 167b, and in *Husband's Message* 31 the adverb of comparison *þonne* also introduces a clause dependent upon this phrase. In the *Guthlac A* context the comparative should be translated by 'too' with the positive of the adjective and 'for' + infinitive substituted for the *þonne* clause (cp. the examples of the construction listed in BT under *þanne*, D. III).

menniscum þrymme. May be treated either as instrumental in function or as the object of the verb 'to serve' represented by the infinitive *þegan*.

æfter þonce. (i) The emendation *æfþonce* 'jealously' is offered by Thorpe, but although the change can be justified graphically quite convincingly, it is unnecessary. (ii) The common use of the adverbial phrase *to þonce* (e.g. *Guthlac* 125, *Andreas* 1112, etc.) suggests that *æfter þonce* may be similarly interpreted with the translation 'willingly' or 'thankfully', but no other example of *æfter* used with substantives in adverbial phrases is recorded, only the prepositional formulae containing the phrase *æfter þam* being comparable. In particular, the frequent collocation of *to þonce* with *þicgan* is advanced in support of 'willingly', *þegan* being taken as an otherwise unrecorded infinitive of *þicgan*. (iii) Kock, 'Jubilee Jaunts and Jottings', *Lunds Universitets Årsskrift*, NF Avd. 1., Bd. xiv, No. 26 (1918), 40, suggests the phrase should be translated 'to reap thanks', comparing *Genesis* 282 *æfter his hyldo ðeowian*, *Genesis* 2284 *dreogan æfter dugeðum*, *Genesis* 291, 2155, etc. This originally local preposition, with the sense 'in order to obtain', after many verbs denotes the direction of an enquiry or the turn of one's desires (see also *Beowulf* 1720, 2179, and Wülfing, *Die Syntax in den Werken Alfreds des Grossen*, ii (1901), §614a for many examples in Alfredian prose). The interpretation to be found in BT under *þanc* III(a) 'following the dictates of pleasure' indicates the meaning which *þonc* should here be given: instead of Kock's 'to reap thanks' is suggested 'in order to obtain pleasure', with *menniscum þrymme* as the object of *þegan* 'to devote oneself to'. (iv) With *menniscum þrymme* as an instrumental phrase, *æfter þonce* may be regarded as the object of *þegan* 'to devote oneself to' (cp. ll. 128b–9a *þurh neþinge wunne æfter worulde*).

þegan. Two interpretations of this otherwise unknown infinitive

form are put forward. (i) The form may represent an alternative strong infinitive for *þicgan* (see BT under *þegan*, where the passage is translated 'for him to wish to get human glory'). But as neither *þicgan* nor *þecgan* (to which *þegan* could be attributed as a late form with simplification of *cg* to *g*) governs the dative, the interpretation is unlikely. It should be noted that Thorpe's 'of human grandeur . . . would partake' cannot be followed unless radical emendation of *menniscum þrymme* to a genitive is made. (ii) Cosijn, 'Anglosaxonica. IV', p. 116, suggests *þegan* is a by-form of *þeowan* 'serve', an interpretation followed in GK and by KD; the verb may be regarded as governing the dative or as followed by *æfter* (see n. on *menniscum þrymme*, above). Cosijn points out that this verb shows traces characteristic of weak verbs of the third class and suggests that beside *þeowan* there must once have been **þeogan*; he notes also that both *ō*- and *ē*-stem weak verb forms are represented in these poems. This *þegan* may be the result of Mercian smoothing from Cosijn's **þeogan*, and *þigað* 461 may similarly reflect the smoothing of *io*. Both forms reflect the fairly common alternation of *g* and *w* in Germanic. H. M. Flasdieck, 'Untersuchungen über die germanischen schwachen Verben III. Klasse (unter besonderer Berücksichtigung des Altenglischen', *Anglia*, lix (1935), 54–6, does not include the *Guthlac A* forms in his discussion of *þĕowian*.

170 *God.* Begins a new section on the fourth line of fo. 34ʳ, heavy punctuation occurring after the last word on the second line and the third being left free. The initial capital *G* stretches from the third to the fifth line and *od* are enlarged minuscules.

173 *feara sum.* Guthlac's essential solitariness is emphasized throughout the poem, so the phrase should here be interpreted 'one of a few', i.e. 'alone'. Comparison with the litotes of *Beowulf* 3061 might point to the interpretation 'a very great man'.

176 *ondwiges heard*, MS. *7wiges heard.* The alliteration shows that 7 is the first element of a compound; *o* is preferred in expansion to *a* which appears only rarely before a nasal consonant in the MS.

177 ff. Thorpe estimates that several lines have fallen out after *wæpnum*, but it is now generally accepted that not more than a couple of words are missing. The older editors place *wæpnum* at the end of l. 177b, take *wong bletsade* as l. 178a, and supply a clause or phrase for l. 178b, e.g. *þa he waldendes beacen* (Grein), *syððan he wuldres beam* (Cremer, *Metrische und sprachliche Untersuchung der altenglischen Gedichte Andreas, Gûðlâc, Phoenix* (*Elene, Juliana, Crist*) (Bonn, 1888), p. 50), and *waldendes tacn* (Cosijn, 'Anglosaxonica. IV', p. 116), producing in l. 177b a rare verse pattern more suitable in the first half of the line (*mid* must be regarded as a syllable of anacrusis, so the occurrence of such a b-verse is unlikely except in a hypermetrical passage). Assmann, Gollancz, and Craigie print *wong bletsade* alone on one line, but, whether or not single verses were purposely composed by Anglo-Saxon poets, there is no other instance in this poem. In the KD text *wæpnum* is placed at the beginning of l. 178 and a lacuna marked by asterisks, an arrangement following the division of the text suggested

by Trautmann, 'Zur Berichtigung und Erklärung der Waldhere-Bruch-stücke', *Beiträge*, v (1900), 174, who supplies *ond wordum* and by Holt-hausen, *Beiblatt*, ix (1899), 356, who supplies *Guðlac*. The stop-gap 7 *wædum* adopted in this edition is metrically like Trautmann's but reflects verses from Ephesians 6 which the poet could have had in mind. Similar phrases occur in *Beowulf* 292 *wæpen ond gewædu* and *Beowulf* 39 *hildewæpnum ond heaðowædum*, and omission might easily have arisen through the likeness of the words in shape.

179 *him to ætstælle*. F. Norman, *Waldere* (London, 1933), p. 38, following Müllenhoff's identification of the meaning of the word with German *Anstand* and *Antritt* in fencing, suggests for *Waldere I* 21 *æt ðam ætstealle* 'at the place where the other man has taken up position', i.e. a place which will be of advantage to one's opponent, because the phrase is followed by *oðres monnes*; but *monnes* can alternatively be linked with *wigrædenne* 22, paralleling *æniges monnes / wig* 14–15, and cannot be accepted as proving so restricted a sense in this context. In *Guthlac A* the position is clearly chosen by the saint himself. The phrase 7 *swa on ætstealles beorh* generally cited from an eleventh-century Portesham charter as containing a third instance of this form is more likely to represent *Stalborough* (see Rune Forsberg, '*Ætstealles beorh* A Place-Name Crux Reconsidered', *Studia Neophilologica*, xlv (1973), 3–19, who points out that there is therefore no evidence for *ætsteall* from place-names). Translations such as 'refection place' (Thorpe), 'as his help' (Gordon, *Anglo-Saxon Poetry*, p. 259) or 'to mark his standard' (Shook, 'The Prologue', p. 7) supply more than is here implicit, and Gollancz's 'to mark his station' is to be preferred. An alternative explanation, first mooted in the notes of Trautmann and Holthausen and accepted by BTs, depends upon taking the phrase with the preceding clause in the sense 'as his station', but seems less satisfactory.

180 *Cristes rode*. An eighth-century Irish canon required a cross to be set up on all consecrated ground (see W. O. Stevens, *The Cross in the Life and Literature of the Anglo-Saxons* (New York, 1904), pp. 57–9) and this may well have been the custom in England too, for Stevens points out that St. Botulf and his companions first set up their cross before doing anything else when founding Icanhoe.

181 *frecnessa fela*. See n. for l. 110. Here, because the phrase follows so closely upon *lorica* imagery, it may recall Ephesians 6: 11 *insidias diaboli*.

182 *þæs Guðlaces*, MS. *þæs guð lace*. Thorpe and Gollancz apparently treat *Guðlace* as a possessive dative, despite the absence of any preposition to support such an interpretation. Malone, in his review of Schaar's *Critical Studies* in *Anglia*, lxx (1951), 446, explains *Guðlace* as a dative of accompaniment, translating 'we and Guthlac ascribe to the Lord the valuable part of that . . .', but such a construction is not found in OE. Schaar, *Critical Studies*, p. 79, argues that a comma should be placed after *dæl* and that both *Guðlace* and *dryhtne* are dependent on *cennað*, but reads too much into the text with his explanation: 'In this way we get the connection between *Frome wurdun monge godes þrowera* and

the rest: many of God's martyrs became bold, and we ascribe a considerable share in this fact to Guthlac, as a model, and to the Lord,
because the latter *him sige sealde ond snyttrucræft.*' Emendation seems
needed. Cosijn, 'Anglosaxonica. IV', p. 116, supplies *eac* before *dryhtne*,
'nächst gott', an emendation perhaps suggested by l. 206. Although
Holthausen, in his review of Assmann, *Beiblatt*, ix (1899), 356, rejects
this on metrical grounds, it must be noted that there are other examples
of A-type verses with anacrusis in the second half-line in this poem.
Holthausen, 'Zu den AE. Gedichten der HS. von Vercelli', *Anglia*,
lxxiii (1955), 277, later suggests inserting *mid* before *Guðlace*. The
simpler change to a genitive *Guðlaces* is here followed, as in KD. It is
unnecessary to read a common noun 'of this warfare' with Kock,
'Jubilee Jaunts', p. 41, though it may well be that the author is indulging
in word-play (see F. C. Robinson, 'The Significance of Names in Old
English Literature', *Anglia*, lxxxvi (1968), 46–7); *þæs* as a specifying
genitive in agreement with *Guðlaces* would allow this pun. For *dæl*
'part, way of life', cp. Luke 10: 42, *þæne selestan dæl* (W. W. Skeat,
The Holy Gospels (Cambridge, 1871–7), Corpus Christi College,
Cambridge MS. 140).

191 *feðehwearfum.* The first element in this *hapax legomenon* is
probably *feðe* 'foot, going on foot' rather than *feða* 'infantry', which
is not used initially in compounds. The only other examples of *hwearf*
'troop' in OE. are *Guthlac* 263, *Judith* 249 *hwearfum*, and a form
sometimes retained in *Battle of Finnsburh* 34; in Middle English it is
used by Laȝamon and there are many West Germanic cognates (see
OED under WHARF, sb. 2).

197 *his sibbe ryht.* Translations such as Gollancz's 'the claims of kin'
are rather vague and take no account of *his*. The phrase, understood as
'his kinship dues', could imply either rights of inheritance (the more
likely interpretation) or duties owed to relatives. As Felix in his account
of Guthlac's conversion tells us that he turned aside both from *patria*
and leadership (§xix), we cannot refer to him for help in restricting the
phrase either to possessions or duties. For the simplex *riht* used with
similar connotations see BT under *riht*, IV and V and GK under *riht*,
2 and 3.

206 *eac Gode sylfum.* There is no need to treat *eac* as an adverb, as in
Thorpe or Shook, 'The Prologue', p. 303. It is a preposition governing
the dative, both in verse (cp. *Battle of Maldon* 11, *Genesis* 2502, and *eac
þon* (*þe*) of *Wife's Lament* 44 and *Aldhelm* 10) and prose (see Wülfing,
Die Syntax, ii. 658–9).

209 *beorgas bræce.* Thorpe's '*the* mountain occupied' is rightly
ignored by later commentators, as neither *bræce* nor his suggested
breace are forms of *brucan* 'use, possess'. The form *bræce* is the preterite
subjunctive singular of *brecan* 'break into' (see BT under *brecan*, I(3)
and BTs under *brecan*, I(4)). Shook's *beorgas* 'the barrows' ('The
Prologue', p. 306) reads more into the text than is justifiable (see also
n. for l. 140).

hy, MS. *he. he* appears occasionally for the nominative plural in OE.

(esp. in the *Regius Psalter* gloss, according to Campbell, §703), but as *hy* and *hi* and less often *hio* and *heo* are the usual forms of this MS. an emendation is chosen here. Thorpe prints *hy* without note, so *hy* appears also in Grein's text; the scribal *he* is recognized only after Schipper's collation, 'Zum Codex Exoniensis', *Germania*, xix (1874), 330. The appearance of *he* in the preceding clause may have led to a mistaken *he* here.

213 *restan ryneþragum. restan* is ambiguous. It may be regarded as a finite verb in a series of co-ordinate clauses (as Thorpe, 'rested *a* space of time'), but is better read as an infinitive after *cwoman*. The meaning of *ryneþragum* is uncertain. The base *þrag* can be interpreted either as 'run, course' or 'space of time'. Thorpe's 'a space of time' is followed in BT, whereas GK suggest *cursus*. Kock, 'Jubilee Jaunts', p. 42, stating that because the original meaning of *þrag* had almost been supplanted 'only a tautological compound like *ryneþrag* would express, unambiguously, the primary idea', manipulates the syntax to produce the translation 'when from their wanderings and races they, weary, came to rest'. There is no need to regard the compound as tautologous, for in *Riddles* 3.58 *rynegiestes* and *Paris Psalter* 19.7 *On rynewǣnum* (J. W. Bright and R. L. Ramsay, *The West-Saxon Psalms* (Boston and London, 1907), p. 41), the element *ryne-* can be translated 'swift'. The translation 'to rest for swift intervals' is attractive, especially in view of Shook's observation that the passage reflects 'the respite theme which is fairly common in apocryphal writings' ('The Prologue', pp. 303–4). Although Shook points out that the poet is here referring to demons rather than the souls of men who have been sinners on earth, the comparison tips the balance in favour of a translation like his 'to rest betimes'.

rowe. row 'quiet' as a noun occurs only here; the nominative singular masculine adjective *row* appears in the *Cura Pastoralis* (Sweet, i (1871) 71.19). Cognate are OHG. *ruowa* and ON. *ró*. The Middle English examples of *ro* in North Midland texts are ON. borrowings (see M. S. Serjeantson, *A History of Foreign Words in English* (London, 1935), pp. 83, 96).

216 *eþelriehte feor. eþelriht* occurs otherwise in *Beowulf* 2198 where it varies *lond* and *eard*, and in *Exodus* 211 where it refers to the promised land; a translation such as 'far from ancestral domain' is therefore suggested. In early Anglo-Saxon England the fens seem to have formed a march-land between Mercia and East Anglia. In Guthlac's times they may well have been desolate, inhabited in only a few scattered places, for Bede describes Ely as surrounded by water and the eighth-century 'Tribal Hidage' indicates that all this region was then lightly populated (see further H. C. Darby, *The Medieval Fenland* (Cambridge, 1940), pp. 7 ff.).

217 *bisæce.* This nonceword is generally explained as either *besēc 'visitation, approach' (e.g. Thorpe, BTs, GK, Williams, KD) or *bisǣt 'taking possession' (with *c* a misreading of *t*—the suggestion of Klaeber, 'Emendations in Old English Poems', *Mod Phil.*, ii (1904), 143). The

existence however in laws and charters of an adjective *bīsæc* 'disputed, contested' and of a passive participle *unbesacen* 'unmolested by litigation, uncontested' suggests its identification as **bīsacu*, 'dispute' (the word may be an additional example of legal terminology in this poem).

218 *ealdfeondas*. Sievers, 'Zur Rhythmik', p. 483, points out that the use of -*as* plurals in *feond* (cp. *feondas* 421) distinguishes *Guthlac A* from the other poems often connected with Cynewulf.

225 *earfeða*. Grein's *earfeðum* is unnecessary. For the intransitive use of *geryman* + *to* 'clear a way to', see BTs under *gerȳman* IV.

229 *hleahtor alegdon*. The striking euphemism of *Beowulf* 3020 is here literal.

235 *deaþa gedal*. Cosijn, 'Anglosaxonica. IV', p. 116, compares the compound *deaðgedal*, but points out that *deaþa* may be a genitive singular from the old *u*-declension (see SB §273 for *u* stem remainders for this noun, older **dauþus*). Elsewhere in *Guthlac A* the word *gedal* appears only as a base element in compounds, but cp. *Phoenix* 651 *þurh his lices gedal*, *Beowulf* 3068 *worulde gedal*, etc.

236 *laþran gemotes*. Cp. *Riddles* 5.10a.

245 *geðringan*. MS. *gedrin | gan* with the second *g* altered from *c*. Although Thorpe records the manuscript *d*, both he and Grein present the emendation *þ* rather than the graphically simpler *ð* of later editors.

246 *fealóg*. This *hapax legomenon* is paralleled by the OHG. *fō(h)-lōgi* cited in GK and BTs. Like the better-represented *fēasceaft* it seems to have had the meaning 'poor, destitute'. The phrase *on his loh* replaces *on his steall* in two MSS. in the *Chronicle* entry for 693, and the related weak verb (*ge*)*lōgian* occurs somewhat more frequently. Stratmann and Bradley, *A Middle English Dictionary* (Oxford, 1891), under *lōȝ*, *looȝ*, list cognate nouns from West Germanic, pointing out that this word is used by William de Shoreham in the sense 'place'; further Middle English examples are grouped under LŌGH n. in *MED*.

251 *hleonað*. This nonceword is often connected with the verb *hlinian* 'lie down' (e.g. GK translate *reclinatorium cubile* and give an incorrect long vowel in the stressed syllable, BT 'a place to lie down in', Gollancz 'a resting-place'), but the BTs explanation of the form as from *hlēo(w)* 'protection' with the addition of the suffix -*noþ* (cp. Kennedy, *The Poems of Cynewulf*, p. 270, 'place of refuge') seems more likely. Another *hapax legomenon* with the same suffix is found in l. 757 *trumnaþe*.

252 *tweoþ*. With MS. emendation from *w* to *þ*: The metre indicates that *tweoþ* is to be decontracted for reading aloud (see §8, p. 59).

262 *ðA*. A new section begins here with a large capital accompanied by a smaller one; the preceding line is empty to mark this division except for *les eower leng:7* at the end. As the next MS. indication of a new section does not occur until l. 404 it is likely that a similar break occurred within the folio lost between fos. 37 and 38 (i.e. ll. 368–9).

263 *hwearfum*. Although it might be argued that the adverbial use of the noun here allows it to be placed in the introductory dip of the verse (as Roberts, 'A Metrical Examination', p. 127), it must be noted that the form alliterates on *w* in *Judith* 249.

268 *in gelimpe*. Interpretations such as the BT 'in chance', Gollancz's 'in changeful state', and Gordon's 'amid change' are contextually unsatisfactory. Cosijn, 'Anglosaxonica. IV', p. 116, citing the passages under *gelimp* IIa 'good fortune, success' in BTs, puts forward 'prosperity', apparently followed by Kennedy, *The Poems of Cynewulf*, p. 271, 'in happy issues'.

271 *us*, MS. *hus*. Comparable insertion of *h* before a vowel without metrical stress is found in *Juliana* 545 *is* (MS. *his*).

272 *eart ðe*. *ðe* may be either an unusual reduction of *ðu* (apparently the interpretation of Grein, Assmann, and Gollancz) or a form reduced from *ðeah* 'however' (cp. *þe* 290 which may however be an oblique form of the pronoun). KD transpose *eart* and *ðe* which, in its new position, might be the relative particle, but in their commentary seem to favour *ðe* 'although' by advancing for comparison *þeah þu lond age* 273; alternatively they suggest a reflexive *ðe*.

274 *mose*. Generally recognized as an oblique form of *mōs* 'food, nourishment', a word found both in verse and prose. Shook, 'The Burial Mound', p. 5, translates *mose* 'in the marsh'; but *mos* 'bog', from which his suggestion derives, has a short vowel and would thus be metrically improbable here and unparalleled in this text. (Moreover, it does not appear in OE. poetry and is first found in late charters.)

285 *inðriceð*. With MS. emendation of first *ð* from *d* and erasure after second *i*. Apparently both here and with *geðringan* 245 the scribe started to write *-drincan*.

287 *breodwiað*. Thorpe's 'drive hence', explained as from *bredan*, cannot be accepted as that verb has a long stem vowel. The verb to which *breodwiað* belongs is represented in *Beowulf* 2619 *abredwade* and *Hildebrandslied* 54 *bretōn*. The OHG. **brëtōn* is generally interpreted 'niederstrecken, schlagen' (see W. Braune and E. A. Ebbinghaus, *Althochdeutsches Lesebuch* (Tübingen, 15th edn., 1969), p. 186), meanings suitable in this passage, whereas the *Beowulf* form is generally glossed 'kill, slay', the intensive prefix accounting for the greater force of *abredwade*.

288 *tergað*. Thorpe's *terað*, followed in the translations of Gollancz, Kennedy, and Gordon, is an unnecessary emendation, for *tergað* is from the weak verb class I *tierwan* 'insult, torment' (cp. *Andreas* 963 *tyrgdon* and see GK under *tyrgan*, BT under *tirgan*, and *OED* under TAR v.[2]).

290 *þe*. See n. for l. 272.

292-3 In previous editions *on ondsware 7 on elne strong* is punctuated as if part of the clause *hine God fremede*, although in such an arrangement *strong* might be expected to have the accusative *-ne* ending. To retain this order haplography could be advanced in support of an emended *strongne*, but with *hine God fremede* placed in parenthesis the emendation is unnecessary.

298 *wærlogan*. Etymologically the word means 'faith-falsifier', and already in OE. it is used especially of the devil and his associates (see *OED* under WARLOCK sb. 1 and 2). The compound appears only once outside OE., applied to the Pharisees in *Heliand* 3816 *te huî gi uuârlogon*

(O. Behaghel, *Heliand und Genesis* (Halle, 6th edn., 1948)). The *OED* examination of the English forms suggests that the word extended also to: '3. A savage or monstrous creature (hostile to men). The word is applied to giants, cannibals, mythic beasts, etc. *Obs.*' in the Anglo-Saxon period, though a survey of the forms listed in BT and GK does not support this assumption. Indeed, the one OE. instance cited under this head in *OED*, from *Genesis* 1266, refers to the people who lived before the flood, and they had broken God's covenant. The Mermedonians, to whom the word is applied by the *Andreas* poet, were treaty-breakers as well as cannibals. Otherwise the earliest instance of this development is fourteenth century, and it might therefore be taken as closely related to the *OED* sense 4 'One in league with the Devil and so possessing occult and evil powers . . .' (a fourteenth-century development). It is unlikely that *wærloga* had any of its later reference to witchcraft in the OE. period; its later semantic development can be attributed to the growing interest of Englishmen, particularly from the twelfth century, in tales of the occult (see Crawford, 'Evidences for Witchcraft in Anglo-Saxon England', *MÆ*, xxxii (1963), 96–116). The final sound of the modern form *warlock* seems first to have been in use in sixteenth century Scotland and is difficult to explain, unless as due to the influence of some other word within the same semantic field.

299 *abonne*, MS. *abunne*. Thorpe's translation 'banish' is possible only in a non-continuous Modern English version, and later editors emend in a suitable form of *abannan* 'summon'. Though *abanne* is usually adopted because of the confusion between *u* and open-topped *a* often found in OE. MSS., here Assmann's *abonne* is adopted, first because *o* predominates before nasal consonants in this MS. and secondly because confusion of *o* and *u* may be a sporadic feature of the Exeter Book (cp. n. for l. 18).

300 *widor sæce*. Thorpe wishes to emend *wiðersæc* into his text on the analogy of *Elene* 569 *wiðersæc*, a suggestion adopted by Grein in his *Bibliothek*, though later ('Zur Textkritik der angelsächsischen Dichter', *Germania*, x (1865), 423) he returns to the simpler MS. reading which does not require adding *ic* before *eow* or reading 7 in the sense 'against'. For the short unresolved second stress in this A-type verse, well attested as a sporadic feature of OE. poetry, see Roberts, 'A Metrical Examination', p. 114.

301 *áteoð*. Metrically a form without contraction is needed here (see §8, p. 59).

308 *earda*. There is a general unwillingness to accept Guthlac's words as ironical at this point, Grein suggesting *earfeða* as the true reading and Cosijn, 'Anglosaxonica. IV', p. 116, advancing an alternative *earmða* (citing *ermþu* 447 in support). KD remark laconically, '"Many dwelling places"—presumably other than the one he has chosen'.

311b–12a Because *wealdan* may govern either the genitive or dative two translations are possible. Although an adverbial interpretation of *weorcum* is fairly widespread (e.g. Thorpe, BT under *weorc* V(b), GK under *wealdan*, Gollancz, and Kennedy), here Gordon's translation

(*Anglo-Saxon Poetry*, p. 261) 'who governs the works of all mighty things' is preferred.

313 *leofes gelong*. Cp. *Beowulf* 2150a *lissa gelong*. Such verses occur sporadically in most long OE. poems (see Klaeber, *Beowulf*, p. 279, and Roberts, 'A Metrical Examination', p. 112). The construction *gelong æt* 'dependent upon' appears also in *Beowulf* 1376–7 and *Wife's Lament* 45.

317 *sealdun*. Thorpe's 'have inflicted' imposes an awkward shift in sequence of tenses. Grein's *raro* is now followed, Cosijn 'Anglosaxonica. IV', p. 116, pointing out that here the adverb should be interpreted *niemals* (like *Vǫluspá* 26.3 *sialdan*); in both litotes accounts for this use of the word.

333 *anade*. The word, apparently from *ān* + Germanic **odus*, occurs again in l. 356 and otherwise only in *Riddles* 60.5. Cognate are OS. *enodi*, OHG. *einoti* and Modern German *Einöde*.

342 *æreste*. Thorpe's attractive translation 'vigils' (as the subject of *binoman* and varied by the following verse) cannot be justified. The form is sometimes regarded as instrumental (e.g. Gordon, *Anglo-Saxon Poetry*, p. 261, 'at his rising up'), but less strained is its usual explanation as a genitive dependent upon *elne* (e.g. Gollancz, 'his power of rising'). The medial syllable *e* shows lowering from *i* under reduced stress.

343 *slæpa sluman*. Though no other plural forms of *slæp* are recorded for OE., this is hardly sufficient reason to adopt Thorpe's *slæpes*. However, given that the next word begins with *s*, it is interesting that Malone ('When did Middle English Begin?') should note *slæpa* as having -*a* for -*es*.

349 *flygereowe*. The form may be treated either as a compound or as two separate words (e.g. Thorpe's 'in flight *the* cruel *ones*'), but it would be perverse not to accept a compound with BT, GK, Grein, Assmann, and KD. The base element, used frequently in verse compounds, remains a feature of late OE. homilies, and *flyge*- occurs as the first element of *Vainglory* 27 *fligepilum*.

360 *Oft worde bicwæð*. Gollancz's 'oft by word addressed him' implies the following lines were spoken to an angel sent to Guthlac by God, but 'him' is a detail not found in the text. The phrase *worde bicwæð*, its verb varying according to context, is probably formulaic: cp. *Andreas* 193, 210, 304, 418.

361 *se þe him*. Cp. *þa þe him* 72 and see §9, p. 69.

365a *ne lete him ealdfeond*. The verse is metrically ambiguous (either A3 or C). Cp. n. for *ealdfeonda* 475a.

368 At this point a break occurs in the poem. A folio is missing, one of several leaves lost from the interior of the Exeter Book. A strip remains, the fold belonging to fo. 44, sticking out before fo. 38ʳ. Förster (CFF, p. 57) assumes that this leaf was cut out clumsily. It must have contained some sixty verse lines, probably continuing the speech begun in l. 361. As *Guthlac A* is divided into sections of about a hundred lines it is likely that a new fitt began very near the top of the recto of the missing folio. This supposition need not indicate an interruption in

Guthlac's speech, for later in the poem his profession of faith runs over from one section into another (ll. 592 ff.).

369 *ær oþþe sið*. Some particle(s) may have been lost from the head of this verse, though it can be scanned as it stands (see Roberts, 'A Metrical Examination', p. 115).

371–2a Thorpe's emendation *deaðe* only partly supports his translation 'by death be sever'd'. The verb *gedælan* is here used with the preposition *wið* (see BT under *wiþ* III(3)) and the passage runs 'My body cannot separate death from this fleeting creation . . .' (cp. Cosijn, 'Anglosaxonica. IV', p. 116). A conflicting interpretation appears in BT under *gedælan*, where the clause is improperly excerpted: 'my body cannot separate [itself] from [*i.e.* avoid] death'.

377 *sarum forsæcen*. A similar phrase occurs in *Elene* 932 *sarum gesoht*, suggesting that the verb base is here *sēcan* 'seek with hostile intent' (BT III); there is no other instance with the intensive prefix *for-*.

382 *fægran*. An unsyncopated comparative is needed by the metre. Cp. 748b and see §8, p. 59.

384 *duge*, MS. *buge*. Thorpe suggests for 384b *þonne hine man buge* 'when it *a* man inhabits'. An ingenious attempt to support the MS. *buge* is made by Shook, 'The Burial Mound', p. 7: 'The shelter of this barrow is such (lit. not less nor more than that) that it 'bows' (i.e. makes stooped) the man who lives daily [in it] in discomfort according to God's will', but the translation of *þonne* is unsatisfactory and no parallels can be adduced for the use of the intransitive *būgan* with the dative. Grein first suggested the generally accepted emendation *duge*, an impersonal use suited to the context. As there is little evidence for the confusion of *b* and *d* in OE. MSS., it is likely that the scribe dittographed *b* from the alliterating sounds of the preceding line.

387 *mare*. Grein suggests the emendation *ma ne*, but the adverbial use of the accusative singular neuter of the comparative is well attested (see GK under *māra*) and a negative particle is not necessary before the infinitive *gelufian*.

389 *lade*. *lad* in the sense 'means of sustenance, provision' does not otherwise appear in OE. verse but may be compared with the phrase *cyrcan lād* used in the charters of Oswald, Bishop of Worcester (see BTs *lād*[1] under IV). This meaning survives in Middle English in the compound *lyflode*, *lyvelode* (see *OED* under LIVELIHOOD for its later history).

390–2a 'then again as before the hate of old foes was hot, cries for a time gave vent to a second outburst of hate, when to the heavens rose the clamour of fiends'. This interpretation, which appears in BTs, requires least possible emendation. The context shows that a passive participle should replace *onwylleð* and the alliteration demands *woð*; *oþerne* is referred back to *nið* and *lythwon* understood as an adverb of time.

onwylled, MS. *onwylleð*. Thorpe's translation 'waken'd' is supported by a tentative emendation to *onweced*. Later editors are satisfied with the graphically simple change to *onwylled* (the simplex *wyllan* 'boil' is also used figuratively).

woð oþerne, MS. *soð oþerne*. The emendation from *soð* to *woð*, first made by Thorpe, is adopted in all subsequent editions. Thorpe also completes this measure with *oþerne*, but the later editors place *ne* at the head of l. 392. Only Gollancz fills up the gap this arrangement leaves in l. 391b, adding *þær* after *oþer* (presumably on the grounds of haplography), a solution approved by Cosijn, 'Anglosaxonica. IV', p. 117. Sievers, 'Zur Rhythmik', p. 517, objects to both verses in the division *woð ôðer / ne lythwôn leôðode*, inclining towards Thorpe's *oðerne* and noting his preference for *lĕoðode*.

lythwon leoðode. Thorpe's 'a while resounded' may perhaps explain the appearance in many OE. dictionaries of a ghost word *lēoðian* 'sing, sound'. Though a plausible invention (cp. *lēoð* 'song', Gothic *liuþôn* 'sing', and OHG. *liudôn* 'sing, rejoice'), its appearance in BT as the verb of this passage and of *Riming Poem* 40 *leoþode* is mistaken. In the latter the rhyming word *freoðode* points to *ĕo*. Two etymologies are possible for **liðian*. In GK and *AEW* it is glossed *führen* and connected with *Riming Poem* 14 *leoþu*(?) 'ship, band of men' (see *OED* under LITH sb[3] and sb[4] for Scandinavian origin and Middle English use), *līþan* 'sail', and OS. *liðôn*; and the GK entry *lēoðian* is given a short vowel in Holthausen's emendations at the end of the dictionary. Alternatively **liðian* may be thought closer to *lið* 'limb', and these *Guthlac A* and *Riming Poem* forms considered the only instances of the simplex found otherwise with the prefixes *ā*, *ge-*, *on-*, and *to-*, e.g. *Genesis* 177 *aleoðode*, *Soul and Body II* 103 *tohleoþode*. It seems pointless to argue the merits of such closely related etymologies when the meaning found for *geliðian* 'unloose, release' satisfies both contexts.

393 *ceargesta*. Either *gæst* 'visitor' (with non-WS. *i*-mutation of *æ/ea*, see Campbell, §188) or *gǣst* 'spirit, ghost' (with Anglian *e* for *ǣ*, see §9, p. 65) may be reflected in this nonceword. R. A. Peters, 'OE. "ceargest"', *Notes and Queries*, ccvii (1960), 167, unable to find 'a single example of OE. *gǣst* written as *gest*' in poetry, prose, glosses, or place-names, interprets this compound 'sorrowful visitor'. Some such meaning as 'woeful demon' is supported by the equivalents in BT and GK.

397 *se hyra gæst*. For the use of the comparative without explicit contextual comparison see for example *Daniel* 206 *hæftas hearan*.

398 *þeara*: see §9, p. 65.

400b-3 Thorpe places *se* in the same verse as *an oretta* and takes *ge* and *cyðeð* separately, translating ll. 400b-2a 'which was greater than / he whom a hero, in our times, / a champion, ye call'. With *an* changed to *on*, *gecyðeð* to *gecyðed*, and *þæt* to *þæs*, Kemble (see Thorpe, p. 504) suggests 'Who was greater than he in battle, in our times, a champion illustrious; therefore, etc.': his 'in battle' for l. 401a, not unsuitable metrically, recalls phrases found in *Widsith* 41 *on orette* and *Exodus* 313 *an on orette* (Krapp's text omits *an*). Grein, placing *se* before *an oretta* in l. 401a, inserts *he* after *þonne* to fill l. 400b, an arrangement followed by Assmann. Gollancz's translation, assuming a pronoun directly after *þonne* 400b, is at odds with his placing of *se* before *an*

oretta in l. 401a: 'What man was greater than he, / the one hero, the one champion, / known in our times...' Holthausen (*Beiblatt*, ix (1899), 356) prefers Gollancz's lineation to Assmann's and suggests reading *ma* for *mara* to avoid an A-type with two syllables of anacrusis in the *b*-verse. Craigie presents a compromise between the Grein and Gollancz approaches, adding [*he*]? after *þonne* to complete l. 400b and emending *gecyðeð* 402 to *gecyðed*.

No emendation is made in the KD text where *þonne se?* ends l. 400b, a new sentence beginning with the following line; they note that the verse *se an oretta* often put forward is 'metrically unusual' and that *se* is unnecessary to it. Schaar, *Critical Studies*, p. 81, objects to this conservative arrangement, presenting instead the syntactically unusual *A ne oretta* 'Never does warrior' and retaining *gecyðeð* with the explanation that *þonne* (*Christ*) *Guthlace gecyðde* can be easily supplied. He argues that *ma* gives doubtful sense because Guthlac's miracles have not yet been mentioned, and that in his reading *oretta* 'does not refer to the hero of the poem'—but poet and audience would have been familiar with the deeds of so popular a saint. His tortuous reading is further elaborated by Malone (in his review of Schaar's monograph, *Anglia*, lxx (1951), 446) who assumes elision rather than Schaar's 'restoration of a lost letter', proposing *a n'oretta*. The KD arrangement freely translated runs: 'What man was greater than he? One hero, a champion, in our times testifies that Christ manifested in his sight more miracles on earth.' Any attempt to introduce Kemble's *gecyðed* into l. 402 produces a clause without finite verb and makes some change in the conjunction *þæt* necessary; emendation from *gecyðeð* to *gecyðde*, though attractive, is unnecessary as *ussum tidum* stands in the same clause.

404 *HE*. A new section begins here on the fifth line of fo. 38ᵛ. The preceding line is empty, except for *gecyðde:7* at the end. *H* is a large capital and *E* the height of the tallest ascenders of the script. In those editions and translations where the fitt divisions are retained, this is numbered V (e.g. by Gollancz), but should be numbered VI to allow for the lacuna between ll. 368 and 369.

405 *onfengum*. With MS. emendation from *o* to *u* in the final syllable. See n. for *ærendu* 162.

406 *reowe*. Two adjectives which to a certain extent overlap in meaning, *rēow* 'fierce' and *hrēoh* 'rough', appear to have influenced one another, the amalgam *hreow* being much used, especially as the second element in compounds (e.g. *wælhreow* and its derivatives). The simplex *rēow* 'fierce' occurs four times in poetry, always alliterating on *r*: cp. *Juliana* 481 *reone* (with absence of *-w-* which should extend throughout the paradigm), *Andreas* 1116 *hreow* and 1334 *reowe*.

408 *sawl*. Is here and at l. 535 metrically disyllabic.

409 *se*. Is reduced from *swa*, as in *Guthlac B* 961. Though the reduction has been considered Kentish in the OE. period (K. D. Bülbring, *Altenglisches Elementarbuch* (*Lautlehre*) (Heidelberg, 1902), §562), the evidence is poor and it is best to regard the reduction as a late scribal feature.

411 *7 þæt frið*. Cosijn, 'Anglosaxonica. IV', p. 117, suggests reading *ac þæt ferð* and treating ll. 409b–10 as a parenthetical clause, but the emendation is unnecessary. l. 411 is a second noun clause, co-ordinate with the clause of l. 410.

412 ff. The poet does not, as Whitelock, *The Beginnings of English Society* (London, 1952), p. 172, suggests, go 'out of his way to create an opportunity to rail at the slackness in monasteries in respect of vigils and prayers', for the theme is already foreshadowed in ll. 60 ff. He criticizes laxities in monastic discipline constructively, explaining that the basic reason for such behaviour is immaturity and forecasting that time will bring wisdom to these erring monks. Other passages within the poem suggest it was made for a monastic audience, especially ll. 460–6. Churchmen found much to criticize in the state of monasteries, even before the Danish attacks on England began, and the *Guthlac A* author is unusual only in regarding such a theme as suitable for vernacular poetry. His concern is perhaps shared by the late poet of *The Seasons for Fasting* which contains a lively account of priestly gluttony (ll. 208–20, singled out by D. Whitelock, 'Anglo-Saxon Poetry and the Historian', *Transactions of the Royal Historical Society*, 4th series, xxxi (1949), 93). No close analogue can be found for this temptation of Guthlac or for his compassionate defence of *geongra monna* 490 who are censured by the devils.

hean. Holthausen, in his review of Assmann, *Beiblatt*, ix (1899), 356, notes that metrically some such form as **hēa[a]n* is needed here; see also §8, p. 59.

415 *hyrda*. The word has the figurative sense normally associated with the L. *pastor*.

420 *þæs ealdres*. There is no general agreement as to the meaning of this phrase. Identifying *ealdor* as the neuter noun 'life', BT produce the unsatisfactory 'so is the wont of youth, where fear of death checks not'. GK suggest the word is to be taken in the sense 'old age', no doubt reflected in Grein's *des Alters* and Kennedy's 'old age', but there are no parallels to support this interpretation. In certain prepositional phrases the neuter noun has the more suitable meaning 'eternity', but not outside such phrases as *to ealdre*. With the masculine noun *ealdor* many interpretations of the passage are possible, from the safe and colourless 'elder' of Thorpe and Gollancz to Gordon's 'the Lord', an over-definite translation when the noun is not limited by a descriptive genitive other than the article *þæs*. Perhaps the most attractive among the possibilities in this context is 'superior, prior', for the word is often used in prose of men of ecclesiastical authority (see BTs under *ealdor* 1(a))(δ). MacGillivray, 'The Influence of Christianity', §190, gives examples of its use for 'abbot' and (§197) generally for older monks; he also lists (§260) as other meanings *prior conventualis; decanus monasterii; senior*.

421 *gefeon*. May be interpreted as having either two or three syllables. Cp. *gefeon motum* 13[b] and the forms discussed in §8, pp. 59–60.

425 *witum wælan*. The verb *wælan*, considered an Anglian feature of

prose vocabulary by Jordan, *Eigentümlichkeiten des anglischen Wort-schatzes*, p. 57, is otherwise represented in verse only in *Andreas* 1361 *witum bewæled*. The similarity between the two phrases may indicate that both poets are drawing on a stock phrase.

441 *anum*. Thorpe (p. 504) equates *anum* here with *agenum*, translating the phrase 'for his own soul'. The adjective is attracted to *feore* though, as GK (under *ān* I) point out, *his anes* might be expected (cp. *his anes gemet* 388).

454 *hean*, MS. *heam*. The usual emendation is adopted, for this final *-m* is hardly the result of inflexional levelling.

458–9 The basic meaning of *myrcels* is 'mark, sign' and there is no evidence that it was ever narrowed in significance to 'tonsure', a sense first given the form by Cosijn, 'Anglosaxonica. IV', p. 117, who suggests also that *þe* 458 should be changed to *þȳ*, explaining ll. 460b–1a as *mit diesem äussern leben manche welche jedoch sündigen*. Further elucidation of his ingenious interpretation is provided by KD who, following Cosijn's explanation for *myrcels*, translate ll. 458a–9: '"by which (*þe* = *þȳ*) the hand of man has changed thee from the beauty of thy appearance", i.e. has shorn him of the glory of his locks'. The inter-pretation is strained, despite the observation 'The thought is continued in ll.460 ff.' GK suggest that in this context *myrcels* may mean *periculum, calamitas*, but Grein's very free *vor dem Ausgang* is followed by *dass* which assumes an emendation of *þe* 458 to *þæt*. Gollancz suggests omitting *þec*, translating ll. 458–9 ('unintelligibly', as KD note) 'because of the sign, which warded the hand of man from off thy noble face'; the Kennedy and Gordon translations are in essentials the same. BT, under *mircels* IV, offer 'on account of the ensign (the cross?) that would turn man's hand from thy face', at least leaving out *æþelum* rather than overlooking its lack of congruence with *onsyne*, but it is unclear whether this understanding of *myrcels* is to refer back to *Cristes rode* 180 or to a mark on Guthlac's face.

Toller (see BTs under *fram* 17) points out that the preposition *fram* is occasionally found in OE. 'denoting ground, reason, cause' (cp. *OED* under FROM 14). If this use of *from* is assumed in l. 459, ll. 456 ff. may be translated: 'then you declared that the Holy Ghost would easily shield you against afflictions for the sake of that sign which would turn the hand of man aside from you, because of the noble qualities of your face'. The spread of *þec* into the dative, found also in l. 278, is a not uncommon feature both of Mercian and of the poetic codices. In case the reading be thought improbable, cp. the *Andreas* poet's description of demons who were rather more easily intimidated by the mark of Christ's cross in their victim's face (ll. 1337–40):

> Syððan hie oncneowon Cristes rode
> on his mægwlite, mære tacen,
> wurdon hie ða acle on þam onfenge,
> forhte, afærde, and on fleam numen.

460–6 No-one has thought to point to this passage as in any way

strange, and editors and translators, if they mark out speeches by inverted commas, include these lines in the speech of the demons. It is however likely that they should be read as an aside by the poet (cp. his interruption of a speech later in ll. 620b–2, where the verses are widely recognized as the narrator's comment). If the audience were a monastic one, the aside would have held considerable point.

461 *þigað*. See n. for *þegan* 169.

472 *martyrhád*. This word, used only here in OE. poetry, appears a few times in religious prose texts (MacGillivray, 'The Influence of Christianity', p. 55), but occurs less frequently than another hybrid of similar meaning, *martyrdom*. The native *þrowung* 'suffering, martyrdom' is the usual word in both verse and prose (verse examples are *Christ* 470, 1129, 1179 and *Kentish Hymn* 28 for Christ's sufferings, and *Guthlac A* 385, 471 and 778 for Guthlac's), and even *martyrdom* is infrequent in poetic texts (*Menologium* 126, 145 and *Resignation* 81).

475 *ealdfeonda*. Cosijn, 'Anglosaxonica. IV', p. 117, suggests the addition of *fela* to this verse, but a decontracted form should be read (cp. §8, p. 59, and see Roberts, 'A Metrical Examination', p. 96 and n. 24).

478 *forscadene*. Cosijn, 'Anglosaxonica. IV', p. 117, argues that the meaning *dispersus*, suitable in the *Cura Pastoralis* (ed. Sweet, EETS (OS), xlv and 1 (1871), 134.16 and 469.11), is unsatisfactory in this context, and suggests '*Abgeschieden' von der himmlischen seligkeit?* Grein seems also to give the prefix *for-* destructive effect, translating l. 478a *Verflucht seid ihr*, and in GK the participial adjective is the only form cited for the sense *condemnare*. The 'scattered' of BT, Gollancz, and Gordon, and Kennedy's 'dispersed', are too weak, yet 'accursed' implies more than can be justifiably read into this context. Some translation such as 'scattered utterly, routed' suits both prefix and *-scadene*.

482 *onwald*, MS. *onweald* with *e* subpuncted. See §9, p. 65.

489 *rume regulas*. See §8, p. 52 and n. 3.

reþe. Here the loss of *h-* is metrically confirmed. Cp. *hreðe* 1140.

490 *templum*. Keiser, 'The Influence of Christianity', p. 39, notes that this learned word may be used both for buildings and figuratively for congregations in verse texts. Either meaning is suitable here. There is no need to argue (with Keiser, who takes *Guthlac A* ll. 30–818 together with *Guthlac B* as one poem) that it must apply to Guthlac's dwelling-place in *Guthlac A* because that is its meaning in *Guthlac B* (cp. n. for *temple* 1002).

494 *wiþ þon*. Both Thorpe and Gollancz misreport *w* as *s*, and Thorpe's readings serve as the base for Grein's edition where *siþþon* is therefore taken as the MS. form; the mistake goes unnoticed by Schipper. Both Assmann and KD note the MS. *w* (*wyn*) but present *siþþon* in emendation, though *wiþ þon* is more suitable contextually. Two examples of the phrase with the sense 'against that' are given in BT under *wiþ* II(7) from the Old English Bede, where it translates *e contrario*, and the use of the prepositional formulae *wiþ þon/þam þe/þæt* is widespread.

496 *þa æfteryld*. This *hapax legomenon*, literally 'after-age', is similar

to another nonceword *æfteryldo* used in the Old English Bede (ed.
Miller, EETS (OS), xcv (1890), I.48.26. The base element of the latter
should be interpreted 'age' (*ævum*), whereas *-yld* is rather 'age, time of
life' (*ætas*). Both Thorpe and Grein present the compound as two
words, Thorpe translating 'The young generations may not at first
bear fruit' and Grein *sie können nach des Alters Weise in ihrer ersten
Blüte sich nicht gebahren* (apparently following the suggestion *ylde* for
yld made in the fnn. of his own edition). Later Grein, 'Zur Textkritik',
p. 424, puts forward the compound *æfteryld* now generally accepted,
e.g. in Gollancz's 'they may not show maturity in their first bloom'.
    504 *aflihð.* Holthausen, *Beiblatt*, ix (1899), 356, first notes that a de-
contracted form is necessary here for the metre (see also §8, p. 59).
    510 *Oft ge in gestalum stondað.* Thorpe translates *on gestalum*
'among thieves', perhaps recalling Luke 10: 30 *incidit in latrones*, and
Gollancz's 'Oft are ye engaged in theft' shows that he too connects this
noun with *stelan* 'steal' and its cognates. Grein gives *in Hinterhalten*
in his translation, an interpretation preferred by Cosijn, 'Anglosaxonica.
IV', p. 117, who, comparing with this verse ll. 534 and 1140, objects to
Gollancz's translation *denn die teufel haben nichts zu stehlen.* In BT
choice is left open between *gestala* 'thief' and *gestalu* 'theft' for this
passage; the only relevant additional information in BTs is that *gestala*
means 'accomplice in theft' rather than 'thief'. Gordon follows Thorpe
with 'Often ye are among thieves', and Kennedy follows Grein with
'Often are ye found in stealthy deeds'.
    The form *gestalum* can, as Schaar, *Critical Studies*, p. 82, observes,
be connected with *stælan* 'accuse'. He translates l. 510a 'You are often
occupied with quarrels', suggesting that the use of *semon* in the following
line leads us to expect a noun *gestāl* 'dissension', cognate with *stælan*
and *onstāl* (cp. BTs *gestāl* 'accusation, charge' and see also M. Förster,
'Der Vercelli-Codex CXVII nebst Abdruck einiger altenglischen
Homilien der Handschrift', *Festschrift für Lorenz Morsbach* (Halle,
1913), p. 163, for four examples in the Vercelli Book homilies). The
verses can therefore be translated 'Often you make accusations' (see
BT under *standan* V), though probably the early ME *is stoken in stall*
(see N. S. Baugh, *A Worcestershire Miscellany, compiled by John
Northwood, c. 1400* (Philadelphia, 1956), p. 155, for examples and
interpretations of this phrase) should be compared and the verse
translated 'Often you stand accused'. Cp. E. G. Stanley, 'Studies in
the Prosaic Vocabulary of Old English Verse' *Neuphilologische Mitteilungen*, lxxii (1971), 415.
    511–12 Critical discussion of these lines was at first complicated by
Thorpe's misreading of *mæg* as *wæg*, his *se us ic se mon-wæg* 'he *who's* to
us man's way' being accompanied by a footnote emendation from *us
ic* to *us is.* Grein supplies *mund* before *sendeð* in l. 511a, following
Thorpe's recommendation for the second half-line, but later ('Zur
Textkritik', p. 424) reads *me þonne [sige] sendeð, se usic senian mæg*
'es sendet mir den Sieg dann, der uns segnen kann'. Schipper, 'Zum
Codex Exoniensis', p. 330, fails to note the MS. *mæg*, as does Gollancz

who reads *me þonne sendeð se usic se mon wæg* 'then He sendeth me, He who for our sakes moved as man'; and the same reading appears in Assmann's revision of the third volume of the *Bibliothek*. Holthausen, *Beiblatt*, ix (1899), 356, suggests *séman mæg statt des sinnlosen se mon wæg*, but the MS. *mæg* is again missed by Hans Gerke (see Holthausen, 'Vergleichung des Gūðlāc-textes mit der hs' *Anglia*, xl (1916), 365, for Gerke's collation of Assmann with the Exeter Book). Kock, 'Jubilee Jaunts', p. 42, can therefore propose *se usic sem on wæg* 'who over us brought peace (reconciliation)', comparing *gesem* and (*ge*)*ner* with the *sem posited, and reinstating Grein's *sige* before *sendeð*. KD first record the MS. *mæg*, reading *Me þonne sige sendeð, se usic semon mæg* for l. 511 with the infinitive *semon* 'reconcile, bring to peace', but, as Schaar, *Critical Studies*, p. 82, points out, *sige* is unnecessary.

515a Cp. *Phoenix* 242 *synnum asundrad*, *Gloria I* 10 *asyndrod fram synnum*, and *Andreas* 1243 *asundrad fram synnum*. Schaar, *Critical Studies*, p. 292, and 'On a New Theory of Old English Poetic Diction', *Neophilologus*, xl (1956), 304, thinks ll. 514–17a lie behind *Andreas* 1241b–4. See also §8, p. 54.

517 *wolde. wolde* for *weolde* occurs again in *Juliana* 562, and late OE. monophthongization, perhaps present in *Maxims I* 85 *lof* and *Maxims I* 139 *lofes* (KD texts have *eo* emendation), may also lie behind the scribal correction from *o* to *e* in *Guthlac A* 190 *hweopan* and the MS. insertion of *e* in *Seafarer* 71 *feorh*. See D. Whitelock's review of K. and C. Sisam, *The Salisbury Psalter* (*RES*, n.s. xi (1960), 420) for the possibility of such monophthongization.

519 *afrum*. The only other occurrence of this adjective in verse-texts is in *Judith* 257 where it again means 'severe in strength, vehement'. Examples of its literal use may be found in the *Leechdoms* and the glosses (see BT and BTs).

528–9 It is curious that this passage is rarely noted by those who try to contrast a *Guthlac A* poet dependent on oral traditions with a *Guthlac B* poet working from a written source.

530 *Geofu*. A new section begins here on the last line of fo. 40ʳ; the preceding line is empty and *cyþað:7* stands right at the end of the line immediately above. Only *G* is a capital, in height about an inch.

533 *foregengan*. Thorpe's suggested emendation *forðgengan* 'a forth goer' is unnecessary. The compound is used here in its literal sense, 'a forerunner' (compare Gollancz's 'advance-guard'), as in *Exodus* 120 and perhaps in the gloss '*antecessor*', *forgencga*, *forstæp* (A. S. Napier, 'Old English Glosses chiefly unpublished', *Anecdota Oxoniensia*, iv (1900), 18, no. 619), and in the sense 'attendant' in *Judith* 127. It is most widely used with the meanings 'predecessor, ancestor'.

535 *sawl*. Cp. n. for *sawl* 408.

540 *nyðgista*. With *y* superscribed above *i* in the manuscript. Assmann thinks this among the changes made in a hand later than the scribe's. It is the only place where *i* is changed to *y*; for examples of changes in *ĭ* see the note for *swylc* 756. The meaning of the base element of *nyðgista* is uncertain (cp. n. for *ceargesta* 393). A similar form occurs in *Beowulf*

2699 *þone niðgæst* (for the dragon), where *gæst* 'visitor' is better contextually than *gǣst* 'spirit, ghost', but here Gordon's 'evil spirits' is preferred to Gollancz's 'hateful guests'.

541–3 Thorpe, suggesting in his footnotes *hwile* for *wel* and *þe þa* for *þe þæt*, translates continuously with little sense: 'He the pain despis'd / of the soul ever, / while in the Protector, / who held him in *his* care / that doubted not . . .' Grein, placing a comma after *wel*, supplies *on frean fultum forð getreowde* between ll. 541 and 542 and emends *mond* to *mod*. Assmann, instead of incorporating into his text the stop-gap verses, prints a row of asterisks between ll. 541 and 542 (numbered ll. 512 and 514 respectively by him). Gollancz leaves no space but, numbering the lines consecutively, notes 'an evident omission of one line' after l. 541, and, adopting Grein's *mod*, translates: 'he despised the pains; (he) ever (trusted) well his Saviour / (for) his soul's (protection), and He guarded his spirit'. Kennedy, *The Poems of Cynewulf* (1910), p. 279, also indicates omission: 'He scorned his sore distress and ever joyed exceedingly in that Protector of his soul . . . who preserved his spirit', whereas Gordon, *Anglo-Saxon Poetry*, p. 265, follows the *Bibliothek* text with: 'He ever scorned well those things which hurt the soul; he trusted in help from the Lord, the Guardian who kept that heart safe.' KD follow Gollancz, printing a row of asterisks between ll. 541 and 542, which are numbered consecutively. Schaar *Critical Studies*, p. 83, suggesting there is no MS. loss, advances a few 'typical slips of negligence':

> He þa sar forseah a þære sawle hæl
> wæs mundbora þe þæt mod geheold
> þæt him ne getweode treow in breostum *etc.*

Neither punctuation nor translation is given, and a comparison with *Juliana* 211b–15 does little to illustrate how the emended passage is to be understood, presumably: 'He despised those pains, the salvation of that soul was always the protector who guarded that spirit so that . . .' The solution is to be admired for its provision of a finite verb between *forseah* 541 and *geheold* 542, but the syntax is awkward.

It is indeed likely that some finite form has been lost from l. 542a. With the insertion of *gemunde* at the beginning of this line the passage becomes intelligible without any alteration other than Grein's *mod*: and the omission of *gemunde* may be ascribed to haplography. Unfortunately, so far as the metre is concerned, there are no parallels closer than ll. 229a and 335a. A free translation runs: 'He despised those sufferings, he always remembered well in his soul that Protector who guarded his spirit, so that . . .'

549 *to deað*. *to*, except in phrases marking time, only infrequently governs the accusative; another Exeter Book example is *Christ* 32 *to þis enge lond*, and see BT and BTs under *tō* III(i) for further examples. Therefore, although the phrase *deman to deaðe* occurs elsewhere, for example *Judith* 196, *Elene* 500, *to deað* need not be emended on grammatical grounds. Metrically too the alteration to *deaðe* is attractive (see

Holthausen, 'Zur altenglischen literatur. IV', *Beiblatt*, xviii (1907), 201), but similar verses are found in the corpus.

550a Cp. *Beowulf* 750 *fyrena hyrde* (of Grendel) and *Christ and Satan* 159 *firna herde.*

559 *husulbearn.* Both this compound and *husulweras* 796 are not otherwise found in OE. The only other use of *husul* as the first part of a poetic compound is in *Daniel* 704 and 748 *huslfatu*, though it is much used in religious prose writings and in the laws.

576b Cp. *Andreas* 1393b *Hit ne mihte swa!* Both poets are using a traditional line-filler in a b-verse, but for some discussion of the supposed indebtedness of the *Andreas* poet to *Guthlac A* see §8, p. 54.

592 *Doð efne swa.* Both Cremer, *Metrische und sprachliche Untersuchung*, p. 46, and Sievers, *Zur Rhythmik*, p. 477, suggest expanding *Doð* for the sake of the metre, but see Roberts, 'A Metrical Examination', p. 115.

594 *wergengan.* The only other examples of this compound are in l. 713 of this poem and in *Daniel* 662 *wildra wærgenga*, where the phrase describes Nebuchadnezzar. Its first element may be either *waru* 'shelter, protection' or *wær* 'pledge, agreement', a similar difficulty of interpretation attaching to the Latinized words from Germanic law-codes (quoted by BT under *wergenga*) *wargangi* and *wargengum*, and to the Warings, i.e. the *Væringi*, who served the Greek emperors of Constantinople as bodyguards (Jan de Vries, *Altnordisches Etymologisches Wörterbuch* (Leiden, 1961), suggests an etymology **wāragangja-* for *Væringi*, comparing ON. *várar* 'pledges', but presents all these compounds with a short vowel in the first syllable). The second of these etymons is preferred and the compound thought similar in meaning to *husulbearn* 559.

613 *leohtes.* Cosijn, 'Anglosaxonica. IV', p. 117, points out that *leoht* here means 'heaven', comparing *Christ* 1463. Cp. also *Genesis* 392, 394, 401, and see BTs I(a) for further examples.

614 *deaðe.* Neither Grein nor Cosijn, 'Anglosaxonica. IV', p. 117, seems willing to recognize this instrumental use of *deaðe*, Grein proposing the graphically simple change to the adjective *deade* and Cosijn either the insertion of *on* or an emendation to *deað.*

617 *habban.* Cosijn, 'Anglosaxonica. IV', p. 118, suggests reading *hebban*, assuming an unnecessary parallelism in meaning between this form and *besingan*, the two infinitives dependent on *sceolon* 614, but there is no difficulty in understanding the passage with *habban.*

618 *IC.* A new section begins half-way down fo. 41ᵛ with a large capital *I* followed by *C* which stands as high as the ascenders of normal script. The preceding line is empty, and the line above that, completely filled, ends with *cyninges:7.*

620b–2 These words are regarded as an aside from the narrator by some (e.g. Thorpe, Gollancz, Gordon), but apparently as an integral part of Guthlac's speech by others (e.g. Grein in his translation, Kennedy, KD); see §5, p. 35.

lufian. Cosijn 'Anglosaxonica. IV', p. 118, suggests changing this infinitive to *lofian* to bring it closer in meaning to *weorþian* 619 which is

also dependent on *wille* 619. The emendation, though supported also by Holthausen in the appendix to GK, would detract from the variation.

622 *in his*. Grein, 'Zur Textkritik', p. 424, suggests these words have been transposed and translates l. 622 *die in ihren Werken seinem Willen folgen*. It seems better, however, to treat *ræfnað* as a singular form, with *-að* for *-eð*, as for example in Gollancz's 'for him who in his works performeth His will'.

624 *lege biscencte*. Thorpe translates 'with flame for drink', adding in fn. 'Lit. having flame served to them for drink'. Grein suggests reading *bisencte*, an emendation supported by Cosijn, 'Anglosaxonica. IV', p. 118, who compares *wraðe bisencte* 666 and *Christ* 1168 *flode bisencan*, as well as by Kennedy's 'engulfed in flame' and Gordon's 'plunged in fire'. Gollancz retains *biscencte*, translating l. 624b 'with flame proffered for drink', and Assmann too reverts to the MS. reading, though the latest editors, KD, object to it because it involves 'a rather violent metaphor'. However, the emended *bisencte* is extended in a way unparalleled for that verb (see the entries for *sencan* with the *be/bi* prefix in GK), making the acceptance of a solitary instance of *scencan* with the prefix *bi-* a no more unattractive proposition. The MS. form is supported by the widespread use of ironic metaphors of serving drink in medieval writings (see Brown, 'Poculum Mortis', pp. 389–99, Smithers, 'Five Notes on Old English Texts', pp. 67 ff., and §6, pp. 37–9).

633 *mid scome scyldum*. Thorpe translates 'with your shameful crimes', suggesting a compound *scomu-scyldum* should be read, but other interpretations proposed are simpler. It is possible to take *scome* as a genitive dependent on *scyldum*, as in Kennedy's 'in your shame and guilt'. Again, *scyldum* may be regarded as instrumental in function, allowing some such translation as Grein's *durch eure Schuld mit Schmach* or Gordon's 'shamefully . . . in your guilt'. Simplest is Gollancz's version 'ignominiously and guiltily'.

650 *mine*. Generally taken as 'my' here, despite the occurrence of a similar verse, *Guthlac B* 909, where 'my' is contextually unsuitable; it is probable both verses represent a formula preserved only in these two poems. Only Cosijn, 'Anglosaxonica. IV', p. 118, tries to emend both, advancing *mirce* 'schwarze', which he puts forward also for *Paris Psalter* 120.6 *min ne*. The emendation, although described as plausible by KD, is graphically unattractive as well as unnecessary. Both *mine* 650 and *minne* 909 will be found in the glossary under *minne* 'evil, wicked', an adjective found some eight or nine times in all in OE. (see H. Meritt, 'The Old English Glosses *deðæ* and *minnæn*. A Study in Ways of Interpretation', *JEGP*, xliii (1944), 441–5, and *Fact and Lore about Old English Words* (Stanford and London, 1954), p. 206).

mánscapan. The use of this word against *peccator* in other OE. texts and the appearance of an accent over its vowel here (to distinguish the less common *mān* from *mănn*) support the usual identification of *mān* as 'evil'; the cognate OS. *mēnskaðo* should be compared.

661 Metrically the line is unusual (see Roberts, 'A Metrical Examina-

tion', p. 115). Probably stress falls upon the attributive dative pronoun, as in *Juliana* 54 *þe to gesingan.*

663 Cp. *Andreas* 1072 *Wendan ond woldon wiþerhycgende.* The compound *wiþerhycgende* is represented otherwise only in *Elene* 951 and *Juliana* 196.

671 *wærnysse.* Cosijn, 'Anglosaxonica. IV', p. 118, suggests the emendation *wærgnysse*, but because simplification in a consonant cluster appears so often in OE. no change is made in the MS. form; the vowel of the accented syllable shows Anglian smoothing (see §9, p. 66). Grammatically *wærnysse* may be interpreted either as a genitive singular dependent on *brynewylm* 672 (e.g. Grein's *den Schwall der Lohglut* or Gordon's 'the surging flame of damnation') or as an accusative singular parallel with *brynewylm* (e.g. Thorpe's 'that ye malediction, / burning heat have', and see Kock, 'Interpretations and Emendations of Early English Texts XI', *Anglia*, xlvii (1923), 267). As a similar opposition of the concepts *wærgnys* and *bletsung* occurs in a famous passage from Deuteronomy 11: 26 ff. *Et propono in conspectu vestro hodie benedictionem et maledictionem . . .* and was probably known to the poet, I prefer to regard *wærnysse* and *brynewylm* as being in variation.

684 *duguð 7 drohtað.* Cosijn, 'Anglosaxonica. IV', p. 118, objecting to Grein's *Gefolgdienst* and Gollancz's 'retinues' for *drohtað*, points out that *drohtað on wuldre* is meant; no more do their *Heershaaren* and 'troops' suit *duguð* here. BT under *drohtaþ* suggest 'virtue and converse', but Kennedy's 'glory and fellowship' is better.

684 ff. A few resemblances between the ending of this poem and the *Vita sancti Guthlaci* are sometimes identified (see particularly nn. for ll. 698–700 and 732, and §4), though, as Schaar, *Critical Studies*, p. 40, notes, except for the part played by St. Bartholomew, the central events in *Guthlac A* and the *Vita* are 'wholly different'.

692a Cp. the use of this formulaic phrase in *Daniel* 725 and *Andreas* 1266.

692b *Ofermæcga.* This nonceword, comparable in form with ON. *ofrmenni* 'mighty champion', is the subject of *spræc* and is varied by *dyre dryhtnes þegn* 693. The earlier editors seem unwilling to accept the form. Thorpe suggests *ofermettum* 'proudly', Grein *ofermægne* (though later his translation contains *übermächtig*, indicating acceptance of the MS. form), and Cosijn, 'Anglosaxonica. IV', p. 118, also notes that an adverb would be attractive beside *spræc* to balance *dæghluttre scán.* The strong form *mæcg* is commoner, but the weak simplex appears in *Fortunes of Men* 52 *mæcga* and similar poetic compounds in *Juliana* 260 *se wræcgmæcga* and *Solomon and Saturn* 90 *guðmæcga* (*-maga* in 2nd MS.). Otherwise the form is recorded only in glossaries, but the poetic examples, all in the nominative, show its use both with and without article and suggest its established use as a noun.

693 *dæghluttre scán.* Both Thorpe and Gollancz read three separate words here, but in other interpretations *dæghluttre* is treated as an adverbial compound, e.g. Grein's *tageshell erglänzend*, and all the clauses of ll. 692b–97 seem best read as having the same subject. Compound

adjectives with the base element *hluttor* occur in *Rune Poem* 30 *glæs-hluttur* and *Meters of Boethius* 5.8 *glashlutre* (and cp. Samuel Fox, *King Alfred's Version of Boethius* (London, 1895), 14, l. 24 *glæshlutru*), indicating that a similarly based adverb is by no means an unlikely form. Either reading is possible. Here a short parenthetic clause is avoided because such an arrangement is unnecessary for the understanding of the passage. There is no reason for the poet to break off at this point to comment on the time of day or the weather and, as he is building up an imposing picture of St. Bartholomew, it is far more likely he should describe the appearance of this messenger from God.

696 *þreamedlum.* The usual editorial *þreaniedlum* (for which early WS. *i*-mutation must be advanced) is unnecessary. See Thomas J. Gardner, '"þreaniedla" and "þreamedla"', *Neuphilologische Mitteilungen*, lxx (1969), 255–61, who assumes a base *þrēamōd and the etymon *þrēa-mōdilan behind the MS. *þreamedlum* and the *ǒreamedlan* of *Solomon and Saturn*, ll. 242 and 430, comparing the second element of the better evidenced compounds *ofermēdla* and *onmēdla*. He notes the similarity of *Riddles* 3. 49–51, where the appearance of *modþrea* 50 lends support to his explanation of the MS. form by 'mental oppressions'.

698–700 For the similarity found by Liebermann between this passage and the *Vita sancti Guthlaci*, see §4. A close parallel with *Andreas* 1443b–5 and 1473–4 is noted by Schaar, *Critical Studies*, p. 294, and 'On a New Theory of Old English Poetic Diction', p. 304, but the likelihood that the correspondences are coincidental points to the use of a traditional pattern and may also tell against Liebermann's identification of l. 699b with a phrase from the *Vita*. See further §8, pp. 54–5.

700a See §8, p. 60, and Roberts, 'A Metrical Examination', p. 109.

703 *se mec.* Mitchell, 'Pronouns in Old English Poetry', *RES*, n.s. xv (1964), 134, points out that *se* usually carries a strong suggestion of the third person and is rarely used in verse if its antecedent is a pronoun in the first or second person; he finds one instance in *Beowulf* 506 *Eart þu se Beowulf, se þe wið Brecan wunne* which he considers sufficient justification for the retention here of *se mec* against Grein's suggested *þe mec.*

706 *on his sylfes dóm.* See §8 (pp. 50–1) for the possibly legal origins of this phrase.

712 *æfstum*, MS. *æftum.* The emendation, first made by Thorpe, appears in all the editions. Both Rieger, 'Die alt- und angelsächsische verkunst', *Zeitschrift für deutsche Philologie*, vii (1876), 52, and Cosijn, 'Anglosaxonica. IV', p. 118, suggest the reading *æfestum*, but this is not adopted as the scribe may have merely simplified a consonant cluster if the syncopated form stood in his exemplar. See also §8, p. 59.

713 *wergengan.* See n. for *wergengan* 594.

716 *on þære socne.* Thorpe's interpretation 'in that sanctuary' is followed in BT and GK. Grein, with *in dem Bezirke*, attempts a freer translation of the phrase, but both Gordon's 'in his refuge' and Kennedy's 'in his holy refuge' follow the usual interpretation of the passage. The only other instance of *socn* in OE. verse is *Beowulf* 1777 *þære socne* where it is best explained as meaning 'visitation, persecution'.

C. L. Wrenn, *Beowulf* (London, 1958), p. 288, regards this use of the word as 'peculiar to *Beowulf*', though Gollancz obviously recognizes its presence in *Guthlac A* 716a which he translates 'amid your persecution'. This seems therefore to be a use of the simplex peculiar to verse-texts but found also in the compound *hamsocn* and paralleled in certain uses of *secan* (see BT under *sēcan* III).

þe. Listed as a causal adverb in GK (under *þe* III), but it should instead be regarded as the relative particle separated from its personal pronoun (see Mitchell, 'Adjective Clauses in Old English Poetry', *Anglia*, lxxxi (1963), 307, who notes *Christ* 1097 *þe . . . his lichoma* as another example of this construction in a verse-text).

722 *ÐA*. The final section of *Guthlac A* begins mid-way down fo. 43ʳ, its opening marked by a large capital *Ð* and a smaller *A*. The preceding line is empty except for *conn:7* at the very end.

732 *smeþe 7 gesefte*. See §4, p. 21 for discussion of Liebermann's suggestion that these words echo a phrase from Felix.

734 *monge mægwlitas*. Cosijn, 'Anglosaxonica. IV', p. 118, wishing to avoid an interpretation such as GK *Tiere von mancherlei Aussehen* suggests reading a genitive phrase *monigra mægwlita* dependent upon *treofugla tuddor* 735; he compares *Guthlac B* 916–19a, observing that the *A* poet also refers only to birds. KD apparently agree that the *A* poet refers only to birds in this passage, but point out that the nominative phrase may be retained with *mægwlitas* 'species' as the subject of *bletsadon* and in apposition to *tuddor* 'race'. There is indeed no need to restrict the meaning of *mægwlitas* to exclude animals. The poet moves from a general description of the welcome back to his hermitage given Guthlac by 'many living kinds' (Gollancz's translation) to mention in particular his reception by the birds of the trees. I suspect that Cosijn wishes to exclude animals from this account of the saint's return (despite l. 741a) because of the great emphasis placed upon bird miracles by Felix in the *Vita*. It should be noted also that the adjective *meagol* is not restricted to the description of birdsong in OE.

735 *tacnum cyðdon*. The phrase is generally clumsily explained, e.g. Gordon's 'declared by signs'. Only GK show any consciousness that such a translation is unsatisfactory, suggesting *durch Signale* for *tacnum* in this context. The word *tacn* is occasionally extended in OE. to denote sounds used as signals and is probably so used here.

736 ff. These verses are variously interpreted. Some regard *heold* as referring back to a time before the saint's return home and, despite the absence of any adverb to support this interpretation, translate the verb by a pluperfect, e.g. Gollancz's 'oft had he held them food, when . . .' and Gordon's 'Often he had held food for them, when . . .' *þonne* 737 may be regarded either as a conjunction, the general reading, or as an adverb, an ambiguity which may explain Kennedy's choice here of a rather free translation 'oft he held out food to them and they were wont . . .' Again, two interpretations are possible for *geoce* 738, which may be either the help given Guthlac by St. Bartholomew or the help given the birds by Guthlac. Only Gordon obviously follows the first of

these alternatives with his 'They were glad of his safety', and the entries
under *gēoc* in BT and GK are ambiguous, as are Gollancz's 'rejoiced in his
succour' and Kennedy's 'rejoicing in his succour'. As the birds are the subject of *gefegon* and as they are *hungrige* some translation such as Grein's
es erfreuten sich der Hilfe durch Futter die Gierigen seems more
suitable.

738 *grædum gifre*. Thorpe translates 'greedily voracious', noting
that emendation to *grædgum* for *grædigum* should perhaps be made. The
suggestion is attractive for two reasons. First, this is the only appearance
of a noun *grǣd* before the modern period, when 'greed' is apparently a
literary loanword from Scots into English in the early seventeenth
century; the word did not have general currency in English until the
nineteenth century (see *OED* entry for GREED sb. and Sir William
Craigie, *A Dictionary of the Older Scottish Tongue* (Oxford, 1937),
under (GREDE,) GREID). Secondly, the adjectives *grǣdig* and *gifre*
are often paired together in a-verses, e.g. *Genesis* 793, *Christ and Satan*
32, 191, *Soul and Body I* 74, *Seafarer* 62, *Soul and Body II* 69, and *Riddles*
84.30, though these verses might suggest the emendation *grǣdge* 7
gifre rather than Thorpe's more conservative *grædgum gifre*. The MS.
form may however be regarded as an adverbial use of the dative plural
of a noun not otherwise recorded for OE., and is so described in BT,
GK, and *OED*. Cognates are ON. *gráðr* and Gothic *grēdus*; see also
AEW under *grǣd* 3 and Jan de Vries, *Altnordisches Etymologisches
Wörterbuch* (Leiden, 1962) under *gráðr*.

741 *wildeorum*. Cosijn, 'Anglosaxonica. IV', p. 119, suggests that
wildrum is necessary for the metre, but similar verse-patterns are found
in other OE. poems (see the examples given by Bliss, *The Metre of
'Beowulf'*, pp. 94–5 and see Roberts, 'A Metrical Examination', p. 112).

742–3 See §8, p. 55, for comparison of these lines with *Andreas*
1581–2. The poetic compound *sigewong* occurs also in *Guthlac B* 921
and *Judith* 295.

744 *geacas gear budon*. The cuckoo as a harbinger of summer is a
familiar tradition in European poetry. The bird is linked with summer by
Alcuin in his *Versus de Cuculo* and *Conflictus Veris et Hiemis*, and
Snorri, *Skáldskaparmál*, c. 78, gives *gauk-mánuðr* as the poetic name for
the first month of summer. Yet the cuckoo more often appears as a
bird of lament in OE.: the voice of *sumeres weard* is mournful (*Seafarer*, ll.
53 ff.); and the sign for a wife separated from her husband to set out on
voyage will be the sad cuckoo's cry (*Husband's Message*, ll. 19 ff.).
Sieper, *Die altenglische Elegie* (Strassburg, 1915), 70–7, notes particularly its function as a messenger of sorrow, sickness, and death. In
early Irish poetry the cuckoo's voice is a signal for a departure on
voyage (K. Jackson, *Studies in Early Celtic Nature Poetry* (Cambridge,
1935), p. 23) and the Welsh poets use it as a symbol of separation from
loved ones (I. Williams, *Lectures on Early Welsh Poetry* (Dublin
Institute for Advanced Studies, 1944), pp. 12–13). The sad call of the
cuckoo, common in Celtic and Slav traditions, is otherwise found in a
Germanic context only in a Swedish proverb which says that a cuckoo

call from the north bodes sorrow and from the south death (pointed out by O. S. Anderson, 'The Seafarer. An Interpretation', *K. Humanistiska Vetenskapssamfundets i Lund Årsberättelse*, i (1937–8), 23). I. L. Gordon, *The Seafarer* (London, 1960), p. 31, suggests that the more immediate source for the cuckoo as a bird of lament in OE. is 'from the same background as the Welsh tradition'. But in *Guthlac A* the cuckoo as a symbol of the coming of the new year need not be thought closer to Celtic than to any other European tradition. N. F. Blake, '*The Seafarer*, lines 48–9', *Notes and Queries*, ccvii (1962), 163–4, has pointed out that *Seafarer* 48–9 and *Phoenix* 242 ff. draw upon the motif of the reawakening of plant-life after winter, used in Christian Latin writings as a symbol of man's resurrection on the Day of Judgement. This *Guthlac A* passage should be cited as another example of the use of this figure: for A. A. Lee, *The Guest-Hall of Eden* (New Haven and London, 1972), pp. 107–8, 'The mythical connotations of a return to Paradise surrounding Guthlac's resurrection are unmistakable'. Although it would be possible to regard Guthlac's triumphant return as here emphasized by pathetic fallacy, this description of the saint's hermitage and especially the phrase *sele niwe* 742 suggest that the symbolism of the reawakening of plant-life was used also to mark the achievement of salvation. We should perhaps remember the poet's question of ll. 26–9: Guthlac has so acted on earth that he will enter heaven *womma clæne* 29 (and cp. ll. 689b–91a and 781–9).

751 *sylfe*. With *y* placed below *e* in the MS. Assmann thinks this correction made by a hand later than the scribe's.

753–4a See §4, pp. 28–9.

756 *swylc*. With *y* placed below *i* in the MS. Other examples of *ĭ* altered to *y* in this manuscript are *Guthlac A* 780 *agyfen*, *Guthlac B* 1289 *lyfte*, *Phoenix* 133 *wynsumra*, *Phoenix* 371 *fylle*, *Panther* 43 *wynsumast*, *Riddles* 1.7 *hlyn*; and *i* is written in above *y* in *Christ* 1088 *bidyrned*.

763 *Wile*. With MS. space between *i* and *l* where a second *l* has been scratched out. This MS. emendation leaves *wile*, the form usual for the third person present indicative of *willan*.

767b–8 These verses should be compared with the words spoken by the angel at the beginning of the poem and esp. l. 8; see further §5.

780 *agyfen*. With *y* changed from *i* in the MS. See n. for *swylc* 756. *worde*. The emendation here to *wurde*, first made by Grein and followed in all the editions, is not adopted because of the indications of sporadic scribal confusion of *o* and *u* throughout the Exeter Book. The symbol *o* is found for *u* in *Christ* 1448 *gotun*, *Riddles* 22.17 *ne onder*, *Judgment Day I* 70 *fol*, *Riddles* 73.1 *wonode*, and perhaps *Guthlac B* 1007 *fonde*. Correction has been made by what may be a later hand than the scribe's from *o* to *u* in *Descent into Hell* 8 *fondon*, and in *Riddles* 60.1 *sonde* the *o* is upon an erasure. Instances of *u* for *o* may also be found: *Guthlac A* 299 *abunne*, *Riming Poem* 63 *burgsorg* (if the first element is *borh*, 'security', but see Stanley, 'Studies in Prosaic Vocabulary', p. 402), *Riddles* 58.15 *furum*, and perhaps *Guthlac A* 18 *nú* (see n.). In the group

w + short vowel + *r* two examples of *o* for *u* occur, in *Christ* 1496 *worde* and *Juliana* 508 *gewordun*, and correction has been made to *u* in *Phoenix* 407 *wordon*; these forms give some support to the emendation *wuldre* put forward by Klaeber for *Phoenix* 386 and regarded as 'tempting' but 'without sufficient justification' by N. F. Blake, *The Phoenix* (Manchester, 1964), p. 79.

790 ff. In these lines the poet's return to his opening theme should be noted; see further §5.

809a Cp. *Beowulf* 1758 *Bebeorh þe ðone bealoniÐ* from Hrothgar's long speech of advice (a similarity noted by Cosijn, 'Anglosaxonica. IV', p. 119).

816 *sibbe* 7 *gesihÐe*. R. B. Burlin, *The Old English 'Advent'*, Yale Studies in English, clxviii (New Haven and London, 1968), pp. 82–5 and n. 6, points out the popularity of the etymology *visio pacis* for Jerusalem in OE. writings; his tentative suggestion that this verse should be emended on the pattern of *Christ* 50a *Eala sibbe gesihÐ* is unnecessary. Robinson, 'The Significance of Names in Old English Literature', *Anglia*, lxxxvi (1968), p. 49, also noting the Latin phrase behind this verse, ingeniously suggests that it is parallel to and in apposition with *Hierusalem* 813, but it is more easily read as in variation with *Godes onsyne* 815.

þær heo soÐ wunaÐ. Thorpe, translating this verse 'where they shall truly dwell', suggests the emendation *siÐÐan wuniaÐ* for *soÐ wunaÐ*, but later editors find no difficulty in the passage. The pronoun *heo* stands for Jerusalem and *soÐ* is adverbial.

817 *ealne widan ferh*, MS. *ealdne widan ferh*. The emendation is made by all the editors, the *d* of *ealdne* being most likely due to dittography.

818 *wynne*. This word is at the end of a line otherwise empty and the sign placed before it indicates that it belongs to the preceding line of text. It is followed by punctuation heavier than any marking fitt divisions within the poem, and the following three lines are empty. All this suggests that a major break in material is indicated.

GUTHLAC B

819 *ÐAET IS WIDE CVÐ*. These capitals, based on the fourth line below the line on which *Guthlac A* 818 *wynne* stands, indicate the beginning of a new poem. The first capital is approximately four times the height of those which follow, and the first two letters of the next word, *WEra*, are smaller again, to fill up the end of the MS. line. For a note on the sixteenth-century scribble above this poem, see n. for l.1 of *Guthlac A*.

827 *neorxnawong*. The form presents no problems of interpretation, the meaning 'paradise' being accepted for all contexts in which it occurs, but its etymology continues to provoke discussion. The recorded forms are summarized in R. Jente, *Die mythologischen Ausdrücke im altengl. Wortschatz* (Heidelberg, 1921), pp. 227–9, together with (§39) many of the etymologies advanced at different times. Jente's monograph

is supplemented by W. Krogmann, 'Ags. neorxenawang', *Anglia*, liii
(1929), 337–44, and further examinations of the word have appeared,
notably by Krogmann, Holthausen, Langenfelt, and Meritt. Alan K.
Brown, '*Neorxnawang*', *Neuphilologische Mitteilungen*, lxxiv (1973),
610–23, should be consulted for details of recent speculation about the
compound.

Many of the etymologies surmised for *neorxnawong* are, so far as the
recognized sound changes and known mythological details are concerned, unlikely, some leading far into the field of comparative religion
with little support in recorded forms and beliefs, and cryptogram
solutions are also offered. Perhaps most convincing is Bradley's interpretation ('The Etymology of *Neorxnawang*', *Academy*, xxxvi (1889),
254), at first opposed because no example of the initial element *nēo-*
was at that time widely recognized for OE. However, Bradley's Gothic
rōhsns (genitive plural *rōhsnsē*), if it were an *i*-declensional noun,
might be supposed equivalent to an OE. *rēxn* or *rēxen* (genitive plural
rēxena). We should then have a compound *nēo-rēxena-wang* 'plain
of the halls of the dead', which seems to parallel closely the Norse
valhǫll 'Valhalla'. It would be tempting also to compare the idea
behind the ON. *nástrondr*, but the similarity should not be allowed to
sway one's decision too far in view of the manifold uses to which other
wishful similarities have been put in discussion of *neorxnawong*. It may
indeed be safer to start with the assumption that this word, used always
of the Christian paradise, must contain some basic notion such as the
hortus splendidus of Ettmüller (*Lexicon Anglosaxonicum*, Bibliothek
der gesammten deutschen National-Literatur, xxix (1851), 239) or the
grene wang of Brown (1973).

827–8a Cp. *Phoenix* 397–8a *nemnað neorxnawong, þær his nænges
wæs / eades onsyn*. The similarities, often remarked, between *Guthlac B*
819–969a and *Phoenix* 393–419 are discussed in §8.

brosnung. This noun does not otherwise appear in the major verse
codices, although the related verb *brosnian* is frequently used in poetry.
The noun is common enough in homiletic materials, Alfredian translations, and interlinear psalter glosses.

829–30a See §8, p. 59, for some discussion of similar passages in
Phoenix and *Andreas*.

835 *þurh ælda tid*. The phrase is very often equated with *per sæcula
sæculorum* (see GK under *yldu* 3 and BT under *ældu* 2). Cosijn, 'Anglosaxonica. IV', p. 118, comparing *Paris Psalter* 70.8 *ylde tid*, suggests
that *ælda* should be regarded as the genitive singular of *ęld* 'senectus'.
Other examples of *ildu* 'old age, decay from old age' are to be found in
BT under *ildu* III and BTs under *ildu* III and IIIa. As Cosijn's explanation suits the context, whereas taking the verse as a calque upon *per
sæcula sæculorum* does not, *ælda* is here taken as the genitive singular
of *ældu* (see Glossary).

838 Guthlac uses similar words in his instructions to his servant in
l. 1176, drawing again on a conventional way of describing life (cp.
Christ 777 *leomu, lic ond gæst*, in variation with *lif* of the preceding line,

and the rather more ingenious use of the formula in *Phoenix* 513 *leomu lic somod, ond liges gæst*). J. L. Rosier, 'Death and Transfiguration: *Guthlac B*', *Philological Essays* (1971), pp. 84–8, describing the *Guthlac B* poet's preoccupation with 'death as a separation of soul from body', points out that this collocation, or a variant, does not occur in any other single text so frequently as in *Guthlac B*, but this is hardly surprising. No other poem in the corpus is so extensively concerned with a deathbed scene.

847 *ahneop*. This preterite singular form may belong either to the seventh class of strong verbs or, with archaic or dialectal *ēo* for *ēa*, to the second class (see Campbell, §§740 and 745 (f)i); a similar uncertainty affects the preterite in *Exodus* 476 *genēop* 'overcame'. Cognate with *ahnēop* are Gothic *dishniupan* 'discerpere', Old Swedish *niupa* 'surripere', ON. *hnupla* 'surripere' and OE. *hnoppian*, 'vellere' (for further cognates see *OED* under NAP vb), but the relationships of the *Exodus* word are less easy to decide.

848 *wæstm*, MS. *wæsten* with *m* written above *en*. The superscribed *m* may be regarded as an emendation for either -*en* or -*n*. Variation between final -*m* and -*em* is found in similar words within the MS., e.g. *Guthlac A* 262 *breahtm* and *Guthlac B* 1325 *breahtem*, and examples of *wæstm* with a svarabhakti vowel occur also, e.g. *Fortunes of Men* 24 *westem*.

852 ff. Cp. *Phoenix*, ll. 404 ff.

856 *scudende*. No other examples of this verb occur in OE. Thorpe gives in his fnn. emendations suggested by Kemble *sceadende* and *scriðende*, translating the verse 'in shame departing', and Trautmann, 'Kynewulf der Bishof und Dichter', *Bonner Beiträge*, i (1898), 14, proposes *scyndende*. Klaeber, *The Later Genesis*, p. 37, prints the MS. form, records these earlier suggestions, and adds that Kemble's *sceadende* must stand for *sceoððende*. Rather than change the text so that it may contain the present participle of *sceadan* 'scatter', *scriðan* 'depart', *scyndan* 'hasten', etc., it seems best to follow Sievers, 'Zur Rhythmik', p. 507, and assume a strong verb *scūdan* (as *AEW*, with cognates Old Frisian *skedda*, OS. *scuddian*, OHG. *scutten* 'schütteln, stossen, schwingen', etc., and OE. *scydd* 'alluvial soil', *scyndan* 'hasten'). This *scūdan* is sometimes connected with Modern English *scud* (e.g. under *scūdan* in GK), but it is not recorded before the sixteenth century and is unlikely to be descended from OE. See *OED* under SCUD v.[1]; Pogatscher's review of Sweet's *A Student's Dictionary of Anglo-Saxon* (Oxford, 1897) in *Anzeiger für deutsches Altertum und deutsche Litteratur*, xxv (1899), 11; and M. S. Serjeantson, *A History of Foreign Words in English* (London, 1935), p. 103, where *scud* is listed among sixteenth-century Scandinavian loanwords.

860–3a These verses contain ambiguities. The verbal phrase *sceoldon . . . ongyldon* (with *ongyldon* an infinitive) may govern either the accusative or the genitive, so that any one or some combination of the following may serve as object: *þære synwræce*, *morþres*, *gyrn*, and *deopra firena*. Because *onguldon* is followed by a genitive in l. 857, a genitive (or indeed two or three parallel genitives) is selected as object in this clause in most

interpretations of the passage; with this approach some emendation of *gyrn* is generally considered necessary. On the other hand, those who take *gyrn* as the object of the verbal phrase find that either verb or object must be given an unusual meaning. The problems are further complicated by the ambiguity in both meaning and case of *synwræce* 860, a compound occurring otherwise only in *Christ* 794 and 1539. Its first element may be interpreted as either *synn* 'crime' or *sin-* 'everlasting', and *wracu* may be referred to senses within the ranges 'suffering' or 'punishment'. As in all three instances the first part of the compound contain *y*, not *i*, *syn-* is taken as *synn* 'crime, sin'; and the implication of *Christ* 1539b–40a *Bið him synwracu* / *ondweard undyrne* is that *-wracu* should be understood as 'punishment'.

Thorpe translates *gyrn* 'severely' but, because he follows the text verse by verse, he does not provide a coherent sentence. Grein, taking *gyrn* as object, translates *ongyldon* by 'leiden', a meaning scarcely to be deduced from other contexts in which the verb appears. Gollancz's version is difficult to reconcile with the original. Although Kennedy gives more consideration to the structure of the passage with: 'In that punishment for sin, guilty in the sight of God, must man and maid by death atone their guilt, their grievous sin, their great transgression', his translation seems to indicate *gyrnes* for *gyrn*. The dictionaries do not give much help with the translation of these lines, for apparently nowhere in either BT or GK is it quoted in full: Köhler (see GK under *gryn*) suggests that *gyrn* is to be understood as *die Sünde der ersten Menschen*, indicating that he thinks both *morþres* and *deopra firena* dependent upon *gyrn*. Williams, *Short Extracts from Old English Poetry* (Bangor, 1909), p. 53, puts forward the emendation *gyrne* which he describes as an instrumentive singular parallel to *synwræce*, but any emendation which involves adding an unaccented syllable to *gyrn* is unsuitable metrically, introducing into the poem a verse-pattern otherwise absent from it and rare generally in OE. It seems best therefore to treat *gyrn* adverbially (with Thorpe) and translate the passage freely: 'since then men and women, guilty against God, had to pay dearly for their sin, their dreadful crimes, in that punishment for their sins, through death.'

863 ff. A similar personification of death appears in *Phoenix* 485 ff. and *Meters of Boethius* 27.11; see further n. for l. 999.

866 *sigetudre*. This nonceword need not be regarded as an unfeeling or careless use of *sige-*, for the poet emphasizes through contrast the inevitability of man's guilt after the fall. The base element *-tudor* occurs otherwise in poetic compounds only in *Genesis* 2766 *magotudre*, *Christ* 629 *magutudre*, and *Paris Psalter* 117.22 *eorðtudrum*.

867 *gynnwised*, MS. *gynnwiseð*. Thorpe's *gen wisod* 'yet . . . directed' suggests that he did not recognize *gynn-*. Grein prints *gynnwised* in emendation of the MS. reading reported by Thorpe, noting that *gin-wisod* might be expected. Toller (see BTs under *gin-wísed*) puts forward *gynnwíse* 'of noble manners' for this context, but there is no reason to disregard entirely the MS. *ð* which indicates emendation to a participial

adjective. Both *gynnwised* and the preterite *wisde* which must lie behind the MS. reading *Daniel* 35 *wisõe* point to the existence of a weak verb *wīsan* 'direct' beside the second-class *wīsian* (or perhaps to an early weakening of the stem syllable in *wīsian*), cognate with OHG. *wīsōn* and ON. *vísa*.

868 *þone bitran drync.* See §6 for discussion of the *poculum mortis* theme.

874 *gebihþum.* The word occurs only here, but its meaning, 'a dwelling, abode', obvious from the context, can be supported by such cognate words as OE. *byht*, *būgan*, ON. *bot* and *bygð*.

875 *stowum*, MS. *stopum*. A similar confusion of *w(wyn)* and *p* occurs in *Juliana* 294 *bisweop* (MS. *bispeop*) and *Riddles* 42.4 *speow* (MS. *speop*), and appears sporadically in other OE. MSS.

876 The need to read *ūrra* as *ūsserra* in the b-verse is first noted by Rieger, 'Die alt- und angelsächsische verkunst', *Zeitschrift für deutsche Philologie*, vii (1876), 52, and subsequently by Sievers, 'Zur Rhythmik', p. 462. See further §8, p. 60.

877 *tælmearce.* The meaning of this *hapax legomenon* presents no difficulty. The first element of the compound occurs in poetry otherwise only in *Andreas* 113 *tælmet* 'measured number'; BT cite *telcræftas* 'arithmetic' (under *tælcræft*) from a homily and a similar *getelcræft* from a late glossary.

878 *Us secgað bec.* A common phrase in homilies; for an example from Wulfstan's sermons see D. Bethurum, *The Homilies of Wulfstan* (Oxford, 1957), p. 155, l. 208. Cp. also *Phoenix* 655 *þæt sindon þa word*, *swa us gewritu secgað.* The clause is often contrasted with the *Guthlac A* poet's references to hearsay in discussion of the sources for the two Guthlac poems (see §4, pp. 28-9).

880 *on Engle.* Here and again in l. 1360 the poet uses a tag not otherwise found in OE. verse. It is suggested in GK under *Engel* that both instances contain the dative singular of a proper name *Engel*, similar to *Ongel* (for Angeln, the continental home of the Angles), to which the dative singular of *Widsith*, ll. 8 and 35 is usually attributed, but the likelihood that we have here the accusative plural *Engle* 'Angli' discourages acceptance of this suggestion. The use of the phrase *geond Bryten innan*, l. 883, implies that *Engle* refers to all the Germanic inhabitants of Britain.

887 *of sidwegum*, MS. *of siðwegum*. The phrase *of sidwegum* (literally 'from the wide ways', i.e. 'from far and wide') occurs also in *Elene* 282, and the compound *sidwegum* again in *Phoenix* 337, so the graphically simple emendation first put forward by Thorpe is accepted. Even Gollancz, who conservatively retains *ð* in his text, translates the phrase 'from distant ways'. BT gloss the otherwise unrecorded *siðweg* 'a road to travel on, high road(?)', translating l. 887b 'from the travelled ways'.

894 *OFT.* A new section begins here, with *O* a largish capital about an inch in height and the following *FT* smaller capitals. A line is left free between this and the preceding section which ends, at an end-line, with *gefremede:-:7.*

897 *eard weardade*. Although found only in the Exeter Book poems *Christ* 772 *eard weardien* and *Husband's Message* 18 *eard weardigan*, this phrase has the appearance of a useful poetic formula. For other instances of rhyming phrases in *Guthlac B* see §8, p. 63.

905 *wrohtsmiðas*. The only other instance of the compound is *Andreas* 86 *werigum wrohtsmiðum* of the cannibals, but -*smið* is a commonly used base element in Anglo-Saxon verse of all periods.

906 *hleoþrum brugdon*. *bregdan* followed by a dative in the sense 'vary, change in' is found again in the Exeter Book in *Panther* 23 *bleom bregdende*. Cp. also *Meters of Boethius* 13.47b *hleoðrum brægdan*. The cognate ON. *bregða* generally governs the dative, but the use of the dative is apparently restricted to verse in OE.

909 *minne*: see n. for *Guthlac A* 650.

912 *adloman*. Except for this form and *Andreas* 1171 *hellehinca* 'the cripple of hell', there is no evidence for lame devils among the Anglo-Saxons (G. P. Krapp, *Andreas and the Fates of the Apostles* (Boston, 1906), p. 135), although such allusions are found in modern European literature. However, the many similarities between *Guthlac B* and *Andreas* show that they derive from a similar background and make it likely that a figure found in one poem should appear in the other. Brooks, *'Andreas'*, p. 103, develops Krapp's suggestion that Satan's lameness resulted from the conflation of his fall from heaven with the story of Vulcan's fall from Olympus, thus giving support to the usual interpretation of *adloman* 'the lame ones of the fire of hell', because 'Vulcan, or Hephaestus, was the god of the fire and forge'. In this orthodox explanation of the compound the element *ād*- is perhaps stretched too far as 'the fire of hell', and the interpretation implicit in Gollancz's 'the fire-mained wretches' is therefore preferred in the Glossary.

Both Trautmann, 'Berichtigungen, Erklärungen and Vermutungen zu Cynewulfs Werken', *Bonner Beiträge*, xxiii (1907), 123, and Meritt, *Fact and Lore about Old English Words* (Stanford, 1954), pp. 5–6, argue that *ādloman* is a corruption of *aðlogan* 'perjurers', a compound which appears in *Christ* 1604 *aðlogum*. The use of rhyme and assonance is an obvious feature of *Guthlac B*, but cannot be advanced to help emend *aðlogan* into the text to parallel *wærlogan* 911 in sound. Moreover, the emendation achieves only a piling up of meaningless variation. Thorpe's suggestion that the scribe left out a nasal consonant in the first syllable involves an unparalleled figurative extension of the concrete *andlōman* 'tools'. It is possible to argue for a compound made up of *ādl* 'illness, disease' and *lama*, with simplication of -*ll*- in the resultant consonant cluster (as found in examples of *ȳfellic(e)*), for the poet must have known Felix's description (§xxxi) of the repulsive demons who tormented Guthlac. With such infirmities these demons, like so many others in hagiographic and patristic writings, must have limped. However, as poetic compounds with *ādl*- as the first element occur only in this poem, and as they refer to the saint's illness, it seems safer to accept *ād* 'fire, funeral pyre', which is found in poetic compounds (e.g. *Beowulf* 3010 *adfære*, *Exodus* 398 *Adfyr*, and *Phoenix* 222 *adleg*).

spiowdon. An infinitive *spīowan* with *īo* from West Germanic *iu* must lie behind this non-WS. form. Sievers, 'Zur Rhythmik', p. 486, points to similar forms in *Christ* 1121 *spēowdun*, *Elene* 297 *spēowdon*, and *Juliana* 476 *spīowedan*.

916–19a These lines reflect the many episodes which centre on birds in the *Vita* and particularly the story of the two swallows (§xxxix) who obeyed the saint's commands as to where to build their nest.

917 *feorhnere*. The context, and especially the phrase *hungre gepreatad* 916, suggests the word here means 'sustenance, food'. Thorpe's 'refuge' may stem from his knowledge of Felix §xxxix, in which the swallows do not presume to choose a nesting-place without Guthlac's instructions. The poet is less generous in judging the motivation of the swallows for visiting the saint: in the life they go to him because of his purity of spirit, whereas in *Guthlac B* they seek food. This discrepancy may suggest that the poet remembered the final passages of *Guthlac A* for which he was providing a companion-piece, but as he is summarizing and as the motif is common enough in saints' lives the contrast cannot be pressed too far.

921 *sigewonge*. See n. for *Guthlac A*, ll. 742–3, for other examples of this word.

922 *þeowon*. This is the only place in either of these poems where *-on* appears in the declension of weak nouns and adjectives, but to emend the form away, as is generally done, would be inconsistent unless all instances of infinitives in *-on* were also changed.

923 *forþum*. Grein's emendation *furðum* is accepted in GK, but goes unmentioned in commentary upon the text except in Cosijn's note, 'Anglosaxonica. IV', p. 119. Because the adverb *furþum* occurs also in ll. 1228 and 1239 and because there are some signs of scribal *o* for *u* in accented syllables throughout the MS. (see n. for *Guthlac A* 780 *worde*), Grein's explanation is here followed without altering the form.

927 *seoslige*. The adjective occurs only here and, as Thorpe (p. 506) notes first, must be related to *sūsl* 'torment'.

931b The scribe has overlooked some preterite auxiliary verb form in this verse, almost certainly the *moste* generally supplied.

932b From this point the poet follows the material of *Vita* §1 fairly closely (see §6).

933 *endedogor*. The impersonal time constructions of *Judith* 287 and *Genesis* 2510–11 suggest that *endedogor* should be taken as a dative singular here and in ll. 1167 and 1201.

942b–44a Although Thorpe reports these verses correctly, Grein assumes some words have dropped out of the text and supplies between ll. 942 and 943 *untrymnes adle gongum*. Holthausen, 'Beiträge zur Erklärung und Textkritik altenglischer Dichtungen', *Indogermanische Forschungen*, iv (1894), 385, improves this stop-gap metrically by placing *seo* before or *þa* after *untrymnes*. Though the invented line is relegated to the footnotes in Assmann's revision of the *Bibliothek*, a line is left free to indicate some omission. Kennedy, despite recognizing the impersonal construction, indicates loss: 'In the gloom of night . . . it

racked his body'. KD's observation that the subject of *wæs* . . . *geþrungen* 'is carried over from *adl*' is puzzling, given a punctuation in which new sentences open with *Him* 939, *He* 940, and *Wæs* 942. Gollancz, Gordon, and BT (see under *onberan*) find no difficulty in translating the passage.

949 *on his dagena tid*. Cp. *Elene* 193 *on his dagana tid*, *Paris Psalter* 77.32 *Hi heora dagena tid* and 88.39 *þu his dagena tid*. Sievers, 'Zur Rhythmik', p. 484, points out that the use of *dagena* '. . . steht metrisch sicher für Cynewulf, Guthlac und die Psalmen auf anglischer, und für das späte Menologium auf sächsischer seite'. He gives examples where the form is needed for the metre: *Christ* 467, 1586, *Menologium* 64, 169; but *Paris Psalter* 101.21 *minra dagena* and 118.84 *ealra dagena* could have the more recently recognized verse-pattern $/ \times / \times$ with *daga*. Examples of *daga* may also be found in this group of poems, e.g. *Guthlac B* 1001.

950 *ælmihtiga*, MS. *hælmihtiga*. Cp. *æfentid* 1215.

955 *inbendum fæst*. The adjective *fæst* is generally followed by the dative case in OE. rather than by *in* or *on*, evidence that the alliteration is correct in pointing to a compound not found elsewhere. The prefix *in-* may be interpreted either as 'inner' or as an intensive; 'inner' is the more usual in a nominal prefix, and is suitable both contextually and in relation to Felix's *intimorum stimulatio*.

956 *lichord onlocen*. Cp. *lichord onleac* 1029. Thorpe (p. 506) comments that the poet uses *lichord* for *lichoma* 'obviously for the sake of the metaphor with onleac'. In the Glossary a direct translation is given, together with the interpretation 'soul', an interpretation which can be supported by comparison with the more widely used *breosthord* (e.g. *Beowulf* 1719, 2792, *Seafarer* 55) and of *sawlhord* and *feorhhord*. See E. G. Stanley, 'Old English Poetic Diction and the Interpretation of *The Wanderer, The Seafarer* and *The Penitent's Prayer*', *Anglia*, lxxiii (1956), 428–9, for OE. poetic use of the figure behind the idea that a man's thought is bound fast within his mind.

960 *færhagan*. The first element *fær-* allows a choice from the range 'sudden, perilous, terrible', but Thorpe's translation of this *hapax legomenon* by 'peril' is over-simple. The word *haga* has the senses 'hedge' and 'hedged/fenced enclosure' in poetic compounds, and 'hedge of terrors' (Clark Hall), 'Calamity that compasses about' (BTs), and 'the encircling danger' (Gordon) are interpretations put forward. However, *-haga* is also used to denote a wedge formation of ranks in fighting, e.g. *Juliana* 395 *cumbolhagan, Elene* 652 *bordhagan, Battle of Maldon* 102 *wihagan* (cf. *Beowulf* 3118 *scildweall, Judith* 305 *scildburh, Battle of Maldon* 242 *scyldburh*, and cognate Germanic compounds for *testudo*), and it proves easier therefore to interpret the sentence in terms of battle, as do Gollancz with 'the sudden onset of fiends' attacks' and Kennedy with 'the perils of the fiend's assaults'.

962 *egle*, MS. *engle*. The word may have been unfamiliar to the scribe, for the same mistake occurs in *Christ* 762 *eglum* (MS. *englum*), although it is twice correctly transcribed elsewhere in the MS. The unconscious substitution of a better-known noun, moreover a word

commoner in religious poetry, may also appear in *Genesis* 328 *engles* (see Sisam, *Studies*, pp. 29–30), despite the good defence of *engles* put up by Stanley, 'A Note on *Genesis B*, 328' *RES*, n.s. v (1958), 55–8.

969 *gedælde*, MS. *ge dæled*. The MS. reading is generally emended to give a finite verb in this clause, Thorpe suggesting *gedældon* 'should part', Grein and Assmann *gedælden* which KD follow, noting that Gollancz's *gedæleð* is unsuitable because 'the context requires a past tense and a plural number'. A simpler change is to argue a scribal transposition of the letters *ed*, perhaps due to the influence of the perfective *ge-*. The scribe may have had *gedælde* in his exemplar, for there are examples of the preterite plural subjunctive in *-e* in these texts (see §9, p. 68).

971 Cosijn, 'Anglosaxonica. IV', p. 119, notes ironically against this line: *Wenn nur 'fyllan' die bedeutung des afries. 'fella' hätte!*

976 ðA. A new section begins on the sixth line of fo. 47ʳ, opening with a capital about an inch in height; the following *A* is smaller. The preceding line is half-empty and ends with *cynnes:7:-*.

978 *adl*: As Klaeber, *The Later Genesis*, p. 55, points out, the metre shows that *adl* should be regarded as disyllabic. Cp. *adle* 1022, *adl* 1064, *sawul* 1089, *sawel* 1264.

980 *bryþen*. The word occurs only here and in *Andreas* 1532 *sorg-byrþen* 'sorrowful drink' in verse-texts. The *Andreas* compound is generally interpreted 'a burden of sorrow' by the older editors of the poem, but *-byrþen* is now recognized as a metathetic form of *bryþen* 'brewing' (Smithers, 'Five Notes on Old English Texts', *Engl. and Germ. St.*, iv (1951–2), 74, n. 9, and Brooks '*Andreas*', p. 114). Thorpe must have been unfamiliar with this word which he thinks a mistake for *brywen*, but later editors do not question the form, and equivalents such as 'brewing, drink' are general in translations and dictionaries. BT cite under *bryðen* one other example from the *Leechdoms* and a second form which is reidentified in BTs as *byrþen* 'burden'. Cognate are OE. *broð* and *brēowan*, OHG. *brod* and ON. *broð* (see *AEW* for further examples).

985 *bædeweg*. The compound appears also in the Old English Bede (ed. T. Miller, EETS (OS), xcv, xcvi, cx, cxi (1890–8), i. 370, ll. 29–31): Ða hi ða betwih him spræcon be haligra fædra life and him betwih bædeweg scencton þæs heofonlican lifes 'qui dum sese alterutrum cælestis vitæ poculis debriarent'. The form is apparently corrupt in two MSS. which read *beadowig* (see Miller, vol. ii, readings for 0 and Ca). Otherwise there is no evidence for *wæg* 'cup' as a by-form of *wæge* 'cup' whose Germanic cognates (see *AEW* under *wæge* 3) are similar in form: OS. *wēgi* and OHG. *weiga*. The Bede translator had before him *poculum* which can mean both 'cup' and 'drink'. Professor Smithers, 'Five Notes on Old English Texts', pp. 68 ff., discussing the *poculum mortis* image in medieval English writings, cites examples which clearly demonstrate both translations of *poculum*, but the ambiguity of *bædeweg* is not noted. The 'cup' interpretation is followed by Grein, Gollancz, and Gordon, whereas Kennedy's 'and then she poured out that bitter potion to Adam' suggests that he recognized the possible alternative

for -*weg* in this compound. This meaning is suitable both in the Bede and in *Guthlac B*. Poetic compounds in -*wæge* appear in *Beowulf* 481 *ealowæge*, 495 *ealowæge*, 1982 *liðwæge*, 2021 *ealuwæge*, and probably *Guthlac B* 991 *deaðweges* (N). The *Beowulf* examples indicate that an OE. poet would most likely have been familiar with -*wæge* as a base on which compounds could be built, and it is generally agreed that the translator of the Old English Bede had some familiarity with poetic vocabulary. It seems best therefore to regard the compound as a by-form of this word. The ambiguity in meaning remains, for in both contexts *bædeweg* may be translated either 'cup' or 'drink'; the overlapping of these senses may be seen also in ON. *veig* 'drink', a word of uncertain etymology (see de Vries, *Altnordisches Etymologisches Wörterbuch*, under *veig*).

The first element of *bædeweg* is obscure. Dietrich's identification of it with *beado* 'battle', adopted in BT but discarded in GK and BTs, may have been based on his knowledge of the *beadowig* forms of the late Bede MSS. It may be related to *bædan* 'urge on, solicit' (see *AEW* under *bǣdan* 1 for cognate verbs, e.g. ON. *beiða* and Gothic *baidjan*). ON. poetic words in *beiði*- are compared with the compound in GK, where the explanation *poculum, quo ut bibatur aliquis instanter rogatur? als allgemeine Benennung des Bechers* appears. In the ON. phrases in which this *beiði*- occurs there is an accompanying objective genitive, as for example *beiði-Týr Bilds hattar* 'Tyr who asks for a helmet', i.e. 'a man of fighting fame and service' (E. V. Gordon, *Introduction to Old Norse* (Oxford, 2nd edn., rev. A. R. Taylor, 1957), p. 216); cp. the entries for *beiði-Hlǫkk, beiði-Rindr*, and *hǫrbeiði-Sif* in S. B. Egilsson, *Lexicon Poeticum antiquæ Linguæ Septentrionalis* (F. Jónsson's edition, Copenhagen, 1931). In the Bede passage *bædeweg* is followed by *þæs heofonlican lifes*, and the relative pronoun *þæs* 985 is probably to be regarded in the same way. It is curious that this element is not otherwise known from OE. sources, but its appearance in both the Bede translation and in *Guthlac B* suggests that it may have had a wider currency.

990 *þone bleatan drync*. The adjective *blēat* appears only here in simplex form in OE. The related adverb occurs in *Beowulf* 2824 *bleate*, and the adjective forms the second element of *Beowulf* 2725 *wælbleate*. A short note on the word's history can be found in *OED* under BLETE; both the noun and adjective forms in *The Owl and the Nightingale* contain the sense 'bare, naked' (see *MED* under BLĒT).

991 *deopan deaðweges*. C. Brown, 'Poculum Mortis', p. 389, first notes the similarity of *Maxims I* 78 *Deop deada wæg dyrne bið lengest*, where he suggests *deaða*, a *u*-stem genitive should be read for *deada*, and he rejects for both passages such translations as the 'deep dead wave' or the 'deep way of the dead'. Some reconsideration of the suitability of either *wæg* 'wave' or *weg* 'way' to this context is necessary. Smithers argues that the idea of a journey to the abode of the dead is implicit in *Vainglory* 55 *neosiþum*, *Rune Poem* 69 *ofer wæg gewat*, and *Seafarer* 63 *hwælweg* (see Smithers, 'The Meaning of *The Seafarer* and *The Wanderer*', *MÆ*, xxvi (1957), 137–53, for discussion of this concept

in early medieval eschatological writings) and that there is evidence that Germanic peoples may have thought of the journey of death as across water (Smithers, ibid., 'Appendix', *MÆ*, xxviii (1959), 100). Certainly *wæg* 'wave' can be read into *Maxims I* 78, and the elaboration of the *sorgbyrþen* metaphor in *Andreas* 1532b–5, where *drync* refers ironically to floods both as floods and as a bitter potion, indicates that it would not be impossible to read *wæg* 'wave' into *Guthlac B* and to interpret *þone bleatan drync* 990 in terms of a deep wave of death. A rather more compressed image of similar effect is *Riddles* 23.13 *mandrinc*. The appearance however of the *poculum mortis* figure in the preceding lines (and see the note for *bædeweg* 985) makes it likely that ll. 990–1 reiterate this image and that the second element of *deaðweges* is *wæg(e)* 'cup' (or 'drink').

duru sylfa. Klaeber, *The Later Genesis*, p. 55, notes that *duru* may be either a nominative form (in which case *sylfa* requires discussion) or an accusative with a subject 'death' or 'man' understood. There is no need to resort to the second of these alternatives: there are other instances of the levelling of -*e* and -*a* in this text; and cp. *Christ* 59 and *Genesis* 570, where *sylfa* also occurs where a feminine ending is to be expected.

995b–6a: see §6, p. 40 and §8, p. 54.

997 *anhoga*. A good account of *anhoga/anhaga* is given by T. P. Dunning and A. J. Bliss, *The Wanderer* (London, 1969), pp. 37–40, who can find no 'differentiation of meaning corresponding to the differentiation of form' and suggest the general interpretation 'one who is alone'. They point out that the unusual extension of the word to gloss L. *unica* in *Phoenix* 87 and 346 may be found here too, for 'Death is the only one of his kind'.

ætryhte. Both here and in l. 1152 *ætryhte* is followed by the dative. Cp. *Andreas* 848 *biryhte* (explained as an adverb in Brooks, '*Andreas*', p. 91).

999 *wiga wælgifre*. The personification of death, introduced early in the poem in ll. 863 ff., is picked up again in Guthlac's words in ll. 1033 ff. It is not a feature of Felix's account of the saint's death. This phrase otherwise occurs only in *Phoenix* 486 and is described by Rankin, 'A Study of the Kennings in Anglo-Saxon Poetry', *JEGP*, ix (1910), p. 73, as 'probably not an old German phrase'. Boethius in his *Consolatio* IV, *metrum* iv (Loeb text, 1973, p. 350) portrays death as drawing near *Sponte sua volucres nec remoratur equos*, but the Anglo-Saxon translator, perhaps accustomed to some such material as in *Guthlac B*, misinterprets the following sentence, turning death into a huntsman: *hwi ne magon ge gesion þæt he spuraþ ælce dæg æfter fuglum. 7 æfter diorum . . .* (S. Fox, *King Alfred's Anglo-Saxon Version of Boethius* (London, 1895), caput xxxix). See also §6, pp. 39–40 and §8, p. 59.

1002 *temple*. Used in this poem for Guthlac's oratory (cp. ll. 1113 and 1149), which is also described as *þæt halge hus* 1290, 1310.

1003 *eþelbodan*. J. R. Stracke, '*Eþelboda: Guthlac B*', *Modern Philology*, lxxiv (1976), 194–5, points out the appropriateness of both

elements of 'homeland-announcer' in this context, noting the homeland is of course heaven.

1007 *fonde.* The MS. form is retained because of signs of confusion between *u* and *o* in the Exeter Book; cp. n. for l. 780 *worde.*

1015b–16a Kock's suggestion, 'Interpretations IV', p. 122, that because the other instances of the compound *meþelcwide* in ll. 1007, 1219, and *Solomon and Saturn* 434 show variation, here *meðelcwidum* must vary *worda* is unconvincing. He argues that (*ge*)*wealdan* can 'take first an instrumental, then, with the same force, a genitive', comparing *Death of Edward* 19–21 where, as in this passage, a syntactically simpler reading is possible.

1019 *gesoht.* Of those who have edited this part of *Guthlac B*, only Williams, *Short Extracts from Old English Poetry* (Bangor, 1909), p. 87, points out that the participle is without the expected inflexion. Cp. *soden* 1150 and perhaps *gesoht* 1145; see also §9, p. 70.

1022 *adle.* See n. for *adl* 978.

1025 *bancoþa.* The second element of this compound is *-coða* 'disease', but the first may be related either to *bana* 'killer' or *bān* 'bone'. The word occurs once in the *Leechdoms* where Meritt (1960 supplement to Clark Hall) identifies it as *bāncoða* 'bone disease', returning, as apparently BTs, to the earlier interpretation of the form (e.g. see GK for Ettmüller's definition); the GK, BT, and Clark Hall entries adopt the *băn-* reading.

1029 *lichord onleac.* See n. for l. 956.

1032 *leomu, lames geþacan.* Thorpe takes *leomu-lames* as a compound, translating the verse 'with covering of clay' and explaining (p. 506) that 'the notion that the body or limbs are formed of clay' underlies the phrase. Grein's *die Gleider auf Lehm gebettet* is reflected in the BT and GK interpretations of the passage, and in Gordon's 'the limbs stretched upon the clay', but in these explanations *geþacan* is given a participial function and a sense it cannot support. The translations of Gollancz, 'these limbs, coverings of clay', and of Kennedy, 'these clay wrappings of the limbs', are better. The phrase *lames geþacan* varies *leomu.*

1034 *laces.* The simplex *lac* 'struggle' is not found elsewhere in OE., although the sense is well known from the many poetic compounds and proper names in which it occurs. (This line is listed, together with *Beowulf* 1584, as showing *lac* in the sense 'offering to a hostile force as to a god (fig.)' in Toronto dictionary specimens available early in 1979.)

1037 *on þisse eahteþan.* Refers back to *niht* 1035, not forward to *dæg* 1038. The German scholars do not misunderstand the grammatical concord here, but Thorpe's translation of ll. 1037a and 1038a together as 'on this eighth / passing day' has left its mark on most subsequent translations of the passage into English, e.g. Gollancz's 'upon this eighth, / this approaching day'.

1038 *dæg scriþende.* The phrase is described under *dæg* in GK as an accusative absolute and is explained *die appropinquante, kurz vor*

Tagesanbruch. Cosijn, 'Anglosaxonica. IV', p. 119, indicates that it is instrumental, but takes it with l. 1037a.

1040 *gesweðrad*, MS. *geswedrad*. Thorpe's unconscious emendation is the form to be found in all the editions.

1042 *gingra geafena*. The phrase occurs twice again in the Exeter Book, referring also to heavenly gifts in *Phoenix* 624 *geongra gyfena*, but to earthly gifts in *Gifts of Men* 2 *geongra geofona*. The adjective is generally understood either as 'young', e.g. Thorpe's 'the young gifts' or Grein's *die jungen Gaben*, or as 'new', e.g. Gollancz, Kennedy, and Gordon. Cosijn, 'Anglosaxonica. IV', p. 119, explains *geong* in this context by comparing with it the OHG. *iucundlīh* 'jocundis, dolcis', an interpretation which has not gained any support. Klaeber, 'Emendations in Old English Poems', *Mod. Phil.*, ii (1904), 141, advances scribal misreading of the exemplar for all three places, explaining '*ginra* > *gingra* > *geongra* is a self-explanatory series'. Noting that *ginne*, a word confined to poetic texts, where it is rare, is particularly liable to misinterpretation by scribes (e.g. *Beowulf* 466 *ginne* for MS. *gimme*), he suggests his underlying phrase *ginra geofena* is merely a 'metrical variant' of the commoner formula *ginfæste gife*, but adds that it is unlikely that the same mistake should be made three times by one scribe and 'probability therefore favours the retention of the MS. *gingra*'. Klaeber does not say how the adjective is to be understood. The more recent suggestion that 'the gifts are perpetually new' (see Blake, *The Phoenix* (Manchester, 1964), p. 86) points to a way in which the phrase may be read. Its use of *geong* may owe something to the biblical promise of *novos caelos et novam terram* to the faithful (cp. *OED*, NEW a. and sb[27], and *niwra gefeana* 833).

lomber. Cosijn, 'Anglosaxonica, IV', p. 119, points out that as *folgian* is rarely followed by an accusative, *lomber* is *der lautgesetzliche dativ* (*statt lember*). Although this interpretation of the form is likely, there is insufficient evidence to determine whether it is accusative or dative. It is labelled dative in SB, §289, n. 1, but Campbell, §635, is content to describe it as 'poetical'.

1053 *geseah*. A pronoun subject is supplied by all the editors except KD, who note that the subject need not always be expressed in OE., comparing *Christ* 602 and 1154; cp. also *Guthlac B* 995. Here *þæs þe* 1053 refers back to *þæs færspelles* 1050, and the text should be punctuated accordingly. It should be noted that Gollancz's placing of *geseah* at the head of the next verse is dependent on the adoption of some overt subject into the text at this point.

1054 *onbæru*. The base element of this *hapax legomenon* presents little difficulty, but the prefix can be interpreted either as *un-* or *ond-*. Thorpe's 'resignation' is, he notes, conjectural. The BT **un + bǣru* 'wrong behaviour, vexation, anger' is forced ('he could not be vexed at it (Guthlac's death), but he shed hot tears'), and their tentative comparison of OHG. *un-gipārida* 'fastidium, ira, rabies' is insufficient to bolster up this explanation. Identification of the prefix with *ond-* has proved more attractive, as evidenced by the GK *abstinentia?*, Clark Hall's

'self-restraint', and the translations of Grein, Gollancz, Kennedy, and Gordon.

1057 *wægdropan*. Cosijn, 'Anglosaxonica. IV', p. 119, objecting to the conceit contained in this compound, suggests the emendation **wængdropan*, both because the phrase *mæstas genas* appears in the *Vita* and to parallel *hleordropan* 1341 more closely, despite recognizing that similar imagery lies behind *teagor yðum weol* 1340. However, the poet does not follow the Latin phrasing blindly, and his use of *wæg-* in this compound may as easily stem from the *Vita* phrase *crebris . . . rivulis*.

1060 *ONgeat*. An empty line in the MS. marks the beginning of a new section, the previous section ending with *wæs:-:7* (the heavy punctuation fills out the line). In *ONgeat* a large capital *O* (almost an inch high) is followed by a script *n* the height of the tallest ascenders used by the scribe.

gæsta halig. Thorpe translates 'holy in soul', suggesting the emendation *gæste*, a normalization not adopted in this edition. Holthausen, in the supplement to GK, compares *gæsthaligra* 873 and *gæsthaligne* 1149, and with his emendation *gæsthalig* produces a verse metrically less unusual; but Roberts, 'A Metrical Examination', p. 134, scans l. 1060a as a hypermetric verse.

1061 *drusendne*, MS. *drusende*. As the verb *ongitan* generally governs the accusative and as *hyge* is masculine, the orthodox editorial emendation is adopted. For a note on the lack of *-į-* in the participle, see §9, pp. 66–7.

1064 *adl*. See the n. for *adl* 978.

1068 *seocan*, MS. *seocnan*. The adjective *sēoc* does not appear with an *-n-* stem in OE. or cognate Germanic languages, so the scribe's *seocnan* may reflect dittography. Thorpe's emendation is therefore accepted.

1072 *sceolon*. As Cosijn, 'Anglosaxonica. IV', p. 120, points out, the poet returns to the plural subject implicit in *herehloðe hellepegna* 1069.

1078 *edleana georn*, MS. *edlea/nan georn*. No weak forms cognate with the strong noun *edlean* are recorded. The KD suggestion of a weak **edleana* would allow treatment of the MS. phrase as syntactically parallel with *sipes fus* 1077; less likely is *edleanan* as object of *niman* and parallel with *upeard*. Here emendation to *edleana* is made, with that form taken as a genitive plural. As the scribe splits the word between two lines, the circumstances favour dittography.

1088b–9a Similar phrasing appears in *Andreas* 294b–5a *þær þe lust myneð / to gesecanne*.

1089 *sawul*. See the n. for *adl* 978.

1091 *eadwelan*, with super- and subpuncted *g* before *ead-* in the MS. see §9, p. 66.

1094 *se wuldormaga*. Like *se wuldormago* 1293 this compound represents the *Vita* phrase *vir dei*. The forms are synonymous for the translators, yet the standard dictionaries list two grammatically distinct words. As there is evidence for the falling together of back vowels in

inflexions in this manuscript, it seems unnecessary to gloss one form under -*măga* and the other under -*magu*. Both strong *u*-noun forms of *mago* and weak *maga* forms occur in OE. (see Campbell, §614, n. 2); the headword *wuldormaga* is used in the glossary for convenience.

1096 *swamode*. Thorpe translates *swamode* 'floated', treating it (p. 506) as a weak verb built on *swam* and adding that he has not found it elsewhere. Dietrich, 'Zu Cädmon', *Zeitschrift für deutsches Altertum und deutsche Literatur*, x (1856), 315, relates the form to *Genesis* 376 *aswamað*, suggesting the meanings (adopted in GK and BT) 'grow dark' for *Guthlac B* 1096 and 'languish, fail, cease' for *Genesis* 376. Cosijn, 'Anglosaxonica. IV', p. 120, points out that in *Guthlac B* the meaning is rather *wälzte sich*, comparing the Middle High German *sweimen* 'sich schwingen', OHG. *sweimen* 'schweben', ON. *sveima* 'soar' and OE. *āswǣmian* [*sic*] from *Genesis*. Kock, 'Jubilee Jaunts', p. 42, suggests that the etymon of *swamode* is **sṷaịm*- 'move (in a vague manner, not in a straight direction, not with a fixed goal)', comparing ON. *sveima* 'wander, stray', OE. *aswǣman* 'move on, wander about' and *aswāmian* 'pass on, disappear' (see also n. for *Guthlac B* 1352 *áswǣman*). Emphatically rejecting Dietrich's interpretation of *swamode*, Kock points out that *nihtrim scridon* 1097 refers to 'the circular motion of the firmament' and that *swamode ofer niðða bearn* answers 'closely' to *scridon ofer dugeðum*. Gollancz translates the form 'floated', whereas Kennedy and Gordon follow Dietrich with 'grew black' and 'grew dark' respectively.

1097 *nihtrim*. Cosijn, 'Anglosaxonica. IV', p. 120, points out that this collective is explained by *feowere . . . dagas* 1134–45, *seofon niht* 1035, and *se seofeða dæg* 1141.

1101 *mid dreame*. May be taken either as 'amid joy, joyfully' or as 'together with a host' (see W. Temple, 'The Song of the Angelic Hosts', *Duquesne Studies Annuale Mediaevale*, ii (1961), 5–14, for *dream* as the company of holy ones singing psalms to the Creator rather than the song sung). The latter is perhaps the more likely because of *ðreata mæstne* 1103, both phrases being references to the host harrowed from hell.

1102 *onwald*, MS. *onweald* with *e* subpuncted. Thorpe suggests *onwealde* 'with power'. Cosijn, 'Anglosaxonica. IV', p. 120, counters GK *potens*, preferring *princeps*, the meaning he mistakenly ascribes to two instances of *onweald* 'power' in the *Cura Pastoralis* translation. The BT suggestion that the more familiar adjective *onwealh* should be read here is tempting, but see BTs *anweald* for the use of this adjective in Ælfric.

1134 *WÆRon*. A new section begins on the fourth line from the bottom of fo. 49^r; the tail of the large wyn descends below the last line of script on this folio, and the following two letters are smaller capitals (the height of the scribe's tallest ascenders). The preceding line is empty, except for *forgiefen hæfde:-:7*.

1135 *þæs se dryhtnes* [*þegn*]. As far as sense and metre are concerned *þegn* provides a satisfactory stop-gap. Grein's suggestion that *þe* should be substituted for *se* is unnecessary (cp. *þes lifes gæst* 1176, *se eorðan dæl* 1366, and *se wuldres dæl* 1368).

1140 *stalgongum.* This nonceword must mean something like 'with stealthy strides' (Gollancz's translation). Although a figurative 'unrelenting' might seem attractive for the prefix, *stal-* is probably cognate with *stalu* 'theft', *stalian* 'steal, proceed stealthily', and with *stæl-* (as in *stælgiest* 'thieving guest', *stælhere* 'marauding band', *stæltihtle* 'charge of stealing', and *stælöing* 'theft'). Thorpe's 'with iron strides' may involve the notion 'unrelenting' or it may be based on a comparison of *stal-* with *stÿle* 'steel', *stÍlan* 'temper', ON. *stäl*, and OHG. *stahal.* His interpretation may have prompted Grein's alternate explanation of *stal-*, in which he relates the form to *stælwirðe* 'robustus, fortis' (the senses later developed by this word, but in OE. it has the sense 'serviceable') and to a form in Lye, *stalferhð* (but neither this nor *staþolferhð* to which Lye refers it is otherwise recorded). Though such compounds as *staðolfæst* 'fixed, steadfast' might be cited as evidence for the use of *staðol-* in *stalgongum*, it is difficult to explain the appearance of *a.* Grein's preferred gloss for *stalgong*, 'gressus furtivus', is compared by him with *stalu.*

1143 *hildescurun.* See n. for l. 1154a for a discussion of the imagery.

1148 *unwenne.* The emendation *unwemne* 'blameless' is made by Thorpe, Gollancz, and Williams, and is implied by Gordon's 'faultless', but is not otherwise found necessary. It should be noted that GK prefer the headword *unwēn*, perhaps because the ON. cognate is *úvænn*, but as the nominative singular masculine *unwēne* is recorded (see BT, Clark Hall), that form is used in the Glossary.

1150 *soden.* This may be an uninflected parallel in poetic variation (see n. for *gesoht* 1019) but can alternatively be explained as an accusative singular masculine form of the participle with syncope and transposition of final *-en.*

1152 *ætryhte.* See n. for *ætryhte* 997.

1154a *awrecen wælpilum.* Cp. l. 1286a. The compounds *wælpilum* and *wælstrælum* do not occur outside this poem, but similar in form, though used concretely, are *Beowulf* 398 *wælsceaftas*, *Battle of Maldon* 322 *wælspere*, etc. The figure of Death in *The Phoenix* is *wæpnum geþryþed* 486, but the *egeslic hunta* 27.13 of the *Meters of Boethius* is less developed; specific shafts of Death appear in OE. poetry only in *Guthlac B*. The examples of the devil's arrows gathered together by E. G. Stanley, 'Old English Poetic Diction', pp. 419–22, emphasize for the most part torment of the spirit. Only in *Juliana* 468–72a do these arrows cause actual bodily affliction. In the source for *Juliana* the devil strikes his victims with blindness, and this is reflected in the words given him by the poet. Stanley (p. 421 and fn.) notes that this use of the figure of the devil's arrows is the poet's addition, but does not point out that in the OE. poem the Latin account's fact of physical blindness is lost in the symbolical development of this theme. Arrows of physical illness are better known from medical writings and iconography. They appear in *Guthlac B* first in ll. 1142b–5a where they are independent of Felix.

1154b *wló.* Thorpe suggests reading *wlonc* 'the high of soul', but the form is now generally connected with *wlōh* 'hem, fringe' (found in

verse in *Juliana* 590 and *Andreas* 1471) and with the adjectives *gewlō*
'adorned' (*Genesis* 1789) and *anwlōh* 'unadorned' (*Daniel* 584, MS.
form). Cognate are OS. *wlōh* 'Flocke' and ON. *ló* (restricted to the
phrase *ló á klæði*); other cognate words may be seen in *AEW* and in
Jordan, *Eigentümlichkeiten*, p. 57. GK, following Dietrich, suggest that
wló 1154 is an adverbial accusative with the meaning *nicht die Faser,
nicht das mindeste*, and that it may have developed in the same way as
the G. *nicht die Bohne* or the OE. *hwōn*. BT assume an adverb 'readily,
easily', which is referred without further comment to their entry for
wlōh. Kock, 'Interpretations VII' (1920), p. 104, elaborates the GK
explanation by suggesting the translation 'could not a funicle' for *wló
ne meahte*; he supports this suggestion with an unnecessary manipulation
of *Christ* 77 *æfter modwisan mod ne cuðes* to produce *mot ne cuðes* 'thou
knowest not a mote'. However, the clause structure shows that *wló* is
best taken as an adverb, and comparison of the *Vita* words *nec tamen
tunc cum eo loquebatur* (Colgrave, p. 154) indicates 'indeed' as a translation; Gollancz's 'scarce' and the 'hardly' of Gordon and Kennedy are
unsuitable because they necessitate omission of the negative particle.

1155 *ellensprǣce*. Kock, 'Interpretations VII' (1920), p. 253, points
out that *ellensprǣce* should be treated as parallel with *hleopor* (as BT),
noting the similarity of *sprǣce ahebban* 1160 and adding that parallel
accusatives are a common Germanic method of variation.

1158 *modglǣdne*. Kock, 'Jubilee Jaunts', p. 43, suggests the emendation *modlǣtne* 'faint at heart', an unrecorded compound, arguing that
the 'dying saint, *unwen, soden sarwylmum*, is surely not called *meðe*
and *modglǣd* in the same breath!' It would be easier to see the logic of
his argument if these cleverly contrasting adjectives were applied to
Guthlac's companion instead of to the saint, who is eager to enter his
heavenly home.

1161 *truwade*. Sievers, 'Zur Rhythmik', p. 486, and Holthausen,
Beiblatt, ix (1899), 356, suggest *trēowde* should be read here, because
they regard *truwian* as having *ū* (so listed in GK and BT; the correct
ŭ is found in Holthausen's corrections in GK).

1173b–5a In his translation Grein presents these verses as reported
speech within Guthlac's words to his companion, and so Kennedy;
Grein later ('Zur Textkritik', p. 424) suggests the new speech should
begin with l. 1173a, a textual division followed in Williams's reader.
Gollancz, Assmann, KD, and Gordon all divide the text as in this
edition.

1175 *asanian*. This verb, cognate with Gothic *sains* and *sainjan*, OHG.
seini 'slow' and ON. *séina* 'tarry, delay', appears once again in English:
7 hit asanode þa on þa ylcan wysan 'and it waned in the same way'
(A. S. Napier, 'An Old English Vision of Leofric, Earl of Mercia',
Transactions of the Philological Society (1907–10), p. 184, l. 57). For
the verse-form see §8, pp. 61–2, and cp. ll. 1177a, 1252a, and 1361a.

1178 *Fyr*. Thorpe, suggesting *fer?* in his footnotes, translates 'go', an
interpretation supported by the *Vita* instruction *perge ad sororem
meam Pegam* (Colgrave, p. 154). Grein's graphically simple change to

fys has been generally adopted, except for the *Fyr* of Gollancz's text, where however the emendation is implied by the translation 'Hasten'.

1180 *on longne weg*. Cosijn, 'Anglosaxonica. IV', p. 120, compares *Phoenix* 555 *on longne sið* and a Middle Dutch phrase from Reinaert, *up mine langhe vaert*, connecting the phrase with the journey of the soul after death. In contrast, the compound *longwoege* (*Lindisfarne Gospels* gloss, Mark 13:34) means 'pilgrimage' (see W. W. Skeat, *The Holy Gospels* (1871), p. 109).

1189 *leahtra lease*. Cp. the compound *leahtorlease* 1087.

1195 *in þeostorcofan*. Both Cosijn, 'Anglosaxonica. IV', p. 120, and Kock 'Interpretations VII', p. 254, point out that this phrase it parallel with *in sondhofe* 1196. The compound *þeostorcofa* appears also in *Elene* 832, and a similar compound is *Phoenix* 49 *heolstorcofan*.

1200 *frean feorhgedal*. Kock, 'Interpretations VII', pp. 254–5, suggests that this phrase stands before the clause to which it properly belongs, pointing out 'what the servant *oncneow* was not *frean feorhgedal*, but *þæt frean feorhgedal feor ne wæs*' and apparently objecting to Klaeber's view, 'Emendations in Old English Poems', *Mod. Phil.*, ii (1904), 144, that *hit* is used impersonally. The absence of *hit* from ll. 1166–7, cited by Kock against Klaeber's interpretation, shows only that such clauses may occur with or without a subject pronoun. The poet tells us two things, that the saint's companion recognizes that Guthlac is dying and that it is not long to his last day. The translators too are unwilling to allow a clause to vary *frean feorhgedal* and so find themselves obliged to treat *endedogor* as in variation with *hit* and *frean feorhgedal*, rather than as a dative dependent on *feor*.

1215 *æfentid*, MS. *hæfentid*. Cp. *us* 271, *ælmihtiga* 950.

1218 *dægwoman*. Kock, 'Jubilee Jaunts', p. 43, points out that *dægwoma* must here mean 'nightfall', noting the common double application of such words as 'twilight', *Dämmerung*, and *crepusculum*, and explains that the angel visited Guthlac in the evening (ll. 1218b, 1242b) and in the morning (ll. 1219b, 1243b). A note on the compound will be found in the discussion of *dægredwoma* 1292.

1220 *gæstes*. This may be either *gæst* 'spirit' (as Thorpe and Kennedy) or *gæst* 'visitor, stranger' (as Grein, Gollancz, and Gordon). Beccel's description of Guthlac's mysterious visitor in the *Vita* does not help towards a decision either way, for he says he has heard the saint speaking *nescio cum quo* (Colgrave, p. 156); Guthlac's own description of the visitor as *angelum consolationis meae* points to *gæst*.

1222a For this verse see §8, p. 62.

1224 *ðA*. A new section begins here, slightly under half-way down fo. 50ᵛ; the initial capital (*c*. one inch in height) is followed by a smaller *A* which is as tall as the scribe's tallest ascenders. The preceding line is empty and the line above that, filled with script, ends with *sindon:7*.

1226 *elnes oncyðig*. In *Elene* 724 the same phrase describes Judas, as do *meðe and meteleas*, (*mægen wæs geswiðrod*) 698 and *hungre gehyned* 720. The adjective *oncyðig* occurs also in *Fates of the Apostles* 106 *werum oncyðig*, glossed hesitantly in BTs 'unknown', but usually

accepted as meaning 'made known' and explained as a by-form of
*ondcȳðig (a form extracted from the *Vespasian Psalter* gloss 24: 7,
unondcȳðignisse for *ignorantiae*: Sweet, *The Oldest English Texts*, EETS
(OS) lxxxiii (1885), 217). This explanation is followed by the latest
editor of the poem (Brooks, '*Andreas*' and '*The Fate of the Apostles*'
(Oxford, 1961), p. 126). Cognate is the OHG. *antkundig* 'wise' and
probably Modern German *Ankündigung*; one instance of an OE. verb
oncȳðan 'to make known' is listed from a charter by BT.

Two explanations are put forward for *oncȳðig* in *Elene* and *Guthlac B*.
The BT equation of the form in these contexts with *uncȳðig* 'ignorant,
unacquainted' lies behind such translations as Gollancz's 'void of
strength' for *Guthlac B* 1226a. This adjective, containing the prefix
un- which is generally privative or pejorative, appears in *Elene* 960
where stylistic arguments support the interpretation 'ignorant, wicked'.
Though both GK (under *oncȳðig*) and Kock ('Interpretations XI',
p. 266) assign to *Elene* 960 *uncȳðig* such meanings as 'wise, knowing',
the occurrence of a gloss *ðone uncȳðig vel unwittende* against *ignorantem*
(W. W. Skeat, *The Gospel According to Saint Luke* (Cambridge, 1874),
p. 7, l. 18) is further evidence for an adjective *uncȳðig* 'ignorant',
cognate with OHG. *unkundig* and ON. *úkunnigr*. There is however no
indication of the semantic extension necessary if it is to be read into
Elene 724 and *Guthlac B* 1226, which may explain why Brooks prefers
to relate these forms to *oncȳð* 'distress' (see *Beowulf* 830, 1420) and
oncȳðdæda 'harmful deeds' (see *Andreas* 1179) when interpreting them
'devoid of'. The explanation of *elnes oncȳðig* as 'revealing courage'
(e.g. in the editions of *Elene* by Grimm (1840) and Gradon (1958)) is
suitable also in the *Guthlac B* context, for the saint is described similarly
elsewhere in the poem (e.g. *mægne modig* 1272, *eadig on elne* 1285,
eadig, elnes gemyndig 1294). Apparently, therefore, *oncȳðig* appears in
both the Vercelli and Exeter Books in the closely related senses 'making
known' and 'made known'.

1234 The lack of alliteration in this line, noted by Thorpe, leads
Grein to supply two b-verses which, though relegated to his footnotes
by Assmann, are calculated for by the indication of omitted verses in his
text. Because there is no obscurity I follow Gollancz and KD in uniting
these verses into one line. The line is not considered in W. P. Lehmann
and V. F. Dailey, *The Alliterations of the 'Christ' 'Guthlac' 'Elene'
'Juliana' 'Fates of the Apostles' 'Dream of the Rood'* (Texas, 1960).
Elsewhere I have proposed that the assonance between the initial
consonant of *lifgendum* and the medial *l* in the homorganic cluster of
nolde is functional ('A Metrical Examination', p. 115); perhaps *Battle
of Maldon* 183 *Ælfnoð and Wulmær, begen lagon* is comparable.

1239b–42a The clause is often curiously treated, *on þone æfteran
ánseld* 1240 being taken as an accusative noun with its modifiers (e.g.
by Thorpe, Grein, Gollancz, Kennedy, and Gordon, and compare GK
and BT under *æftera*). Cosijn, 'Anglosaxonica. IV', p. 120, first points
out that *seld* is neuter and that *on þone æfteran* and *geargemearces*
should be taken together, quoting from the Old English life of Guthlac

in support of his reading: cp. the underlying *Vita* phrases, *A secundo etenim anno, quo hanc heremum habitare coeperam* . . . (Colgrave, p. 156). The clearest explanation of the phrase in BTs is to be found under *gēargemearc*, where *ānseld* is described as neuter and the passage translated 'directly after I had begun the second year of my inhabiting the hermitage'.

1248 *life*, MS. *lifes*. The emendation is made by all the editors. The scribe, perhaps following his exemplar mechanically, may have expected l. 1248a to form a syntactic group, therefore writing a genitive form for the dative necessary in this context.

1264 *sawel*. See n. for *adl* 978.

1280 *woruld miste oferteah*. Thorpe's 'o'er veil'd the world with mist' is accompanied by the suggested emendation *worulde*, but this is unnecessary as both inflected and non-inflected forms of the accusative singular of *woruld* are found in OE. In the *Bibliothek* fnn. Grein suggests *mist* for *miste*, but his translation some years later shows his satisfaction with the MS. *miste*, rendered by *mit Nebel*.

1281b–2a Thorpe makes his verse division here between *ofer* and *tiht-londes frætwa*, 'when night clos'd over / the cultur'd land's adornments', noting (p. 507) his concern about both *tiht* and the 'integrity of the line'. In the *Bibliothek* text Grein also ends l. 1281 with *ofer*, reading *tihte londes frætwa* for l. 1282a, but in his fnn. reveals his dissatisfaction with this arrangement by putting forward *liht* for his *tihte*. His translation indicates a different manipulation of the text: *und das Dunkel der Nacht / überlagerte des Landes Zierden* . . . Finally, in 'Zur Textkritik', p. 424, he arrives at the division which has prevailed, taking *þrong niht ofer tiht* as one verse. A suggested *ofertyht* 'a covering, what is drawn over' appears in BT under *tyht* III (the cognate *ofertēon* and Mod. G *überzug* are advanced in its support). Klaeber's discussion of the passage ('Guthlac 1252 ff.', *Beiblatt*, xv (1904), 345–7) provides a useful review of many of these interpretations. He argues convincingly for the simplex *tiht*, comparing *Christ* 811 *on tyhte*, *Phoenix* 525 *on tihte*, and *Elene* 53 *on tyhte*. In these phrases *tiht* has the sense 'motion'. Klaeber suggests for *tiht* 'a semasiological development parallel to Latin *tractus*, German *Zug*'. With these, which develop the meanings 'extension, expanse, region', he compares OE. *byht* 'bend', Low German *Bucht* and its Modern English equivalents *bight* and *bought*, OE. *gang* 'path', Modern English *bed* (of a river), OE. *rād* and *sund*. Citing such common poetical phrases as *wonga* (*floda, geofenes*) *bigong* as parallel with *ofer tiht / londes frætwa*, he explains that *þrong* is used intransitively with the sense 'pressed on, forced its way' of *Genesis* 139 *þrang þystre genip*. In contrast, the translations of Gollancz, Gordon, and Kennedy all treat *londes frætwa* as variation of *tiht* 1281 or of *woruld* 1280, placing *þrong niht ofer tiht* in parenthesis. Corruption is sometimes still advanced, as by Wyld, 'Diction and Imagery in Anglo-Saxon Poetry', *Essays and Studies*, xi (1925), 67, whose 'night pressed on and blotted out the beauty of the land' is without the support of a proposed textual emendation, and by Campbell (BTs *Enlarged Addenda*

and Corrigenda), under TYHT, where *ofer byht* is proposed and *Riddles* 7.3 and 22.12 compared.

1284 *burgsalu*. Occurs also in l. 1331 and *Panther* 50. See further §8, p. 57.

1288 *scirwered*. Cp. *Exodus* 125 *Scean scir werod*, where the most recent editors (E. B. Irving and P. J. Lucas) read *scirwerod* 'brightly clad'. The adjective occurs also in *Beowulf* 496 *scencte scir wered* (see Crawford, *Scirwered: Beowulf* 496a', *Notes and Queries*, ccxii (1967), 204–5), and is adopted into W. F. Bolton's edition of 1973. A compound adjective *scirwered* is generally read in *Guthlac B* 1288 (comparable in formation with *Genesis* 812 *unwered*, *Beowulf* 606 *sweglwered*, and *Judith* 230 *scirmæled*), except for Kemble's fanciful suggestion (see Thorpe, p. 507) that the line expresses 'the bright troop of angels, such as we read of at the death-bed of saints'.

1291 *from ... oþ*. F. Wullen, 'Der Syntaktische Gebrauch der Präpositen *fram*, *under*, *ofer*, *þurh* in der angelsächsischen Poesie', i (Kiel, 1908) and ii *Zeitschrift für englische Philologie*, xxxiv (1911), 421–97, cites (i. 28) three further examples of this succession of pre-positions, also from texts with a Latin original: *Elene* 140, *Paris Psalter* 129.6 and *Meters of Boethius* 20.10; *a ... usque* is demonstrably behind the *Paris Psalter* 129.6 and *Guthlac B* instances.

1292 *dægredwoma*. The compound appears also in *Andreas* 125, varying *leoht* in a similar but simpler description of dawn. Comparable is *dægwoma* 'herald of the day', found only in *Guthlac B* 1218 and *Exodus* 344. Brooks, '*Andreas*', p. 67, cites a third example from Ælfric's *Colloquy* (from the Garmonsway edition), but the word there is *dægred*. The base element -*woma* in these compounds, as in OE. *wōm* and ON. *ómi*, must mean 'sound, noise', the sense it has in other poetical compounds in which it appears, e.g. *hildewoma* 'noise of battle' in *Andreas* 218, *Juliana* 136, 663; *heofonwoman* 'noise of the heavens' in *Christ* 834, 998; see also *wiges woman* 'noises of battle' in *Andreas* 1355, cp. *Elene* 19; *wintres woma* 'tumult of winter' in *Wanderer* 103. P. O. E. Gradon, *Elene* (London, 2nd edn., 1966), p. 26, points out that the cognate *weman* 'allure, entice' suggests that *woma* also held the sense 'harbinger, one who speaks', a meaning she thinks implicit in *dægwoma* and *dægredwoma*, explaining the formula *swefnes woma* found in *Elene* 71 and *Daniel* 110, 118, and 538 as 'the revelation of a dream'. T. P. Dunning and A. J. Bliss, *The Wanderer* (London, 1969), p. 71, argue convincingly for a transition from 'noise' to 'terror' in the phrase *wiges woma* found in *Andreas* 1355, *Elene* 19, and *Juliana* 576, and suggest that *dægwoma* and *dægredwoma* 'should be compared with the modern "crack of dawn"'.

1293 *wedertacen*. The following adjective *wearm* shows that *wedertacen* is here a sign of good weather. A similar marking is found in the phrase *Azarias* 96 *wearme wederdagas*. The sense 'fine weather' is implicit in *Exodus* 75 *wederwolcen* (the pillar of cloud protects the Israelites from sun) and *Andreas* 1697 *þa wederburg* (after the conversion of its inhabitants, the city must have been blessed with good weather), but not in

Andreas 372 *Wedercandel swearc.* The use of *weder* as a first element in compounds is not restricted to poetic texts in the OE. period, for the adjective *wederfeste* 'weather-bound' appears in the *Chronicle* entry for 1049 (Laud MS.).

1302 *halge heafdes gimmas.* All the examples of this image for 'eyes' in OE. are found in the Exeter and Vercelli codices. Three instances of the compound *heafodgimm* (*Andreas* 31, *Christ* 1330, and *Maxims I* 44) are all in contrast with words for true inner vision, and the adjective *halge* must here carry some such overtones. The image appears also in *Andreas* 50 *heafdes sigel* (see the commentary in Brooks's edition for this emendation of the MS. *segl*).

For D. G. Calder, 'Theme and Strategy in *Guthlac B*', *Papers on Language and Literature*, viii (1972), 240, ll. 1300–4 focus on beauty, for him a key theme of the poem: 'his face coruscates from heaven's splendour. He has attained the counterpart to heaven's own pure and artificial beauty, one wherein his righteous "former deeds" have reconciled the alienation of deed from ideal, of act from loveliness'.

1305 *ĐA.* A new section begins here, near the foot of fo. 51ʳ; the initial capital, about an inch in height, is followed by a smaller *A*. The preceding line is empty, and the line above that, filled with writing, ends with *dreā:7*.

1308 *belifd.* Thorpe suggests reading *belifen*, but perhaps meant *belifend*, as he translates l. 1308a 'remaining under air'. The word is understood in the sense 'lifeless' by later translators and commentators. KD refer *belifd* 'to a verb *belibban*, "to deprive of life", not elsewhere recorded', but should have noted that three instances of *belifian* 'deprive of life, kill' are listed from Ælfric's homilies in BTs. Although Toller thinks this verb built on *lif*, it is possible that all contain the late re-formed *lifian* from *libban*, and that *be-* is privative in force. Semantic clash with *belibban* 'live by, subsist' may explain the infrequent examples of the alternative meaning. The contracted *belifd* should be compared with *gynnwised* 867.

1317a For a note on the scansion of this verse see §8, p. 62.

1320 *eal innanweard.* The phrase is grouped syntactically with what precedes by Grein, Assmann, KD, Kennedy, Gordon, Craigie, and Bolton, with what follows by Thorpe, Gollancz, Williams, and Wyatt, as here.

1326 *onsprong*, MS. *onþrong*. Thorpe retains *onþrong*, translating 1326a 'rush'd towards *the* land', but making little sense of the passage. Grein puts forward the unlikely *erbebte* for *onþrong*, noting however that some emendation is needed and suggesting *onþrom* from **on-þrimman* (cognate with *þrymm* 'host'). The graphically more attractive emendation *onsprong* 'cracked with the shaking' is suggested in BT under *onþringan*. This *onspringan* 'spring asunder' (cp. *Beowulf* 817 *seonowe onsprungon*) is suitable after *Beofode þæt ealond* 1325, and *onsprong* preserves the assonance which is a feature of this poem; *onspringan* in the sense 'spring forth' is found in *Andreas* 1635, *Phoenix* 63, and a sermon (A. Napier, *Wulfstan, Sammlungen der ihm zugeschriebenen Homilien* (Berlin, 1883), 206, l. 18: not a Wulfstan homily).

1328 *unhyðig*. Thorpe's emendation, *unhydig* 'unheedful', is adopted by Craigie and Williams, but the form *unhyðige* is used of the Anthropophagi when they find the prison empty of the foreigners they had hoped to eat (*Andreas* 1078). It seems unlikely that the mistake assumed by Thorpe should have been made by two scribes. The adjective can be explained literally as 'without booty' and hence as 'hapless, unlucky'.

1329 *wæghengest*. The compound, found also in *Elene* 236, is similar to the ON. *vágmarr*.

wæterþisa, with *w* subpuncted in MS. *þiswa*. Cp. *The Whale* 50 *wæterþisa wlonc*. The element *-þis(s)a* appears also in *Andreas* 257 *mereþissan*, *Andreas* 446 *mereþyssan*, *Andreas* 1657, 1699, and *Elene* 238 *brimþisan*, and has some such meaning as 'stormer'. There is apparently a feminine cognate *-þise* in *Riddles* 27.10 *mægenþisan* 'violence'. For a discussion of the illusory simplex *þys*, see E. G. Stanley, 'Some Notes on *The Owl and the Nightingale*', *English and Germanic Studies*, vi (1957), 39–41; see *AEW* under *ðyssa* 'Toser' for other Germanic cognates.

1330 *under sorgum*. Grein suggests reading *under sargum*, his translation *unter dem Traurigen* corresponding to Gollancz's 'beneath the sorrowing wight'; no emendation is made in Gollancz's text. Wyatt, Kennedy, and Gordon all follow Grein. The emendation destroys the contrast the poet makes between the speed of the boat and the griefs it contains.

1331 *ofer burgsalo*. See n. for l. 1284.

1331b ff. The passage is discussed in §8, pp. 56–7. *Hapax legomena* include *lagumearg*, *hærnflota*, and *sondlond*, the last of these perhaps invented to rhyme with *grond* 1335 and to add to the assonance in its own line. The phrase *æfter sundplegan* 1334 is used only in this poem and *Phoenix* 111.

1338 *bililene*. Generally the emendation *bilidenne* is adopted, but for the sporadic simplification of *-nn-* compare *mine* 650.

1339 *wopes hring*. The phrase occurs also in *Andreas* 1278, *Elene* 1131, and *Christ* 537. The noun *hring* may denote either shape or sound, both being favoured by readers of these passages. Two explanations are possible for the dependent *wopes*, but 'cry of grief, weeping' is preferred to 'loud cry, shout'. For a full discussion of the four passages see K. R. Brooks, 'Old English *wopes hring*', *English and Germanic Studies*, ii (1948–9), 68–74. His interpretation rests on *wop* 'weeping' and *hring* 'circle'. He compares the imagery of *Beowulf* 189 ff. and 1992 ff. and the use of the passive participle *soden* in *Guthlac B* 1073, 1150, 1262 and *Andreas* 1239, assuming therefore that a metaphor, expressed by the verb *seoðan* and drawn from the image of a cauldron boiling over, lies behind *wopes hring* 'outpouring of tears'. The figurative use of the verb *weallan* and of the cognate noun *wylm* in his explanation is well attested: cp. the examples gathered together by E. G. Stanley, 'Old English Poetic Diction', pp. 429–31. A good short account of *wopes hring* appears also in Brooks's edition of *Andreas*.

1340 *gemonade*. Though *(ge)monian* is generally followed by an

accusative of person and genitive of thing, a construction with the dative of the person is noted by Cosijn, 'Anglosaxonica. IV', p. 120, in the *Cura Pastoralis* translation. As examples of the verb followed by a form which may be either accusative or dative for the person occur, e.g. *Genesis* 1029 *me*, the dative construction may have been more widespread than these two instances suggest.

teagor. The form is found only in *Guthlac B*, and could be explained as showing the historically expected OE. development from Germanic *tagur (cp. Gothic *tagr*), and representing the form **teaχur < tæχur*, which Campbell, §235, n. 1, posits in explanation of the Anglian *tēar*. However, beside this *tēar* with loss of a single consonant there are found forms in which gemination occurred, and in them a medial consonant remains, whether represented in spelling by -h- or -hh-, e.g. *tæher*, *teher*, *tehher* (see Campbell's index, under *tēar*). The *ea* of *teagor* may be analogical from *tēar*, and the *g* may reflect late-WS. confusion of *h* and *g*.

1343 *láce.* This form may be either the accusative singular with feminine inflexion (see doubtful entry in BT under *lāc* III) or the dative singular of a neuter noun (see GK under *lāc* 5). The accusative singular *lac* 1298 and the absence of clear examples of this noun with feminine inflexions in *Guthlac B*, although negative evidence, favour the latter interpretation. The clause should be compared with *Elene* 1199 *sende to lace.*

to soð. Holthausen, 'Zur altenglischen Literatur. IV', *Beiblatt*, xviii (1907), 201, suggests *sōðe* for the metre, but cp. ll. 935b, 947b, 1026b, 1029a, 1144b, 1326a, and 1334b for similar verses.

1346 *fusleoð agol.* Cosijn 'Anglosaxonica. IV', p. 120, compares *Christ* 623 *fusleoð galan* and *Beowulf* 1424 *fuslic f(yrd)leoð*. A note on other examples of this figure of speech can be found in Stanley, 'Old English Poetic Diction', p. 431.

1349 *dreogan dryhtenbealu.* Thorpe translates as 'endure evil extreme', noting (p. 507) that '*dryhten* here seems a mere intensitive', an explanation followed by BT, GK, Clark Hall, Kennedy, and Gordon. Both Grein and Gollancz give the meaning 'lord' to the first element, Gollancz translating *dryhtenbealu* 'at his master's bale'. Their understanding of the compound is supported by the appearance of *þeodengedal* in the next line. Cp. *Fortunes of Men* 55 *dreogan dryhtenbealo.*

1350 *þroht, þeodengedal*: cp. *Christ* 1266–7:

> Þær him sorgendum sar oðclifeð,
> þroht þeodbealu, on þreo healfa.

In both passages *þroht* seems an adjective by position and is so treated in GK and BT. Kock, 'Jubilee Jaunts', p. 11, points out that the only other instance of *þroht* in OE. verse is a noun form, *Elene* 704 *ond þes þroht to ðæs heard*, and that there is a separate adjectival *þrohtig*, e.g. *Riddles* 85.4 *þreohtigra*. These forms correspond to ON. *þróttr* and *þróttigr*. Though KD prefer still to explain the *Christ III* and *Guthlac B* instances of *þroht* as an adjective, Kock's suggestion should not be

lightly disregarded. That two nouns may stand in apposition with one another within the same verse (whether shading into attributive use or not) is widely recognized, and only a few of the examples listed by Kock need be cited: *Beowulf* 2198 *eard, eðelriht,* 2493 *eard, eðelwyn* (both with C. L. Wrenn's punctuation), *Guthlac B* 1146 *ár, onbehtþegn.*

1352 *áswæman.* Thorpe and Gollancz translate this verb 'pine', Grein *sich härmen,* and Gordon 'grieve', an interpretation supported by examples of the verb in this sense drawn together in BT under *swæman* and in BTs under *áswæman* from late OE. homilies and biblical translations. An alternative interpretation is put forward by Cosijn, 'Anglo-saxonica. IV', p. 120, who suggests that *áswæman* here parallels *þonan . . . hweorfan* in sense, an interpretation which helps increase the often admired 'elegiac' qualities of the speech, but adds more than the text warrants; Wyatt *An Anglo-Saxon Reader* (Cambridge, 1919), p. 289, favours 'wander about'. Craigie, *Specimens of Anglo-Saxon Poetry* II (Edinburgh, 1926), p. 75, prints *á swæman,* yet another possible interpretation.

1360 *on Engle.* See n. for l. 880.

þara þe. S. O. Andrew, *Syntax and Style in Old English* (Cambridge, 1940), §122, points out that *accennedne* 1361 indicates a singular antecedent for *þe,* and suggests *þara* may therefore be a scribal interpolation. Translators tend either to neglect the singular inflexion of *accennedne* (e.g. Grein), or to waver between both plural and singular antecedents (e.g. Gollancz). The difficulty does not seem to have been noted by anyone else and is probably illusory. As B. Mitchell, *A Guide to Old English* (Oxford, 1971), §187.3(d) points out, the verb of an adjective clause headed by *þara þe* may be either singular or plural, the plural tending to be the norm (for an example of the singular see *Elene* 974–5). It seems logical therefore to extend this licence and to suggest that in such circumstances *þe* as object of a clause headed by *þara þe* may be either singular (as *accennedne* here indicates) or plural.

1365 *winiga,* MS. *wimga* > *wiinga*(?). Thorpe reads *wunga,* which, emended to *wonga,* allows him the translation 'departed, *the* plains' protector'. Grein at first accepts Thorpe's *wonga,* but later, 'Zur Textkritik', p. 424, suggests *winiga* 'amicorum', the form now generally adopted as convincing on grounds both of sense and palaeography. In phrases varying *winiga hleo* (i.e. ll. 1363a and 1364a) a genitive plural again specifies persons, so stylistic probability is also on the side of *winiga.* For this poetic genitive plural cp. *Beowulf* 2567 *winia bealdor.*

1379 *drusende.* This is the last word on fo. 52ᵛ. The upper part of next folio has been cut away, with loss of approximately six lines of text. As a new gathering begins with fo. 53 it is not known how much material has been lost from the MS. at this point (see also §2, p. 13).

Glossary

The words are glossed in alphabetical order. Thus æ comes between *ad* and *af*. The prefix *ge-* is disregarded in verbs, which are listed after the alphabetical order of the simplex. The letters þ and ð, taken together as one letter, follow *t*.

Where variant forms occur within the text for any one word, the form which occurs first is generally used as headword. Preterite-present verbs are glossed under infinitive forms, as are most participial adjectives. References to very common forms and uses are abbreviated by the use of the symbol '&c', and the regular inflected forms of nouns, adjectives, and weak verbs are only occasionally recorded. Minor spelling variations, discussed in §9, are on the whole omitted. Hypothetical forms are marked with an asterisk. The dagger is used for words found only in these poems. No attempt is made to show in the Glossary the accent marks of the manuscript or the capitals either of the manuscript or of the edited text, and the expansions from manuscript abbreviations are silently given.

ā adv 'always' 13, 344, 541, 632, 763, 839, 1190, 1255, 1262, 1371
ābannan stv 7 'summon, call' 2pl pr sj *abonne* 299(N)
ābēodan stv 2 'order, direct' inf 1374; 'offer' pp. *āboden* 309; 'relate, announce' pp. *āboden* 723, 3s pr ind *ābēodeð* 5, 3s pt ind *ābēad* 160, 685
ābrecan stv 4 'break' pp. *ābrocen* 1367
ac conj 'but' 11, 20, 151, 188, 202, &c, 831, 836, 846, 925, 963, &c
ācennan wkv 1 'beget, be born' 825, 1361
ācol adj 'terrified' 692
ācweðan stv 5 'speak' 3s pt ind *ācwæð* 1347
ād m. 'funeral pyre' 668
ādl f. 'disease, pain' 886, 940, 955, 978(N), 1017, &c
†*ādloma* m. 'fire-maimed wretch' 912(N)
†*ādlþracu* f. 'force of the disease' 962
†*ādlwērig* adj 'exhausted by the disease' 1008
ādrēogan stv 2 suffer, endure' inf 516, 3s pt ind *ādrēag* 532, 539; 'practise' 3s pr ind *ādrēogeð* 92
æ f. 'law' 23, 55
†*æboda* m. 'preacher' 937
†*æbylg* n. 'anger' 1237
ædre adv. 'immediately' 1199; 'fully' 1377
æfæst adj 'pious, steadfast, religious' 526
æfen n. 'evening' as 1277, gpl *ēfna* 1242
æfenglōm m. 'twilight' 1291
æfentīd f. 'evening' 1215(N)

æfest m/f. 'envy' 187, 712(N)

(*ge*)*æfnan* wkv 1 'perform, carry out' 15, 844, 1108; 'bring about' 1237

ǣfre adv 'ever' 612, 866, 1119, 1229, 1237, 1260, 1360

æfter adv 'afterwards' 27, 855

æfter prep + d 'after' 23, 211, 471, &c, 836, 877, 943, &c; 'from, according to' 493, 532; 'with' 169(N); 'for' 129, 399; 'along, in' 875, 883, 1275

æfter þon adv phrase 'then, therefore' 1178

æftera cpv adj 'second' 1240(N)

†*æfteryld* f. 'maturity' 496(N)

ǣghwǣr adv 'everywhere' 601

ǣghwylc pron 'each one, everyone' 33, 1000

ǣht f. 'possession' 418

ǣhtwela m. 'wealth, riches' 388

ǣlan wkv 1 'burn' 1065

ælde plm. 'men' 755, 821, 926, 975, 1142, *ęlda* 824

ældu f. 'youth' 109; 'old age' 835(N)

ælmesse f. 'almsgiving, alms' 77

ælmihtig adj 'almighty' 242, 533, 555, 760, 822, 930, 950(N), 958, 1100

ǣmen adj 'uninhabited' 216

ǣnig pron 'anyone, any' 755, 987, 993, 1126, &c; *ǣnges* 1129, *ǣngum* 1229; adj 'any' 1247

ǣnlicra cpv adj 'more excellent' 1320(N)

ǣr adv 'formerly, before, earlier' 27, 143, 369, &c, 859, 876, 1014, &c; *ǣror* cpv 210; *ǣrest* spv 179, 455, 562, 607, 826, 983; *tō ǣr* 'too soon' 844

ǣr conj + sj 'until' 1020, 1222

ǣr þon (*ǣr ðon*) adv phrase 'before' 50, 1162

ǣrende n. 'message, tidings' 5, 162, 724, 1296

ǣrest spv adj 'first' 109, 437, 496, 821, 975

ǣreste, see *ǣrist*

ǣrgewyrht n. 'former work, deed of old' 987, 1079

ǣrist m/f/n. 'rising, getting up' 342(N); 'resurrection' 1100

æt prep + d 'at, in' 1, 443, 889, 922, 982, &c; 'to, towards' 312; 'to, close to' 559; *gehȳran æt* 'belong to' 33; 'from' 258

ǣt f. 'food' 736

ætryhte prep + d 'close to' 997(N), 1152

ætsteall m. 'station' 179(N)

ætwist f. 'substance, form' 500

æþele adj 'noble, excellent' 926, 1105, 1146, 1278, 1287, &c

æþeltungol m. 'noble star' 1314

æþelu pln. 'excellencies' 43, 97, 459(N)

ǣwiscmōd adj 'ashamed' 924

āflēon stv 2 'flee from' 3s pr ind *āflīhð* 504(N)

āfor adj 'fierce' 519

āfrēfran wkv 1 'comfort' 315, 1021

āfyllan wkv 1 'beat down, level' 285

āfyrhtan wkv 1 'frighten' 1326

āfyrran wkv 1 'remove, expel' 669, 748

āfȳsan wkv 1 'urge, impel on' 939

āgalan stv 6 'sing' 3s pt ind *āgōl* 1346

āgān pt prs vb 'own, possess, have' inf 482, 681, 3pl pr ind *āgun* 79, 2s pr sj *āge* 273, 3s pt *āhte* 523

āgēotan stv 2 'pour out, shed' 3s pt ind *āgēat* 522

āgiefan stv 5 'give, grant' pp. *āgiefen* 660, *āgyfen* 780; 'answer, reply' 3s pt ind *ondcwis āgeaf* 1026, *āgeaf ondsware* 1163, 1224

āglǣca m. 'miserable being, monster' 575

āgongan stv 7 'come to pass, happen' pp *āgongen* 470

āgyfen, see *āgiefan*

āhebban stv 6 'raise up, raise (one's voice, clamour), utter (speech)' inf 1156, 1160, 3pl pt *āhofun* 905; 'raise up, lift' 3s pt ind *āhōf* 1104, 1300; 'stir up' 3pl pt *āhōfun* 229; 'exalt, lift up' 3s pt ind *āhōf* 399, 772

†*āhnēapan stv 7 'pluck' 3s pt ind *āhnēop* 847(N)

āhwyrfan wkv 1 'turn away, turn aside' 459

ālecgan wkv 1 'withhold, deprive of' 3s pr ind *ālegeð* 92(N); 'lay down, give up' 3pl pt *ālegdon* 229

ālyfan wkv 1 'allow, grant' 423, 481, 612, 1248

ān adj 'one, alone, single' 242, 250, 269, &c, 1000; asm *ǣnne* 27; *āna* pron 'alone' 101, 158, 207, &c, *ǣghwylc ānra* 'everyone' 33

ānad n. 'solitude' 333, 356

†*ānbūend* m. 'hermit' 88

ānemnan wkv 1 'declare' 42

ānforlǣtan stv 7 'forsake, relinquish' 187, 641

ānhoga m. 'a solitary' 997

ānhȳdig adj 'steadfast, resolute' 897, 978

ānseld n. 'hermitage' 1240(N)

ār m. 'messenger, servant' 684, 920, 1146, 1217, 1327

ār f. 'honour, grace' 450, 480, 620, 766

ārǣran wkv 1 'raise up' 149, 179, 1312

āreccan wkv 1 'tell, relate' 891, 1122, 1322

ārīsan stv 1 'rise, arise' pp *ārisene* 39, 3pl pr ind *ārīsað* 32, 3s pt ind *ārās* 1101, 1108, 1293

ārlēaslīce adv 'wickedly, impiously' 565

ārlic adj 'fitting' 526

āsānian wkv 2 'grow weak' 1175

āscīnan stv 1 'shine' 3s pt ind *āscān* 1308(N)

āsettan wkv 1 'place, set down' 701

āspringan stv 3 'fall away from, fail' 3s pr ind *āspringeð* 20

āstīgan stv 1 'climb, rise' inf 26, 3s pt ind *āstāg* 263, 392, 661, 1104

āsundrian wkv 2 'cut off, separate, sever' 515, 1177

āswǣman wkv 1 'grieve' 1352(N)

ātēon stv 2 'set out upon, undertake' 2pl pr ind *ātēoð* 301(N)

atol adj 'dire, terrible' 116, 562

āttor n. 'poison, venom' 668, 912

āþrēotan stv 2, impers 'weary' 3s pt ind *āþrēat* 844

āwa adv 'always, forever' 670, *āwo* 786, 1043

āwinnan stv 3 'gain, get' 2s pt ind *āwunne* 469
āwo, see *āwa*
āwrecan stv 5 'strike, pierce' pp *āwrecen* 1154, 1286
āwreðian wkv 1 'support, sustain' 324
āwyrgan wkv 1 'curse, damn' pp npl *āwyrgde* 255, 911, *þā āwyrgdan* 25

bǣdewēg n. 'drinking vessel, cup' 985(N)
bǣlblǣse f. 'blazing flame, blaze of fire' 676
bām, see *bēgen*
bān n. 'bone' 380, 698
bāncofa m. 'bone dwelling, body' 942, 954
bāncoþa m. 'bone disease, illness' 1025(N)
bānfæt n. 'body' 1193, 1265
bānhūs n. 'body' 1367
bānloca m. 'bone enclosure, body' 980
bāt m. 'boat' 1328
bēacen n. 'sign, beacon' 1309
beald adj 'bold, brave' 1025
bealdor m. 'prince, master' 1358
bealonīþ m. 'baleful malice, evil' 809
bēam m. 'tree' 847; 'light, beam' 1309
bearn n. 'child, son' 430, 787, 854, 1097, 1130; 'son' (in address) 1076, 1080, 1166
bearu, -wes m. 'grove, wood' 148, 429
bebod (*bibod*) n. 'command, decree' 34, 75, 807, 843
bēc, see *bōc*
bēgen num 'both' n *būtū* 380, 928, g *bēga* 87, 523, d *bām* 870
behlehhan stv 6 'laugh at, rejoice in' inf 1357
behycgan wkv 3 'consider, think about' inf 1349
gebelgan stv 3 'enrage, anger' pp *gebolgne* 287, 303
belibban wkv 3 'deprive of life' pp *belifd* 1308(N)
bēn f. 'prayer' 777
bend m/f. 'bond, fetter' 573
benumene, see *beniman*
bēo, bēoð, see *wesan*
bēodan stv 2 'threaten, menace' 3pl pt *budon* 564, 3s pt sj *bude* 915; 'announce' 3pl pt *budon* 744
beofian wkv 2 'tremble, quake' 1325
beorg (*biorg*) m. 'hill, mound' 140(N), 148, 175, 192, 209, &c; 'grave' 1193
beorgan stv 3 + d 'protect, prevent the happening of' 3pl pr ind *beorgað* 809, 3pl pt *burgun* 730; inf *gebeorgan* 990
†*beorgseþel* m/n. 'hill-dwelling' 102
beorht adj 'bright' 777, 798, 843, 854, 941, 1106, 1191, &c
beorhte adv 'brightly' 1284
beorn m. 'man, hero, warrior' 1328, 1358
beran stv 4 'bear, display' inf 345, 3pl pr ind *berað* 798, 3s pt ind *bær* 170; inf *geberan* 497; 'carry, bring' 3pl pt *bǣron* 117, 729

besingan stv 3 'bewail' inf 615

beswīcan stv 1 'deceive' inf 568, pp *beswicene* 625

betran, betre, see *gōd* adj

bewitigan wkv 2 'observe, watch' 199

bi prep + d 'by, through' 70; 'about' 1234; *bi sǣm twēonum* 'throughout the world' 266, 1359; *Bi hwon* 273

bibēodan stv 2 'bid, command' 1s pt ind *bibēad* 1297, 3s pt ind 697

bibod, see *bebod*

bibūgan stv 2 'avoid, turn aside' inf 868, 990

bicuman stv 4 'arrive' 3s pt ind *bicwōm* 1098

bicweðan stv 5 'declare, say' 3s pt ind *bicwæð* 360

bīdan stv 1 'stand, remain, endure' inf 779, 787, 3s pr ind *bīdeð* 67, 3s pt ind *bād* 329, 914, 952, 1136, 1284; + g 'wait for, await' inf *bīdan* 289, 3s pr sj *bīde* 236, 3pl pr ind *bidað* 84, 3s pt ind *bād* 217, 550, 941, inf *gebīdan* 378; 'experience' inf *gebīdan* 835, 2pl pr ind *gebīdað* 636, 2pl pr sj *gebīden* 509

biddan stv 5 + a(person) & d(thing) 'pray for' inf 479, 3s pt ind *bæd* 332; 'ask' 3s pt ind *bæd* 1158

bidēaglian wkv 2 'conceal, hide' 1252

bīding f. 'rest, repose' 209

bidrēosan stv 2 'deprive of' pp *bidrorene* 626, 901

bidrīfan stv 1 'drive' 3s pt ind *bidrāf* 597

bifæstan wkv 1 'secure, commit' 1193

bifēolan stv 3 'consign to' pp *bifolene* 626

bifōn stv 7 'surround, encompass' pp *bifongen* 994, *bifongne* 627

biforan prep + d 'before' 974 (in post position)

bigān anom vb 'spend, pass' inf 104

bigongan stv 7 'attend to, foster, cherish' 3pl pr ind *bigongað* 805, 3s pr sj *bigonge* 28

bigytan stv 5 'get, obtain' 3pl pr ind *bigytað* 25

bihealdan stv 7 'see, behold' inf 815, 3s pt ind *bihēold* 105; 'guard, look after' 3s pr ind *bihealdeð* 318

bihelian wkv 1 'hide, bury' 1353

bihōfian wkv 2 impers + g 'behove, have need of' 361

bilēosan stv 2 + g 'deprive of' pp *biloren* 1170, 1327

biliðan stv 1 'depart', pp *bilidene* 'deprived of' 1338

bilūcan stv 2 'lock, shut up' 3s pr sj *bilūce* 1194, 3s pt ind *bilēac* 1245

bimīðan stv 1 'hide, conceal' pp *bimiþen* 147

bimurnan stv 3 'mourn for, care for' 3pl pr ind *bimurnað* 130

†*bimūtad* pp 'changed, turned' 71(N)

(ge)bindan stv 3 'constrain, bind, oppress' 3s pt ind *bond* 696, pp *gebundne* 886

binēotan stv 2 + g 'deprive of' pp *binotene* 900

biniman stv 4 'deprive of, take away from' pp *benumene* 625, 3pl pt *binōman* 342

biorg, see *beorg*

†**bisacu* f. 'dispute' *bīsæce* 217(N)

†*biscencan* wkv 1 'give to drink' pp *biscencte* 624(N)

biscirede, see *byscyrian*

bisena, see *bysen*

bisencan wkv 1 'sink, plunge' 3s pt *bisencte* 666

biseōn stv 5 'look' 3s pt ind *biseah* 1302

gebisgad, see *bysgian*

bittor adj 'cruel, bitter' 868, 985, 1025

bitwēon prep + d 'between' 1218

biǒ (*biþ*), see *wesan*

biþeccan wkv 1 'cover, cover over' pp *biþeaht* 1031, 3s pt *biþeahte* 1281, 2s pt sj *biǒeahte* 1377

biþencan wkv 1 'remember' 1296

biwerian wkv 1 'forbid' 848

blāc adj 'shining, bright' 1331

blǣd m. 'glory, bloom' 43, 102, 497, 931; 'well-being, weal, joy' 422, 439, 1374

blēat adj 'wretched' 990

blēd f. 'shoot, fruit' 847

blēo n. 'form' 911

bletsian wkv 2 'bless' 178, 608, 733

blētsung f. 'blessing, favour (of God)' 672

blindnes f. 'blindness' 628

blis f. 'joy, exultation' 954, 1082, 1106, 1317, 1374

(*ge*)*blissian* wkv 2 + d 'rejoice (in), be glad' 497, 722

bliǒe adj 'happy, joyful' 335, 439, 608, 787, 942, 944

blōd n. 'blood' 380

blōdgyte m. 'bloodshed' 305

blōdig adj 'blood-stained, bloody' 289, 698

blondan stv 7 'mingle, blend' pp *geblonden* 668

blōwan stv 7 'bloom, blossom' pp *geblōwen* 'blossoming' 743, -e 1275

bōc f. 'book' npl *bēc* 528, 878

bodian wkv 2 'proclaim, preach' 1115

bold n. 'building, dwelling' 84, 140

bolgenmōd adj 'enraged in mind, angry' 557

gebolgne, see *belgan*

bona m. 'slayer, killer' 87, 429, 523

bōt f. 'remedy, cure' 628

botl n. 'building, dwelling, house' 329, 383

brǣgdwīs adj 'wise in deceit, crafty' 87

breahtm m. 'noise, tumult' 262, 910, 1325

brecan stv 4 'force one's way in, storm' 3s pt sj *brǣce* 209(N)

gebrēdan, see *bregdan*

brēgan wkv 1 'frighten, terrify' 564

bregdan stv 3 'fling, drag' inf *bregdon* 676; 'turn, change' 3pl pt *brugdon* 906(N), 910; 'draw' inf *gebrēdan* 1165

brēme adj 'famous' 883

gebrengan wkv 1 'bring' 3pl pt *gebrōhton* 557

†*breodwian* wkv 2 'strike, strike down' 3pl pr ind *breodwiaǒ* 287(N)

brēost f/n. 'breast, mind' 543, 654, 798, 804, 843, 954, 964

brēosthord n. 'treasure of the breast, mind' 944
brēostsefa m. 'mind, heart' 309, 335
brimwudu m. 'ship, boat' 1331
(*ge*)*bringan* stv 3 'lead, bring' 3s pr sj *bringe* 48, 2pl pr ind *gebringað* 378
brōga m. 'terror' 84, 140
brondhāt adj 'ardent, burning' 964
brosnung f. 'corruption, decay' 828
brōþor m. 'brother' 714, 1358
brōþorsibb f. 'brotherly love' 804
(*ge*)*brūcan* stv 2 + g 'enjoy, make use of, spend' inf 35, 211, 220, 338, 745, 931, 1191, 3s pr ind *brūceð* 383, 3pl pr ind *brūcað* 21, 75, 759, 3pl pt *brucan* 417, pp *gebrocen* 422
bryce m. 'injury, breaking' 698, 729
brȳd f. 'woman, wife' 870
bryne m. 'fire, flame' 573
brynewylm m. 'surge of flame' 672
bryþen f. 'brewing, drink' 980(N)
(*ge*)*būgan* stv 7 'occupy, take possession of, live in' inf 102, 1240, 3pl pr ind *būgað* 298, pp *gebūen* 305
būgan stv 2 'sink' pp *bogen* 1024
burg f. 'city, dwelling-place, dwelling' 812, 883, 942, 1367, ds *byrig* 1191
burgsæl n. 'city-hall, castle, dwelling' apl *bugsalu* 1284, -*o* 1331(N)
burgstede m. 'citadel' 1317
būtan conj + ind 'but that' 132
būtan prep + d 'without' 245, 678, 841; 'except for, save' 1231
būtū, see *bēgen*
bycgan wkv 1 + g 'buy, purchase' 76
gebyldan wkv 1 'make bold, embolden' 475
byre m. 'child, descendant' 985
byrelian wkv 2 'pour out, serve' 3s pt *byr(e)lade* 870, 982
gebyrman wkv 1 'ferment, brew' 981
byrnan stv 3 'burn' inf 192, 3s pt ind *born* 938, 964, 980
byscyrian wkv 1 'separate from, deprive of' pp *byscyrede* 145, 895, *biscyrede* 673, *biscirede* 1074
bysen f. 'example' 175; 'parable' gpl *bisena* 528
(*ge*)*bysgian* (*bisgian*) wkv 2 'afflict' 1012, 1018, 1136, 1197
bysgu f. 'affliction, disgrace' 546, 714, 1110
bytla m. 'builder' 148(N), 733

campode, see *compian*
cearful adj 'sorrowful, full of care' 264, 577
†*ceargēst* m. 'woeful demon' 393(N)
cearu f. 'grief, sorrow' 223
ceaster f. 'city, castle' 17
cempa m. 'warrior, soldier' 91, 153, 180, 324, 402, &c, 889, 901
cennan wkv 1 'give birth to' 52; 'ascribe to' 183
gecēosan stv 2 'gain, obtain' pp *gecorene* 59, 797, *gecorenne* 1004, 3s pt ind *gecēas* 880, 935

cild n. 'child' 1361

cirm m. 'noise, clamour' 264, 393

cirman wkv 1 'shriek, yell' 908

clǣne adj 'clean, pure' 29, 536, 799, spv 822

clǣne adv 'wholly, completely' 580

cleopian wkv 2 'cry, call' 264

clom m. 'bond, fetter' 598; 'grip, grasp' 540

gecnāwan stv 7 'perceive' 3s pt ind *gecnēow* 957

cnēo n. 'knee' dpl *cneowum* 1041

cnēoris f. 'generation' 819

cōlian wkv 2, 'grow cool, cool' 38, 1307

compian wkv 2 'fight' 345, 643

condel f/n. 'lamp, candle' 1290

corðor n. 'band, company' 908

gecostian wkv 2 'try, tempt' 153, 536, 580

costung (*-ing*) f. 'temptation, tribulation' 38, 438

cræft m. 'power, craft' 87, 198

cuman stv 4 'come, approach' inf 23, 29, 366, 777, 951, 3s pr ind *cymeð* 10, 510, 1350, 3s pt ind *cwōm* 140, 148, 185, 684, 732, &c, 1272, 1282, 1291, 1344, *Cōm* 1141, 3pl pt *cwōman* 212, 350, *cwōmun* 894, 2s pt *cwōme* 455, 3s pt sj *cwōme* 432, 3pl pt sj *cwōme* 237

cunnan pt prs vb 'know, understand' pp *cūð* 536, 819, 2s pr ind *const* 1045, 1377, 3s pr ind *conn* 721, 3s pt *cūðe* 295, 1pl pt sj *cūþen* 751; 'be able to, can' 2pt pr ind *cunnon* 479

cwealm m/n. 'death, destruction, slaying' 23, 223, 224, 858

(*ge*)*cwēman* wkv 1 + d 'please, give pleasure to' 306, 462, 949, 1085

cweðan stv 5 'say, speak' 3s pr ind *cwið* 4, 3s pt ind *cwæð* 239, 3pl pt *cwǣdon* 192, 206, 577

cwic adj 'alive, living' 1249

cwide m. 'speech' 1223

cwiþan wkv 1 'lament' 223

cyme m. 'coming, arrival' 830, 972, 1223

cyn(n) n. 'race, kin' 311, 413, 683, 755, 821, 864, 917, 975, 988, &c

cyning m. 'king' 17, 91, 682, 822

cyrran wkv 1 'turn' 908

cyst f. 'best, choicest' 853

(*ge*)*cȳðan* wkv 1 'reveal, make known' 94, 402, 403(N), 448, 529, &c, 1160, 1182, 1222, 1249

dǣd f. 'action, deed' 80, 123, 240, 254, 466, &c, 949, 1085

dæg (pl *dag-*) m. 'day' 51, 610, 618, 772, 949(N), 969, 1001, 1038(N), 1098, &c

†*dæghlūttre* adv 'brightly as by day' 693(N)

dæghwām adv 'daily' 80, 386

dægredwōma m. 'break of day, crack of dawn' 1292(N)

dægwōma m. 'nightfall' 1218(N)

dǣl m. 'part, share, portion' 183, 247, 381, 516, &c, 1366, 1368, dpl *dālum* 54

gedǣlan wkv 1 'divide, separate' 3, 54, 227, 331, 372, &c, 969(N)

daru f, 'hurt, harm' 700

dearninga adv 'scarcely' 1252

dēað m. 'death' 224, 235(N), 240, 372, 379, &c, 830, 841, 858, 863, 871, &c

dēaðberende adj 'death-bearing' 850

dēaðgedāl n. 'separation of death' 963

†*dēaðmægen* n. 'deadly band' 895

dēaðsele m. 'hall of death' 1075

†*dēaðwēge* n. 'deadly cup' 991(N)

dēgle, see *dygol*

dēma m. 'judge' 618, 703, 783, 1188

(*ge*)*dēman* wkv 1 'judge' 493; 'condemn' 549, 554; 'adjudge, assign' 379, 1059; 'praise, glorify' 527

dēofol m/n. 'devil' 850, 895

dēop adj 'deep' 991, 1292; 'stern, awful' 669; 'heinous' 858, 863

dēope adv 'sternly' 554; 'deep' 583; 'hard, deeply' 1349

dēophycgende adj 'deep-thinking, wise' 1112

dēophȳdig adj 'deep-thoughted, wise' 1001

dēoplīc adj 'deep, profound' 1130

dēoplīce adv 'profoundly, deeply' 1121

dēor n. 'animal' 276, 907

deorc adj 'dark' 1098, 1218

dēore adj 'dear, beloved, precious' 69(N), 871, 1059, *dȳre* 693

dēore adv 'cruelly' 969

dēormōd adj 'bold in mind, brave' 952

dēorwyrðe adj 'of greath worth, precious' 183

dim adj 'wretched, grievous' 1162

dōgor n. 'day' 56, 321, 1038

dol adj 'dull, foolish' 464

dōm m. 'ordinance, law' 14, 56; 'will, determining' 111, 135, 706(N); 'decree, judgement' 444, 601, 669, 1362; 'glory, honour' 610; 'might' 772; 'doom, judgement' 972

dōmēadig adj 'blessed with power, mighty' 727, 952

dōmfæst adj 'just, righteous' 1083

(*ge*)*dōn* anom vb 'do' imp pl *Dōð* 592, 3pl pr ind *dōð* 61, 129, inf *gedōn* 314, 700

dragan stv 6 'draw oneself, go' inf 727

drēam m. 'joy, pleasure' 3, 11, 123, 195, 330, &c, 830, 901, 1083, 1101(N), 1304; 'rejoicing, melody' 1316

drēogan stv 2 'keep up, endure' inf 235, 259, 341, 635, 680, 1349, 3s pr ind *drēogeð* 386, 1355, pl pr ind *drēogað* 49, 219, 3s pt ind *drēag* 524, 3pl pt *drugon* 115, 1s pt sj *druge* 487

drēorig adj 'sad, mournful' 1085, 1139

gedrēosan stv 2 'fall' inf 372

droht m/n.? 'manner of life' 1162

drohtað m. 'fellowship' 684(N)

drūsian wkv 2 'become slow, droop' pr ptc *drūsendne* 1061(N), 1379

dryht f. 'people'; pl. 'men' 1130

dryhten m. 'lord, master'; 'the Lord'; 14, 54, 69, 80, 90, &c, 841, 893, 901, 963, 1067, &c

dryhtenbealu n. 'loss of a lord' 1349(N)

drȳman wkv 1 'be joyful, rejoice' 14

drync m. 'drink, draught' 868, 990

dryre m. 'decline, ceasing' 830

gedūfan stv 2 'plunge, dive' inf 583

dugan pt prs vb, impers + d 'befit' 3s pr sj *duge* 384(N)

duguð fm. 'excellence, virtue, salvation, glory' 479, 684(N), 895, 1075; 'men' 893, 1061, 1098

*durran pt prs vb 'dare' 1s pt *dorste* 1211

duru f. 'door' 991

gedȳgan wkv 1 'escape, survive' 436

dȳgle adj 'secret, hidden' 159, 215

dȳgol n. 'darkness' 466, *dēgle* 952

dȳre, see *dēore*

dyrne adj 'hidden, secret' 466, 493

ēac adv 'also' 166, 300, 1182, 1192, 1374

ēac prep + d 'besides' 206(N)

ēaca m. 'addition, increase' 381

ēad n. 'bliss' 1192

ēadig adj 'happy, blessed' 2, 176, 441, 555, 590, &c, 880, 937, 1005, 1026, 1105, &c

ēadwela m. 'riches, blessedness' 1091, 1118

eafora m. 'child'; pl 'men' 855

ēage n. 'eye' 166, 414, 1254, 1301

eahtan wkv 1 + g 'persecute' 88, 346

eahtian wkv 2 'think, consider' 336

eahteþa num 'eighth' 1037

eald adj 'old' cpv *yldran* 4, 500; cpv as sb 'elder' 750, 973

ealdfēond m. 'devil' 141, 203, 218, 365, 390 &c

ealdian wkv 2 'grow old' 43

ealdor m. 'elder, superior' 420(N)

ealdor n. 'life'; 'eternity' in dative phrases 636, 786, 1119, 1229

ealdorgewinna m. 'deadly enemy' 534

ealdorlegu f. 'course of life, death' 1260

eall adj & sb 'all' 17, 42, 50, 68, 96, &c, 832, 892, 1103, 1130, 1184, &c

eal(l) adv 'completely, entirely' 414, 1320

ealle adv 'completely, entirely' 299, 1171

ealles adv 'completely, of all' 469, 601, 662

ēalond n. 'island' 1325

eam, see *wesan*

eard m. 'dwelling, land, home' 220, 256, 297, 308, 351, &c, 897, 1182, 1366, 1372

eardfæst adj 'settled, established' 786

eardian wkv 2 'dwell, live' 55

eardwīc n. 'dwelling-place' 853

earfeðe n. 'hardship, suffering' 194, 207, 225, 245, 432, &c, 1065, 1355

earm adj 'poor' 77; 'wretched, miserable' 210, 297, 339, 405, 437, &c, 904, 912

earnian wkv 2 + g 'earn' 795

eart, see *wesan*

ēastan adv 'from the east' 1291

ēastortīd f. 'Easter' 1102

ēaðe adv 'easily' 242, 250, 457, 488, 556

ēaðmēdu f/n. 'humility' 103, 328, 480, 776

ēaðmēdum adv. 'humbly, with humility' 920

ēaðmōd adj 'humble, obedient' 525, 599, 1301

ēaweð, see *ȳwan*

ēce adj 'eternal' 15, 62, 67, 126, 172, &c, 880, 930, 1079, 1100, 1182, &c

†*edergong* m. 'beggary, penury' 11(N)

edlēan n. 'reward' 1078(N)

edwīt n. 'reproach' 488

edwītspreca m. 'scoffer, detractor' 447

ēfna, see *ǣfen*

efne intensifying adv 'even, just' 592, 973

eft adv 'afterwards, again' 196, 281, 355, 390, 428, &c, 908, 910, 920, 1186, 1243; 'back' 365, 687, 924

eftcyme m. 'return' 736

ege m. 'terror, awe' 686

egeslīc adj 'horrible, fearful' 141

egle adj 'hateful, loathsome' 405, 962(N)

egsa m. 'terror, fear' 72, 86, 167, 203, 339, &c

ēhtend m. 'persecutor' 525

ellen n. 'strength, fortitude, courage' 158, 190, 203, 293, 328, &c, 897, 940, 950, 978, 1026, &c

ellenheard adj 'courageous' 1165

†*ellensprǣc* f. 'brave speech' 1155(N)

ellenweorc n. 'brave deed' 641

ellorfūs adj 'ready to depart elsewhere, dying' 1054

ende m. 'end, ending' 135, 225, 369, 678, 835, 1022, 1037; 'end, death' 443, 1206

endedōgor n. 'final day' 933(N), 1152, 1167, 1201, 1285

endian wkv 2 'end, make an end' 50

enge adj 'cruel' 997

engel m. 'angel' 2, 4, 11, 88, 112, &c, 945, 1124, 1132, 1192, 1242, &c

†*engelcund* adj 'divine' 101

ēode, see *gān*

eom, see *wesan*

eorl m. 'man, brave man' 1108, 1165, 1206

eorðe f. 'earth' 2, 15, 43, 119, 220, &c, 933, 1102, 1127, 1366, 1377

eorðlīc adj 'earthly' 97, 261

eorðware plm. 'earth's inhabitants' 607

eorðwela m. 'earthly wealth' 62, 319

ēow, see *gē*
ēower poss adj 'your' 241, 261, 466, 707, &c
ermþu, see *yrmðu*
ēst f. 'grace, favour' 826
geēþan wkv 1 'make easy, alleviate' 1206
ēðel m. 'native land, country' 67(N), 261, 277, 355, 801, 844, 852, 1091
†*ēþelboda* m. 'land's apostle, missioner' 1003(N)
ēþellond n. 'native land' 656
ēþelrieht n. 'hereditary right, ancestral domain' 216(N)

fācen n. 'sin, evil' 586, 1071
fæc n. 'space of time, period' 214
fæder m. 'parent, father' 825; 'Father' 533, 657, 801, 945, 1236; 'father (confessor)' 1012, 1211
fǣge adj 'doomed to death, fated' 310, 560, 1031, 1058, 1346
fæger adj 'fair, beautiful' 1, 48, 382, 629, &c, 825, 1181, spv *fǣrestan* 836
fægre adv 'pleasantly, beautifully' 152, 653
fǣhð f. 'hostility, enmity' 186
fǣle adj 'gracious, good' 173
fǣmne f. 'woman' 1344
fǣrestan, see *fæger*
†*fǣrhaga* m. 'sudden onset' 960(N)
fǣringa adv 'suddenly' 939
fǣrscyte m. 'sudden shooting, sudden dart' 186
fǣrspell n. 'sudden message, dreadful news' 1050
fæst adj 'firm, fast' 955, 1032, 1274
fæste adv 'firmly' 960
fæsten n. 'fasting, fast' 808
fæstlīc adj 'firm' 773
fæðm m. 'embrace' 782
faran stv 6 'go, journey' imper s *far* 291, *Fyr* 1178(N), 3s pr ind *fareð* 382, 3s pt ind *fōr* 1329
fēa pl adj 'few' 59, 173
feallan stv 7 'fall' inf 283; *gefeallan* 'fall upon, rush to, i.e. strike' 3s pt ind *gefēol* 1008
†*fēalōg* adj 'destitute' 246(N)
fēdan wkv 1 'feed' 274
fela n. indecl 'a great number, many' 59, 110, 143, 181, 189, &c, 872
feng m. 'grip, grasp' 436
gefēon stv 5 'rejoice, rejoice in' inf 13, 421, 2pl pr ind *gefēoð* 508, 3pl pt *gefēgon* 213, 738
fēond m. 'devil, demon, enemy' 136, 152, 186, 201, 265, &c, 864, 902, 915, 961, 982
feor adj 'far' 216
feor adv 'far, distant' 1166, 1200, 1206
fēores, *-e*, *-a*, see *feorh*
feorggedāl (*feorhgedāl*) n. 'death' 1178, 1200

feorh (*feorg*), *fēores* n. 'life' 90, 130, 243, 291, 396, &c, 994, 1036, 1058; in phrases meaning 'forever' *tō fēore* 13, *widan ferh* 817, *tō widan fēore* 840

feorhcwealm m. 'death' 915

feorhgedāl, see *feorggedāl*

feorhgiefa m. 'Giver of life' 1239

feorhhord n. 'life's treasure, soul' 1144

†*feorhloca* m. 'breast' 653

feorhneru f. 'sustenance, food' 917(N)

feorweg m. 'distant path, remote journey' 257

fēowere num 'four' 1134

fēran wkv 1 'go, depart' 6, 691, 1295

ferh, see *feorh*

ferian wkv 1 'carry, bring' 1306

ferð m/n. 'mind, spirit' 923, 1012, 1021

ferðwērig adj 'soul-weary, sad' 1157

†*fēðehwearf* m. 'host on foot, drove' 191(N)

fīftȳnu cdl num 'fifteen' 936

findan stv 3 'find, come upon, discover' 3pl pt *fundon* 270, 349, 913, 3s pt *fonde* 1007(N), *fond* 1147; 'find, obtain' pl pt *fundon* 628, 889, 918; 'visit, call upon' 3s pr ind *findeð* 59

fīras plm. 'men' 864, 1250, gpl *fȳra* 988

firen f. 'crime, wickedness' 265, 508, 627, 858, 863, *fyrene* 1071

firenful adj 'sinful' 560

firenlust m. 'sinful desire' 803

flacor adj 'flickering' 1144

flǣsc n. 'flesh' 994

flǣschoma m. 'fleshly covering, body' 586, 1031, *flǣshoman* 374

flānþracu f. 'arrow-clash, force of arrows' 1144

flēon stv 2 'flee, fly' imper pl *flēoð* 257, 3s pt ind *flēag* 917, 3pl pt *flugon* 737

†*flygerēow* adj 'wild-flying, fierce in flight' 349(N)

geflȳman wkv 1 'put to flight' 136

folc n. 'troop, host' 285; 'people' 820, 1239

folctoga m. 'leader of a host, captain' 902

foldærn n. 'earth-house, flesh' 1031

foldbūend m. 'dweller upon earth, man' 64, 872

folde f. 'earth, ground' 396, 743, 808, 823, 1311

foldweg m. 'earthly path, earth' 1250

foldwong m. 'earthly plain, earth' 1326

folgian wkv 2 'follow' 1044

fōr f. 'journey' 566

for prep + a/d 'for, on behalf of' 200, 341; 'on account of, because of' 208, 238, 294, 458, 639, &c, 933, 1110, 1257

forbēodan stv 2 'forbid' pp *forbodene* 847

forberan stv 4 'bear with, endure' 3pl pr ind *forberað* 804, 1s pt ind *forbær* 488

fore prep + d 'from' 11, 147, &c, 959; 'through, out of, on account of'

19, &c; 'for, on behalf of' 353, 402 (post position), &c, 1051; 'before, in the presence of' 88, &c, 1041, 1188, &c

foregenga m. 'advance-guard, forerunner' 533(N)

forespreca m. 'spokesman' 265

forgiefan stv 5 'give, grant' inf 327, pp *forgiefen* 1133; 'give up, commit' pp *forgiefene* 461

forgieldan stv 3 'give' inf 588

forgripan stv 1 'grasp, assail' 2pl pr sj *forgripen* 375

forht adj 'frightened' 310, 961, cpv 201

forhycgan wkv 3 'neglect, despise' 3s pt *forhogde* 741

forlǣtan stv 7 'leave, surrender' 1s pr ind *forlǣte* 1174, 3s pr ind *forlǣteð* 3, 3s pt ind *forlēt* 330

forlēosan stv 2 'leave, forsake' 3pl pr ind *forlēosað* 503

forsǣcan wkv 1 'seek with hostile intent, attack' 2pl pr sj *forsǣcen* 377(N)

forscādan stv 7 'scatter, rout' pp *forscādene* 478(N)

forsēon stv 5 'scorn, reject' 3s pt ind *forsēah* 96, 541, 2pl pt *forsēgon* 630

forsittan stv 5 'neglect' 3s pt ind *forsæt* 340

forstondan stv 6 + d 'withhold, block' inf 702

forswelgan stv 3 'swallow, devour' inf 193

forswiðan wkv 1 'overcome' 966

forð adv 'forth, forward, away' 36, 75, 841, 969, 1039, 1044, 1134, &c

forþon adv 'therefore, accordingly' 46, 65, 316, 526, &c, *Forðan* 378; *forþon* conj 'because' 469

forþryccan wkv 1 'oppress, overwhelm' 1198

forðsið m. 'journey forward, death' 939, 1050, 1148, 1181, 1346

forþum, see *furðum*

forðweg m. 'onward course, departure' 801, 945

for ðȳ conj 'because' 1185

forwyrnan wkv 1 + g 'deprive of' 164

fōt m. 'foot' dpl *fōtum* 285

frætwan wkv 1 'adorn, deck out' 806

frætwe plf, 'trappings, adornments' 1059, 1282

frāsung f. 'temptation' 189

frēa m. 'Lord' 1080; 'master, lord' 1148, 1200, 1222

frēcne adj 'horrible, dangerous' 191, 566

frēcne adv 'horribly, boldly' 974

frēcnes f. 'danger, hazard' 110(N), 181

frēfran wkv 1 'console, comfort' 77

fremde adj 'foreign, strange' 64

(*ge*)*fremman* wkv 1 'make, bring about' 207, 292, 466, 586, 715, &c, 859, 875, 893, 1100

frēodryhten m. 'noble lord' 1021

frēond m. 'friend' 291, 453, 715, 1012

frēorig adj 'chilled, freezing' 1157

†*frēorigferð* adj 'sad in soul' 1344

†*frēorigmōd* adj 'sad in mind' 888

(*ge*)*freoðian* wkv 2 'keep, protect' 152, 243, 396, 411; + d 442

†*freoðuweard* m. 'guardian of peace' 173

frignan stv 3 'ask, inquire' inf 1010, 1211, 2s pr ind *frignest* 1228; *gefrignan* 'find out by asking, hear' 1pl pt sj *gefrūnen* 1360

frið m/n. 'peace, truce' 257, 310, 411

frōfor f. 'comfort, consolation' 136, 508, 888, 923, 936, 1211, 1236

from prep + d 'from, out of' 256, 277, 366, 514, 988, 1104, 1291, 1311; 'because of' 459(N)

from adj 'strong, bold' 181, 349, 902

fromlīce adv 'strongly, boldly' 453

fruma m. 'noble man, lord' 773; 'beginning' 823, 982, 988

frumbearn n. 'firstborn' 1071

frymþ f. 'creation' 820; *æt frymðe* 'at first' 1(N)

fugol m. 'bird, fowl' 743, 917

full adj + g 'full of' 205

fultum m. 'help, aid' 189

fundian wkv 2 'strive after, desire' 6, 1089, 1264

furþor adv 'further' 1222

furðum adv 'at first, indeed' 1228, 1239, *forþum* 923(N)

fūs adj 'striving forward, eager, ready to go, hastening' 801, 945, 1044, 1050, 1077, 1148, &c

fūslēoð n. 'dirge' 1346

fyl m. 'destruction' 548

fyllan wkv 1 'fulfil' 971; *gefyllan* 'fill' 653, 1317

fyr, see *faran*

fȳr n. 'fire' 191, 374, 634

fȳra, see *fīras*

fȳren adj 'flaming, fiery' 1311

fyrene, see *firen*

fyrn adv 'formerly, long ago' 869, 973, 1258

fyrndagas plm 'days of yore' 629

†*fyrngewyrht* n. 'ancient decree' 971

fyrst m. 'space of time, period' 110, 326, 836

fyrstgemearc n. 'appointed time' 1036

fȳsan wkv 1 reflexive 'hasten, depart quickly' 1266

gǣst m. 'a spirit, soul' 5, 28, 36, 89, 100, &c, 944, 967, 1045, 1060, 1115, &c; *līfes gǣst* 'principle of life' 838, 1176; *frōfre gǣst* 'spirit of consolation' 136, 936; *hālig gǣst* 'the Holy Spirit' 361, 456; 'demon, (accursed) spirit' 25, 116, 297, 339, 405, 437, &c, 904

gæst m. 'stranger, visitant' 1220(N); some instances of *gǣst* might be placed here.

gǣstcund adj 'spiritual, divine' 771

†*gǣstcwalu* f. 'death of the soul' 679

gǣstgedāl n. 'separation of the soul and body, death' 862, 1138

†*gǣstgemynd* f/n. 'inmost thought' 602

gǣstgerȳne n. 'spiritual mystery' 248, 1084, 1113

†*gǣstgewinn* n. 'soul torment' 589

gǣsthālig adj 'holy in spirit' 873, 1149, 1241

gǣstlīc adj 'spiritual' 155, 177, 630

gafulrǣden f. 'tax, tribute' 986

galdor n. 'divination, prophetic speech' 1207

gān anom vb 'go' 3s pt *ēode* 1005; *gegān* 'get by going, gain' inf 272, 3s pt *geēode* 158; 'happen' 3pl pt *geēodon* 753; 'come upon, overtake' 3s pr ind *gegǣð* 499

gē pl pron 'you' 240, 256, 299, 301, 308, &c, a/d *ēow* 243, 244, 246, 258, 300, &c

gēac m. 'cuckoo' 744

geafena, see *giefu*

gēar n. 'spring' 744; 'year' 936

gēara (*gēaro*) adv 'formerly' 40, 630

geard m. 'dwelling-place' 791, 1221, 1267

†*gēargemearc* n. 'reckoning by years' 1241(N)

gēaro, see *gēara*

gearu adj 'ready' 1175, gearo 292, asm *gearene* 913, asf *gearwe* 889, npl *gearwe* 89, 724

(*ge*)*gearwan* wkv 1 'prepare, make ready' 100, 690, 802, 3s pt *gyrede* 177

gearwe adv 'well' 1045

gēað f. 'foolishness, folly' 504, 1233

gebǣru f. 'behaviour, bearing' 416

gebed n. 'prayer' 809

†*gebihþ* n.? 'abode, dwelling' 874

gecost adj 'tried, proven' 91

gecynd n. 'kind, variety' 44

gedāl n. 'parting' 235

gedēfe adj 'fitting, seemly' 579, 610

gedwola m. 'error' 259

gefēa m. 'joy, bliss' 1, 48, 382, 691, 833, 837, 1079, 1090, 1181, &c

gefēalīc adj 'joyous' 657, 825

gefērscype m. 'brotherhood, fellowship' 1258

gefrǣge adj + d 'famous among' 820

gegnunga adv 'directly, certainly' 813

gehāt n. 'promise, vow' 941

gehþa f. 'sorrow, anxiety' 1208

gehwā pron + g 'each' asm *gehwone* 555, gsn *gehwæs* 311, 512, dsm *gehwām* 321, 1242

gehwylc pron + g 'each, every' 43, 45, 56, 63, 332, &c, 926, 965, 1075, 1244, 1255

gehygd f/n. 'thought, meditation' 473, 807

gelād n. 'way, path' 1292

gelēafa m/n. 'belief, faith' 652, 798, 1111

gelīc adj 'like, similar' 117, 664

gelimp n. 'prosperity' 268(N)

gelōme adv 'often' 7

gelong adj + *on*/*æt* 'dependent on' 252, 313

gemāna m. 'society, companionship' 670

gemet n. 'measure, portion' 388
gemete adv 'meetly, in a proper manner' 501
gemetfæst adj 'moderate, modest' 1107
gemōt n. 'meeting, assembly' 127, 236
gemynd f/n. 'remembrance, memory' 118, 168, 215, 474, 877
gemyndig adj (+ g) 'mindful (of)' 89, 154, 446, 1294
gēn adv 'yet, still' 521, 538, *þā gēn* 515
gēna adv 'still, again' 155, *þā gēna* 233, 446, 1270
geneahhe adv 'frequently, earnestly' 697, 719
gener n. 'refuge' 290
genge adj 'current, prevalent' 765
genip n. 'mist, darkness' 350, 970
genōg adj 'enough' 295
gēoc f. 'aid, comfort, help' 89, 137, 367, 738
gēocend m. 'Preserver, Saviour' 1133
gēocor adj 'sad, grievous' 976, 1048, 1138
geofu, geofona, see *giefu*
geoguð f. 'youth' 21, 104, 419, 495, 499, &c
gēomor adj 'sad' 1208, 1354
gēomormōd adj 'sorrowful' 1060, 1220
gēomrian wkv 2 'mourn, sigh' 1048
geond prep + a 'throughout' 30, 39, 68, 270, 501, &c, 865, 883
geong adj 'young' 490, 870, 1048, gpl *gingra* 'new' 1042(N); cpv 1062
georn adj + g 'eager for, desirous of' 867, 1045, 1078, 1267, 1299
georne adv 'eagerly, gladly' 107, 124, 177, 552, 805, 815, 1084, cpv 138, spv 357
geornlīce adv 'eagerly, readily' 602
gēotan stv 2 'pour out, tell forth' inf 1056, 3pl pt (sj?) *gutan* 1233
gerȳne n. 'secret, mystery' 644, 1121
gesǣlignes f. 'happiness, blessedness' 12
gesceaft f/n. 'thing created, creature' 50, 638, 760; 'creation' 371, 629, 777, 1117
gesēfte adj 'soft, mild' 732
geset n. 'seat, habitation' 1268
gesihð f. 'sight' 759, 816(N); 'sight, presence' 841
gesiþ m. 'companion, retainer' 1295
gestāl n. 'charge, accusation' 510(N)
gestrēon n. 'possessions, riches' 78
gesund adj 'sound, unharmed' 701
gesynto f. 'health, salvation' 332
getimbre n. 'building, foundation' 18, 485
getrēowe adj 'true, faithful' spv 709
geþaca m. 'covering, wrapping' 1032
geþeaht f/n. 'counsel' 1216
geþeahting f. 'counsel, design' 646
geþōht m. 'thought' 800
geþonc m/n. 'thought' 368, 1253
geþyld f/n. 'patience' dpl *geþyldum* 'patiently' 483, 914

geþyldig adj 'patient' 600
geþyncðe f. 'honour, dignity' 605
geweald n. 'power, control' 29, 415, 523, 596, 694
geweorc n. 'work, deed' 529, 882
gewin(n) n. 'conflict, struggle' 115, 134; 'strife, hardship' 932, 1081; 'attack' 961
gewinna m. 'opponent, enemy' 275
†*gewinworuld* f. 'world of turmoil' 857
gewit n. 'mind, reason' 376
gewita m. 'witness' 752
gewitnes f. 'testimony, cognisance' 720, 758
gewyrht n. 'work, deed' 70
giedd n. 'song' 1233
giefan stv 5 'give' 3s pt ind *geaf* 869
giefu f. 'gift' 606, 765, 1246, gpl *geafena* 1042; 'grace' 100, 124, 357, 893, 1115, *Geofu* 530, as *gife* 771 gpl *geofona* 1303
(ge)gieldan stv 3 'give, pay, requite' inf *gyldan* 434, *gegyldan* 471, 3s pr ind *gieldeð* 124, 2pl pr ind *gieldað* 464
gielpan stv 3 + d 'exult over, boast in' inf 239, 3pl pt *gulpon* 265
gielpcwide m. 'boastful speech, boasting' 1235
gielplīc adj 'boastful, ostentatious' 167, 419
gīeman wkv 1 + g 'heed, care for' 150
gierela m. 'garb, apparel, clothing' 167, 419
gīet adv 'yet, still' 1221
gif conj 'if, whether' + ind 34, 276, 280, 289, + sj 236, 291, 433, + ind/sj 195, 592, 842, 1159
gife, see *giefu*
gīfre adj 'greedy, eager' 375, 407, 738, 996
gim(m) m. 'jewel' 1212, 1302
gingra, see *geong*
git dual pron 'you two' 1371
gītsung f. 'covetousness, desire' 150
glædmōd adj 'joyful in mind, happy' 1062, 1303
glǣm m. 'splendour, radiance' 1278, 1289
glēaw adj 'wise, prudent' 914, 1221
glēawmōd adj 'wise in mind, prudent' 1002
glēawnes f. 'wisdom, prudence' 802
gnornian wkv 2 'lament, mourn' 232, 429, 679, 1209, 1266
gnornsorg f. 'grief, sorrow' 1335
gnornung f. 'grief, sorrow' 544
God m. 'God' 5, 21, 28, 40, 72, &c, 820, 826, 848, 867, 873, &c
gōd adj 'good' 36, 170, 394, 580, cpv *betre* 'better' 75, 217, 378, 654, 779, *sēlla* 'better, greater' 278, 492, 1268, spv *sēlast* 'best' 1348, 1359
gōd n. 'good; property, goods' 71, 107, 120
godcund adj 'divine' 248, 530
goddrēam m. 'heavenly joy' 630, 1299
†*godscyldig* adj 'guilty against God, impious' 862

godspel n. 'gospel' 1115

gomen n. 'joy' 1354

gong m. 'going, journeying' 731; 'attack' 1017; fig. 'stream (of words)' 1161

gongan stv 7 'go' inf 571, 1002, 3s pr ind *gongeð* 42, 3pl pr ind *gongað* 813

grǣd m. 'hunger, greed' dpl *grǣdum* 'greedily' 738(N)

grāp f. 'grasp, clutch' 407, 996

grēne adj 'green' 232, 477, 746

grēot n. 'earth' 1335

†*grēothord* n. 'earthen treasure, body' 1266

grētan wkv 1 'approach, speak to, greet' 5, 357, 1157; 'touch, harm' 377; *gegrētan* 'assail, oppress' 316

grim adj 'fierce, cruel' 547, 571, 589, 679

grimme adv 'terribly, cruelly' 986

grimnys f. 'severity, harshness' 578

grindan stv 3 'grind against' 3s pt ind *grond* 1335

gromheort adj 'fierce-hearted' 569

gromhȳdig adj 'fierce-minded' 375

grund m. 'bottom, abyss' 563

gryre m. 'terror, horror' 571

guma m. 'man' 35, 495, 1204, 1362

gyfl n. 'food, morsel' 850, 1301

gyld n. 'payment' 765

(*ge*)*gyldan*, see *gieldan*

gylp b. 'boasting' 662

gylt m. 'sin, crime' 461

†*gynnwised* adj 'well-directed, knowledgable' 867(N)

gyrede, see *gearwan*

gyrn m/f/n. 'grief, affliction' 446; adv 'sorely, dearly' 862(N)

gyrnan wkv 1 + g 'desire, want' 320; *gegyrnan* + a 'obtain by seeking' 72, 258

gyrnwracu f. 'vengeance for injury' 434

habban wkv 3 'have, hold' inf 584, 617, 1055, 1s pr ind *hafu* 1067, 3s pr ind *hafað* 4, 87, 647, 3pl pr ind *habbað* 800, 3s pr sj *hæbbe* 389, 2pl pr sj *hæbben* 672, 3s pt *hæfde* 694; as aux + uninflected pp 309, 422, 426, 436, 546, &c, 1133, 1207

hād m. 'rank, degree' 4, 31, 60(N), 500, 1361; 'kind' 52; 'manner' 94(N)

hǣdre adv 'clearly' 1283

hæft m. 'captivity, bondage' 597; 'captive' 725

(*ge*)*hǣlan* wkv 1 'make whole, heal' 705, 885, 928, 1245

hǣlend m. 'Saviour' 604

hæle(*ð*) m. 'hero, warrior, man' 683, 890, 928, 1129, 1145, 1203

hǣlu (*hǣlo*) f. 'salvation' 171, 435, 683; 'safety' 397; 'healing' 890

†*hærnflota* m. 'sea-ship' 1333

hālig adj 'holy, blessed' 10, 31, 34, 65, 90, &c, 842, 896, 922, 925, 938, &c

halsian wkv 2 'entreat, adjure' 1203

hām m. 'home' 10, 69(N), 83, 98, 149, &c, 834, 871

hāt adj 'hot, burning' 979, 1055, 1143, 1209, 1336, &c, spv 1020

hātan stv 7 'command, bid' 3s pt ind *hēt* 687, 1370, 1374, *hěht* 703;
  gehātan 'threaten, promise, vow' 2s pr ind *gehātest* 271, 3s pr ind
  gehāteð 363, 3pl pr ind *gehēton* 234, 447, 570, *gehēhton* 548, 2pl pr sj
  gehāten 240, 2s pt sj *gehēte* 456

hāte adv 'hotly, intensely' 1330

hě, *hēo*, *hit* pers pron 'he', 'she', 'it' nsm *hě* 15, 27, 48(N), 51(N), 56,
  &c, 831, 833, 868, &c, nsf *hīo* 2, 3, *hēo* 770, 816, 983, 1193, nsn *hit*
  42, 384, 576, 1124, 1195, 1200, asm *hine* 99, 105, 114, &c, 886, 918,
  927, &c, *hyne* 127, 552, asn *hit* 469, 1321, gsm/n *his* 14, 24, 27, &c,
  843, 846, 882, &c, gsf *hyre* 849, 984, 1184, dsm/n *him* 5, 98, 100, &c,
  827, 880, 915, &c, dsf *hyre* 1182, 1192, npl *hȳ* 1, 65, 73, &c, 842, 845,
  855, &c, *hī* 219, 220, 230, &c, 873, apl *hȳ* 221, 411, 430, 466, 844, gpl
  hyra 80, 89, 90, &c, 854, 968, 1177, dpl *him* 15, 20, 25, &c, 870, 974

hēaf m. 'lamentation, wailing' 616, 1047

heafela m. 'head' 1270

hēafod, *hēafdes* n. 'head' 73, 1302

hēah adj 'high' asf *þā hēan* 412, cpv nsm *hȳra* 397(N), spv *hȳhst-* 16, 63,
  73

hēahgetimbru npl 'lofty buildings' 584

hēahþrym m. 'great glory, high praise' 1324

hēahþu f. 'high place, glory' 796, 938, 1088

healdan stv 7 'keep, hold to, support' inf 34, 717, 842, 1263, 3s pr ind
  healdeð 16, 249, 310, 397, 3pl pr ind *healdað* 90, 157, 810, 3pl pr sj
  healden 55, 3s pt ind *hēold* 736, 3pl pt *hēoldon* 729; *gehealdan* 'keep,
  guard' inf 1058, 3s pt ind *gehēold* 542

healf f. 'side' 133

hēan adj 'low, mean, humble' 454(N), 925, 995, 1353

hēan, see *hēah*

hēanmōd adj 'humble in mind, abject' 1379

heard adj 'brave, strong' 176, 275, 545, 953, 977, 1109

hearmstæf m. 'grief, affliction' 229

hēarsume, see *hȳrsum*

hebban stv 6 'lift, raise' pp *hæfen* 262, 3pl pt *hōfun* 412, 899, *hōfon* 730

hefegian wkv 2 'make heavy, grow heavy' 956, 1029

hefig adj 'heavy, grievous' 885, 1009, 1052

hel(l) f. 'hell' 582, 616, 677, 1104

heldor n. 'hell-door' 559

†*helleþegn* m. 'hell-fiend' 1069

help f. 'help, assistance' 683, 890, 922

helpan stv 3 + g 'help' inf 717

helwaru fpl. 'body of inhabitants of hell' 572

hēo, see *hě*

heofon m. 'heaven' 16, 31, 52, 66, 98, &c, 1104, 1212, 1283, 1302, 1316

heofoncund adj 'heavenly, celestial' 83, 171

heofoncyning m. 'heavenly king' 617, 807

heofonlīc adj 'heavenly, celestial' 1290, 1310, 1323
heofonrīce n. 'kingdom of heaven' 611, 789, 837
heolster m. 'place of hiding, darkness' 83
heonan adv 'hence, from here' 1036
heorde, see *hyrde*
heorogrim adj 'war-grim, exceeding grim' 979
heorte f. 'heart' 368, 582, 611, 799, 1009, 1052, 1143, 1205, 1209, &c
hēr adv 'here' 14, 23, 27, 250, &c, 892, 931, 948, 1129, 1248; *hēr on* 'on here' 256, 373
†*herecirm* m. 'war-shout' 900
†*herehlōð* f. 'hostile troop' 1069
herenis f. 'praise' 616
herian wkv 1 'praise, extol' 1s pr ind *herge* 611, 3s pt *herede* 121
hī, see *hē*
hider adv 'hither, to here' 274, 711
hige, see *hyge*
†*hildescūr* m. 'war-shower, flight of missiles' dpl -*un* 1143
him, see *hē*
hinder adv 'down' *on hinder* 676
hine, see *hē*
hingong m. 'going hence, departure' 811
hinsīþ m. 'journey hence, death' 1357
hīo, *hit*, see *hē*
hīw n. 'shape, form' 710, 900, 909
gehlæstan wkv 1 'load' 1333
hlāford m. 'lord, master' 1053, 1357
hleahtor m. 'laughter, exultation' 229
hlēo m. 'protection, protector' 1012, 1061, 1365
hlēolēas adj 'unprotected, shelterless' 222
†*hlēonað* m. 'shelter' 251(N)
hleonaþ, see *hlinian*
hlēor n. 'cheek, face' 334
hlēordropa m. 'tear' 1341
hlēotan stv 2 + *g* 'gain, obtain' inf 972, 1041
hlēoþor n. 'sound, speech' 685, 906, 1156, 1319, 1323
hlēoþrian wkv 2 'speak, cry out' 513
hlinian wkv 2 'lean, slope' pr ptc asm *hlingendne* 1147, 3s pr ind *hleonaþ* 73
hlīsa m. 'reputation, fame' 60, 157
hlōð f. 'company, band' 896, 915
hlūd adj 'loud, ringing' 900
hlūttor adj 'clear, pure' 106
hof n. 'house, dwelling' 1147
hold adj 'gracious, kind' 280, 1353
holdlīce adv 'graciously' 604
hond f. 'hand' 131, 259, 283, 303, 322, &c, 916, 951, 1300
hrā n. 'body' 283
hraðe adv 'quickly, soon' 422, *eft hraðe* 687, spv 1109

hrēmig adj + d 'exulting in' 1106

hrēow f. 'sorrow, penitence' 10

(*ge*)*hrēowan* stv 2 + d 'grieve' 3s pr ind *hrēoweð* 811, 3s pt ind *gehrēaw* 714

hrēowcearig adj 'troubled, sorrowful' 1053

hrēðe, see *rēþe*

hreþer m. 'breast, bosom' 938, 979, 1020, 1052, 1129, &c

hreþerloca m. 'breast' 1263

hrēðlēas adj 'inglorious, joyless' 906

hrīnan stv 1 + d 'touch, strike' inf 283, 410, 520; *gehrīnan* + a/d 'reach by touching, reach' 3s pt ind *gehrān* 1027

hring m. 'ring, circle' 1339(N)

hrōf m. 'roof' 1312

hrōpan stv 7 'shout, cry out' 3pl pt *hrēopun* 906

hryre m. 'fall' 730; 'fall, death' 829, 1093

hū adv 'how, in what way' + direct question 366, 1011, + indirect question 95, 337, 879, 884, 1022, 1161, 1322; *hū* 'the more' 20(N), 138

hungor m. 'hunger' 275, 916

hungrig adj 'hungry' 737

†*hunigflowende* adj 'flowing with honey, mellifluous' 1276

hūru adv 'indeed, truly, however' 361, 769, 1221, 1234, 1356

hūs n. 'house, dwelling-place' 251, 562, 677, 802, 1290, 1310

hūsel n. 'host, Eucharist' 1300

†*hūsulbearn* n. 'communicant' 559(N)

†*hūsulwer* m. 'communicant' 796

hūþ f. 'booty, plunder' 131

hwā pron 'who, what' asn *hwæt* 1252, is *bi hwon* 273

hwær adv 'where' 55

hwæt adv 'what, lo' 108, 517, 752, 1227

hwæþre adv 'however, yet' 233, 446, 520, 557; + indirect question 'whether' 352

hwearf m. 'crowd, troop' 263(N)

hweorfan stv 3 'turn, go, depart' inf 572, 837, 1354, 1379, 3pl pr ind *hweorfað* 812

hwider adv 'whither, to where' 26(N)

hwīl f. 'space of time, time' 423, 481, 1225; *hwīlum* 'at times' 86, 907, 908, 910, 916, 919

hwon, see *hwā*

hwonan adv 'whence' 1223

hwonne conj 'when, until' 111, 237, 779

hwōpan stv 7 + d 'threaten' 3pl pt *hwēopan* 190

hwylc pron 'who', 'which', 'what' 400, 748

hycgan wkv 3 'think, ponder' 3s pt *hogde* 1253; *gehycgan* 'resolve, hope for' inf 47, 2pl pr ind *gehycgað* 465

hyge m. 'mind, heart' 66, 545, 1020, 1048, 1053, 1061, 1139, &c, *hige* 368

hygegēomor adj 'sad in mind, sorrowful' 885, 928, 1156, 1336

hygerōf adj 'stout-minded, valiant' 953

hygesnottor adj 'wise of mind, prudent' 1109

hygesorg f. 'sorrow of mind, anxiety' 1009, 1205-, 1245

hȳhst-, see *hēah*

hyht m. 'hope' 63, 90, 98, 171, 318, &c, 925, 953, 1088

gehȳnan wkv 1 'oppress, humble' 572, 597

hyne, see *hě*

hȳra, see *hēah*

(ge)hȳran wkv 1 + a 'hear, learn' 108, 1049, 1120, 1170, 1212, 1316, &c; + d 'listen to, obey' 280, 364, 454, 604; *gehȳran æt* + d 'belong to' 33

hyrcnigan wkv 2 'listen to, obey' 1006

hyrdan wkv 1 'make hard, brace' 1270

hyrde‚ m. 'guardian, keeper, shepherd' 217, 318, 415, 550, &c, *heorde* 747

hyre, see *hě*

hȳrsum adj 'obedient' 368, *hēarsume* 705, 725

(ge)hyrwan wkv 1 'despise' 65, 491

hȳðʼ f. 'harbour, port' 1333

ic 'pers pron I' ns 7, 243, 244, 246, 250, &c, 1013, 1027, 1040, &c, as *mec* 241, 242, 252, &c, 1208, 1242, *mē* 249, 310, &c, 1227, gs *mīn* 482, ds *mē* 240, 247, 250, &c, 1016, 1019, 1065, &c, a/d *mē* 253, 1027, 1064, 1070

īdel adj 'empty, vain' 86, 166, 216, 308, 418, &c

ides f. 'woman' 983, 1232

ilca pron '(the) same' 973

in prep + d 'in, on, at, by, among' 46, 98, 111, &c, 834, 839, 843, &c, post position (preceding verb) 1008, 1024, 1142, *in innan* preceded by d 1367; + a 'in, into' 29, 31, 107, &c, 1085, 1102, 1105, &c; + a/d 95, 137, 348, &c, 965, 1091, 1099, 1195

in adv 'in, inside' 863, 940, 1005, 1028, *þǣr in* 19

inǣlan wkv 1 'burn, kindle' 668

†*inbend* m/f. 'inner chains' 955(N)

inbryrdan wkv 1 'incite, inspire' 654

ingong m. 'entrance, entry' 562, 993

inlȳhtan wkv 1 'enlighten, illumine' 99, 655

innan adv 'inside, (from) within' 883, 938, 979, 1052, 1271, &c, post position (quasi prep) 1065

innanweard adj 'inward, interior' 1320

inne adv 'inside' 1003

inþriccan wkv 1 'press forward, push' 285(N)

is, see *wesan*

iū adv 'long ago, formerly' *gēara iū* 40

lāc n. 'battle, struggle', 1034(N); 'offering, oblation' 1111; 'gift, message' 79, 307, 1298, 1343

lād f. 'sustenance, sufficiency' 389; 'course, journey' 1332

(ge)lǣdan wkv 1 'bring, take' 7, 85, 131, 188, 253, &c, 1297, 1305, 1343

lǣl f. 'wound, weal' 699

lǣne adj 'fleeting, transitory' 3, 120, 151, 330, 371, 967, 1120

(*ge*)*lǣran* wkv 1 'teach, instruct' 24, 138, 279

lǣs n. 'less' 79

lǣsast, see *lȳt*

lǣstan wkv 1 'perform, carry out' 24, 843, 845, 1171, 1259; *gelǣstan* 'serve, avail' 376

læt adj 'late, sluggish, tardy' nsf *latu* 903, 1265

lǣtan stv 7 'allow, permit' inf 199, 1259, *lēton* 520, 948, 3s pt ind *lēt* 777, 951, 1055, 3s pr sj *lēte* 365; 'let alone, give up' inf *lǣtan* 126

†*lagumearg* m. 'sea-horse, ship' 1332

lām n. 'clay, earth' 1032, 1194

lande, see *lond*

lār f. 'teaching, instruction, learning' 117, 252, 364, 453, 620, &c, 846, 1006, 1120, 1126, 1170

lāreow m. 'teacher' 359, 1004

lāst m. 'track, footprint' 289; *lāst weardian* 'remain behind' 1338

late adv 'slowly' 1164, 1225

lātteow m. 'leader, lord' 364

latu, see *læt*

lāð adj 'hateful, hostile' 85, 577, 595, cpv 236, spv 588

lāð n. 'evil' 313, 699

laðian wkv 2 'invite, call' 363

lāðspel n. 'hateful message' 1343

leahtor m. 'crime, sin' 832, 947, 1189; 'frailty' 1072

leahtorlēas adj 'faultless' 1087

lēan n. 'reward' 15, 92, 123, 588, 784, 1087, 1093, 1170, 1303

lēanian wkv 2 'reward, pay' 449

lēas adj + g 'free from, void of' 832, 925, 947, 1189

lecgan wkv 1 'lay' 2pl pt *legdon* 713

lēg, *lēge*, see *līg*

legdon, see *lecgan*

legerbedd n. 'bed of sickness, death-bed' 1032

lengu f. 'length' 512

lēof adj 'dear, beloved' 726, 797, 1062, 1076, 1164, 1225, &c, cpv 307, 551, spv 427, 655, 689, 1004, 1014, 1063, 1173, 1180, &c

lēof n. 'love' 313

†*lēofian* wkv 2 'delight, be dear to' 139(N)

lēoflīce adv 'kindly, lovingly' 784

lēoht n. 'light' 8, 486, 583, 659, 1282, 1308; 'light, heaven' 613(N); 'light, glory' 1369

lēoht adj 'bright, heavenly' 652, 834, 1111, 1289; 'light, fast-running' 1332

lēohte adv 'brightly, clearly' 768

lēohtfruma m. 'Source of light' 593, 609

lēoma m. 'light, radiance' 655, 659, 1310

leomu, *leoma*, see *lim*

leoðode, see *liðian*

gelettan wkv 1 'hinder' 359, 1236

līc n. 'body' 3, 699, 829, 838, 929, 967, 1072, &c

līcfæt n. 'body-vessel, body' 1090, 1369

līchoma m. 'body-home, body' 163, 193, 228, 338, 371, &c, 1099, 1376

līchord n. 'body-treasure, soul' 956(N), 1029

līf n. 'life' 20, 62, 74, 85, 99, &c, 829, 834, 838, 929, 932, &c; 'living thing' 512

līffruma m. 'Giver of life, God' 637

lifgan wkv 3 'live' inf 273, 831, pr ptc *lifgend-* 818, 1099, 1234, 3pl pr ind *lifgað* 460, 2pl pt *lifdon* 624

līfgedāl n. 'parting from life, death' 1046

līfweg m. 'life-way, path of life' 768

līfwela m. 'life-riches, wordly wealth' 151

līg (lēg) m/n. 'flame' 193, 375, 595, 624, 1072

ligesearu n. 'lying art, wile, snare' 228

lim (leom-) n. 'limb' 221, 838, 956, 1029, 1032, 1046, &c

†*limhāl* adj 'limb-whole, unharmed' 689

gelimpan stv 3 'happen, befall' 3s pt ind *gelomp* 520, 665, 3pl pt sj *gelumpe* 194

liss f. 'mercy, grace' 613, 834, 1076

līþe adj 'pleasant, gentle' 363, 768

liðian wkv 2 'release, unloose' 3s pt *leoðode* 392(N)

lof m/n. 'praise' 24, 159, 393, 491, 527, &c, 963

lombor n. 'lamb' 1042(N)

lond n. 'land, country' 139, 146, 151, 273, 307, &c, 831, 1282

long adj 'long, lasting' 120, 904, 1046, 1090, 1180, &c, cpv *lengra* 1034

longað m. 'desire' 316, 330, 359

longe adv 'long, for a long time' 7, 624, 642, 832, 1171, 1259; cpv *leng* 236, 261, 424, 1058; *lenge hū* + cpv adv 'the longer the . . .' 20(N), 138

†*longfyrst* m. 'long space of time' 947

longsum adj 'long, enduring' 794

(ge)lufian wkv 2 'love, treat with kindness' 79, 109, 138, 161, 387, &c

lufu f. 'love, favour' 38, 92, 462, 652, 769, 964, 1076, 1173, 1189, 1257

lust m. 'pleasure, joy' 113, 417, 524

(ge)lȳfan wkv 1 + d 'allow, permit' 214, 409, 593; + a 'believe, trust in' 637

lyft m/f/n. 'air, heavens' 120, 221, 392, 412, 427, &c, 1289, 1308, 1315

lyftlācende adj 'hovering in the air' 146

lyre m. 'loss, damage' 829

lȳt adv 'little, not at all' 238, 252, 316, 726, 774; cpv *þȳ lǣs (þæt)*, see *sě*; spv *lǣsast* 'least' 338, 769

lȳtel adj 'little' 214, 423, 481

lȳthwōn adv 'a while, for a little' 392

mā cpv adv 'more' 518; as indeclinable noun + g 403

mæcg m. 'kinsman, man' 861, 1219

mǣg m. 'man, kinsman' 195

mæg, see *magan*

mægen n. 'power, might, strength' 46, 260, 282, 311, 325, &c, 977, 1086, 1272; 'effort, feat of strength' 1107

mægencræft m. 'mighty power' 1132

mægenfæst adj 'strong, vigorous' 474

mægenspēd f. 'strength, might' 639

†*mægenþegn* m. 'mighty man' 1126

mæg(e)ð f. 'maiden, woman' 861, 1342, 1376

mǣgð f. 'tribe' 762

mǣgwlite m. 'appearance, form' 460; 'species, kind' 734(N)

mǣnan wkv 1 'lament, mourn' 430, 1233

mǣran wkv 1 'celebrate' 507

mǣre adj 'famous, renowned' 71, 881

mǣst, see *micel*

mǣte adj 'moderate, poor, mean' 53, cpv 46(N)

mæðlan wkv 1 'speak' 1202

magan pt prs vb 'be able to, have power to, (I) can' 1s pr ind *mæg* 244, 2s pr ind *meaht* 1015, 3s pr ind *mæg* 35, 242, 278, 347, 371, &c, 993, 1070, 1pl pr ind *magun* 32, 93, 284, 2pl pr ind *magon* 702, 3pl pr ind *magun* 496, 1s pt *meahte* 486, 2s pt *meahtes* 469, 3s pt *meahte* 358, 576, 989, 1023, 1055, 1057, 1109, &c, 3pl pt *meahton* 187, 3s pr sj *mæge* 868, 891, 1321, 3s pt sj *meahte* 433, 1159, 1225, 1251

magu m. 'young man, servant' 1010

mān n. 'sin, evil' 96

gemanian (*gemonian*) wkv 2 'admonish' 1208; 'remind' 1340(N)

manna, see *mon(n)*

mānsceaþa m. 'evil foe' 650, 909

māra, see *micel*

māre adv 'more' 387

martyre m. 'martyr' 514

martyrhād m. 'martyrdom' 472

mē, mec, see *ic*

meagol adj 'earnest, firm' 734, 919

meaht (*miht*) f. 'strength, power' 185, 240, 413, 695, 881, 884, 926, 1158

meaht, meahte, meahtes, meahton, see *magan*

meahtig adj 'mighty' 788, 1243

mearclond n. 'borderland, wasteland' 174

mearh m. 'horse' gpl *mēara* 286

melda m. 'informant, teller' 1230

mengu indeclinable f. 'host, troop' 68, 185, 201, 237, 279, &c

mennisc adj 'human' 168, 909, 919, 1122

meodume adj 'small, little' cpv 384

meord f. 'pay, reward' 1041, 1086

meotud m. 'Creator, God' 147, 358, 366, 576, 708, 959, 1041, 1132, 1243

gemētan wkv 1 'meet' 1; 'come upon, find' 531, 922, 1015

mēðe adj 'weary, sad' 1015, 1110, 1158, 1261, 1337

meþelcwide m. 'speech, conversation' 1007, 1015, 1219

gemeðian wkv 2 'weary, exhaust' 977

micel adj 'great, big, large' 53, 326, 531, 1010, 1110, 1342, cpv *mār-*

168, 198, 237, 247, 270, &c, spv *mǣst*(-) 207, 910, 1103, 1127, 1282; sb 'much, great possessions' 320

micle adv 'much, greatly' 1125, 1247, cpv *māre..þonne* 'more than' 387(N)

miclum adv 'greatly' 1197

mid prep + a 'with, in' 14, 90, 303, &c, 999, 1215, 1372; + d 'with, among, amid, by means of' 79, 89, 177, &c, 1101, 1192; + a/d 'with, among, between' 237, 258, 338, 578, &c, 1258

midd adj 'mid, middle (of)' 1151

middangeard m. 'world' 30, 39, 53, 68, 270, &c, 865

mihta, see *meaht*

milde adj 'mild, gentle' 739, 788, 1007, 1107

milts f. 'mercy, kindness' 21, 331, 639, 959

mīn, see *ic*

mīn poss adj 'my' 243, 258, 260, &c, 1011, 1020, 1036, &c

minne adj 'mean, vile' nplm. 909, *mine* 650(N)

mislīc adj 'various, diverse' 874, 898

mist m. 'mist' 1280

mīþan stv 1 'hide, conceal' inf 708, 2pl pr ind *mīþað* 465, 1s pt ind *māð* 1255, 3s pt ind *māð* 1345

mōd n. 'mind, heart' 26, 65, 96, 106, 118, &c, 962, 977, 1068, 1086, 1110, &c

mōdcearu f. 'sorrow, grief' 195, 1010, 1342

mōdgeþanc m/n. 'mind' 1197

mōdgian wkv 2 'exult' 323

†*mōdglæd* adj 'glad in spirit, happy' 1158(N)

mōdig adj 'brave, courageous' 267, 695, 1272

mōdsefa m. 'mind' 387, 959, 1337

†*mōdsēoc* adj 'sick at heart' 1261

mōdsorg f. 'distress of mind, sorrow' 1051

molde f. 'earth' 989, 1230

moldweg m. 'way upon earth, earth' 1039

mon(*n*) m. 'man' 26, 46, 130, 147, 154, &c, 865, 874, 989, 1126, 1164, &c, gpl *manna* 1173; indef pron 'one' 274, 279

gemonade, see *gemanian*

mon(*n*)*cynn* n. 'mankind' 198, 440, 514, 739

mondryhten m. 'lord, master' 1007, 1051, 1151, 1337

monfaru f. 'moving host' 286

monig (*mong-*) adj 'many, many a' 39, 118, 734, 898; pron 'many' 30, 174, 181, 264, 323, &c, 884

monigfeald adj 'manifold' 644, cpv 1247

†*monlufu* f. 'human love' 353

monþēaw m. 'manner, custom' 507

morgen m. 'morning' 1219, 1243

morþor m/n. 'death' 861

mōs n. 'sustenance, food' 274(N)

mōst, *mōst-*, see **mōtan*

*mōtan pt prs vb 'be able, be permitted, (I) may' 1s pr ind *mōt* 717,

1040, 2s pr ind *mōst* 6, 3s pr ind *mōt* 785, pl pr ind *mōtan* (-un, -um) 13, 22, 132, 220, 314, &c, 1191, 3s pt *mōste* 744, 779, 831, pl pt *mōstun* (-um, -an, -on) 210, 226, 424, 549, 632, 837, 840, 1187, 3s pr sj *mōte* 28, 2pl pr sj *mōten* 613, pl pt sj *mōsten* 410, 482, 1371

gemunan pt prs vb 'remember' 3s pt *gemunde* 97, 3 pl pt sj 750

mundbora m. 'protector' 542, 695, 788

mundbyrd f. 'protection, aid' 185, 881

mundian wkv 2 'protect' 260

murnan stv 3 'mourn' pr ptc *murnende* 430

mūð m. 'mouth' 1122, 1272

*mynnan wkv 1 'be impelled, direct onself to' 1088

mynster n, 'monastery' 416

myrcels m. 'sign, mark' 458(N)

myrðra m. 'murderer' 650

nǣfre adv 'never' 10, 92, 376, 636, 640, &c, 1013, 1170, 1173, 1210

nǣgan (*nēgan*) wkv 1 'speak to, address' 1063, 1227; *genǣgan* 'approach, assail' 290, 1153, pp *genęged* 1013

nǣnig pron 'not any, none' 865, 890, 923, gsn *nǣnges* 827

næs, see *wesan*

næss m. 'headland, cliff' 563

nalæs (*nales*) adv 'by no means, not at all' 117, 261, 461, 583, 616, &c; *nales þy* 150, see *sē*

ne adv, neg particle 'not' 46, 61, 130, &c, 987, 993, 1023, &c; conj 'nor' 19, 227, 283, 313, 320, &c, 1069, 1070, 1121, linking disjunct phrases 310, 384, 579, &c, 828, 829, 830, &c

nēah adj 'near, nigh' 93, 172, 189, 336, 970, spv *nyhst-* 'next' 445, 1018, 1168

nēah prep + d 'near, close to' 1143 (post position)

nēalǣcan wkv 1 'draw near to, approach' 1033, 1139

nearu adj 'narrow, oppressive' asm *nearone* 598, dpl *nearwum* 540

nearwe adv 'narrowly, closely' 1013, 1210

nearwum adv 'narrowly, hard' 1153

nēgan, see *nǣgan*

nelle, see *willan*

nemnan wkv 1 'name, tell' 93

nemne conj 'unless' 367

nēod (*nyd*) f/n. 'need, necessity' 241, 329, 697, 1095

nēol adj 'deep, bottomless' 563

nēorxnawong m. 'paradise' 827(N)

nēosan wkv 1 + a/g 'seek, attack' 350; 'seek out, visit' 719, 920, 958, 1001, 1146, 1217, 1365

nēotan stv 2 + g 'make use of, enjoy' inf 832, 1373

(ge)nergan wkv 1 'save, protect' 241, 553, pr ptc adj 598

nergend m. 'Saviour' 640, 658

nēðing f. 'audacity' 128

niht f. 'night' 350, 1018, 1028, 1035, 1218, 1281, 1287; *nihtes* 'by night' 128, 610, 1210

†*nihtglōm* m. 'night-gloom, darkness of night' 943

nihthelm m. 'cover of night' 970

†*nihtrīm* n. 'a number of nights' 1097(N)

nihtscūa m. 'shade of night, darkness' 998

niman stv 4 'take, take up abode in' inf 1078, 1372; 'feel' 3pl pt *nōman* 218; *geniman* 'take, feel' 3s pt ind *genōm* 741; 'seize, take' 3s pt ind *genōm* 846, 2pl pt *genōman* 701

nis, see *wesan*

nið m. 'grief, trouble' 49; 'attack' 241, 553, 648; 'violence, enmity' 141, 390, 525; *niþa* 'violently' 290

niþer adv 'down, downward' 563

*niððas plm. 'men' gpl *niðða* 640, 1097

nīwe adj 'new' 742, 823, 833

genīwian wkv 2 'renew, make new' 953

nō emphatic neg adv 'not at all, not ever' 18(N), 201, 269, 302, 331, &c, 833

nōht adv 'not' 1171

nolde, see *willan*

†*norðrodor* m. 'north-firmament, northern sky' 1279

nū adv 'now' 6, 9, 35, 42, 49, &c, 1166, 1257, 1263, 1268, 1298, &c; conj 307, 317, 717; correlative 1044–5; *nū gēna* 'even now' 155; *nū ðā* 'now' 1231

nȳd, see *nēod*

nȳdcosting f. 'painful trial, affliction' 1153

nȳdgedāl n. 'forced dissolution, death' 445, 934, 1168

nȳdwracu f. 'violence' as *nȳdwræce* 553

nȳhst-, see *nēah*

nȳðgīst m. 'malicious spirit' 540(N)

of prep + d 'from, out of' 44, 57, 106, 196, 212, &c, 822, 847, 866, 887, 938, &c, postponed 1363

ofer prep + a 'over, above, against' 49, 62, 311, &c, 848, 872, 1097, &c; 'up over' 1292; 'after' (of time) 947, 1171; + d 'over, above, on' 73, 1098; + a/d 755, 1127, 1230

oferbīdan stv 1 'survive' pp *oferbiden* 546

ofercuman stv 4 'overcome' pp *ofercumen* 438

oferfeohtan stv 3 'conquer, vanquish' 3pl pr ind *oferfeohtað* 803

oferhygd f/n. 'arrogance, pride' 269, 634, 661

oferlēoran wkv 1 'deviate from, transgress' 726

†*ofermæcga* m. 'very strong man, illustrious being' 692

ofersēon stv 5 'observe' 1pl pt *ofersēgon* 266

oferstīgan stv 1 'defeat' 3s pt ind *oferstāg* 230

ofertēon stv 2 'draw over, cover' 3s pt ind *ofertēah* 1280

oferþēon stv 1 & 3 'excel, surpass' 3s pt sj *oferþunge* 431

oferwinnan stv 3 'overcome' 3pl pr ind *oferwinnað* 25, 3s pt ind *oferwon* 152, 180

†*oferwlencu* f. 'arrogance, ostentation' 418

ofestlīce, see *ofostlīce*

ofestum adv 'quickly' 1297

ofgiefan stv 5 'give up' inf 232, 477, 3s pr ind *ofgiefeþ* 2

ofostlīce adv 'speedily, quickly' 1201, *ofestlīce* 1327

oft adv 'often, constantly' 84, 108, 140, 160, 266, &c, 884, 894, 1208, 1217, spv *oftost* 1348, 1355

oftēon stv 2 + g(thing) & d (person) 'take away from, deprive of' 1pl pt *oftugon* 467

oftost, see *oft*

ofunnan pt prs vb + g (thing) & d (person) 'begrudge a person something' 3s pr ind *ofonn* 85

ombehtþegn (*onbehtþegn*) m. 'servant' 1000, 1146, 1199, 1294

†*ombiehthēra* m. 'obedient servant, vassal' 599

on prep + a 'in, at, during' (time); 'on, upon'; 'unto, into'; 71, 133, 257, &c, 827, 855, 857, &c, post position 995; + d 'in, on, by' 16, 51, 61, &c, 831, 844, 874, &c; + a/d 15, 112, 175, &c, 841, 927, 935, &c; *on betran* 'to a better end' 378; 'among' 244, 271

on adv 'on'; *hēr on* 'here upon' 256, 373; *on hinder* 'backwards, back' 676; *on innan* 'within' 1271

onǣlan wkv 1 'fire, kindle' 955

†*onbǣru* f. 'composure' 1054(N)

onbehtþegn, see *ombehtþegn*

onberan stv 5 'weaken' pp *onboren* 944

onbid n. 'waiting, interval' 904, 1046

onbryrdan wkv 1 'stimulate, stir' 335

oncnāwan 7 'know, recognize' 3s pt ind *oncnēow* 1199

oncweþan stv 5 'answer' 3s pt ind *oncwæð* 1023

oncyrran wkv 1 'turn away' 365

oncȳðig adj + g 'revealing, making known' 1226(N)

7 (*ond*) conj '& (and)' 2, 3, 7, &c, 825, 838, 839, &c

onda m. 'anger, terror' 565; *ondan niman* 'become angry' 218; *on ondan* + d 'against' 346, 773

†*ondcwis* f. 'answer' 1026

ondgiet n. 'understanding' 766

ondgiete f. 'mind' 112

ondlong adj 'continuous, whole' 1277, 1287

ondsaca m. 'adversary' 210, 233

ondswarian wkv 2 'answer' 590

ondswaru f. 'answer' 293, 1163, 1224

ondweard adj 'present' 1083, 1142

ondwīg m/n. 'resistance' 176(N)

onfeng m. 'grasp, attack' 405, 519

onfōn stv 7 'receive, obtain' 3pl pt *onfēngon* 974

ongēan prep + d 'against' 239 (post position), + a/d 302 (post position)

ongietan stv 5 'understand, perceive' pp *ongieten* 1207, 1/3s pt ind *ongeat* 1060, 1220, 3pl pt *ongēaton* 552

ongin(n) n. 'undertaking' 277, 355

onginnan stv 3 'begin' pp *ongunnen* 980; 'try, endeavour' imp s *Ongin* 290, 3pl pt *Ongunnon* 569; in periphrastic construction, denoting

simple action of the infinitive 1/3s pt ind *ongan* (*ongon*) 101, 726, 1001, 1010, 1061, 1110, 1114, &c

ongyldan stv 3 + a/d 'pay for, be punished for' inf *ongyldon* 861, 3pl pt *onguldon* 857, 986

onhǣle adj 'secret, hidden' 297, 351, 534

onhrēran wkv 1 'stir up, agitate' 37

onhyldan wkv 1 'bow, sink' 334, 1213, 1270

onlūcan stv 2 'unlock' pp *onlocen* 956, 3s pt ind *onlēac* 1029, 1144

onmōd adj 'resolute, steadfast' 745

onsǣgan wkv 1 'cause to sink down, prostrate' 1162

onsecgan stv 3 'offer, make (sacrifice)' 3s pt *onsægde* 1111

onsendan wkv 1 'send, dispatch' 711, 776, 937, 1238, 1303

onsettan wkv 1 'impose' 697

onsittan stv 5 'fear, dread' 1s pr *onsitte* 1070

onspringan stv 3 'burst forth, spring forth' 3s pr ind *onsprong* 1326(N)

onstæl m. 'arrangement, disposition' 824

onstǣlan wkv 1 'bring against, accuse of' 468

onsȳn f. 'lack, want' 828

onsȳn(n) f/n. 'face' 143, 459, 500, 707, 718, &c, 1184, 1188

onsȳne adj 'visible' 1254

ontȳnan wkv 1 'open, reveal' 9, 487, 992, 1301

onwald adj 'powerful, mighty' 1102(N)

onwealda m. 'Ruler' 638

onwendan wkv 1 'turn away, avert' 376, 469

†*onwille* adj 'desired' 728

onwrēon stv 1 'reveal' 3s pt ind *onwrāh* 147, 162, 3s pt sj *onwrige* 1161

onwyllan wkv 1 'cause to boil, become violent' 391

geopenian wkv 2 'open' 993

ord m. 'beginning' 532

ōretta m. 'warrior' 176, 344, 401, 569

oreþe, see *oroð*

orlege n. 'battle, warfare' 196, 455, 564

oroð m. 'breath, breathing' 1024, 1155, 1165, 1226, 1271, &c

orsāwle adj 'without soul, lifeless' 1194

orwēna adj + g 'despairing of, hopeless' 627

orwēnnys f. 'hopelessness, despair' 575

oð prep + a 'until, to' 1256, 1277, 1312

oðberan stv 4 'bear forth' inf 303

oðbregdan stv 3 'take away, carry off' pp *oðbrōden* 854

ōþer pron 'the one . . . the other' 119 . . . 127; adj 'other' 5, 391, 1119, 1215

oþþæt conj 'until' 134, 147, 498, 546, 1291

oþþe conj 'or' 27, 281, 343, 369, 751, 891

ōwiht f/n. 'anything' 319

gerǣcan wkv 1 'obtain by effort, attain' 171

rǣd m. 'counsel, advice' 278

rǣdan stv 7 + d 'gave the disposal of, dispose of' inf 132

ræfnan wkv 1 'do, perform' 622, 792

rǣran wkv 1 'raise' 24, 160; 'excite, stir up' 186

rǣsan wkv 1 'rush' 406, 995

rǣst f. 'rest' 12, 25, 221, 1095, *ręste* 363

rēaf m. 'spoil, booty' 132

reccan wkv 1 'recite, tell over' 3s pt reahte 160; *gereccan* 'direct, train, ordain' pp *geræhte* 768, 3s pt *gerehte* 96, *gereahte* 135

reccan wkv 1 + g 'have a care for' 291

regul m. 'rule, standard' 489

rēonigmōd adj 'weary in spirit, sad at heart' 1096

reord f. 'voice, speech' 160, 734, 743, 898

gereordan wkv 1 'give food to, refresh' 1300

reordian wkv 2 'speak' 1025

rēow adj 'fierce, cruel' 406(N)

restan wkv 1 'rest' 213

rētan wkv 1 'cheer up' 1062

rēþe (*hrēðe*) adj 'savage, cruel' 489(N), 1140

rīce adj 'powerful, great' 995

rīce n. 'kingdom' 660, 682, 792, 1302

rīcsian wkv 2 'reign, tyrannize' 871, 3s pt *rixade* 864

rīm n. 'number' 32, 498, 891, 1135

gerīsan stv 1, impers + d 'befit' 3s pt ind *gerās* 1114

rixade, see *rīcsian*

rōd f. 'cross' 180

rodor m. 'firmament', pl. 'heavens' 682, 792, 1096, 1312

rōf adj 'valiant' 1095

†*rōw* f. 'rest, quietness' 213(N)

rūm adj 'lax' 489

rūmmōd adj 'liberal in giving' 78

rūnwita m. 'wiseman, sage, one acquainted with mysteries' 1095

ryht adj 'true, right, lawful' 78, 682; 'erect' 1312

ryht n. 'law, justice' 810; 'dues' 197(N)

ryht adv 'rightly' 32

rȳman wkv 1 'manifest, clear a way' 767; *gerȳman* + *tō* 'clear the way to' 225

†*ryneþrāg* f. 'swift interval, snatched moment' 213(N)

sacu f. 'strife' 678, as *sæce* 300

sǣ m/f. 'sea' 266, 1359

sæce, see *sacu*

sǣd n. 'seed' 45

sǣl f. 'time, prosperity' 35

gesǣlan wkv 1 'manage, bring about' 347

sǣmra cpv adj 'worse, inferior' 492

sǣne adj 'sluggish' 343

sār n. 'pain, suffering' 377, 408, 433, 515, 541, &c, 957, 965, 1027, 1030, 1073, &c

sārbenn f. 'painful wound' 1019

sārig (sarg-) adj 'sad, grieving, sorrowful' 887, 1356

sārigferð adj 'sorrowing in one's soul, sorrowful' 1352, 1378

sārslege m. 'painful blow, wounding blow' 227

†*sārstæf* m. 'bitter word' 234

†*sārwylm* m. 'surging pain' 1150

†*sāwelcund* adj 'spiritual' 317

sāwelgedāl n. 'parting of soul and body, death' 1035

†*sāwelhūs* n. 'house of the soul, body' 1030, 1141

sāw(u)l f. 'soul' 2, 12, 22, 122, 227, &c, 929, 1089, 1264

scæd n. 'shade' as 675, npl *scadu* 1288

sceal, scealt, see *sculan*

sceaða m. 'criminal, raider' 127

scēawian wkv 2 'look at, behold' 54, 80, 414, 718

scencan wkv 1 'pour out, give to drink' 984

(ge)sceþþan stv 6 + d 'injure, hurt' inf 226, 3pl pt *scōdun* 544, 3s pt sj *scōde* 443; 3s pt ind *gescōd* 425, 870

sceþþend m. 'adversary, marauder' gpl *sceðþenra* 404(N)

(ge)scieppan stv 6 'make, create' pp *sceapen* 677, 3s pt ind *scōp* 495; 3s pt ind *gescōp* 606

(ge)scildan, see *(ge)scyldan*

scīma m. 'radiance, splendour' 1286

scīnan stv 1 'shine' inf 1283, 3s pt ind *scān* 693, 1288, 1330

scīran wkv 1 'distinguish, discern' 505

scīrwered ptc adj 'clothed with radiance' 1288(N)

scolu f. 'host' 204

scomu f. 'shame, humiliation' 204, 633(N), 856

scond f. 'shame', ds *sconde* 'shamefully' 675

scrīðan stv 1 'go by, pass' pr ptc *scrīþende* 1038(N), pp *scriþen* 1039, 3pl pt *scridun* 969, *scridon* 1097

*scūdan stv 2 'hasten, skitter' pr ptc *scūdende* 856(N)

scūfan stv 2 'thrust, shove' inf 675, pp *scofene* 633(N), 856

sculan pt prs vb 'ought to, (I) must' 1/3s pr ind *sceal* 7, 26, 63, &c, 1030, 1189, 1195, &c, 2s pr ind *scealt* 273, 582, 1168, pl pr ind *sceolon* 614, 635, 680, 1072, 3s pt *sceolde* 104, 192, 235, &c, 971, 1284, 1342, pl pt *sceoldon (-an)* 231, 477, 664, 860, 3s pr sj *scyle* 1022

*scyccan wkv 1 'urge, egg on' 3s pt *scyhte* 127(N)

scyld f/m. 'guilt, crime' 478; dpl *scyldum* 'guiltily' 633(N)

(ge)scyldan (-scildan) wkv 1 'shield, protect' 242, 404, 457, 556

scyldig adj 'guilty' 204, 505

scyndan wkv 1 'hurry' 1331

scyppend m. 'Creator' 664, 1158

sĕ, sēo, þæt def art 'the, that' nsm *sĕ* 4, 16, 46, &c, 852, 896, 925, &c, nsf *sēo* 2, 45, 146, &c, 903, 962, 970, &c, nsn *þæt* 277, 355, 739, 904, 1076, 1080, &c, asm *þone (ðone)* 477, 533, 571, &c, 821, 868, 990, &c, asf *þā* 109, 301, 412, &c, 926, 976, 992, &c, asn *þæt* 62, 106, 126, &c, 957, 1290, 1310, &c, gsm *þæs* 26, 60, 69, &c, 973, 1067, 1131, &c, gsf *þǣre* 68, 541, gsn *þæs (ðæs)* 75, 83, 134, &c, 1050, dsm *þām (ðām)* 10, 91, 192, &c, 834, 836, 871, &c, dsf *þǣre (ðǣre)* 716, 822, 860, 983, &c,

dsn *þām* (*ðām*) 3, 196, 333, &c, 831, 866, 1147, &c, ism *þȳ* 73, 132, 702, isn *þȳ* 1301, npl *þā* 18, 91, 421, &c, 905, 975, 985, apl *þā* (*ðā*) 25, 49, 56, &c, 851, 1168, 1296, &c, gpl *þāra* 528, 606, 709, 892, dpl *þām* (*ðām*) 241, 661, 894, 1110; sb pron 'that one, he, she, it', nsm *sě* 1, 28, 400, &c, nsf *sēo* 214, nsn used emphatically *þæt* (*ðæt*) 18, 91, 517, &c, 819, 870, 1008, &c, asn *þæt* 72, 271, 483, &c, 947, 1351, dsm *þām* 98, npl *þā* 55, 287, 493, &c, apl *þā* 299, gpl *þeara* 398(N), dpl *þām* 19, 993; (note emphatic nsn *þæt* with pl vb, 18, 91, and 796);

  rel pron 'that, who, which, what' nsm *sě* 63, 92, 106, &c, 1000, 1242, nsf *sēo* 965, nsn *þæt* 93, 851, asm *þone* 869, *sē mec* 'whom' 703, asn *þæt* 1258, gsn *þæs* 985, dsm *þām* 642, 1084, 1099, 1354, npl *þā* 81, 91, 115, &c, apl *þā* (*ðā*) 51, 52, 58, &c, 1172; with relative particle *þe* 'that, who, which, what' nsm *sě þe* 85, 99, 241, &c, 1284, 1337, 1351, asm *ðone þe* 104, gsm *þæs þe* 131, 1207, 1228, gsn *þæs þe* 379, 426, 465, &c, dsm *þām þe* 92, 173, 346, 1348, *sě þe him* 'him who' 361, npl *þā þe* (*ðā þe*) 14, 23, 31, &c, gpl *þāra þe* (*ðāra þe*) 155, 268, 417, &c, 1360, dpl *þām þe* 124, 161, 622, *þām þe him* 'over whose' 72;

  adv use of gsn *þæs* 'in respect of this' 32, 252, 361, &c, 1034, 1054, intensifying adv 'so' 867, 1130; conj *þæs* 'since' 1135, conj + rel particle *þæs þe* 'the time in which, when' 341, 1053, 1142; adv use of isn *þȳ* 'thereby, therefore' 201, 491, *nales þȳ* 'not that' 150; *þȳ læs* conj 'lest' 757, *þȳ læs þæt* 'lest' 1232, and see *for ðȳ*; use of isn *þon* in adverbs and prepositional formulae, *Tō þon* 'thereupon' 218, *wiþ þon* 'against that' 494(N), and see under *æfter*, *ær*, and *for*

se þeana, *se þeah*, see *swā*

sealdun adv 'seldom' 317(N)

searo n. 'artifice, guile' 850

†*searocǣg* f. (?-*a* m.) 'treacherous key' 1145

searocræft m. 'treacherous art, wile' 142, 568, 674

sēcan, *sōhte* wkv 1 'seek, look for' 82, 128, 480, 492, 561, &c, 878, 927, 1082, 1141, 1279, &c; *gesēcan* 'seek out, visit' 197, 354, 522, 887, 1037, 1089, 1145, 1244; 'attack, seize' 281, 957, 1019, 1030

(*ge*)*secgan*, (*ge*)*sægde* wkv 3 'say, utter, tell' 41, 119, 234, 244, 295, &c, 878, 1027, 1116, 1179, &c, imp s *saga* 1192

sefa m. 'understanding, mind, heart' 473, 570, 1048, 1077, 1116, 1123, 1138, &c

sēfte adj 'soft, comfortable' 165

sēl cpv adv 'better' 20

sēlast, -*a*, *sēllan*, see *gōd* adj

seld n. 'seat, dwelling-place' 585

sele m. 'hall, dwelling' 742

(*ge*)*sellan* wkv 1 'give, grant' 1s pr *sylle* 367, 3s pr ind *syleð* 767, 3pl pr ind *sellað* 77, 3s pt *sealde* 100, 112, 184, 202, &c, 849, 3pl pt *sealdon* 413, pp *geseald* 784, 3s pt *gesealde* 103

sēman wkv 1 'reconcile' inf *sēmon* 511(N)

sendan wkv 1 'send' 321, 511, 767

sēoc adj 'weak, sad' 1068(N), 1077

seofeða num 'seventh' 1141

seofian wkv 2 'sigh, lament' 230

seofon cdl num 'seven' 1035

gesēon stv 5 'see, behold, look at' inf 486, 1080, 1187, pp *gesewen* 1128,
    1313, 3s pr ind *gesihð* 56, 3s pt ind *geseah* 712, 1053, 2s pt sj *gesāwe* 468

†*sēoslig* adj 'afflicted, troubled' 927(N)

sēoðan stv 2 'boil, cause to well up' *soden* 1073, 1150, 1262

setl n. 'seat, dwelling-place' 144, 165, 244, 278, 383, &c

setlgong m. 'setting-journey, setting' 1214, 1279

(*ge*)*settan* wkv 1 'set, establish' 51, 58, 434, 488, 535, &c, 1022

sib(*b*) f. 'peace, harmony, friendship' 12, 197(N), 716, 816(N), 1082,
    1173, 1262

sibgedryht f. 'peaceful band' 1372

sīd adj 'wide, extensive' 1123

sīde adv 'far and wide' 882

sīdweg m. 'distant way' 887(N)

siex cdl num 'six' 51

gesīgan stv 1 'sink' 3s pt ind *gesāg* 1269

sige m. 'victory' 184

sigedryhten m. 'victorious Lord, God' 1238, 1375

sigehrēðig adj 'rejoicing in victory, triumphant' 732

sigelēas adj 'without victory, defeated' 302, 476, 651

sigelēoð n. 'song of victory' 1315

†*sigetūdor* n. 'victorious race' 866

sigewong m. 'victorious plain, place of victory' 742, 921

sigor m. 'victory' 1080

sigorfæst adj 'firm in victory, victorious' 965, 1244

sigorlēan n. 'reward for victory, prize' 878, 1370

†*sigortācn* n. 'victorious sign' 1116

†*sigorwuldor* n. 'triumphant glory' 122

sihste ord num 'sixth' 1150

gesincan stv 3 'sink' 3s pt ind *gesonc* 1142

sincgiefa m. 'giver of treasure, generous lord' 1352

sind, *-on*, *-an*, see *wesan*

sindrēam m. 'eternal joy' 839, 1043

singales adv 'continually, always' 219

singan stv 3 'sing' 1s pr *singe* 609, 3pl pt *sungon* 1315

sinhīwan plm. 'couple' 851, 968

sinnan stv 3 'care for' 1s pr *sinne* 319

sinneht(*e*) f. 'unending night, darkness' 678

sīð adv 'afterwards' 369, 876, 1118, *þā sīð* 1023

sīð adj 'after' cpv nsf *sīþre* 45

sīð m. 'journey' 144, 302, 354, 726, 1045, 1077, 1175, 1375

sīðfæt m. 'journey' 1378

sīðfrom adj 'eager to be going' 921

sīðian wkv 2 '*journey*' 924

sīððan (*siþþan*) adv 'afterwards, since' 667, 706, 751, 774, 839, 852, 860,
    866, 984, &c, *siþþam* 136(N), *siþþan āwo* 'ever afterwards' 1043; conj
    'after, once' 99, 152, 175, 208, 504, &c, 935, 1049, 1176, 1239, 1254

sittan stv 5 'sit, settle' 3s pr ind *siteð* 478; *gesittan* 'sit down in, settle' 3pl pr ind *gesittað* 82, 122, 3s pt ind *gesæt* 158, 174, 3pl pt *gesæton* 144

slǣp m. 'sleep' 343(N)

slīðen adj 'cruel, hard' 992

slūma m. 'slumber' 343

smēþe adj 'smooth' 732

smolt adj 'pleasant, calm' 742

snel adj 'quick, strong' 1330

snottor adj 'wise, prudent' 35, 1145

snūde adv 'at once, quickly' 704

snyrian wkv 1 'hasten' 1332

snyttru f. 'wisdom' 163, 473, dpl *snyttrum* 'wisely, prudently' 764

snyttrucrǣft m. 'wisdom, prudence' 184, 1128

sōcn f. 'visitation, persecution' 716(N)

somud adv 'together' 1372; post position prep + a 'together' 838

somwist f. 'life together' 968, 1177

sōna adv 'immediately' 992, 1023

†*sondhof* n. 'sand-dwelling, grave' 1196

†*sondlond* n. 'sandy shore' 1334

song m. 'singing' 1323

sorg f. 'sorrow, grief, trouble' 219, 230, 295, 317, 354, &c, 1019, 1040, 1068, 1092, 1137, &c

†*sorgcearu* f. 'sorrowful anxiety, care' 966

sorgian wkv 2 'sorrow' 238

sorgwylm (-*wælm*) m. 'surge of grief, wave of sorrow' 1073, 1262

sōð n. 'truth' 244, 295, 468, 494, 759, &c, 957

sōð adj 'true' 1264, 1343; adv 'truly' 816, *sōþra* 'more truly' 1123(N)

sōðfæst adj 'firm in truth, faithful' 22, 506, 567, 790

sōðlice adv 'truly' 651

spēd f. 'success' 254

spēdig adj + d 'successful, rich' 695

spelboda m. 'messenger, prophet' 40(N)

spell n. 'discourse, conversation' 1160

*spīowan wkv 2 'spit, spew out' 912(N)

spōwan stv 7, impers 'succeed' pp asf *spōwende* 254, dsf *spōwendre* 621

sprǣc (*sprēc*) f. 'speech, conversation' 254, 621, 1005, 1160, 1220

sprecan stv 5 'speak' 3s pt ind *sprǣc* 200, 692, 1294, 1pl pt *sprǣcon* 1172

gespurnan stv 3 'tread upon, spurn' 3s pt ind *gespearn* 1334

gestǣlan wkv 1 + d(person) & a(thing) 'accuse' 1071

†*stalgong* m. 'furtive step, stealthy pace' 1140(N)

staþelian wkv 2 'make firm, fix' 66, 1110

staþol m. 'foundation, i.e. root' 1274

stedewong m. 'open place, plain' 875

stefn f. 'voice, sound' 919, 1322

stenc m. 'smell, fragrance' 1318, 1322

stēor f. 'punishment' 510

steppan stv 6 'step, advance' 3s pt ind *stōp* 1140

gestīgan stv 1 'climb, ascend, mount' inf 791, 1s pt ind *gestāg* 307, 3s pt ind 428, *gestāh* 175; 'board, get into (a boat)' 3s pt ind *gestāg* 1328

stihtung f. 'arrangement, direction' 1131

gestillan wkv 1 + g 'cease from' 1094

stille adv 'still', *lǣtan . . . stille* 'let alone, let be' 199

stincan stv 3 'smell sweetly' 3pl pr ind *stincað* 1274

stondan stv 6 'stand' 1s pr *stonde* 246, 373, pl pr ind *stondað* 88, 256, 510(N), pl pt *stōdan* 191, *stōdun* 724; 'remain, continue' 215, 746; 'stand firm' 323, 474

stōw f. 'place, spot' 146, 159, 215, 875, 1274

strong adj 'strong' 293, 1140

stronglīce adv 'strongly' 903

stund f. 'hour, time' 903, dpl *stundum* 'from time to time' 1271

stȳran wkv 1 'govern, check' 420

sum sb 'one', pl 'some' 60, 81, 398, 709, 876(N), *fēara sum* 'alone' 173(N), *wundra sum* 'a particular marvel' 517

sumor m. 'summer' 1273

sundplega m. 'tossing of the sea' 1334

sunne f. 'sun' 1214, 1313

sūsl n. 'torment' 667

swā adv 'thus, in this manner' 70, 133, 200, 323, 344, &c, 854, 996, 1105, 1219, 1276, &c; intensive adv 'so' 246, 431, 1121; in adv phrases *efne swā* 592, *swā þēah* 493, 940, *se þēah* 961, *swā þēana* 110, *se þēana* 409(N); conj 'so' 129, 219, 246, 276, 373, &c, 907, 974, 1109, 1114, 1118, &c, correlative *swā þæt . . . swā* 'even as . . . so' 40–2

swǣs adj 'dear, beloved' 984, 1080, 1166

swāmian wkv 2 'move, wander' 1096(N)

swāt n. 'blood' 522

sweart adj 'dark, dismal' 651, 667, 678

swearte adv 'darkly, miserably' 625

swebban wkv 1 'send to sleep' 3s pr ind *swefeð* 221

swecc m. 'smell, scent' 1273

swefeð, see *swebban*

swēg m. 'sound' 1315, 1322

swegelcyning m. 'heavenly king' 1082

swegl n. 'heaven, sky' 486, 585, 625, 785, 1313, 1330

†*sweglbeorht* adj 'heaven-bright' 1214

swegldrēam m. 'heavenly joy' 1125

†*sweglwuldor* n. 'heavenly glory' 1187

†*sweglwundor* n. 'heavenly wonder' 1318

swelgan stv 3 'swallow, imbibe' 1pl pr sj *swelgen* 764

swencan wkv 1 'trouble, afflict' 452, 570, 806, 1137

sweorcan stv 3 'darken, grow dark' 3s pt ind *swearc* 1052, 1279

sweord n. 'sword' 302

sweostor f. 'sister' 1179

swēte adj 'pleasant, sweet' 1318, spv *swētast* 1273

(*ge*)*sweðrian* wkv 2 'weaken, abate' 113, 352, 1040, 1288

geswīcan stv 3 + g 'give up' imper s *geswīc* 278

swice m. 'delaying, wait' 1034

swincan stv 3 'labour, toil' 3pl pr ind *swincað* 810

swiþ adj 'strong, harsh' 142, cpv *swiðra* 230

swiþe (*swiðe*) adv 'greatly, very much, fervently, strongly' 234, 452, 570, 1070, 1356, *ealles tō swiðe* 662; intensive adv 'very, much' 977, 1166, 1268, 1299, cpv *swiþor* 1125

swylc demonstrative pron & adj 'such' 355, 1119, 1128; adv 'thus' 756(N)

swylce adv 'so, likewise' 1301; conj 'such as, like' 1272, 1311, *swylce ēac* 'so also' 166

swylt m. 'destruction, death' 851

swyltcwalu f. 'death-pang, death' 561

sȳ, synd, see *wesan*

syleð, sylle, see *sellan*

sylf pron 'self' 58, 82, 142(N), 197, 206, &c, 991, 1092, 1234

symbeldæg m. 'feast-day' 165

symle adv 'always' 348, 393, 785, 888, 913, 966, 1212, 1238

synfull adj 'sinful' 674

synn f. 'crime, sin' 113, 506, 515, 550, 568, &c, 1070

synwracu f. 'punishment for sin' ds *synwræce* 860(N)

tācn n. 'sign, signal' 735(N)

†*tælmearc* n. (?) 'measured time, date' 877

teagor (*tēar*) m. 'weeping, tear' 1056, 1340(N)

tempel n. 'church, oratory' 490(N), 1002, 1113, 1149

(*ge*)*tēon* stv 2 'take, lead' inf *getēon* 574, *tēon* 649, 3s pt ind *getēah* 851; *sið tēon* 'undertake a journey, journey' 3pl pt *tugon* 144, 3s pt sj *tuge* 354; 'draw (breath)' inf *getēon* 1024, 1155, 3s pt ind *tēah* 1271

tēona m. 'injury, hostility' 426

tēoncwide m. 'abusive speech, taunt' 448

†*tēonsmið* m. 'evil doer, tormentor' 205

tergan wkv 1 'torment, insult' 288(N)

tīd f. 'time' 36, 45, 114, 118, 154, &c, 835, 877, 949, 967, 970, &c, dpl *tīdum* 'at times' 211

†*tīdfara* m. 'traveller under summons' 9(N)

tiht m. 'expanse' 1281(N)

tima m. 'time' 754

getimbran wkv 1 'build' 250; 'establish, implant' 770

tinterg n. 'torture, torment' 211, 649

tō prep + d 'to, towards' 10, 47, 66, &c, 836, 851, 894, &c, post position 84, 253, apparently + a 225, 549(N); 'to, for, as' 98, 131, 179, &c, 916, 1005, 1112; + inf 531; + infl inf 406, 539, 1066, 1089, 1249; adv phrases *tō þonce* 'gratefully' 125, phrases meaning 'forever' *ā tō fēore* 13, *tō widan ealdre* 636, *āwo tō ealdre* 786, *tō worulde* 814, *tō widan fēore* 840, *æfre tō ealdre* 1119

tō adv 'too' 585, 662, 844, 1077, 1343

tōberan stv 4 'bear off, carry away' 3pl pr ind *tōberað* 289

tōlȳsan wkv 1 'unloose, release' 1289

tor m. 'tower' 1311

torht adj 'bright, beautiful' 9, 487, 1295, spv 645

torn n. 'grief, anger' 205, 288, 487, 1056

torn adj 'grievous' 448

torncwide m. 'bitter speech' 574

torne adv 'grievously, bitterly' 1340

†*tornmōd* adj 'raging, furious' 649

†*tornwracu* f. 'fierce vengeance, grievous revenge' 301

tōweard adj 'approaching, near' 114

tredan stv 5 'walk on, tread on' 3pl pr ind *tredað* 288

†*trēofugol* m. 'bird of the trees, bird' 735

trēow f. 'truth, faith' 340, 448, 543

getrēowan wkv 1 'trust in, believe in' 1s pr ind *getrȳwe* 645, 3s pt *getrēowde* 435

trēowe adj 'faithful, true' 1295

†*trumnaþ* m. 'strengthening, confirmation' 757

truwian wkv 2 + g 'trust, have faith in' 1161(N)

trymman wkv 1 'make strong, strengthen' 107, 133, 190, 362, 960, 1116

getrȳwe, see *getrēowan*

tūddor n. 'race, kin' 735, 824

twēgen num 'two' nm. 114, nn. *tū* 968, af. *twā* 133

twelf num 'twelve' g *twelfa* 709

twēogan wkv 2 'doubt, be uncertain' inf 754; impers + a (person) 'seem doubtful' 3s pr ind *twēoþ* 252; *getwēon* 'hesitate, falter' 3s pt *getwēode* 340, 543

twēone distributory numeral 'two' *bi sǣm twēonum* 'between the seas, on earth' 266, 1359

tȳdre adj 'weak, feeble' 757

tȳdrian wkv 2 'grow weak, decay' 18, 1265

þā (ðā) pron & def art, see *sě*

þā (ðā) adv 'then, thereupon' 262, 390, 412, &c, 823, 932, 936, &c; in adv phrases *þā gēn* 'yet' 515, *þā gēna* 'yet, still' 233, 446, 1270, *þā sīð* 'after some time' 1023, *nū ðā* 'now' 1231

þā (ðā) conj 'when, as' 148, 158, 230, &c, 855, 1104, 1375; correlative 'when . . . then' 454–6, 1098–1101, 1197–99

þǣr adv 'there' 11, 13, 143, &c, 833, 839, 873, &c, *þēr* 421(N); 'to there' 140; *þǣr in* 'therein' 19

þǣr (ðǣr) conj 'where' 10, 16, 121, &c, 827, 917, 1003, &c; 'to where' 896, 951, 1344

þæs, see *sě*

þæt pron & def art, see *sě*

þæt conj + noun clause 'that' 67, 108, 192, &c, 845, 931, 958, &c; 'that, so that' 28, 48, 101, &c, 868, 905, 924, &c; *swā þæt . . . swā* 'even as . . . so' 40-2

þætte conj 'that' 449, 820, 981, 987, 989

geþafian wkv 2 'support, obey' 600

þe (*ðe*) relative particle 'who, which, that, &c' 18, 19, 49, &c, 859, 886, 891, &c; see under *sě* for *sě þe* etc; *þēah þe* 'though' 240, 377, 466, 481, 516 (*ðēah þe*), 872

þēah adv 'however, yet' with proclitic *swā* (*se*) 493, 940, 961(N)

þēah (*ðēah*) conj usually + sj 'though, although' 273, 299, 374, 380, 487, 915, 967, 1064, 1164

þēah þe (*ðēah þe*) conj + sj, see under *þe*

þēana adv 'however, yet' + proclitic *swā* (*se*) 110, 409(N)

þēara, see *sě*

þearf, see *þurfan*

þearfendlīc adj 'poor, needy' 431

þearl adj 'severe, excessive' 547, 978

þēaw m. 'custom, way' 161, 267, 398, 419, 502, &c

þēgan, see *þěow(i)an*

þegn m. 'servant, follower' 547, 693, 696, 708, 1114, 1216, 1231, 1243

þencan wkv 1 'think, intend' 289, 303, 306, 3pl pt *þōhtan* 327

þendan conj 'while, as long as' 376, *þenden* 929

þēod f. 'people' 267, 502, 1231

þēoden m. 'Master, Lord' 385, 778, 1066; 'lord, master' 1014, 1114, 1174, 1198; (of the angel) 1216, 1256

†*þēodengedāl* n. 'death of a master' 1350

(*ge*)*þēon* stv 1 'prosper' 3s pr ind *þihð* 398, 3s pt ind *geþāh* 537

þēostorcofa m. 'dark chamber, tomb' 1195

þēostra, see *þýstru*

þēow m. 'servant' 157, 314, 386, 579, 600, 896, 951

þēowa m. 'servant' ds *þēowon* 922(N)

þěow(i)an wkv 2 & 3 + d 'serve, devote oneself to' inf *þēgan* 169(N), 3pl pr ind *þeowiað* 69, 502, *þeowiaþ* 80, *þeowað* 91, *þīgað* 461(N), 3s pt *þeowde* 740

þěs, *þēos*, *þis* dem adj 'this' nsm *þěs* 53, 296, 304, 1091, 1176, nsf *þēos* 279, 373, 1022, 1064, nsn *þis* 1030, 1046, 1265, asm *þisne* 1256, asf *þās* 119, 125, 371, 741, 967, 1068, 1085, 1120, asn *þis* 244, 307, 455, 1193, gsm *þisses* 383, gsf *þisse* 337, 946, 1037, *ðisse* 1028, gsn *þisses* 74, 278, dsm *þissum* 256, dsf *þisse* 47, 1018, npl *þās* 70, apl *þās* 2, 3, 284, gpl *þissa* 752, dpl *þissum* 376; dem pron 'this' asn *þis* 1171, npl *þās* 753

þicgan stv 5, 'accept, partake of' inf 125, 483

þider (*ðider*) adv 'thither, to there' 22, 1044; conj 'whither, to where' 6

þīgað, see *þěow(i)an*

þīn poss adj 'your' nsm *þīn* 1358, asm *þinne* 1223, asf *þīne* 1174, asn *þīn* 283, gsn *þīnes* 291, dsf *þīnre* 459, 1257

þingian wkv 2 + *ongēan* 'address, accost' 239

þolian wkv 2 + g 'lose, forfeit' 222; 'endure, suffer' 1056, 1066

þon, see under *æfter*, *ær*, *for*, *tō*

þonan adv 'from there, from that place' 144, 325, 1353

þonc m. 'thanks' 169(N), 471, *tō þonce* 'gratefully' 125; 'thought' 914

þoncian wkv 2 + g(thing) & d(person) 'give thanks to, thank' 605, 778

þonne (*ðonne*) adv 'then' 4, 190, 511, 1038

þonne (*ðonne*) conj 'when, whenever' 1, 27, 72, &c, 1212, 1350; 'than' (following cpv) 126, 168, 279, &c, 1035, 1059, 1126, &c
þracu f. 'violence' as *þræce* 267
þrāg f. 'time, season' 1184, 1195, 1350
þrēa m/f/n. 'threat, menace' 431, 547, dpl *þrēam* 'cruelly' 1198
þrēamēdla m. 'mental oppression' 696(N)
geþrēan wkv 2 'chasten, correct' pp nplm. *geþrēade* 74
þrēat m. 'troop, band' 286, 691, 902, 1103, 1314
geþrēatian wkv 2 'urge, press' 916
þringan stv 3 'press (forward), throng' inf 896, 3s pt ind *þrong* 1281, pp *geþrungen* 934, 943, 3s pt ind *geþrong* 863; *geðringan* 'oppress, gain by pressing forward' inf 245(N); 'press in, come' pp *geþrungen* 934
þroht m. 'oppression, hardship' 1350
þrōwere m. 'sufferer, martyr' 161, 182
þrōwian wkv 2 'suffer' 204, 408, 573
þrōwing f. 'suffering' 385, 471, 778
þrym(m) m. 'glory, majesty, power' 74, 169, 646, 1103, 1364
†*þrymcyme* m. 'glorious coming' 1256
þrȳnes f. 'Trinity' 646
þū pers pron sg 'you' *þū* (*ðū*) 6, 271, 273, &c, 1015, 1020, 1021, &c, enclitic *þe* (*ðe*) 272(N), 290, a *þec* 7, 274, 281, &c, 1203, *þē* 452, 1013, 1017, &c, d *þec* 278, 458, *þē* 8, 275, 280, &c, 1011, 1206, 1231, &c, a/d *þec* 1215, *þē* 1262, *þē sylfa* 468
þurfan pt prs vb 'need' pr ptc *þearfende* 1347; as auxiliary 1/3s pr ind *þearf* 46, 282, 754, 1356, 2pl pr ind *þurfun* 673, 3s pt *þorfte* 337, 833, 3pl pt *þorftan* (*-on*) 239, 421, 452, 3pl sj *þurfe* 758
þurh prep + a 'through, by means of' 41, 58, 75, &c, 826, 835, 850, &c; 'in, with' 417, 610, 685, &c, 1361; 'for the sake of, because of, on account of' 641, 987; 'through, during' 214
þurhtēon stv 2 'carry out, accomplish' pp *þurhtogen* 426
þurst m. 'thirst' 275
þus adv 'thus, so' 452, 1011, 1015
þȳ, þȳ lǣs, see *sě*
geþȳdan wkv 1 'join, attach' 998
(*ge*)*þyncan* wkv 1 impers + d 'seem, appear' 3s pt *þūhte* 440, 518; *gesewen þūhte* 1128; *Is . . . geþūht* 1016; *wæs . . . geþūht* 1123
þyslīc adj 'such' asm *þyslīcne* 1014
þȳstro (*þēostru*) f. 'darkness, cloud' 635, 696, 1281

ufan adv 'from above' 612, 937, 958
ufancund adj 'heavenly, celestial' 686, 1124, 1242
uncer dual poss adj 'our' 1189
uncūð adj 'unknown, strange' 141, 1217
uncȳððu f. 'strange place' 855
under prep + a/d 'under, beneath, in' 31, 52, 120, &c, 1280, 1289, 1308, &c
underþȳdan wkv 1 + d 'subject (to)' 603
ungēaro adv 'shortly, soon' 281

ungeblȳged adj 'undismayed' 941
unhwīlen adj 'lasting, eternal' 1087, 1093
unhȳðig adj 'unhappy' 1328(N)
unlæt adj 'quick, ready' 1034
unnan pt prs vb 'grant' inf 930
unrōt adj 'sad' 1064, 1260
unscyldig adj 'innocent, guiltless' 687
unslāw adj 'not slow, quick' 950
unsnyttru f. 'folly' dpl *unsnyttrum* 'foolishly' 859
unsōfte adj 'severely' 886, 1107
untrymnes f. 'weakness, infirmity' 1017
unwēne adj 'hopless' 1148(N)
ūp(p) adv 'up, on high, aloft' 97, 263, 484, 776, 791, 1024, 1155, 1311
†*ūpeard* m. 'dwelling on high' 1078
ūphladan stv 6 'draw up' pp *ūphlæden* 1278
ūplīc adj 'celestial' 681
ūprodor m. 'firmament, heaven' 782
ūpweg m. 'ascent' 1306, 1366
ūre poss adj 'our' nplm *ūsse* 750, 973, gpl *ūssera* 753, *ūrra* 876(N), dpl
    ūssum 401
ūre, ūs, ūsic, see *wē*
ūt adv 'out' 299
ūtsīþ m. 'departure' 1267
ūttor cpv adv 'more utterly' 126
ūðgenge adj 'not to be held, alien' 852

wacian wkv 2 'keep watch' 115
gewadan stv 6 'go' 3s pt ind *gewōd* 940, 1028
wǣg m. 'wall' ds *wāge* 1269
wǣgan wkv 1 'afflict' inf *węgan* 370
†*wǣgdropa* m. 'water-drop, tear' 1057
wǣghengest m. 'ship' 1329
wǣlan wkv 1 'vex, torment, afflict' 425
wælgifre adj 'murderous, bloodthirsty' 999
†*wælpīl* m. 'deadly dart, death-pang' 1154(N)
wælræst f. 'death-bed' 1033, 1368
†*wælstrǣl* m/f. 'fatal arrow, mortal pang' 1286
wǣpen n. 'weapon' 89, 178, 284, 304
wǣr f. 'protection' 360, 690, 746; 'covenant, promise' 775, 1172
wærc m. 'pain' 1028
wǣre, see *wesan*
wǣrfæst adj 'constant' 1190
wǣrloga m. 'promise-breaker, traitor, devil' 298(N), 623, 911
wærnys f. 'evil, damnation' 671(N)
wǣron, see *wesan*
wǣstm m/f/n. 'fruitfulness, fruit' 44, 848
wæterþisa m. 'ship, boat' 1329(N)
wāge, see *wǣg*

waldend m. 'Ruler, Lord' 594, 666, 763, 800, 845

wana m. 'lack, want' 1354

wānian wkv 2 'lament' 1073

warnian wkv 2 'deny oneself something' 1183

wāst, wāt, see *witan*

gewāt, see *gewītan*

wāð f. 'wandering, roving' 145, 212

wē pers pron 'we' npl *wē* 32, 34, 49, &c, 1360, apl *ūsic* 511, gpl *ūre* 289, dpl *ūs* 48, 280, 766, 878; a/dpl *ūs* 93, 271, 528, 764

wēa m. 'woe, misery' 615

wealdan stv 7 + a/g/d 'ordain' 3s pr ind *wealdeð* 512; 'rule, command the mastery of, control' inf *wealdan* 702, 1159, 3s pr ind *wealdeð* 17, 241, 312(N), 3pl pt *wēoldon* 268, 3s pt sj *wōlde* 517(N), inf *gewealdan* 1016, 1226

weallan stv 7 'well up, surge' inf 1057, pr ptc asm *weallendne* 615, 3s pt ind *wēol* 979, 1340

weard m. 'guardian' 105, 115, 231; 'Lord, Guardian' 611, 789, 929, 1204

weardian wkv 2 'occupy' 897, 1129, *lāst weardian* 'remain behind' 1338

wearm adj 'warm' 1293

weaxan stv 7 'grow' 3s pr ind *weaxeð* 249, 3s pt ind *wēox* 395

wēdan wkv 1 'rave' pr ptc nplm *wēdende* 907

†*wedertācen* n. 'sigh, weather-sign' 1293(N)

wefan stv 5 'weave, destine' pp *wefen* 1351

weg m. 'way, path' 8, 37, 99, 1180(N)

wegan stv 5 'bear, feel' inf 61, 3s pt ind *wæg* 1009, 1051, 1137, 1335, 1341

wel(l) adv 'well, fully' 541, 581, 1171

wela m. 'weal, happiness' 828

wēn f. 'likelihood, probability' 1016

wēnan wkv 1 + g 'expect, hope' 76, 291, 508, 663, 673

wendan wkv 1 'change, turn' 44, 57, 758

weorc n. 'work, deed' 61, 312(N), 362, 581, 622, &c, 857, 948, 1304, 1373; 'pain, suffering' 1269

(*ge*)*weorðan* stv 3 'become, be' (both with predicate and as passive aux) inf *weorðan* 305, 1230, (*ge*-) 64, 1261, 3s pr ind *weorþeð* 660, 3pl pr ind *weorþað* 71, 3s pt ind (*ge*)*wearð* 93, 153, 174, &c, 852, 879, 1197, &c, pl pt *wurdon* (-*um*) 181, 633, 856, 881, 3s pr sj (*ge*)*weorðe* 369, 765, 3pl pr sj *geweorþen* 380, 3s pt sj *worde* 780(N); *wæs . . . geworden* 'was brought about' 749; impers. *Hū gewearð þē* 'How did you come to be' 1011

weorþian wkv 2 'honour, worship' 156, 619, 800, 918

weorðlīce adv 'worthily, honourably' 324

weorðmynd f/n/m. 'honour, glory' 463

weorud n. 'host, troop' 134, 247, 395, 594, 894

wēpan stv 7 'weep' inf 1074

wer m. 'man' 108, 503, 590, 749, 819, 849, 925, 984, 1105, &c

werge adj 'accursed, evil' 451

wērge, see *wērig*

wērgenga m. 'follower' 594(N), 713

gewērgian wkv 2 'weary' 1269

werian wkv 1 'defend, hold' 351

wērig adj 'weary' 212, 1363

wērigmōd adj 'weary in mind' 255

wesan stv (defective) 'be' inf 260, 603, 665, &c, 3s pt ind *wæs* 98, 110, 114, &c, 823, 825, 827, &c, negated *næs* 903, 961, 966, pl pt *wǣron* 205, 406, 547, &c, 1134, 3s pt sj *wǣre* 411, 441, 1124, 3pl pt sj *wǣre* 872

  bēon forms: 3s pr ind *biǒ* (*biþ*) 1, 11, 20, &c, 1034, 1348, 1354, pl pr ind *bēoǒ* (*bēoþ*) 59, 73, 78, &c, 1038, imp s *bēo þū* 1064, 1077, 1175

  other forms: 1s pr ind *eom* 314, 599, 651, &c, 1077, 1268, *eam* 246, 2s pr ind *eart* 9, 272, 579, 3s pr ind *is* 37, 53, 242, &c, 819, 890, 1016, &c, negated *nis* 277, 309, 312, &c, 1065, 1081, 1091, &c, pl pt *sindon* (*-an*) 8, 30, 38, &c, 1223, *sind* (*synd*) 18, 91, 251, &c, 3s pr sj *sȳ* 698

west adv 'west, westwards' 1213

wēsten m/n. 'wilderness, wild place' 81, 208, 296, 899, 935

wēþe adj 'gentle, pleasant' 8

wīc n. (pl frequently with sg meaning) 'dwelling-place, home' 284, 298, 702, 894, 1365

†*wīceard* m. 'dwelling-place' 935

wīd adj 'wide' 296; *widan* in phrases meaning 'forever' 636, 817, 840

wīde 'far and wide, far' 145, 536, 819, cpv *widor* 300; *wīde 7 sīde* 'far and wide' 882

wīdeferh m/n. 'a long time' as used adverbially 603, 671

wīf n. 'woman, wife' 846

wiga m. 'warrior' 999, 1033

wiht f/n. 'anything' 277, 312, 313, 425, 699

†*wilboda* m. 'messenger of joy, angel' 1246

wilde adj 'wild' 276, 907

wildēor n. 'wild beast' 741(N)

willa m. 'will, wish, desire' 82, 95, 348, 358, 362, &c, 828, 845, 867, 873, &c; dpl *willum* 'at will, willingly' 199, 1373

willan anom vb 'will, wish, desire, be about to' 1s pr *wille* 243, 257, 378, &c, 1027, 1263, negated *nelle* 1259, 2s pr ind *wilt* 280, 3s pr *wile* 241, 346, 763, pl pr ind *willaǒ* 34, 60, 124, &c, s pt *wolde* 169, 196, 407, &c, 930, 1006, 1229, negated *nolde* 945, 1234, pl pt *woldun* (*-um*, *-an*) 353, 468, 483, &c, 842, s pr sj *wille* (*wylle*) 272, 593, 640, &c, 3pl pr sj *willen* 224

willian wkv 2 + g 'desire' 37

wilnian wkv 2 + g 'desire, ask for' 70, 290, 1185

windan stv 3 'move, waver' 3s pt ind *wond* 294

wine m. 'friend, lord' 1063, 1227, 1339, 1347, 1365(N)

winedryhten m. 'friend and master' 1011, 1202

winemǣg m. 'kinsman, friend' 1364

winescype m. 'friendship' 1172

winnan stv 3 'strive for, strive after' 3s pt ind *won* 399, 3s pt sj *wunne* 129; *gewinnan* 'conquer, triumph' 3s pt ind *gewon* 450

winter m/n. 'winter, i.e. year' 498

wīs adj 'wise' 800

wīscað, see *wȳscan*

wīsdōm m. 'wisdom' 156, 503, 529, 763, 1131, 1246

wīse f. 'way, mode' gpl *wīsna* 1161

wīsian wkv 2 'direct, show' 362, 444

wist f. 'food, feast' 463

wit dual pers pron 'we two' n *wit* 1172, 1186, 1190, 1258, a/d *unc* 1186, 1258

witan pt prs vb 'know' 1/3s pr ind *wāt* 1086, 1092, 1221, 1351, 1352, 2s pr ind *wāst* 1021, 3pl pr *witon* 67, 90, 3s pt *wiste* 1003, 1339, 3s pr sj *wite* 891, 1247

gewitan stv 1 'depart, go away' pp *gewiten* 1365, npl -*e* 1134, 2s pr ind *gewītest* 276, 3s pt *gewāt* 325, 1327, pl imp *Gewitað* 255

wīte n. 'pain, torment' 425, 469, 517, 713, 885

wītedōm m. 'prophecy' 41

witian wkv 2 'appoint, assure' pp asf *witude* 918

wið (*wiþ*) prep + a 'towards, with' 411, 716, + a/d 1262; + d 'against' 203, 240, 323, &c, 960, 1335; + d 'from' 3, 241, 553, &c, + a/d 228, 331, + a 371; *wiþ þon* 'against that' 494(N)

wiþerbreoca m. 'adversary' 294

wiþerhycgende ptc adj 'hostile, malevolent' 663

wiðhycgan wkv 3 + d 'set oneself against' 2pl pt *wiðhogdum* 631

wiðstondan stv 6 'withstand, resist' inf 994, 3s pt ind *wiðstōd* 903

wlencu f. 'pride' 208, 503

wlite m. 'beauty, splendour' 44, 1314

wlitig adj 'beautiful, fair' 817, 1117, 1304

wlō adv 'indeed' 1154(N)

wolcen n. 'cloud' 1280

wōlde 517, see *wealdan*

wom(m) m/n. 'impurity, sin' 29, 587

won(n) adj 'dark' 1028, 1280

wong m. 'field, place, plain' 178, 231, 304, 352, 477, &c, 1275

wonian wkv 2 'weaken, fade' 57; *gewonian* 'abate, infringe' 3s pr *gewonade* 775

wonsǣlig adj 'wretched' 946

wōp m. 'weeping, lamentation' 615, 636, 905, 1047, 1339(N)

word n. 'word, speech, command' 41, 58, 61, 294, 308, &c, 842, 848, 1016, 1063, 1094, 1126, &c

wordcwide m. 'speech' 1159

woruld f. 'world' 37, 47, 105, 125, 129, &c, 892, 932, 946, 982, 1047, &c

†*woruldbliss* f. 'worldly joy' 164

worulddrēam m. 'worldly joy' 1363

woruldgestrēon n. 'wordly riches' 70

woruldlic adj 'wordly' 403

woruldlif n. 'wordly life, life in this world' 1169, 1185

228 *Glossary*

woruldryht n. 'law for the world, law' 57(N)
wōð f. 'sound, cry' 263, 391(N), 899
wracu f. 'strife, hostility' as *wræce* 199; 'hardship' 1081
wræce, see *wracu*
wræcmæg m. 'banished man, outcast' 129, 231, 263, 558
†*wræcsetl* n. 'place of exile' 296
wræcsīð m. 'exile journey, exile', 509, 623, 688, 1074
wrāð adj 'hostile' 558, 666
wraþu f. 'help, support' 249, 1363
wrecan stv 5 'wreak, avenge' 3pl pr ind *wrecað* 288; 'press, drive' 3s pt ind *wræc* 1329
wrōht m/f. 'strife' 391
wrōhtsmið m. 'strife-worker, worker of evil' 905(N)
wuldor n. 'glory' 8, 25, 76, 86, 145, &c, 1081, 1117, 1246, 1286, 1304, &c
wuldorcyning m. 'King of glory' 596, 793, 849
wuldorfæst adj 'fast in glory, glorious' 817
wuldorlēan n. 'reward in glory, glorious reward' 1373
wuldormaga (-o) m. 'glorious man' 1094(N), 1293
wund f. 'wound' 284, 698
wundor n. 'wonder, miracle' 156, 403, 517, 529, 752, 882, 892, 1127, dpl *wundrum* 'wondrously' 1117, *tō wundre* 'in this wondrous way' 370
wundrian wkv 2 'marvel' 1232
(ge)wunian wkv 2 'remain, abide, inhabit' 19, 81, 137, 249, 360, &c, 840, 948, 999, 1033, 1190, &c
wylm m. 'surge' 191, 374
wyn(n) f. 'delight, pleasure' 2, 105, 139, 164, 166, &c, 1108, 1206, 1364, dpl *wynnum* 'joyously, pleasantly' 814, 1275
†*wyncondel* f. 'joyful light, sun' 1213
wyndæg m. 'joyful day, day of gladness' 632
wyntīc adj 'joyful, pleasing' 824
†*wynmæg* f. 'joyous maiden' 1345
wynsum adj 'pleasant' 1321
wyrcan wkv 1 (intrs) 'work, do' 3s pr ind *wyrceð* 756, 3pl pt *worhton* 974; *gewyrcan* (trs) 'make, work' 3s pt *geworhte* 823, 2pl pr sj *gewyrce* 300
wyrd f. 'fate, destiny' 1057, 1345
†*wyrdstæf* m. 'decree of fate' 1351
wyrm m. 'serpent' 846, 911
wyrpe f. 'change, improvement, relief' 47, 509, 636
wyrs cpv adv 'worse' 665
wyrt f. 'plant' 1275
wȳscan wkv 1 + g 'wish for, desire' 3pl pr ind *wȳscað* 76, *wiscað* 223

yldran, see *eald*
ymb prep + a 'about, around' 114, 737, 1287, 1290, 1310
ymbstondan stv 6 'stand around, encircle' 3pl pt *ymbstōdan* 262
yrfestōl m. 'home, seat' 1319
yrming m. 'wretch' 272

yrmðu (ermþu) f. 'misery, distress' 11, 19, 447, 933
yrre adj 'angry' 190
yrringa adv 'angrily' 484
yrsian wkv 2 'enrage' 200
ȳt(e)mest spv adj 'utmost, final' 443, 1167
ȳð f. 'wave' 1340
ȳwan (ēawan) wkv 1 'reveal, show' 86, 143, 502

LIST OF PROPER NAMES

Ādam m. Adam n 826, d *Ādame* 853, 869, 981, 983
Bartholomēus m. Bartholomew n 723
Bryten f. Britain a 883, a/d *Brytene* 175
Crist m. Christ n 402, 598, g *-es* 23, 38, 153, &c, d *-e* 306, 577, 797
Ēue f. Eve n 869, 981, d *Ēuan* 853
Engle mpl Englishmen apl 880(N), 1360
Gūðlāc m. Guthlac n 95, 170, 206, &c, 879, a 348, 530, 913, g *-es* 137, 182(N), 188, &c, 1305, d *-e* 111, 327, 449, &c, 976, 996
Hierusālem f. Jerusalem a 813

Appendix I

The Three Utterances

(Text from L. Dudley, *Egyptian Elements in the Legend of the Body and Soul* (Baltimore 1911), p. 165: Bibliothèque nationale MS. Latin 2628, Fos. 103ᵛ–5ʳ.)

Quando vero boni angeli inueniunt animam iustam suam esse
sociam gaudent omnes et demones contristantur. Angeli
dicunt: Noster est ille uir quia in bello fortis est,
stabilis in acie, arma pauli custodiens, id est scutum
fidei, et gladium spiritus sancti, loricam iusticiae et   5
galeam salutis et nunquam inermis fuit. Fidelis est et
lenis est: amans dominum ualde misericors est. Omnia
sustinuit propter dominum omnipotentem, sperans futura.
Tunc dicunt angeli: Suscitate eam leniter de suo corpore,
ut quod ei parauit dominus uideat bonus. Tunc dicit   10
anima hominis iusti: Magnum est lumen! Angeli dicunt:
Maius tibi futurum est. Uidebis claritatem domini facie
ad faciem non per speculum neque per uelum quemadmodum
uidebant filii israelis faciem moysi. Dicit denuo anima:
Magna est leticia; Cui respondetur ab angelis: Maior tibi   15
futura est. Tunc uidet angelorum multitudinem in obuiam
sibi uenientium et canentium. Hi sunt qui uenerunt ex magna
tribulatione et lauerunt stolas suas in sanguine agni.
Dicit tercio anima: Suaue est iter. Angeli respondent:
Suauius tibi est futurum. Deducimus te ad tabernacula   20
sanctorum carentia in iustorum habitatione. Tunc dicunt
angeli: Suscitate eam leniter de suo corpore, et ut nichil
timoris, nichil doloris uideat. Diuidite, uos in duos
choros, ut alius sit proueniens, alius consequens, et
cantate illi de canticulis dauid ubi manifesta . . .   25
beatitudinem anime intrantis in domo domini dicit:
Beatus quem elegisti et assumpsisti domine, inhabitabat
in tabernaculis tuis. Replebimur in bonis domus tue:
sanctum est templum tuum, mirabile in equitate. Non est
acceptio personarum ibi et nobilitas generis, sed reddit   30
dominus unicuique secundum opera sua. Et ibunt impii in
ignem eternum, iusti autem in uitam eternam in sæcula
sæculorum. Amen.

Appendix II

Gregory: Introduction to the life of Friardus

(Texte from *PL*, lxxi. 1054–5.)

Multi variique sunt gradus per quos ad coelorum regna conscenditur, de quibus, ut opinor, et David dicit, quia *ascensus in corde deposuit* (*Psal.* lxxxiii. 6). Accipiuntur ergo hi gradus diversorum operum ad cultum divinum profectus, et nullus in his gressum figere potest, nisi fuerit, sicut sæpe testati sumus Dei adjutorio provocatus. Sic enim Psalmographus in illo mediæ profectionis gradu loquitur, dicens: *Nisi Dominus ædificaverit domum, in vanum laborant qui ædificant eam* (*Ps.* cxxvi. 1). Quod adjutorium, non modo martyres, verum etiam et illi quos sacræ vitæ roboravit aucitoritas [*Ed.*, celebravit], jugiter inquirentes, ad hoc quod sitis disiderii spiritalis promebat alacres pervenerunt. Nam si ad martyrium mens accensa est, hujus adjutorii opem poposcit martyr ut vinceret; si jejunii observantiam adhibere studuit, ut ab eo confortaretur afflictus est; si castitati artus reservare voluit impollutos, ut ab illo muniretur oravit; si post ignorantiam pœnitendo converti desideravit, ut ab eo nihilominus sublevaretur cum lacrymis flagitavit; et si quid operis boni exercere eorum quispiam meditatus est, ut ab hoc adjutorio juvaretur expetiit. Per hos ergo scalæ hujus ascensus tam difficiles, tamque excelsos, tam arduos, cum sint diversi, ad unum tamen Dominum per hujus adjutorii opem conscenditur. Idcirco semper ille poscendus, ille quærendus, ille invocandus erit, ut quod de bono mens concipit, adjutorio suo ipse perficiat, de quo et nobis sine fine oportet dicere: *Adjutorium nostrum in nomine Domini, quo fecit cœlum et terram* (*Ps.* cxxiii. 8). Sicut et ille beatissimus, de quo nunc nobis futurus est sermo, qui inter diversas vel tentationes, vel cruces sæculi, semper hujus adjutorii munimen expetiit.

Appendix III

Rex aeterne Domine

(Text from J. Stevenson, 'The Latin Hymns of the Anglo-Saxon Church, with an interlinear Anglo-Saxon gloss', *Surtees Society*, xxiii (1851), 30–1: Durham, Cathedral MS. B.III.32. The relevant verses are printed, together with the Old English gloss.)

Rex aeterne Domine		cyning ece ó eala ðu drihten
Rerum Creator omnium		gesceafta scyppend ealra
Qui eras ante secula		þu ðe wære ǽr worulde
Semper cum Patre Filius		æfre mid fædor sunu
Qui mundi in primordio	5	þu ðe middaneardes on fruman
Adam plasmasti hominem		gesceope mann
Cui tuae imaginis[1]		þam þinre anlicnysse
Vultum dedisti similem.		andwlitan þu sealdest gelicne
Quem diabolus deceperat		þæne deoful beswác
Hostis humani generis	10	feond mennisces cynnes
Per pomum ligni vetiti		þurh æppel treowes þæs ealdan
Mortis propinans poculum.		deaðes scencende drenc
Quique clausis in tenebris		se ðe beclesed on þeostrum
Gemebat in suppliciis		geomrode on witum
Cujus tu formam corporis	15	þæs þu hiw lichoman
Assumere dignatus es		geniman gemedemod þu wære
Ut hominem redimeres		þæt mann þu alysdest
Quem ante jam plasmaveras		þæne ær eallunga þu gesceope
Ut nos Deo conjungeres		þæt us gode þu geðeoddest
Per carnis contubernium.	20	þurh flæsces gemænnysse
Quem editum ex virgine		þæne acennedne of fæmnan
Pavescit omnis anima		forhtað ælc sawul
Per quem et nos resurgere		ðurh ðæne 7 we arisan
Devota mente credimus.		estfullum mode we gelefað.

[1] Editor notes '*imagini* originally in Durham MS.'